Political Power: USA/USSR

SPONSORED JOINTLY BY

THE RUSSIAN INSTITUTE

AND

THE INSTITUTE OF WAR AND PEACE STUDIES

COLUMBIA UNIVERSITY

Political Power:

USA/USSR

BY

Zbigniew Brzezinski

AND

Samuel P. Huntington

1964

Chatto & Windus

LONDON

Published by
Chatto and Windus Ltd
42 William IV Street
London W C 2

To TIMOTHY and IAN

Contents

PREFACE   xi

INTRODUCTION   3
    Contrasts and Comparisons   7
    The Theory of Convergence   9

PART I: THE POLITICAL SYSTEM

Chapter One: Political Ideas and Politics   17
    Ideological Commitment and Political Beliefs   17
    The Traditional Background   24
    The Outlook of the Political Leaderships   35
    The Functions of Ideology and Political Belief   45
    The Value and Viability of Ideology   56

Chapter Two: The Political System and the Individual   71
    Ideological and Instrumental Political Systems   71
    Socialization and Politization   76
    Political Participation and Control   90
    Alienation and Dissent   104
    Science and Social Manipulation   121

Chapter Three: Political Leadership   129
    Access to Leadership   130
    Professional Politicians: Electoral and Bureaucratic   141
    Cincinnatus and the Apparatchik   150
    Circulation of Leaders   173
    The Problem of Succession   182

Chapter Four: Power and Policy   191
    The Relation between Power and Policy   191
    Bargaining and Deciding   193
    The Policy-Making Process   202
    The Dimensions of Policy-Making   224

viii   *Contents*

PART II: THE DYNAMICS OF POWER: RESPONSES TO COMMON CRISES

Chapter Five: The Struggle for Power   235

Stages of Conflict   238
Khrushchev's Struggle   240
Kennedy's Struggle   253
Policies, Appeals, and Power   263

Chapter Six: The Ambivalence of Power   269

Khrushchev and the Consumer-Goods "Debate," 1960-1961   272
Kennedy and Civil Rights, 1961-1963   283
Means, Ends, and Power   295

Chapter Seven: The Intractable Problem of Power: Agriculture   301

Economic Context and Contrasts   301
The Structure of Power   305
Ideology and Myth   310
Palliatives and Compromises   318
The Politics of Change   326

Chapter Eight: Civil Power in Political Crisis: Zhukov and MacArthur   331

Civilian Control   332
Military Leaders   339
Political Discord   342
Political Supremacy and Political Harmony   358

Chapter Nine: Foreign Dilemmas of Power   367

Intervention: Cuba and Hungary   367
Alliance-Management: France and China   388

CONCLUSION   409

Strengths and Weaknesses   409
Convergence or Evolution   419

APPENDIX: Soviet and American Societies   439

REFERENCE NOTES   441

INDEX   451

TABLES

page

Circulation of Periodical Literature, USSR and USA   89

Social Status and CPSU Membership, 1961   100

National Origin and Access to Political Leadership in the Soviet
Union   132-133

Per Cent in Soviet Union of Men Who Became White-Collar
Workers   137

Curriculum of the Four-Year Party School   145

Primary Occupations of Top Political Leaders, USSR and USA   153

Primary Occupations of Administration Leaders, USA   158

Primary Institutional Connection of Top Soviet Leaders   161

Education and Party Membership: Soviet Union   169

Leadership Tenure in Congress   176

Changes in CPSU Politburo-Presidium and CC Secretariat, 1919-
1961   178

Turnover in Central Committee Membership, 1917-1961   179

Turnover at the Top, USSR and USA, 1917-1964   183

Number of Pictures of Top Soviet Leaders in Izvestia and Pravda   185

Major Policy Innovations, USSR and USA, 1945-1963   231

Grain Hectarage and Production, USSR and USA   302

Man Hours Used per Quintal of Output, USSR and USA   303

Preface

THE IDEA of this book was born in a convention-crowded Washington hotel lobby in September 1959. A few hasty words exchanged by the two authors led to further discussions and some preliminary outlining. In the spring of 1961 we initiated at Columbia University a joint graduate seminar on comparative American and Soviet politics. We taught the same seminar a year later. It furnished us with the opportunity to expose our preliminary ideas to an intelligent and critical audience. Our very special thanks go to our seminar students: their interest and lively participation, their criticisms and suggestions made an invaluable contribution to this project.

We began to write in the spring of 1962. Each chapter was outlined jointly, and written and rewritten by each of the authors. Each of us contributed sections on both political systems. The resulting manuscript is completely a joint product. In the course of our work, our ideas evolved and took shape. Without giving away our argument, let it be said that we started much more sympathetically inclined to the views summarized in the Introduction. The Conclusion reflects the research, debate, and thought that went into writing the book.

To avoid approaching the subject purely from the American perspective—and both authors are, after all, products of the American intellectual environment—we visited several foreign countries, where we held extensive conversations with leading intellectuals and presented the preliminary versions of some of our chapters to special seminars. In this connection, we recall with particular pleasure the stimulating meetings that we, jointly or singly, had in Kyoto, chaired by Professor Masamichi Inoki; in Tokyo, one presided over by Professor Tadao Ishikawa and another by Mr. Yoji Hirota; in Calcutta, one organized by Professor N. C. Bhattacharyya and a second by Mr. K. K. Sinha; in Bombay, arranged by Mr. V. B. Karnik; at Sapru House in New Delhi, organized by Dr. M. L. Sondhi and chaired by Professor A. Appadorai; with various helpful Soviet professors and intellectuals in

Moscow, Leningrad, and Tashkent; and with many distinguished western European scholars.

Our work on this book began when Brzezinski was at Harvard and Huntington was at Columbia. It ended with Huntington at Harvard and Brzezinski at Columbia. The great bulk of the work, however, was done when both authors were at Columbia between 1960 and 1962. The book is jointly sponsored by the two institutes at Columbia University with which the authors have been associated. Our sincerest gratitude goes to the Russian Institute and to the Institute of War and Peace Studies for their generous support. We are particularly grateful to their directors, Professors Henry Roberts and later Alexander Dallin of the Russian Institute and Professor William T. R. Fox of the Institute of War and Peace Studies, who encouraged and assisted us in every way possible. We received additional support from three other sources. The Guggenheim Foundation awarded a fellowship to Brzezinski in 1962; and, in a gratifying example of inter-university comity, Harvard University during 1962-1963 helped to support Huntington's research on this Columbia project. For this assistance, we are happy to express our respective gratitude to Guggenheim and to Harvard. Finally, at the invitation of the Rockefeller Foundation we were able to spend several weeks writing our manuscript at the Villa Serbelloni in Bellagio, Italy. The quiet atmosphere and beautiful surroundings of the villa certainly eased the normal pains of literary effort.

We have other important intellectual debts to acknowledge. Professors Merle Fainsod (Harvard University) and H. Douglas Price (Syracuse University) read the entire manuscript and Professor Walid Khalidi (American University in Beirut) read part of it. Their thoughtful and helpful comments, criticisms, and advice have contributed much to the substance of the book. At various stages in our work, we benefited greatly from the penetrating advice and suggestions of Professors Max Beloff (Oxford University), Cyril Black (Princeton University), and David B. Truman (Columbia University) concerning the general approach, structure, and contents of the book. We are also grateful to the research assistants who, at one time or another, helped us in gathering material: William E. Jackson, Jr., George Murray, Carole Parsons, Charles A. Sorrels, Robert Steele, Rudolf Tokes, and David Williams. Our thanks also go to Mrs. Ellen H. Bernstein, Mrs. Christine Dodson, and Mrs. Shirley Johannesen Levine, for their valuable contributions in editorial and research assistance.

As usual, the acknowledgment to the wives comes last—but probably because they are always first: first to criticize, first to encourage; first to impose on our "precious" time and first to sustain us when somehow there is not enough time; they will also be the first to bring us down to earth if the critics like our book and the first to praise us if they do not. That is why, in many ways, this is also their book.

S.P.H.
Z.B.

October 1963

Political Power: USA//USSR

Introduction

THE Soviet and American governments are rivals. Fifteen years of competition have extended this rivalry from diplomacy to military affairs, economics, science, education, culture. Each side's failures and successes in foreign policy are ponderously weighed by pundits and journalists; the balance of power in military force and technology is probed and analyzed; rates of economic growth are compared and debated; scientific achievements in space and on earth are trumpeted and deprecated; anxious count is kept of the annual crops of grain and of engineers. These subjects are important. But in the last analysis, the performance of each country in each of these areas depends upon the workings of its political system. All the key choices in all areas of competition are made through politics. The strengths and weaknesses of the political system determine the wisdom or folly of its actions in diplomacy, strategy, economics, or science. The fundamental competition is political.

While much has been written about the specialized competitions, the competition between the political systems has been neglected. In the past decade many exciting advances have been made in the study of comparative politics, yet students of Soviet politics and students of American politics have remained largely outside these developments. Each group has tended to study its own system as an end in itself and, implicitly, as a system so *sui generis* as to forbid comparison with others. The esoteric cult of Kremlinology on the one hand has been matched by the worship of American "uniqueness" on the other.

The purpose of this book is to compare these two political systems and to answer three broad questions:

(1) What are the principal similarities and differences between the Soviet and American political systems?

(2) What are the strengths and weaknesses of each system?

(3) Are the two systems becoming more alike or less so?

Closely related to these are a host of secondary questions about the salient features of the two systems. Do both systems have

3

ideologies which guide the leaders in the exercise of power? Does ideology help or hinder the systems in making rational political decisions? How do the two systems educate their citizens for their political roles? In which system do the citizens participate more broadly and effectively in politics? In which system is there more alienation and dissent, and how do the systems handle them? In which are the political leaders more professionally skilled in wielding power? Which has a more effective method of recruiting political leaders and of regularly changing the wielders of power? Through what methods do the political leaders exercise their power? "The power of the President," Harry Truman said, "is the power to persuade." Is this also true of the First Secretary of the Communist Party of the Soviet Union? In formulating policy in each system, what are the roles of professional politicians, civilian bureaucrats, military leaders, industrial managers, intellectuals, public opinion? Which system is more successful in giving coherence and direction to its policies? Which is more successful in innovating major policies and providing for flexibility in policy? These are some of the specific questions with which we will be concerned in comparing the strengths and weaknesses, the similarities and differences of the two systems.

Political systems should not be studied in terms of barren institutional comparisons: it makes little sense to compare Congress to the Supreme Soviet or an American election to a Soviet one. At the other extreme, it also makes little point to formulate abstract categories of comparison so rarefied as to be drained of practical relevance. What really counts in a political system? Systematic political analysis must distinguish the more important from the less important or it fails to be analytical and becomes merely encyclopedic. To make this distinction, the system of analysis must be rooted in values and purposes consciously chosen by the analyst. The purposes of comparison must dictate the method.

We are students of politics; we write this book in that capacity. And here we are concerned not with vices and virtues but with strengths and weaknesses. Moral judgments have been passed often enough—and with predictable results—on both sides of the Iron Curtain. In this volume we aim to keep our analyses free of our preference for constitutional democracy. Too often in the United

States people have assumed that because the American system provides more liberty and is therefore more desirable it must also be stronger. This is bad logic bred of wishful thinking. Our values are not necessarily history's values. A system devoted to individual liberty and well-being may or may not be more capable of surviving effectively than one based on different principles. The decisive question is which system provides an ordering of power more adequate to cope with the challenges of the age. It is this question which guides our choice of four subjects for comparison.

First, a key factor in the analysis of political systems is the relation between *political ideas and politics*. The outlook of the political leaders and their followers is conditioned by the cumulative historical experience of their respective countries. This experience creates varying degrees of receptivity to political ideologies. A political system is effective to the extent that the history behind it has brought about an underlying consensus on an ideology or a set of beliefs, to the extent that these beliefs legitimize the system, and to the extent that they furnish the leaders with a hierarchy of goals to guide policy choices and a reasonably effective method of analyzing policy problems. Politics is not only the exercise of power; it is also a matter of will. An outlook which involves unrealistic goals, or no goals at all, or which rests on irrelevant analytical categories, can be a guide to disaster.

Second, each political system shapes and is shaped by the society of which it is a part. The political system imposes demands on the members of society. The extent to which the latter accept and respond to them is determined largely by the processes through which individuals are turned into citizens. In addition, the members of a modern society both participate in the political system and exercise some controls over it. The forms of participation and control and the nature of the balance between them are key elements in the strength of the system. In every society, also, there are varying degrees of dissatisfaction and indifference, with which the political system must have means of coping. All these questions broadly concern the relation between *the political system and the individual*.

Third, the strength and effectiveness of a system obviously depend upon the character of its *political leadership*. The key questions here concern the education and training of the leadership, the sources from which it is recruited, the methods of advancement up the political ladder, the organizational framework of leadership, and the regularity of turnover and circulation among leaders. A political system in which leaders are recruited by birth rather than by achievement and from a small number of families rather than from society at large, who are dilettantes rather than professionals in politics, who advance to the top through family connections, and who either grow old and stale in office or circulate through offices in a rapid game of musical chairs, is weaker than one where these conditions do not prevail.

Fourth, political leaders exercise power by applying their values and ideologies to the *processes of policy-making.* Each system must have ways of recognizing the problems confronting society, of mobilizing support for alternative solutions to them, of formulating the issues for decision, and of implementing the policies once they have been decided upon. To govern is to choose. And the processes of policy-making affect the choices (or the lack of choices) of the political leaders. The same processes determine to what extent policies in one area are coordinated with policies in other areas and the speed and flexibility with which new policies can be introduced.

These four subjects—political ideas, the system and the individual, political leadership, and policy-making processes—in large part determine how well a political system functions. For this reason they are the primary concerns of this book. In the second part of the book, several case studies deal more specifically with the ways in which power is acquired, exercised, and limited in the two systems; with the intractable problems which agriculture poses for the political process; with the assertion of civilian supremacy over the military establishment; and with some specific aspects of alliance relationships and forceful intervention. While each case study focuses on a specific issue, their purpose is to illustrate or develop the generalizations made about the two systems.

CONTRASTS AND COMPARISONS

Although there have been no systematic comparisons of Soviet and American politics, many current ideas have implications for such a comparison. Some of these are popular and unsophisticated; others reflect an elaborate theory of history. Virtually all focus upon the similarities and differences believed to exist between the two systems now and in the future. Two of these are sufficiently prevalent or influential to deserve mention here.

One common image assumes a sharp contrast between the two:

> The Anglo-American relies upon personal interest to accomplish his ends and gives free scope to the unguided strength and common sense of the people; the Russian centers all the authority of society in a single arm. The principal instrument of the former is freedom; of the latter, servitude. Their starting-point is different and their courses are not the same; yet each of them seems marked out by the will of Heaven to sway the destinies of half the globe.

These words were written by Alexis de Tocqueville in 1834. Today they are repeatedly invoked in discussions of the two systems. We quote them here, however, not to support a point but to illustrate the "black-and-white" image of Russian and American politics. In the years since *Democracy in America,* this image has been an extremely prevalent one. The Revolution of 1917 gave it a renewed relevance. Slavery and freedom; dictatorship and democracy; communism and capitalism; collectivism and individualism; the totalitarian state and the constitutional one: how easy and appropriate it is to pin one label on the United States and its opposite on the Soviet Union. The human mind craves simple distinctions; and Russians, Americans, and Europeans all have their own motives for embracing the "black-and-white" approach. For the Russian the Soviet Union is the leading socialist state, the spearhead of the worldwide communist revolution. The United States, as the strongest of the capitalist powers, is the center of "reactionary imperialism." The American puts different words on the same differences and reverses the value assigned to them. The European combines the American and Russian formulas in a variety of permutations, in all of which, however, Europe is seen as embodying the virtues of both with the vices of neither: freedom without license; socialism without slavery. In one form or another the "black-and-white" approach seems to meet everyone's need.

We would be the last to deny the obvious differences. Too often, however, in the Russian, American, and European versions of the "black-and-white" formula, the distinctions are not analyzed;

they are simply asserted. Political reality, however, cannot be captured in a static dichotomy. It is a commonplace in the West that the Marxist formula that assumes the increasing misery of the proletariat and the increasing intensity of class conflict has little relevance to the American economy. John Kenneth Galbraith once pointed out that the "conventional wisdom" embodied in the commonly expressed axioms concerning the American economic system also failed to describe American economic reality. One main theme of this book is that the "conventional wisdom" of the "black-and-white" approach in its Marxist, American, and European versions furnishes an inadequate guide to the significant similarities and differences. To be specific, the "black-and-white" approach fails on two counts.

First, by starting from two stereotypes, it limits its vision too narrowly. It entirely overlooks the possibility that viewing the Soviet and American systems in a broader compass might reveal significant points which they have in common, and which distinguish them from other political systems. To name only a few key similarities: the governments are on a continental scale; they involve the commingling of a variety of peoples, often with consequent racial (or ethnic) tensions; the societies have experienced rapid technological and economic change and share in some regards a similar respect for material and technical values; historically each society was closely related to but not an integral part of the western European political system; each society sees itself as the particular embodiment of universally true principles; international responsibilities have become increasingly important in shaping their major domestic political dilemmas. When compared to the complex political systems of western Europe, with their intricate class structures and multiplicity of political cultures, the political systems of the United States and the Soviet Union seem to share a homogeneity, a unity, and a simplicity which are missing on the Continent. Confronted today with many of the same challenges—economic, military, and political—the two systems have not reacted along entirely different lines.

Second, starting from *a priori* assumptions about the nature of the differences between the two systems, the "black-and-white" approach tends to neglect other important differences—ones which may be at least as significant as those which are summed up in the stereotypes of "freedom and slavery," "communism and capitalism." These easy contrasts are not entirely divorced from underlying reality. In general, they all have to do with the different relationship between the political system and society. In the Soviet Union, individual liberty is limited by the state, and economic activity is directed by the state. In the United States, the state is responsible to society and it is limited by the economic and social functions performed by autonomous institutions. These are crucial differences but they are not the only important ones. Two others not usually covered in the common formulas concern the role of ideology and the selection and character of the political elites in the two systems.

THE THEORY OF CONVERGENCE

The "black-and-white" image predominated during the early years of the Cold War. It was a static conception. In the late 1950s it began to be replaced by the more dynamic theory of convergence of American and Soviet societies. This idea exists in a variety of forms and varying degrees of refinement. The basic theme is that the Soviet Union and the United States are becoming more alike. In its most widely held forms almost all the change is seen as occurring within the Soviet Union. Implicit in the theory is the image of a static America and a dynamic Soviet Union. The United States is seen as affluent and free; the Soviet Union is gradually moving in this direction. On the other hand, the United States is also viewed as comfortable and inflexible, while the Soviet Union is viewed as flexible, developing, responsive to new needs. If Khrushchev has accomplished nothing else, he has popularized that image of the Soviet Union as a highly dynamic, pragmatic society. And many intellectuals and politicians in Asia attach higher value to the society which is changing than to the society which serves as the standard for change. They are more impressed with the rapid Soviet industrialization than with the fact that the total economic product of the United States is still about twice that of its rival. Similarly, they are more impressed with first steps toward liberalization in the Soviet political system than with free speech and popular elections in the United States.

The wider acceptance of the convergence theory was stimulated by the events in the Soviet Union in the decade following the death of Stalin. The end of the atmosphere of terror; the closing of labor camps; the subordination of the secret police; the denunciation of the "crimes of the Stalinist era"; the absence of an all-powerful tyrant, and the collective exercise of power between 1953 and 1957 and in more restricted form after 1959; the greater freedom for a while permitted writers, artists, and scientists; the encouragement of criticism and discussion on specific limited issues; the greater sensitivity of the regime. to public opinion; and, above all, the pragmatic, free-wheeling, open political style of Khrushchev: all these are facts. The believers in convergence argue that these developments are only the first steps to more fundamental changes in the Soviet political and social systems. "Liberalization" is not just a restricted phenomenon, nor simply one phase in a cycle which will eventually produce renewed terror and coercion. They say that it is a secular process which will develop and spread and which is the inevitable concomitant of the industrialization of the Soviet Union and its new role in international politics.

The argument that industrialization will produce increasing liberalization and therefore convergence is not always explicitly formulated. It appears, however, that industrialization has three consequences which are held, in varying ways, to stimulate tendencies toward convergence.

First, industrialization and urbanization, it is said, give rise to a common culture found in all modern societies. The industrial process imposes uniformities in equipment, skills, technique, and organization. Managers and workers in the two societies perform similar tasks and hence develop similar outlooks and similar ways of life. Industrial culture is the same in Sverdlovsk and Detroit. Eventually this culture will produce similar political institutions. As the industrial process gives rise to certain common forms of factory organization which most efficiently serve the requirements of that process, so also certain common forms of political organization will be developed which are most appropriate to the needs of that society. This is, in effect, anti-Soviet Marxism: the forces of production will shape the social context of production, which in turn will determine the political superstructure.

Second, industrialization produces increasing diversity and complexity in society. More and more technical specialties develop;

interest groups multiply; more intricate forms of social organization arise. An industrial society is necessarily pluralistic. If it is to function efficiently, the specialized interests within it must, first of all, be given autonomy to apply their specialized knowledge. Physical scientists, medical experts, pedagogues, military strategists, engineers, even economic planners, must be free to use their skills and expertise. The laws of physics, of strategy, of engineering, and even of industrial management and economics are universally true and eventually must be respected as such by all modern societies. Hence ideological and political claims must be limited. Industrialization increases the number of interest groups which make positive demands on the political process. In the early stages of industrialization the Communist Party could pre-empt the scene: it articulated and imposed the demands for industrialization on an agricultural society. Relatively few other industrial interest groups existed. As a result of its success in industrializing the country, however, the previous vacuum has been filled. Large numbers of established groups are now said to exist: they make claims for resources on the political system. The function of the Party will no longer be to impose new demands on the system itself but to play a mediating, brokerage role, comparable to that of governments and political parties in Western democracies.

Third, industrialization creates affluence. Affluence undermines political disciplines and ideological orthodoxy. The historical function of the Communist Party was to industrialize the Soviet Union. It could justify its monopoly of power only so long as sacrifice was required to achieve this end. Now, sacrifice is no longer economically necessary, and hence the Communist Party is no longer politically necessary. The balance of production will increasingly shift from producer goods to consumer goods. What place is there for revolutionary *élan* in a high-mass-consumption society? Ideological fervor is characteristic of only the early phases of the industrialization process. The age of ideology has already come to an end in western Europe, the United States, and Japan. It will soon come to an end in the Soviet Union. With rare exceptions, affluent countries are also democratic ones. If Khrushchev does succeed in raising the Soviet standard of living above that of the United States, he will not achieve communism; he will bury it.

These arguments for convergence as a result of industrialization are often supplemented by the argument for convergence as a result of mutual influence and contact between nations. The Soviet Union and the United States, it is said, will enter into a phase of "mutual discovery," in which they will learn from each other. Modern technology and communication make it impossible for any nation to be an island. One important aspect of the 1950s was the increased contacts between people in the Soviet Union and foreigners. With improved travel and communication, these contacts will multiply in the future. A machine, a technique, or even a form of social organization which works in one society will be imported into the other. Since the Soviet Union has been more of a closed society than Western countries, it will inevitably experience the greatest immediate changes resulting from this increased contact.

Probably the most sophisticated theory supporting convergence is that developed by W. W. Rostow in *The Stages of Economic Growth*. He argues that a society is ripe for Marxism only in the early stages of the industrialization process. Marx himself developed his theory from observing those stages in England in the middle of the nineteenth century. The dislocation of Russian society in World War I came just at the moment in Russia's "take-off" into sustained economic growth when Russian society was peculiarly susceptible to the appeals of Marxism and peculiarly vulnerable to take-over by Marxist groups. Marxism generally has an appeal in the developing areas of the world and relatively little appeal in the highly developed industrial societies of western Europe, North America, and the British dominions.

According to Rostow, the latest stage in the industrialization process is that of high mass consumption. The United States has reached this stage. Western Europe is entering it. Eventually the other industrializing societies will approach it or reach it. In such a society, a high-powered political dictatorship cannot survive. Communism, as Rostow puts it, is a "disease of the transition." Societies outgrow it as they move into the more advanced phases of economic growth; "Communism is likely to wither in the age of high mass-consumption. . . ." [1] * The leaders of the Soviet Union, Rostow argues, "almost certainly" understand this problem. They will do their best to postpone a high-mass-consumption economy

---

* Reference notes begin on page 441.

or to alter it to make it compatible with continued dominance of the Communist Party. But, in the end, the probabilities are that sustained economic growth will undermine communism.

The convergence thesis shapes the images of the Soviet and American systems in the minds of public officials, intellectuals, and scholars in Japan, in India, elsewhere in Asia, and in the Middle East. It is also prevalent in the United States. In different form it is espoused by the Titoist communist movement and is, indeed, implicit in much of the Titoist criticism of Soviet communism. And from the opposite corner of the communist world, "convergence" is, in effect, one of the charges which the Chinese Communists level at their former Soviet comrades.

Convergence serves many needs. To Americans and western Europeans it offers what appears to be the only way out of a hopeless and endless conflict. To neutralists it provides the historical sanction for their position. To the Titoists it justifies their isolation from the rest of the communist community. To the Chinese it explains why they, in contrast to the Soviets, remain uncorrupted orthodox Marxist-Leninists. The theory of convergence is not only an abstract intellectual position but also a source of optimism for many and of justification for all. The only apparent dissenters from the theory are the Soviet leaders themselves, who resolutely adhere to their own version of the "black-and-white" concept. In June 1963, indeed, L. F. Ilyichev, Secretary for Ideological Affairs of the Communist Party of the Soviet Union (CPSU), in listing several "pernicious" clichés, noted:

> Some time ago there appeared a theory, according to which socialism and capitalism, in spite of their fundamental difference, are allegedly developing in the same direction—that the compulsory economic imperatives of total industrial development will gradually lead to a hybridization of the two systems, to their synthesis, to the formation of a single mixed society by means of the internal change of socialism and some modernization of capitalism. This is frank social demagogy. The imperialist ideologists speculate on socialist terminology. They are not beyond adopting a few ideas of socialism in order to deceive the working people, to delude them with socialist slogans, since they have in their hearts no positive ideals which could promise the people any prospects of hope for the future. Like any reactionary concepts, the latest fancies of anticommunism have no future at all.

And yet even the Soviets themselves have their own long-run convergence thesis that the entire world will eventually be communist: "Your grandchildren," as Khrushchev said, "will play under red flags." In one form or another, the convergence idea appears to be a pervasive belief throughout the world.

A closer look at the similarities and differences between the two political systems will help to determine whether this idea is justified.

PART I

The Political System

◆◇◆

CHAPTER ONE

Political Ideas and Politics

IDEOLOGICAL COMMITMENT AND POLITICAL BELIEFS

THE TERM "ideology" does not have the same meaning for an American as for a Russian. On the whole, Americans avoid using it when referring to their own political preferences or individual political beliefs. Similarly, the two major American political parties never refer to their programs as ideological declarations. The President never speaks of the ideology of his Administration. In the discussions concerning the need for a more conscious sense of national purpose,[1] the dominant viewpoint by far was that there is no American ideology and that it would be harmful to try to invent one.

At the same time, Americans are inclined to describe the views held by the Soviet leaders or by Communists in general as "ideological." Communists are often said to be blinded by their ideological prejudices. Implicit in this is the notion that ideology and reality are two entirely different things. It is assumed that to be ideologically motivated is to be unrealistic, irrational, dogmatic, and fanatical. However, since the communist leaders seem to act intelligently and efficiently and in recent years have demonstrated impressive technical skills, there is also a growing tendency to assume that the Soviet leaders are really quite cynical in their use of ideological slogans, that they do not believe in their ideology but merely use it to mislead their opponents and to mobilize their supporters. In either case the term "ideology" has a pejorative meaning in the prevalent American usage. A sensible, rational person can be idealistic but should not be ideological. Implicit in this viewpoint is the belief that all intelligent and realistic people think alike, that there is an objective reality which anyone can perceive. Those who think the Russians are fanatical often tend to be convinced that a total showdown between America and Russia is inevitable; those who think the Russians are cynical tend to believe that it is only a matter of time before all Soviet-American differences are resolved in a quiet "businesslike" way.

17

To a Soviet Communist, on the other hand, to be ideological *is* to be historically conscious, to be purposeful, and to be idealistic in a practical sense. Idealism without ideology is at best sentimentality, at worst cynicism. To be truly idealistic, one must be conscious of one's purposes, of one's place in history, of one's relationship to the continually changing social-economic reality. The Soviets are proud to describe themselves as ideologically motivated. Their ideology is said to express the interests of the masses and is therefore allegedly the truly humanistic and democratic one. The Soviet leadership often boasts about the superiority of its ideological program and proclaims the continual necessity to imbue every Soviet citizen with a profound dedication to the Marxist-Leninist ideology. It also makes real understanding with others conditional on the sharing of a common outlook. Nikita Khrushchev expressed the basic communist commitment when he said, "Friendship is real and strong when people share the same views about events, about history, about life. If you do not share the philosophy of the Communist Party because you have your own principles and your own views, then it is possible to maintain good relations with Communists, but it is difficult to achieve a deep friendship as we understand it."

The Russians, furthermore, discriminate between "good" and "bad" ideologies, and between the "conscious," "rational" communist ideology, which is said to dissect and analyze reality scientifically and develop a program expressing the interest of "the masses," and those ideologies which merely express the interests, often not even in a fully conscious manner, of narrow, exploitative classes. They are thus quite willing to use the term "ideology" while speaking of the views and attitudes of their opponents, including the Americans. Since to them an ideology is the expression of the interests of a particular class, and since monopoly capitalism is said to dominate America, the prevalent American ideology is a capitalistic, bourgeois one, articulated by the various leading spokesmen of the dominant interests. The Russians often cite the lack of ideological differences between the two major American political parties as proof of this. They readily admit that conflicting utterances are quite frequent in America, but this to them is not necessarily an expression of democracy. Rather, this is said to reflect either the clash of conflicting monopoly interests or merely the fact

that many Americans are politically not fully conscious and hence
have not articulated systematically the ideology of their class. Thus,
unlike Americans, the Soviets view ideology as a general social-
political phenomenon, present in all societies.

The difference is significant, for it reflects quite distinctive conceptions of the relationship between politics and ideas. These
conceptions in turn are themselves important, for they reveal the
underlying attitudes, beliefs, and doctrines that shape the political
style of the respective countries. The very attitude of a Russian or
an American to the term "ideology" is in itself indicative of his
"ideological" inclinations. Basically, the difference involves one
outlook which consciously stresses purpose in all social-political
activity and relates it to a scheme of history, and another which
tends to be more spontaneous and focuses primarily on specific
situations. Thus, if "ideology" means a set of political ideas that
are overt, systematic, dogmatic, and embodied in a set of institutions, the Soviet world outlook can justifiably qualify for the label.
The Soviet political ideas are overt in the sense that there are
certain officially proclaimed "texts" which contain the basic doctrines and guides to action. They are systematized in the sense that
these texts are regularly revised and brought up to date in the light
of both experience and the needs of the ruling elite.[2] They are institutionalized in the sense that they have been proclaimed to be the
official ideology of the Soviet state, binding upon every citizen,
embodied in the ruling Communist Party, and articulated by appointed "ideologues." They are dogmatized in the sense that, until
any of its tenets have been officially revised or repudiated, the
ideology is to be accepted without reservation by anyone who
wishes to describe himself as a Communist.

Communist ideology has developed through the progressive re-
definition of orthodoxy. Deviations are either suppressed or extir-
pated. American political ideas, on the other hand, are more complex but less explicit; they have grown through accretion. Over the
course of centuries new ideas and concepts are added to but not
necessarily integrated into older ones. In the broadest terms, the
results of this process can be thought of as three strata: an inherited tradition of law and constitutionalism, to which ideas of
natural rights and liberalism were added in the eighteenth century,
and on which were superimposed concepts of democracy and

majority rule in the nineteenth. The resulting amalgam lacks the coherence and the concreteness to qualify as an ideology. Only the constitutional strand furnishes a close parallel to the Soviets'. Here there are overt texts in the form of the Constitution, the Bill of Rights, and authoritative interpretations such as *The Federalist.* These texts are reasonably systematic and are regularly annotated, revised, reinterpreted, and brought up to date in the light of new circumstances. The Presidium of the Communist Party redefines the meaning of class struggle for a thermonuclear world; so also the Supreme Court redefines the meaning of "due process of law" for the welfare state. The constitutional tradition is thus institutionalized in the sense that it has a "carrier" in the Supreme Court and the judicial system. It is dogmatized in that the constitutional interpretations of these bodies are binding upon officials and citizens until subsequently changed by the Court.

The actual process of constitutional revision, moreover, has its parallels with ideological revision in the Soviet Union. Changes in the meaning of the American Constitution or the Soviet ideology usually occur at times of acute controversy or crisis. The changes are then justified through written statements (judicial opinions, Party resolutions) in which previous interpretations are denounced or reversed and a new "true" interpretation of the doctrine or Constitution is justified through logic, textual analysis, appeals to history and the intentions of Lenin or the Founding Fathers, and the "felt needs" of current conditions. And just as there are conflicts between dogmatists and revisionists in the interpretation of communist doctrine, so also are there conflicts between narrow constructionists and broad constructionists in the interpretation of the American Constitution.

The Constitution and constitutionalism, however, make up only part of the American political tradition. The other elements lack most of the characteristics of an ideology. The "overt texts" of liberalism and democracy are too scattered and disputed to be recognized as such. The position of Locke in the history of liberalism is hardly comparable to the position of Marx in the history of Marxism. Similarly, few Americans could agree on a "systematized" current elaboration of liberal and democratic ideas binding on the present reality. Who is the genuine interpreter of the American values and tradition: Barry Goldwater or Arthur Schlesinger?

Both are rooted in the common past, but they disagree sharply on its current meaning. This is as if the Soviet system could tolerate at one time Soviet equivalents to Gomulka and Mao Tse-tung. And certainly, with the exception of certain fringe groups which see themselves as the singular standard bearers of the *true* tradition, there is no comparable current institutionalization of the original doctrines as there is in the Soviet Union. American political institutions have been shaped by constitutional, liberal, and democratic ideas, but the doctrines have not been institutionalized in a living carrier ("a living church"), such as the Communist Party is in the Soviet Union. Because of this it has been more difficult—outside the realm of constitutional doctrine—to dogmatize the original principles, even though some of them (for example, the sanctity of private property or the automatic social good of private initiative) occasionally have been elevated into the realm of the absolute. Nonetheless, the absence of official arbiters and the plurality of current meanings attached to liberalism and democracy effectively exclude over-all dogmatization.

The Soviet ideological commitment is based on a series of basic and absolute assumptions concerning reality: they are alleged to provide all-embracing answers to such key philosophical and social questions as what is the nature of man, what is his relationship to his environment, what forces cause historical change, and what are the ultimate purposes of social organization. This part of the ideological commitment can be described as its *doctrinal* component; it is unchanging (or static) and is based primarily on the historical and philosophical writings of Marx and Engels. Ideology also involves an *action program,* designed to implement most effectively through political and social action its basic doctrinal assumptions. This action program is very specifically related to the conditions and opportunities prevailing in any particular phase of history and in any particular geographical and social-economic context. While based on the doctrine and reflecting its philosophical principles and biases, the action program is subject to revision by the leaders in the light of experiences and necessity. Thus it is dynamic.

Much effort, however, is expended to demonstrate that such revisions do not involve any basic departure from the doctrinal part of the ideology but are merely "creative" adaptations of it. The conscious and subjective identification of the communist leaders with the ideology produces an ideological commitment, even if these leaders are primarily preoccupied with specific political activity. Lenin's contribution, for instance, has been primarily in the realm of the action program, although he occasionally dabbled in doctrinal matters.[3] Khrushchev's much more limited contribution to Marxism and Leninism has been entirely in the realm of the action program.

The Soviets attempt to link doctrines and programs together through logic and analysis sanctioned by power. They are obsessed with "the unity of theory and practice." The more amorphous American values and doctrines are seldom directly related to political action. Americans see a natural gap between principles and expediency. The requirements of the two are assumed to conflict, and a politician is usually thought to act according to one or the other. To the communist politician, on the other hand, the correct line is always *both* principled and expedient. Expediential actions must be formulated and expressed in terms of basic doctrine: basic doctrine must be applied expedientially. Since politics is necessarily the art of the possible, Americans often view politics and politicians as unprincipled and even corrupt. The general principles of the American political beliefs are usually thought to be inoperative in day-to-day political action. Indeed, statements of general principles (for example, in a presidential inaugural address) often derive their appeal and authority precisely from their failure to imply a particular course of political action. Contrast, for instance, outstanding presidential addresses with the reports of Soviet leaders to Party congresses. The latter are typically elaborate and lengthy efforts to relate fundamental Party doctrine to the concrete program which the leaders see as immediately necessary. The presidential address which makes a mark on history,* on the other hand, is not devoted to specific legislative proposals but rather restates in eloquent and memorable language the fundamental beliefs of the American creed. If the President goes on to trace out the implications of his generalities for specific programs, his speech ceases to

---

* Washington's Farewell Address, Jefferson's First Inaugural Address, Lincoln's Gettysburg and Second Inaugural Addresses, Franklin D. Roosevelt's First Inaugural Address and "Four Freedoms" speech, Kennedy's Inaugural Address.

be a sermon accepted by all and becomes a partisan plea debated by many.

With respect to political issues, the Soviets ask, "What is the correct line?" Americans ask, "What is the correct position?" The difference in terminology reflects differences in political thinking. The communist "line" is the link between fundamental doctrines and stands on particular issues: it defines the meaning of the doctrines in a particular historical context and the relation between a stand on one issue and stands on other issues. The American, however, does not have a line; he only has ad-hoc "positions." The position which he takes on one issue may be quite discrete and unrelated to positions on other issues and to his general political beliefs. Soviet political action is justified by the line which links it to general doctrine. American political action is justified by an immediate consensus quite distinct from the consensuses which may be developed on other issues and from the over-all agreement on the key elements of the American political beliefs.

The foregoing discussion points to the advisability of avoiding the term "ideology" when speaking of the looser, vague, less formal, and unstructured American counterpart. Sociologists have sometimes described the American as being a "value system"—that is to say, a generalized over-all outlook shared by most Americans, involving certain fundamental preferences, prejudices, and often unverified and unarticulated assumptions, without any formal structure and official interpreters. This value system lacks a formal specific doctrinal component, although its philosophical roots can be traced to some common sources, for example, Locke and the so-called "liberal consensus." However, the recognition of a common source has not much current political relevance, since a great many Americans act in keeping with these basic assumptions without necessarily accepting them philosophically. (This is particularly true of American Catholics, who naturally see themselves as part of another philosophic tradition.) Similarly, it would be difficult to speak of any specific, conscious action program insofar as the American value system is concerned. Rather, there are certain generally accepted methods for handling problems as they arise, and there is a reasonably widespread consensus as to which methods are not in keeping with "the American way of life." The common assumptions concerning acceptable means of political action add up to a set of

American political beliefs, a term we prefer to the more obscure and pedantic "value system." While in some respects they perform the same political function, we will henceforth refer to the Soviet *ideology* and to the American *political beliefs.*

THE TRADITIONAL BACKGROUND

The Soviet ideology and the American political beliefs are the products of the accumulated social experience of the two societies, which sets their respective political styles. A brief glance into the more recent past might thus set the stage for a discussion of their current functions.

Most of Russian history has involved a combination of political autocracy and doctrinal absolutism. Pre-Soviet Russian political history, in the period paralleling American growth, was characterized by an increasing gap between social development and the prevailing political institutions. Russia by the nineteenth century had expanded geographically into Asia, reached the Pacific, and planted its flag on the frontiers of British India, while in the West the partition of Poland made Russia, for the first time in its history, into a central European power. The Russian empire became a major factor in the European international system, with the concomitant exposure of Russia to European influence. This influence was at first limited to the upper reaches of Russian society, to the younger officers and intellectuals and, later in the nineteenth century, to the gradually emerging merchant, industrial, and professional middle class. The bulk of Russian society—the peasantry—remained relatively immune, and the autocratic czarist system was not endangered as long as the disaffected elements lacked the political basis of mass social unrest. The political system, proudly describing itself as autocratic and fiercely resisting any diminution in its power, was bolstered by an official state ideology with strong religious overtones and messianic aspirations. The notion of a "third Rome" was useful to the autocracy, since it combined the appeal of state nationalism, which was attractive to the more politically conscious, with the appeal of Russian Orthodox religious sentiment, which turned the people against alien national and religious forces.*

---

* "He who deserts the Orthodox belief ceases to be a Russian not only in his thoughts and acts but also in his way of living and in his dress,"

The traditional autocracy, however, rooted as it was in the background of centuries-long Mongol oppression and repeated foreign invasions, was gradually undermined by the increasingly restless and radical intelligentsia and later by the social-economic changes wrought by the impact of the first phases of the industrialization in Russia. The Russian intelligentsia, made conscious of Russia's social-economic backwardness by greater contacts with the West, and oppressed by the political tyranny of the autocratic order, responded in a variety of ways, ranging from utmost pessimism to naïve utopianism. Some, like P. U. Chaadaev, saw no salvation for Russia since it had been nurtured in a climate devoid of legality or moral sense of justice.[4] Others, like K. Aksakov, veered to the belief that there was a long-range advantage in this historical circumstance:

> A Russian, whatever his calling, evades the law whenever he can do so with impunity, and the government does exactly the same. All this is distressing and hard to bear at present, but so far as the future is concerned it is an enormous advantage. It proves that in Russia there is no ideal, invisible government lurking behind the visible government as some sort of apotheosis of the existing order of things.[5]

But, whatever their image of the future and their analysis of the past, most agreed that, to correct the present, several basic social ills had to be eliminated. Serfdom was seen as perhaps the most burning social problem and its abolition the point of departure for subsequent reforms. But concerning the latter there was no con-

---

declared Konstantin Pobedonostsev, the reactionary Over Procurator of the Holy Synod and the czar's chief political ideologue at the end of the nineteenth century, urging the authorities to restrict mass education primarily to the inculcation of loyalty and to the acquisition of skills in basic trades and arts. Pobedonostsev's image of the ideal society—with state religion, family training, and indoctrination of the intellectuals all within a rigid legal framework—bears a striking resemblance to the rigid social order advocated by Plato in his *Laws*. Indeed, one is tempted to compare Russia to a tough urchin sporadically exposed to very strict re-education programs often under strong but conflicting doctrinal guidance (the czar's or Stalin's). By way of analogy, America matured under circumstances similar to some contemporary "progressive" educational programs: it could do much as it pleased in the context of relative material plenty and physical security.

sensus. Some (as the Populists did) saw salvation in the traditional peasant commune, an institution said to incarnate all the special virtues of the Russian soul. Others wanted to encourage the development of a free-holders class of independent farmers. Some pleaded, "God save Russia from the bourgeoisie!" while others incanted, "God give Russia a bourgeoisie!" [6] Some cursed and rejected the West; others preached the advantages of learning and imitating its experience.

In going to the peasant—as the Populists attempted to do in the second half of the nineteenth century—or in trying to stir up the small but disaffected new proletariat—a vocation increasingly popular among the intelligentsia toward the end of the century—the alienated Russian intellectual was seeking the social base for his political action. Often not finding it, he turned to direct political action which, because of the intolerance and the overwhelming preponderance of autocracy, frequently meant isolated acts of political terrorism. Thus developed the tradition of conspiratorial activity, based on faith, fanaticism, and fratricide, and imbued with a strong dose of romanticism.*

This tradition's concomitant was a marked inclination toward political messianism—a preoccupation with abstract, absolute principles, often with overtones of utopianism—almost as a form of psychological compensation for the hardships and dangers of the revolutionaries' tenuous links with life and for the alienated intel-

---

* The following account of a gathering of the young revolutionaries on New Year's Eve of 1880, in the midst of sweeping arrests, conveys the particularly romantic flavor of that generation: "On a round table in the middle of the room a vase was placed, filled with pieces of sugar, lemon, roots, sprinkled with arac and wine. It was a magic sight when the arac was fired and the candles extinguished. The flickering flame, mounting and waning, lighted the severe faces of the men surrounding it; Kolodkevich and Zheliabov stood closest. Morozov took out his stiletto, then another, then another, placed them, crossed, on the vase and, without preparation, with a sudden impetus, the powerful, solemn melody of the well-known *haidamak* song was heard: 'Hai, ne dyvuites, dobryie ludi, shcho na Ukrainie povstaniie.' The sounds of the song spread and mounted, they were joined by fresh voices, and the shimmering flame flickered, bursting out with a red glow, as if steeling the weapons for struggle and death. . . ." Olga Lubatovitch, *Byloe* (June 1906), pp. 123-124, quoted in J. Kucharzewski, *Od Bialego Caratu do Czerwonego* (Warsaw, 1931), V, pp. 304-305.

lectuals' sense of political and social frustration. The quest for absolute answers, a characteristic of minority social groups that reject the existing social order, expressed itself in a wide variety of political programs and pamphlets, most of them stated with self-righteous conviction. This subterranean political dialogue was made more radical by the police repressions which mounted in intensity toward the end of the century. The autocratic tradition of czardom in general was not conducive to the emergence of a variety of political viewpoints, based on the pragmatic principle of agreement to disagree. As a result, the politically thinking segment of Russian society did not develop an appreciation of the complexities of social-economic reforms or of the desirability of a legal order, and those few Russians who did tended to be government bureaucrats,[7] who necessarily shared the fate of the state that they served. For the most part, Russian intellectuals "were pushed into abstract thought which, untempered by contact with reality, assumed the form of growing radicalism, and the radicalism in thought in turn led to radicalism in action." [8]

Just as the Civil War in America is a watershed in American economic history, so in Russia the emancipation of the serfs in 1861 can be seen as creating the conditions for the subsequent rapid industrial development, encouraged in a large part by the government's realization that without it the national security of the country would be threatened. In the second half of the nineteenth century Russia, while still lagging economically in comparison to western Europe, began to develop rapidly its railroad networks and its industrial sector. Favorable conditions in the world grain market in the 1890s encouraged extensive investments in the railroad network, with consequent demands for heavy industry. Russia's industrial growth during the decade spurted ahead at an average annual rate of approximately 8 per cent. By 1914, the economy was producing annually 5 million tons of pig iron, 4 million of iron and steel, and 40 million of coal. This economic development was accompanied by a major population explosion; in 1861 the czarist empire numbered approximately 74 million inhabitants, and by 1917 the number had grown to 170 million. Considering the impact of economics on ideology, even more significant is the fact that in the territory which remained Soviet after the Revolution the number of urban inhabitants had increased from about 7 million in

1861 to 20 million in 1917, thus involving the appearance of first-generation proletarians, divorced from their traditional environment and, as studies elsewhere show, highly susceptible to radical appeals.[9]

The paradox of Russia's economic development is that in large part it was stimulated by the security interests of an autocratic state which required a traditional social order for its stability. Yet the very process of industrialization and modernization disrupted the traditional society, while the awareness of more developed societies elsewhere encouraged the appearance of political and social ideologies which tried to simplify complex social processes, gave all-embracing explanations for the existing inadequacies, and offered guides to action. An advanced society such as America or England experienced its growth without the image of a more developed economy to serve as a beacon and a goal. But in Russia the very awareness of backwardness made the social development dependent on political action, especially since the society was already guided by a political autocracy. In that sense, the Russian experience has certain parallels with the existing tendencies in some of the under-developed nations.

The initial impact of economic development was thus a stimulus to intense ideological preoccupation; Marxism made its first appearance in this context and was subsequently adapted by Lenin to the specific Russian conditions. Perhaps in time, with the social wounds healed by further growth, more moderate tendencies would have prevailed, and the split of the Mensheviks and Lenin's Bolsheviks may be viewed as portending such a development. History ruled otherwise, however, and the calamitous collapse of czardom—in a domestic revolution caused by an external military defeat—brought to power a political elite imbued with radical ideological inclinations reflecting the tensions and the utopian aspirations of a society in rapid transition.*

---

* We cannot enter into the complex matter of the reasons for the success of the Bolsheviks and the failure of their rivals, but the following from A. Ulam, *The Unfinished Revolution* (New York, 1960) seems particularly perceptive: "The ideal society for revolutionary Marxism is the one that is 'arrested' in its response to industrialization; where large-scale industry and urbanization make simple anarchism obsolete and syndicalism unavailing from the point of view of the radical

Thrust into power by a combination of fortune and accident, the new revolutionary elite ceased to be a product of such a transition and became its master. They could now impose even more forceful, rapid, and extreme measures of social change—all in keeping with their aspirations but also in effect making their permanent revolution the basis for their power. Thus an isolated group of alienated political radicals, with an ideology which was the offspring of a reactionary autocracy and of the social-economic dislocation and other iniquities of industrialization, became the makers of a new society in which their political power and their total social-economic reconstruction of society, on a scale unprecedented in history, were consciously based on their ideology.

American political experience lacks the tension, the anguish, and the drama of Russian political development. Ideology and revolution are the key words for Russia; consensus and evolution describe America. The colonists of the seventeenth century brought with them English law and constitutionalism and the English class structure. The former flourished across the Atlantic, but the latter withered and died. Social and economic inequalities persisted in the New World, but they were supplemented by opportunities which Europe lacked. It was impossible to maintain a landed, European-style aristocracy, and the upper classes which did exist could not keep their monopoly of political power long. In the northern colonies political dominance easily passed to the coastal merchants and yeomen farmers. Eighteenth-century ideas of liberty and natural rights found a congenial home in that middle-class atmosphere, the introduction of liberalism occurring without the revolutionary struggles which accompanied it in the British Isles. The Americans, as Tocqueville said, were "born equal." This happy circumstance colored the rest of American history.[10] Unchallenged by an aristocracy, the middle class adjusted more easily to the introduction of democracy in the first half of the nineteenth century. By the

---

worker; where the relative newness of industrialization has not entirely killed off the peasant mentality; where a large part of the population consists of peasants tilling their small holdings; and where the political process and class divisions, whatever the official form of the state, do indeed give the worker the impression of the state as the 'executive committee of the exploiting class' " (p. 153).

1840s constitutionalism, liberalism, and democracy had become firmly lodged in the main current of American thought.

In other countries similar ideas had been employed for conflicting purposes. In America they joined in the service of a middle-class society. The moral absolutes of liberalism theoretically could, and at times did, conflict with the demands of the masses. Similarly, ideas of popular government were logically incompatible with a constitutional heritage of checks and balances and judicial review. At other times, constitutional requirements and legalistic procedures seemed to put fetters on liberty. In general, however, ideas which were logically contradictory nonetheless lived together more or less in political harmony. The cement in the American amalgam was the ambiguity and fuzziness of the ideas which composed it. The only major ideological controversy grew out of the struggle between North and South over slavery. Social, economic, and geographical factors gave the South a distinct outlook and interest which seemed increasingly threatened by the growth of industry and population in the North and the expansion of the nation westward. In the conflict that followed, the South rejected the democratic strand in the American tradition and combined selected elements of the liberal and constitutional strands with the familiar conservative ideas in defense of the status quo. The result was a distinct, although ephemeral, outbreak of political and social thought dissenting vigorously from the emerging American consensus.[11] Appomattox, however, re-established that consensus by force of arms. This consensus furnished the framework for the rapid economic development that followed the Civil War, giving rise to vigorous clashes between laissez-faire liberals and reform liberals at the end of the nineteenth century and in the first decades of the twentieth. These debates occurred, however, within a heritage of shared values accumulated during the course of two and a half centuries.

Russian politics in the nineteenth century was marked by the weakness of the doctrines of constitutionalism, liberalism, and democracy which were the very heart of American politics. By the turn of the century, moreover, American thought was shifting from moral absolutism to modern relativism. In both countries the dominant trends for the twentieth century were set by the reform movements at the end of the nineteenth. But in Russia the reform movements were conspiratorial and revolutionary: they opposed the official orthodoxy of the regime with an equally intense, absolutist political orthodoxy of their own. In America the dominant orthodoxy of free enterprise was opposed in the 1880s and 1890s by Populist doctrines equally moralistic and absolute. About the turn of the century, however, reform liberalism began to change. It was increasingly shaped by social Darwinism, pragmatism, economic determinism, and Freudianism.[12] The intellectual weapons of the reformers against the stand-patters were such as to undermine faith in all absolute values, not just conservative ones.* In Russia the relatively simple doctrinal absolutism of Pobedonostsev was displaced by the relatively more sophisticated ideological absolutism of Lenin. In the United States, the stern but simple moralism of McKinley was eventually replaced by the relatively carefree pragmatism of Franklin D. Roosevelt.

This contrasting ideological evolution reflects original differences in society and the consequent differences in social development. Russia's intellectual reformers lacked a sufficiently strong middle class or a sufficiently politically conscious peasantry with which to identify themselves. Necessarily, the reformers were driven to conspiratorial actions and messianic hopes. In the United States, on the other hand, the struggle between reform and laissez-faire liberalism occurred within a framework of shared middle-class values. In addition, the reformers were linked to definite social groupings —Southern and Western farmers, middle-class professionals, small businessmen, labor—and could advance the claims of these groups in an atmosphere of relative freedom and political opportunity. To achieve their goals, the reformers did not need new doctrinal absolutes. If they could undermine the old absolutes, the natural workings of the pluralistic political order would accomplish the rest. The reformers could safely resort to skepticism and relativism to attack the values of their opponents because there were so many values which they and their opponents shared and which were

---

* "The apostle of relativity," Charles A. Beard subsequently observed, "is destined to be destroyed by the child of his own brain. . . . I wish we could find some way of getting rid of conservative morality without having these youngsters [the New Dealers] drop all morality." Quoted in Eric F. Goldman, *Rendezvous with Destiny* (New York, 1952), pp. 200, 361.

beyond question by either. Appropriately enough, pragmatism or instrumentalism, as Dewey called it, was the distinctively American contribution to twentieth-century philosophy. The test of truth lies in its practical consequences: such a doctrine could flourish only in a society where there was little disagreement on underlying values. Pragmatism was the natural child of the liberal consensus. When fundamental values were challenged, however, the pragmatic test was no longer sufficient. Dewey himself shifted toward a natural-rights philosophy when confronted with the rise of Nazism in the 1930s.[13]

Political consensus also gave political debate in America an empirical cast. Consensus implied that political controversies could be resolved largely through analytic means.[14] Extensive investigation of the facts was the proper way to approach any political issue. Policy could be the child of study and research. These expectations were frequently unwarranted. Nonetheless, they gave a distinctive tone to political controversy. American reformers typically were concerned with exposing the extent to which actual conditions deviated from accepted middle-class values. They could think in terms of muckraking rather than assassination because of the general agreement on what was muck and what was not. Thus reform took a practical, empirical course devoted to exposing facts rather than asserting values. The difference in the two environments is reflected in the differences between Lenin and Steffens and between the contents of *Iskra* and those of *McClure's.* The Bolshevik attacked with the revolutionary manifesto, the American reformer with the Brandeis brief.

The deeply ingrained American fear of "established religion" also contributed to the widespread suspicion of any dogmatic ideological outlook. The early colonists' intense desire to avoid the religious persecution and dogma associated with the established state church of England was later translated into the doctrine of official state neutrality toward religion and the peaceful coexistence of a variety of religions. Although those conditions were often violated in practice, they were an integral part of the prevailing constitutional myth, and eventually set the religious pattern for the country. In turn, this tradition created a mental outlook which favored ideological relativism rather than dogmatic commitment.

The Russian Orthodox Church, on the other hand, combined

dogmatic belief with political subservience. The church was a state institution and taught obedience to the state. Orthodoxy in dogma and compliance in politics made for an entirely different tradition, much more compatible with subsequent ideological orthodoxy, albeit an atheistic one. The Bolshevik revolution first brought to power an essentially internationalist and intellectual communist leadership—one in which a significant role was played by Poles, Jews, Letts, and others, none of whom had been shaped by the Russian Orthodox tradition. In the thirties, however, Stalin's massacre of those elements brought into the Party a whole new generation, composed essentially of peasant bureaucrats who, although rejecting their peasant fathers' religiosity, were nonetheless predisposed toward a compliant acceptance of dogma. Furthermore, their traditions, unlike those of their internationalist Bolshevik predecessors, were "nativist," and they accepted the new orthodoxy with a typically peasant devotion to the "Holy Motherland." This new generation, combining communist orthodoxy with orthodox patriotism, set the style for Soviet "national communism," which was at the core of the later Soviet inability to adjust to the new reality of communist internationalism and contributed to the splits with the Yugoslavs, the Poles, the Albanians, and, finally, the Chinese.

Despite their differences in political heritage, the United States and the Soviet Union have certain similarities in contrast to western Europe. Both Russia and America in the nineteenth century lacked the intense and widespread ideological pluralism which in Europe was not restricted to narrow groups of intellectuals but actually was capable of activating the masses. The "spring of nations" of 1848 was an expression of the conflicting appeals of romantic nationalism, liberalism, and even incipient proletarian self-consciousness. It had no echo among the American or Russian masses. By the end of the century, when the social base for ideological pluralism began to emerge in Russia, there was still no political room for it. In America, there was political room but no social need. The ideological homogeneity of the United States was thus natural and spontaneous. In Russia, it was artificial and forced. The czarist government, however, proved incapable of maintaining it. The Bolsheviks substituted a new, virile, messianic ideology with more popular appeal than czarism and buttressed with the ruthless suppression of all bourgeois and Marxist opposition. By the 1930s they had effectively achieved the ideological uniformity which the traditionally minded czars with their more restricted range of techniques had never been able to accomplish. Thus, ideological homogeneity in the Soviet Union is the product of revolution; in the United States it is the result of the absence of revolution.

In both countries the dominant political ideas have been closely linked with nationalism. The United States and the Soviet Union are the first two major countries to define themselves purely in political terms. Even their formal designations illustrate this: they are not primarily geographical designations (such as England, France, America, or Russia) such as have traditionally served to identify nations. "To be an American," C. J. Friedrich has said, "is an ideal; while to be a Frenchman is a fact." [15] The same could be said of the Soviet Union: to be a Soviet citizen is an ideal. It means identification with and acceptance of definite political concepts. A Soviet or American citizen is loyal not only to a national community (as is an Englishman or Frenchman) but also to a "way of life" defined largely, although not exclusively, in terms of distinctive political and economic beliefs. Hence, too, each society harbors a pervasive fear of offbeat or subversive ideas: a fear consciously embodied in Soviet governmental policies directed at "bourgeois influences" and unconsciously embedded in American popular attitudes on subversion.* Historically, however, the political definition of nationalism helped both societies to integrate potentially disruptive ethnic and regional loyalties. Ukrainians and Uzbeks can never be Russians, but they can be Soviet citizens. In the 1790s the Constitution and the principles it reflected gave Americanism a political definition acceptable to both Virginians and New Yorkers. And because Soviet and American nationalism have not had to compete with a multiplicity of ideologies, they have also tended to be free of the more extreme romanticism and emo-

---

* When asked why they thought American Communists were dangerous, 8 per cent of a cross section of the American public mentioned espionage, 8 per cent mentioned sabotage, and 28 per cent mentioned "Communist ideas" which would convert others. Samuel A. Stouffer, *Communism, Conformity, and Civil Liberties* (Garden City, N.Y., 1955), pp. 157-58.

tionalism found in western European nationalism. Political ideas have reinforced nationalism but also reshaped it.

THE OUTLOOK OF THE POLITICAL LEADERSHIPS

Khrushchev is hardly a creative doctrinal thinker, but his political pragmatism does not prevent him from being a truly committed Communist. Kennedy was not just an unprincipled "organization man," but his obvious consciousness of the American political tradition did not prevent him from being a true political pragmatist. While both had thus much in common, there are certain fundamental differences in their basic outlook on politics which are broadly revealing as far as the respective political beliefs of the two countries are concerned.

In December 1961, *Izvestia* published the first interview with an American President ever to appear in the Soviet press. It is useful to compare this interview with two more serious ones from among the many given by Khrushchev for foreign consumption, for instance, with Walter Lippmann in April 1961 and with Iverach McDonald, foreign editor of the London *Times*, in January 1958.[16] Even when speaking to a Western audience for the purpose of allaying their fears, Khrushchev reiterates certain fundamental assumptions which reflect his ideological conditioning. His image of the world is dynamic, with a concrete sense of "history" being on his side, and with capitalism inevitably being supplanted by socialism.[17] Related to this is his rigidly black-and-white conception of the world basically divided into two hostile systems, the capitalist one inherently "blinded by hatred for our country and for the other socialist countries and for our communist ideas." [18] Needless to add, the socialist system is said to be superior in all respects, while capitalism is naturally warlike and exploitative. The United States President, Khrushchev argues, would be unable to negotiate disarmament or to accelerate American economic growth because the "Rockefellers" and the "Du Ponts" would not let him.[19] Insofar as his own domestic affairs are concerned, Khrushchev is convinced that the dictatorship of his party will remain a necessity especially as the state withers away. "The Party has a stronger foundation than the government bodies. It grew up and exists not as a result of some obligations of a legislative kind. Its development

is conditioned by the political views of people, that is, from proposi-
tions of a moral factor. And humanity will always need moral
factors." [20]

Walter Lippmann summed him up as "a true believer that communism is destined to supplant capitalism as capitalism supplanted
feudalism. For him this is an absolute dogma, and he will tell you
that while he intends to do what he can to assist the inevitable,
knowing that we will do what we can to oppose the inevitable, what
he does and what we will do will not be decisive. Destiny will be
realized no matter what men do." [21] Much the same has been said
by Khrushchev, privately and publicly, to many others. For this
reason his prescription for the West is closely bound up with his
long-range perspective. As he once put it to Adlai Stevenson, "You
must understand, Mr. Stevenson, that we live in an epoch when one
system is giving way to another. When you established your republican system in the eighteenth century the English did not like it.
Now, too, a process is taking place in which the peoples want to
live under a new system of society; and it is necessary that one
agree and reconcile himself with this fact. *The process should take
place without interference."* [22]

President Kennedy's prescriptions for the Russians were strikingly and revealingly different. His underlying theme was that "If
the Soviet Union looked only to its national interests and to providing a better life for its people under conditions of peace . . . there
would be nothing that would disturb the relations between the
Soviet Union and the United States." [23] His central objection to
communism was its denial of freedom of choice to the people who
fall under it, and he pointed to Soviet efforts at communizing the
world as the source of American-Soviet tensions. His broader
perspective was open-ended: there was little indication as to where
the world, in his view, is heading, while in his emphasis on the
right of each nation "to live in different ways" there was no concrete delineation of programmatic or institutional alternatives. The
President did not try to suggest what are some of the basic factors
of world change, and he did not base his views on any self-evident
historical or philosophical premise. In the critical words of a
friendly observer, "Kennedy's weakness is that big plans and grand
designs seem to bore him. He lives in the now. He is a tactician,
more interested in political manipulation than in public education,

and this leaves him without a goal to which the day-to-day decisions can be related." [24] *

If that was a fair assessment of Kennedy, how much more true it is of his successor and most of his predecessors. Kennedy, to a greater extent than most Presidents, had at least a deep feeling for history, a respect for intellectual achievement, and a vigorously analytical mind. His personal sense of mission, his vision of America pioneering a new, even if undefined, world order, and his compelling leadership compensated for the traditionally pragmatic and rather short-range outlook of American society, and of most American Administrations, including in some ways even his own.

That perhaps is the key to the differences in outlook of the Soviet and American political leaderships. The Soviet leadership is highly motivated by a goal; its immediate objectives are derived from and related to its over-all purpose. This purpose is the victory of communism in the struggle with world capitalism. On the international scene, according to the Soviet view, conflict between communist and capitalist states is inevitable, even though wars between them are no longer "fatalistically" inevitable. But no real conflict can or should exist within a socialist society. Any conflict which does occur is a holdover from the capitalist era or the work of capitalist agents. The end of external conflict will come only with the end of the "external" capitalist world. World peace requires world socialism, and the forces of history are inevitably marching in this direction. The outlook of the Soviet leadership thus stresses internal unity and external struggle to achieve a long-range goal.

The American approach is quite different. American thinking has not been generally at home with the idea of permanent and inevitable conflict among nations. In Kennedy's view the struggle

---

* President Kennedy's advisers were similarly described by another sympathetic observer: "There was not a reformer among them, as far as anyone could tell. Pragmatism—often of the grubbiest kind—was rampant. 'Facts' were often valued beyond their worth. 'Ideology' was held in contempt—too much so, perhaps—and was described as a prime source of mischief in the world. But if there were no do-gooders around, and no planners, and not even, really, very much in the way of plans, there were large thoughts and large intentions and very long looks into the future." Richard Rovere, *The New Yorker,* November 30, 1963, pp. 51-52.

between the United States and the Soviet Union was the result of certain specific causes, such as the expansionist motives of the present Soviet leadership, which are not inherent in the situation and the removal of which would bring about peace. Khrushchev sees peaceful coexistence as a tactical necessity; Kennedy saw it as a genuine possibility. Khrushchev saw the victory of communism as predetermined; Kennedy saw the future as open-ended. While the Bolsheviks reject domestic conflict, American thinking accepts conflict within American society as natural and healthy: checks and balances in government, competition between parties, competition in the economy, competition among ideas. Madison's encomiums of conflict in *The Federalist* contrast markedly with Lenin's emphasis on the "monolithic unity" of the party. This domestic conflict, however, does not involve fundamental antagonisms such as those that the Soviets assume to exist between socialist and capitalist states. Nor is there any overriding goal or predetermined outcome. Hence, the conflicts among interests, parties, and political ideas can be resolved through discussion and negotiation. To the Bolshevik, politics is the craft of conflict; to the American, it is the art of compromise.

The American attitude toward compromise derives from a suspicion of concentrated power. "Power naturally grows," John Adams warned early in the Republic's history, ". . . because human passions are insatiable. But that power alone can grow which already is too great; that which is unchecked; that which has no equal power to control it." This theme is a recurring one in the American political tradition. It is reflected in antitrust legislation and the regulation of trade unions. Political power, however, is even more suspect than economic power, and this distrust is embodied not only in the constitutional separation of powers but also in the continuing deep-lying suspicion of men who appear to crave power.

The Soviet conflict theory involves a professional and systematic approach to politics, with primary emphasis put on the need for the elite to acquire skills in political combat. The training programs of the Party, its official histories, the speeches of its leaders all stress a militant approach: need for vigilance, ideological purity, determination, "steel-like" character, and so on. Although derived from a doctrine of economic determinism which stresses that social relations are inherently antagonistic until the "socially just" society is built, the theory emphasizes the primacy of conscious political action. The Marxist doctrine is the basic source of the leadership's commitment to an apocalyptic and utopian image of the future and to the persistent conviction that the vehicle of history is the class struggle. This struggle is directed at those who are regarded as enemies, irrespective of their own subjective feelings. A "bourgeois democracy," a feudal dictatorship, a socialist party are seen as enemies even though some of them may not feel hostile toward either the Soviet state or communism. Absence of such hostility is a consideration which the Soviet leaders may weigh from a *tactical* point of view, but in itself it does not determine the long-range relationships between the enemies and the Communists.

Furthermore, the combination of Marxist doctrine, Russian revolutionary experience, social-economic backwardness, and the vested interest of the ruling Party resulted in a series of further postulates, particularly in the realm of the action program, which constitute the Soviet political elite's ideological framework. Probably the most important of these is the Soviet conviction that the construction of "socialism" requires that power be wielded solely by the Communist Party. This belief, in part arising from the Russian experience and in part reflecting the institutionalized vested interests of the ruling elite, has become a fundamental thesis. It colors particularly the Soviet appreciation of changes occurring in the underdeveloped parts of the world. Similarly, the Leninist concepts of the seizure of power, with their emphasis on violent revolution, went far in the direction of establishing the supremacy of "consciousness" over "spontaneity" in historical processes, thereby consolidating the importance of the party as the organized and conscious agent of history. The basic organizational principles which the Communists apply to society are rooted in the conviction that most social ills are derived from private ownership; under certain circumstances even an inefficient public or state ownership (as, for instance, in Soviet agriculture) is to be preferred to private ownership.*

---

* Khrushchev expressed his bias quite openly. In a major speech on agriculture, delivered in 1958, he said that some regions "had con-

Considering the ideological commitment of the Party as well as Russia's specific revolutionary history, it is understandable why the political elite attaches so much importance to "theoretical" contributions. A Soviet leader knows that his hold on power will be far more secure if he seals it with a "creative" ideological achievement of some significance. For example, Khrushchev's political climb reached its summit when he was repeatedly acclaimed at the 22nd CPSU Congress in October 1961 for his allegedly important contributions to the theoretical elaboration of the meaning of the Soviet Union's present "transition to communism," a matter hitherto only vaguely defined. Similarly, Stalin's exegesis of Lenin's writings was hailed by his supporters as a major contribution (the official ideology was renamed during his lifetime Marxism-Leninism-Stalinism), while the writings of his erstwhile competitor, Trotsky, were denied any theoretical merit. Thus power determined ideological merit. Khrushchev's successor will also find it opportune to leave his mark on the Party's ideology.

In terms of their relationship to the ideology, Soviet leaders can be divided into three broad groups: the communist "experts" (the "Gosplanners" or high-level bureaucrats who specialize in technical-operational matters, such as Mikoyan, Ustinov, Kosygin); the "ideologues" (Suslov, Kuusinen, Ilyichev—specialists in agitation and propaganda [*Agitprop*] and doctrinal matters who are the watchdogs of ideological purity); and the "action-program generalizers" (Khrushchev, Kozlov, Brezhnev, Polyansky, Shelepin, who provide the integration for the system as a whole). The division between experts and ideologues is more objective than subjective. Both are loyal and dedicated, but with the development of a more advanced society the Party has to absorb the new, highly trained professional elite and provide it with skilled leader-

---

tributed a high percentage of the increase of the production of meat," but that these regions could not be considered as "leading ones" because the increase had come from the private plots. "Therefore, no matter how high the increase of production of meat as a whole, if the share of this increase contributed by the collective farms and the state farms is insignificant one has to say this region lags behind." (*Plenum TSK KPPS 15-19 Dekabra 1958,* [stenographic report], Moscow, 1958, p. 41.)

ship, risking the concomitant danger of a gradual change in the Party's orientation. In part purposely to balance this, in part by a process of reaction, there has developed within the Party a professional cadre of "ideologues," a group of specialists in doctrinal matters, who bear little resemblance to the creative revolutionaries of the twenties. The growth of Agitprop, its professionalization, is in itself a reflection of the Party's sense that its ideology must be protected against the erosive effects of time and social change. Nonetheless, as the ideologues become more bureaucratic, the ideology must become more ritualized and routine.

In revolutionary times (in early post-1917 Russia or in China today) there is a fusion between the generalizers and the ideologues, symbolized by Lenin or Mao Tse-tung. With stability, a differentiation takes place, and experts begin to threaten the party professionals. This was especially true during the Malenkov-Khrushchev conflict from 1953 to 1957. Khrushchev counteracted this by stimulating increased activity by the Agitprop and by assigning greater responsibility to the third group, the party "generalizers"—professionals who implement the action program without extremes of either dogmatism or sheer pragmatism, knowing that their power requires ideological backing. He thus compensated for the increased stature of the experts which was inevitable in the light of Soviet industrial-technical development. It is likely that in the future the Party will continue to be dominated at the top by the action-program generalizers, since it is they who provide integration for the Party, which is both an ideological and a bureaucratic organization.

These leaders are conscious of the Party's organizational commitment to the ideology on which its claim to power rests. For this reason, domestic reforms and campaigns are a constant feature of the system. Since these leaders matured within an established collectivist society when the revolution was already over, much of this tends to be translated into the drive for higher production and a better standard of living at home, with external communist expansion serving as a source of revolutionary satisfaction. Ideology is thus routinized. Nonetheless, a skeptical leader would run serious risk of undermining his power if he were to allow himself openly to question the ideology. In the shaping of policy he may ignore it in the sense that he will not ask himself whether

a partial truth. The intellectual in politics may be either an ideologue or an expert. In the latter capacity, he plays a major role in American politics. Political leaders in and out of power demand the services of intellectuals expert in all the substantive areas of policy, in communications, in testing public opinion, in framing electoral strategy, and, not the least, in speech writing. The intellectual *qua* expert probably plays a more important role in American politics than in that of any other country, including the Soviet Union. Political leaders, however, have little use for the intellectual *qua* ideologue. The expert is a specialist with a defined competence in a particular field. The ideologue is a specialist in ideology, but ideology is the intellectual effort to define and to relate over-all goals, immediate policy objectives, political strategies and tactics. Such formulations can at times serve the purposes of the politician if he is out of power. Once he is in power, however, ideological formulations become a restraint and an embarrassment to him. The intellectual-ideologue must become either a compromiser or expert, or he soon finds himself on the outside again, making much the same criticism of the new Administration which he had previously made of the old.

The principal habitat of the ideologue in American politics is the minor parties, ideologically oriented pressure groups such as Americans for Democratic Action or the Committee for Constitutional Government, the journals of opinion, and the universities. Ideological critics also appear at times in the House of Representatives and the Senate, but there they are always small minorities, never members of the "club," and usually without significant status or power. In American politics, ideology can thus serve as a basis for systematic critique of politicians in power and as a basis for a systematic program for politicians out of power.* But it cannot serve as a guide or rationale for the Administration in power.

---

devils who cannot afford any character at all because they have no friends in parliament. Oh, these moral dandies! these spiritual toffs! these superior persons! Who is Joe anyhow that he should not risk his soul occasionally like the rest of us?" Hesketh Pearson, *G.B.S.* (New York, 1942), p. 156.
* The prototype of the ideology for the politician-out-of-power is Herbert Croly's *The Promise of American Life* (1909); and even Theodore Roosevelt out of power was not entirely comfortable with Croly's ideological formulations.

THE FUNCTIONS OF IDEOLOGY
AND POLITICAL BELIEF

Political ideas may perform various functions in a political system. They may help legitimize the system; they may aid in social integration; they may assist in conservation and innovation. In some measure but in different ways, Soviet ideology and American political beliefs perform each of these functions.

Soviet ideology, pointing to certain allegedly fundamental laws of historical change, asserts that the Soviet Union represents the highest form of social organization ever achieved by man and is thus not only in keeping with the laws of history but in its forefront. It thus justifies the power of the elite and the existing system. The divine right of kings made it a sin to oppose a royal command (except for the highly complex issue of morally justified regicide); the Soviet ideology makes opposition to the regime— irrespective of its motives—a crime against the people, an act directed at the historically ordained course of social change. It is hence not accidental that offenses against the political or social order are punished with the greatest severity. Furthermore, by asserting that the ideology is based on a scientific approach to social affairs, the Soviet regime claims legitimacy on grounds which have a certain intellectual appeal to those circles of the twentieth-century world which feel that human reason should be applied to social engineering, irrespective of the wishes of the "unenlightened" masses. This minimizes the costs (sacrifices, terror, and the like) which the elite might exact in order to rule satisfactorily.

Although the American beliefs lack the overt and doctrinal elements of the Soviet ideology, they also play a crucial role in legitimizing the American system. In Soviet ideology as formulated by the party leadership, there is a single source of legitimacy, and an institution or practice either is or is not legitimate in terms of that formulation. In the United States there are multiple sources of legitimacy, and legitimacy is a matter of degree. Each of the major sources—constitutional tradition, liberal values, popular consent—can be given a variety of meanings and interpretations. What are the bounds of constitutionality? What is the content of liberalism? What does the public want? One element in the constitutional tradition may be at odds with another, one liberal value infringe on a second, a later popular majority contradict an earlier one. The principal institutions of the system were sanctioned originally by a written constitution which in many respects was neither liberal nor democratic. The evolution of the system during the nineteenth century made it more liberal and democratic and thus enhanced its legitimacy. Today the political system as a whole is legitimate because it is generally constitutional, liberal, and democratic. This comprehensive legitimacy, however, does not extend to all of its parts.

In the Soviet Union a new institution or practice is endowed with legitimacy at birth: legitimacy is a prerequisite to existence. In the United States, new institutions and practices develop more or less spontaneously in response to social and political needs. In most instances only subsequently are they brought within the framework of legitimacy: existence comes before legitimacy. The Founding Fathers generally viewed factions and political parties as quite nefarious, and gave them no sanction in the Constitution. Yet, inevitably, the social-economic pluralism of American life brought them into existence. They were justified in terms of democratic practice, but for a long while they lived in a limbo-like state of semi-legitimacy. Eventually they became more or less accepted as an essential part of the living Constitution. The growth of national power vis-à-vis that of the states, the development of presidential power, and the expansion of the federal bureaucracy have also taken place in response to felt needs but have only gradually acquired legitimacy. Most informed observers today would recognize political-interest groups as an essential part of the political system. Their legitimacy, however, still remains in doubt: to many Americans they constitute a flagrant challenge to constitutional government, liberal individualism, and the realization of the popular will. In the Soviet Union an institution or practice can lose legitimacy as quickly as it gained it, and loss of legitimacy is usually synonymous with loss of existence. The Machine Tractor Stations, said by Stalin to be an essential element in the socialization of the countryside, were both liquidated in fact and ideologically repudiated by his successors within a few months. In the American system, on the other hand, the loss of legitimacy, like its acquisition, is a long-drawn-out process. Slavery undoubtedly furnishes the most notable example. Although originally accepted as legitimate and sanctioned by the Constitution, slavery gradually lost its legitimacy with the rise of liberal, democratic, and humanitarian ideas in the North during the nineteenth century. Since it retained its legitimacy in the South, the question eventually had to be resolved by war.

Slavery, however, was the exception because in this case ideological, sectional, economic, and constitutional issues accumulated so as to create an irreparable split. Many institutions and practices in the American system exist indefinitely in a state of partial legitimacy. The Senate and the Supreme Court, for example, are difficult if not impossible to justify in terms of democratic theory. This partial legitimacy, this uncertainty about ever being entirely beyond challenge, acts as a key restraint in the exercise of political power. Supreme Court action, legitimate in terms of constitutional tradition and liberal values, is often limited by the Court's awareness of its lack of legitimacy in terms of popular consent. Conversely, presidential actions fully legitimate in terms of popular approval may be held up by apparent lack of constitutional sanction. What is legitimate in terms of one American political idea can almost always be challenged in terms of another. The system functions, however, as long as all major political groupings feel that they have a potential stake in all the major American political beliefs and as long as neither the democratic nor the liberal nor the constitutional strand becomes the exclusive property of one group. As it is, the sources of legitimacy which may be invoked by a group in one political controversy may well be invoked by its opponents in another.

The legitimizing function in both systems is closely related to the function of social integration. For citizens to share in certain beliefs they must make almost automatic responses to certain key notions, symbols, or aspirations. Such responses create social cohesion and make the functioning of the system possible. Political indoctrination of the citizen, by making him nationally conscious, integrates him socially and politically, and this inevitably makes for the further spreading of the elite's ideology or political beliefs. The Red Flag with the hammer and sickle has very specific ideological overtones: it symbolizes the workers' and peasants' state; similarly with the other symbols or national heroes in both states.

Until quite recently, the Soviet regime did not support its power through the legitimizing and integrating functions of its official ideology. During the thirties, Russian society was subjected to extremely rapid and forced social changes, with millions of peasants uprooted and pressed into collective farms, with millions of new city dwellers (the urban population increased from 26.3 million in 1926 to 56 million in 1939) living in highly inadequate housing space and employed in state-owned enterprises, with the remnants of the middle class (from both the pre-revolutionary and the New Economic Policy periods) being forcibly liquidated. In these circumstances, the Soviet rulers relied primarily on terror—and they justified it ideologically by proclaiming that the class struggle inevitably intensifies with the construction of socialism.

With the passage of time, a new society took shape, and the principle of the mounting class struggle was finally denounced in 1956. A new generation of engineers, technicians, managers, professionals, and bureaucrats had been produced, to whom the Soviet system was increasingly the source of satisfaction and rewards. A positive commitment could gradually replace the earlier reliance on violence, while Russia's increased international stature and technical achievements gratified the Russian's sense of national pride. Indeed, as far as the masses are concerned, the legitimacy of the regime as well as the political integration of society has been achieved less by conscious mass acceptance of the ideology as such than by the linkage of the regime and its doctrine to such nationally satisfying achievements as the launching of the sputnik and Gagarin's and Titov's orbital flights, as well as by improvements in the material welfare of the people. Precisely for this reason Soviet leaders have said again and again that Soviet space achievements—and victories in sports—prove the historical superiority of their ideology. In their view this linkage is part of the "unity" of theory and practice. In effect, however, they are using scientific achievements to justify their ideology, just as at times Americans have used the abundance of their continent to prove the superiority of free enterprise and the democratic way of life.

This Soviet tendency to blend ideological objectives with industrial achievement and modernization was illustrated by the new CPSU Program, adopted with much fanfare in 1961. The Program discussed at length the significance of the transition to communism,

the alleged passing of the Soviet Union from one historical phase
to another, the progressive transformation of the Soviet state from
a dictatorship of the proletariat into a socialist democracy, relating them closely to international changes, especially the collapse
of the colonial system and the alleged emergence of the "socialist
world system" as the decisive factor in determining further international developments.

Within this essentially ideological framework, however, the
program was concerned primarily with specifying the expected domestic achievements to be reached by 1980, the target date for
completing the construction of "the material-technical base of
communism." By doing so in great factual detail, the Program
combined continued stress on Soviet industrial development with
increased emphasis on improving the well-being of the average
Soviet citizen. Specific targets were outlined, but the eventually
affluent society was still to be strictly collectivist, with little indi-
viduality in child-rearing and personal ownership. The Program
concluded, "Under the experienced leadership of the Communist
Party and under the banner of Marxism-Leninism, the Soviet people have built socialism. Under the Party leadership and under
the banner of Marxism-Leninism, the Soviet people will build
the communist society."

The Program is significant in several ways. It shows, first of all,
the system's continued inclination to formulate social and political
objectives within an ideological framework, using ideological categories of thought. It reveals the presence of a persistent social
myth—that the Soviet Union is a society without class conflict.
A corollary is the Party's fear of those social developments which
point in the direction of social individualism, achieved either
through acquisition of property or humanistic nonideological education. The concrete expression of the ideology is the regime's preoccupation with productive achievement at home and the promotion of continued communist revolution abroad. Thus the
ideology, with its stress on historical change, creates a built-in
compulsion in the ruling Party for permanent social engineering,
which in turn permits the Party to lay claim to continued power.

It is revealing to compare this communist Program with the
product of the President's Commission on National Goals, namely
its 1960 report on "programs for action in the sixties." The Soviet

document was an official statement, prepared by the Secretariat of the CPSU, discussed by the Party Presidium and its Central Committee, before its open publication and "approval" by the 22nd Party Congress. The American report was prepared by a group of leading private citizens, at the invitation of the President of the United States. The Soviet program, sometimes called a new manifesto, to all intents and purposes became binding upon publication, although a few minor textual corrections were made subsequently. The American report expressed the hope that by stimulating a discussion it might help to achieve not unanimity but a "national consensus." While the Soviet document is lengthy and detailed, the American report is brief (twenty-three printed pages), and is mostly a series of vague and general tenets. Characteristically, more detailed and provocative statements come in the form of appended essays submitted by individual leading Americans and representing only their own opinions, without the commission's endorsement. Based largely on the implicit American myth of the harmony of interests (in some ways strikingly similar to the Russian notion of the classless society) and basically reflecting the values of a middle-class society, the American document sought to establish the widest possible basis for consensus, but at the price of specificity. The Soviet document justified continued Party direction of social change; the American one justified the existing American social system.

The Founding Fathers anticipated the Commission on National Goals by making the Constitution brief and general, leaving the specifics to be filled in by experience. Their true genius, it has been argued, was revealed not in what they said but in what they left unsaid. As a result, the Constitution provided the basis for unity among a number of states with a common culture but different social conditions and often conflicting economic interests. The pattern of vagueness and silence embodied in the Constitution also characterizes more broadly the role of American political beliefs in integrating American society. Soviet ideology integrates to the extent that it clarifies goals and illuminates the course of action thought necessary to achieve them. American political beliefs integrate, in large part, to the extent that they obfuscate, to the extent to which they can mean many things to many people. They help to create the illusion of multiple alternatives which, in turn, broadens the identification of the people with the system. In fundamentals, only one alternative exists in the American system as in the Soviet. The many specific alternatives, however, coupled with the vagueness of political beliefs, create the impression that fundamental changes are always possible.

In a broad sense, Soviet ideology requires that the political system move continually toward a predefined goal. To a Soviet Communist, stability is illegitimate. To an American, sudden change is suspect. American political beliefs preclude any drastic change in the political system and assume no final goal toward which the system should be moving. The basic beliefs can change only gradually. Hence, political innovations must be marginal and designed to improve what is assumed to be the general correspondence between ideal and reality. Action, improvement, dynamism are highly valued in the United States, but in terms of unceasing tinkering around the edges.

In addition to legitimizing and integrating the system, the political ideology or beliefs also play both an innovative and a conservative (or restrictive) function. In the Soviet system, the linkage of the ideology to the ruling party, which sees itself as a unique possessor of the truth and therefore not only destined but obliged to exercise a monopoly on power, has resulted in continuous internal pressure in the ruling elite to effect social changes in keeping with "the laws of history." Thus the preoccupation of the elite with moving Soviet society from one stage—for instance, that of completing the construction of socialism—to another—that of the extensive building of communism—is not merely a word game or myth-making. It reflects a purposeful effort to make changes in social organization correspond to changes in technical development and in the so-called social consciousness of Soviet citizens. As the Soviet economy matures and Soviet citizens become accustomed to both an industrial and a socialist order,* the ruling elite sets new objectives in keeping with the foreordained march toward communism. This then justifies its power and avoids the inherent danger that,

---

* As of 1961, three-fourths of the Soviet population had been born after the Revolution.

once economic maturity is achieved, communist dictatorship becomes obsolescent even in terms of the Marxist-Leninist ideology
itself.

This pressure for innovation thus stems both from the ideological orientation of the ruling elite and from its collective
vested interest in power. At the same time, however, it stifles individual initiative, since inevitably such initiative could threaten the
elite's claim to monopoly. The inescapable consequence is a highly
centralized social-economic system, which perhaps could be justified during the initial stages of the social-economic revolution,
but which increasingly becomes a liability to the smooth functioning of the system once it reaches a certain measure of maturity
and stability. One of the most enduring legacies of Stalinism has
been the spread of the bureaucracy through the entire system and
the unwillingness of individuals to innovate on their own initiative. It was in direct reaction to this condition that Khrushchev
in December 1961 criticized an agricultural scientist who persisted
in applying methods which he knew to be wrong. "You say: Comrade Khrushchev has said this and that. Am I to be the highest
authority on agricultural matters? You are the president of the
Ukrainian Academy of Agricultural Sciences, while I am the Secretary of the Party Central Committee. It is you who must help me
in these matters, and not I who must help you [applause]. I can
be wrong. And if you are an honest scientist you must say: Comrade Khrushchev, you do not understand this question correctly."

However, while seeking to encourage creative innovation at the
bottom, Khrushchev is certainly unwilling to yield in any signifi-
can measure the Party's ideological primacy and political monopoly. Thus criticism and innovation from below will be either
restricted to purely mechanical-operational matters or stifled from
the top whenever it exceeds those bounds. Therefore it is safer
for the lower echelons not to exercise any excessive initiative.

A related aspect is the general restrictive impact of the ideology
or political beliefs on the choice of alternatives available to the
leadership. The preference of Soviet leaders, already cited, for
even an inefficient collective farm system over the more productive private plots illustrates a strong collectivist bias. (Similar
but reversed examples are available in the American experience—
for instance, in the opposition to TVA or public power in general.)

This restrictive effect in turn encourages the conservative tendencies induced by the dogmatic aspects of the ideology. Since whatever the leaders do is automatically justified ideologically, specific policies tend to be elevated into the realm of dogma. When the time comes to change, the dogma has to be revised accordingly, and this can be done only if there is in power an unchallenged political arbiter, such as Stalin. Without him, innovations can run headlong into political opposition which is fortified by dogmatic claims.

In the period after Stalin's death, a number of major domestic reforms were carried out in the USSR. Many were actively opposed within the leadership by various party leaders, including Molotov, Malenkov, and Kaganovich, who claimed that these steps involved fundamental departures from the ideology. While their opposition to Khrushchev's increasing power was probably the paramount factor, their claim that he was abandoning the true principles of Marxism-Leninism-Stalinism was nonetheless a source of political embarrassment to him. Indeed it was in part to overcome precisely this ideological challenge that he finally made an all-out attack on Stalinism, first at the 20th Party Congress in 1956 and then at the 22nd in 1961, thereby rejecting his opponents' ideological claims and establishing himself as the true "Leninist" leader of the CPSU, with all the related ideological prerogatives.

As Khrushchev's close associate Anastas Mikoyan put it in his speech at the 22nd Party Congress on October 20, 1961, "These differences with the conservative-dogmatist group were not just differences on some particular organizational or separate political questions. No; they concerned the definition of the Party's entire policy at the new stage of historic development—in fact, its basic policy line." The ideological orientation of the system thus made it insufficient merely to criticize the preceding "administration" (something quite common in America). Stalin had to be *condemned for ideological errors.**

---

* Khrushchev's spokesman, Leonid Ilyichev, itemized Stalin's errors in detail: at least six major errors in Marxist philosophy, at least six in Marxist economic theory, at least four in the field of Party-historical science, and total negligence of Marxist jurisprudence. (See Ilyichev's speech of December 26, 1961.)

By appealing to traditional dogma Molotov—like Goldwater in the United States—was attempting to mobilize support based on certain deeply ingrained principles. Molotov, however, had no choice but to operate within the Party elite, and there the tradition of Party discipline, buttressed by Khrushchev's control over the machinery, worked against him. In the much looser American structure, it is more feasible to exercise a conservative influence by appealing to the underlying political beliefs of most Americans, thereby obstructing innovation from the top. At the same time, because of the pluralistic nature of the American system and the undogmatic character of the political beliefs, innovation and initiative on the lower echelons not only are encouraged but actually are part of the country's traditional respect for achievement. Thus in the Soviet Union the ideological pressure for innovation operates from the top down, even though it occasionally generates a dogmatic tendency within the political elite, while widespread stagnation of initiative is induced at the bottom; in the United States political beliefs can be effectively used to obstruct innovating initiatives at the top (for example, opposition to the Kennedy program in Congress) even though individual initiative at the bottom not only is encouraged but is a fundamental part of the American system of beliefs.

Paradoxically, these differing conditions tend to have a similar effect on the political attitudes of the intellectuals of the two countries. In both cases they stimulate the sense of political frustration or even alienation. In Russia the intellectual, while perhaps attracted by the notion of centralized, rationally directed social engineering, is repelled by the doctrinal rigidities of the system, and the absence of any alternatives tends to paralyze his political initiative. Internal emigration is the most frequent consequence,*

---

* The Soviet minister of culture, Mrs. Ekaterina Furtseva, addressing the 22nd Party Congress in 1961, stated, "The new Communist norms of social relations are being established in the most varied fields of the Soviet people's life. It must be said, without hesitation, however, that in literature as in art very few works—I have in mind not so much quantity as quality—reflect this remarkable, great process of our times. It is possible to study life only if the artist is firmly linked with the people about whom he writes. Yet it must be said frankly that some writers and art workers still live divorced from life."

while the more numerous professional intelligentsia seek fulfillment in nonpolitical technical specialization. In America, the intellectual enjoys almost unlimited freedom of political expression
but he has access to the top policy decisions primarily as a specialist. Furthermore, the interlocking of interest groups and the
conservative function of the prevailing political beliefs hamper any
significant policy shifts or reforms. Elsewhere in the modern age
—be it in nineteenth-century Europe or in today's new nations—
intellectuals have tended to exercise a major influence on political
events. The political neutralization of intellectuals in both Russia
and America appears to be a strikingly similar effect of the special
roles played by the highly doctrinaire Soviet ideology on the one
hand and the intensely anti-dogmatic American political beliefs
on the other.

The differences in role between Soviet ideology and American
political beliefs are highlighted when Khrushchev's changes in
ideology are compared with those which took place in American
values during the mid-twentieth century. In the Soviet Union the
changes were directly associated with the struggle for power after
Stalin's death and with policy innovations to rectify evils which
had developed during the period of Stalinist stagnation. They were
concrete and conscious acts of political leadership. They date almost specifically from the 20th Party Congress. In the United
States during the three decades after 1920 a fundamental change
occurred away from the individualistic, moralistic values of the
Protestant ethic, with their emphasis on achievement, to the more
tolerant, group-centered values of the 1950s, with their emphasis
on the present.[25] Like the changes in Soviet ideology, this shift occurred in a changing economic and social structure. But unlike the
Soviet change, it had its origins in society rather than in the political system. It was unconscious, spontaneous, gradual, pluralistic,
and virtually impossible to identify until it had taken place. The
changes in Soviet ideology were initiated by the political leadership
in response to its political and social needs. The changes in American values took place with little purposeful action or awareness on
the part of political leaders. Nonetheless, both the Soviet and the
American changes had important consequences for political leadership: they significantly altered its styles and methods, and drastically changed the environment of policy-making, making accept-

able in the 1950s policies which would have been unthinkable in the 1920s. Like those of the Soviet people, American attitudes toward the shift in values were ambiguous: some critics welcomed it and condemned the "errors" of the 1920s, but others seemed to view it with nostalgia and regret. All, however, more or less accepted the change as a fact of history. In contrast to the sharp and conscious change in Soviet ideology, the glacier-like quality of the shift in American values made it seem quite irreversible.

THE VALUE AND VIABILITY OF IDEOLOGY

Ideology and political beliefs thus play significant roles in the Soviet and American political systems. Ideology gives the Soviet leaders a framework for organizing their vision of political developments; it sets limits on the options open to them as policy makers; it defines immediate priorities and longer-range goals; and it shapes the methods through which problems are handled. The American political beliefs condition the specific style of leadership —its emphasis on the immediate, its stress on the empirical and pragmatic approach, its suspicion of long-range commitments, and its preference for compromise. In key areas of domestic policy, such as agriculture, the impact of political ideas in the two countries is visible and important.[26] Their impact, however, is most visible and most important in the field of foreign affairs. Here the two systems are confronted with many similar problems. Here, consequently, the ways in which political ideas shape their approaches to these problems are relatively clear. Here, also, it is possible by comparing the roles of Soviet ideology and of American political beliefs to furnish some idea of the advantages and disadvantages which each gives its proponent in grappling with the problems of international politics. In weighing these advantages and disadvantages, several differences between Soviet ideology and American beliefs are particularly relevant.

First, the Soviet view of the relation between domestic politics and international affairs differs sharply from the traditional American view. The Soviet Communists reject the conception that international affairs involve principally the interplay of nation-states attempting to promote their national objectives; rather, they view the world as a continuing struggle among various interests—domestic, social, economic, and political, as well as national. The interplay between nation-states is merely an aspect—often only a formal one—of international affairs. In the Soviet view, for true understanding one must seek to establish the correlation of the various forces that are dynamically coexisting within a given society and chart their likely pattern of behavior as well as their likely influence in the future. This preoccupation with the nature of the domestic dynamics of other societies and the realization that economic processes create political problems which are international often results in a more meaningful appreciation of reality than arguments about "traditional national goals," or moralistic pronouncements that democracies are inherently peaceful and more powerful while dictatorships are warlike and ultimately doomed. For all its limitations, Soviet ideology at least seems to point to some of the inner mechanisms of international affairs. That is so because Marxism itself was a response to an international process which has become a paramount force of change in our age: the Industrial Revolution.

The approach of Western statesmen still is often derived from an image of international affairs shaped by the emergence of nation-states. It tends to be both legalistic and static while the Soviet is political and dynamic. America came of age when still relatively isolated, with nationalism as its main perspective. As long as mass emotionalism was not politically determinant, international politics could operate relatively stably on the basis of certain commonly accepted rules. But the intervention of mass public opinion, rallying around nationalist and ideological symbols (democratic or totalitarian), has necessarily transformed interstate political conflicts also into doctrinal ones, with profound social-economic overtones.

The communist realization, even though not often successfully exploited in policy, that the key to the future of our era lies in the transformation of the colonial and underdeveloped parts of the world, preceded similar recognition on the part of Western chancelleries by several decades. The focus on long-range social-economic and political trends, increasingly accepted in the West since World War II, had doubtless contributed to a more mature appreciation of international issues than the somewhat artificial view of them as a matter of legal-diplomatic maneuvering between nation-states. For all its methodological shortcomings and doc-

trinal biases, Lenin's pamphlet (written in 1916) on "Imperialism—the Highest Stage of Capitalism" probed much more deeply
into the dynamics of what has lately become one of the most
important factors of change in the world than did the contemporary
utterances of Western leaders.

Perhaps the most thoughtful American counterpart to Lenin was
President Wilson, a politician and a scholar. Yet in his approach
to international affairs he was preoccupied with the interplay of
nation-states; he had little or no concern for the internal social-
economic and political dynamics that affect their behavior and
little or no understanding of the trends of world change. The emphasis is primarily on "equality of rights" of states on territorial
issues (for example, access to seas of nation-states), with a brief
reference to the "impartial adjustment of old colonial claims." [27]
The over-all outlook is static, reflecting a legalistic conception of
world affairs, even while partaking of the underlying American
political beliefs with their inherent sympathy for otherwise undefined democracy and independence for all peoples. The Wilsonian
approach dominated American thinking about international affairs
until after World War II. Only then, as a result of hard experience,
did Americans slowly come to accept the proposition that foreign
policy involved the manipulation of social and economic forces
within other nations as well as the management of relations among
nations.

A second difference in attitudes toward international relationships is based on the Soviet view of politics as constant flux, contrasted with the traditional American belief in the possibility of
both stability and progress. The Soviet approach to international
affairs is characterized by an intense preoccupation with change.
This awareness of continuing change, and the conviction that they
alone understand its inner nature, encouraged the Soviet leaders
to believe that they have unraveled the internal logic of history
and that their policies are not merely an aspiration but a "scientific" calculation.* They feel that their ideology provides a method

---

* Their conviction that social-economic trends, as evaluated by them,
inevitably dictate their victory is not to be dismissed lightly as a mere
act of faith; the Soviets have been doing some empirical calculation to
prove their point. An authoritative example of such evaluation is a
study written in 1961 by Professor Stanislav Strumilin, a leading

for understanding and evaluating the historical phases on the way to the final goal. In policy-making, these phases are not so broad as the historical Marxist stages, such as feudalism or capitalism. Rather, they identify the character of the specific period within the present epoch, as, for instance, a revolutionary phase, a quiescent phase, a phase dominated by aggressive imperialism, or a phase in which the essential force changing history is "the liberation struggles of the colonial peoples." Once properly understood, the nature of the particular phase reveals who the main enemy is and what measures ought to be adopted.

The following sequence of questions is usually examined by the Soviet leaders when defining their policy: What is the nature of the present historical phase? What is the meaning of the relationships prevailing between economic forces and political institutions? What direction are they taking? Who is our major enemy? Is the enemy subjective or objective? (For instance, Japan at one time was "subjectively" hostile in its policy while "objectively" a progressive force since its industrialization was subverting the feudal order.) Who are our allies, subjectively and/or objectively? At which point will we part with our allies? What will be the nature of the next phase? What ought to be the pace of our efforts to stimulate further change? At almost every important turning point in Soviet policy, such questions have come to the fore and have often resulted in heated debates and conflicts. But, once understanding and evaluation have been achieved, the debate ceases and the policy is set.

How often have American statesmen asked themselves questions like these? The Soviets want the policy which is correct for a specific phase of historical development, but pointed always

---

Soviet ideologue, on "The World Twenty Years from Now." By projecting in some detail existing demographic and economic trends, and then evaluating them, first on the assumption that the present communist world will not expand territorially, and, second, on the assumption that it will expand by absorbing 30 per cent of the neutral countries and 10 per cent of the present "imperialist" countries, he reaches the conclusion that in either case there are "reliable signs that . . . imperialism is definitely embarked on a period of decline and fall." *Kommunist*, No. 13, September 1961; full translation in *The Current Digest of the Soviet Press*, Vol. XIII, No. 38, October 18, 1961.

toward a purposeful goal. The Americans want a policy which either will furnish an ad-hoc solution of the immediate problem or will be correct under all historical circumstances. They are not accustomed to thinking in terms of phases of historical evolution. Soviet communism combines a philosophy of progress with a theory of history. Americans tend to have one without the other. Traditionally, Americans have believed in progress. This has, however, been a vague belief in the inevitability and naturalness of progress, and unlike the Soviet idea it has been divorced from explicit theory of the phases of historical development. At least until recently American political thinking lacked not just a theory of history but also a sense of history. American political ideas were predominantly liberal in character, and liberalism is the least historically conscious of the major European ideologies.

In the 1950s several American thinkers developed theories of history. These gave order and sequence to the stages through which the Western world had moved from traditional agrarianism to modern industrialism. Derived from Western experience, the theories suggested the stages through which the more backward countries would probably progress also. They notably failed, however, to set forth a clear image of the next stages of the highly developed societies or to derive political goals for tomorrow from yesterday's perceived thrust of history. Their analysis of the past was acute, their image of the future hazy. They produced a theory of history and a philosophy of progress for the underdeveloped areas, but only a theory of history for their own society.

While Americans have tended to think in terms of natural and painless progress for themselves, they have also tended to think in terms of natural stability in relations among nations. This stability is disturbed only when governments engage in aggression or intervention in the affairs of other countries. Until recently, Americans have also thought that stability in the domestic politics of other countries meant the absence of revolution or rapid evolution. Maintaining the status quo meant the prevention of change. This view contrasts with the Soviet emphasis on the universality of change. To the Soviets the status quo is change. For Khrushchev, "the social and economic revolution now in progress in Russia, China, and elsewhere in Asia and Africa *is* the status quo, and he wants us to recognize it as such. In his mind, opposition to this revolution is an attempt to change the status quo. Whereas we think of the status quo as the situation as it exists at the moment, he thinks of it as the process of revolutionary change which is in progress." [28]

Asking the right questions, however, is only the first step toward the right answers. At times, the ideology creates difficulties in responding to change. It can cause an excessively dogmatic evaluation of the situation, stimulate premature optimism, or simply mislead. The elevation of certain formulas into dogma, furthermore, makes it difficult to revise the Soviet outlook, especially when there is some division within the leadership. At such a juncture, opposition to innovation can use dogma as a weapon in the struggle for power. When Khrushchev wanted to modify the principle of the inevitability of war because of growing Soviet understanding of nuclear weapons, his opponents could charge him with revisionism. (Nonetheless, he did win out over them.)

The Soviet ideological outlook, for all its awareness of change, has one fundamental flaw: it underestimates the force of nationalism and prevents the Soviet leaders from realizing that their own communist "internationalism" is in itself quite nationalistic. As a result, Soviet leaders have frequently adopted an insensitive and overbearing attitude toward other nations, to the detriment of Soviet interests; eastern Europe is one example. Similarly, the Soviet leaders failed properly to assess the force of nationalism in the Middle East and Africa, whereas the West, after an initially slow start in perceiving the change, was able to adjust pragmatically to the new nationalist leaderships. This makes for a major liability in the Soviet world outlook.

A third difference in international outlook is that the Soviets stress basic conflict between communist and capitalist countries, whereas Americans tend to believe in a natural harmony of interests among states. In the American view, wars would be avoided if each government pursued only its true national interests. Peace is the natural and preferred condition. Wars have specific causes which reasonable men should be able to control or eliminate. War is justified only on behalf of basic principles and ideals. When it is justified, it must be waged vigorously for the complete vindication of the principles at stake and for a quick restoration of the peace. The concept of unceasing limited violence is foreign to the American mind. In the Cold War this attitude made Americans unhappy with the protracted struggle in Korea, Vietnam, and Cuba. It also made them unwilling to accept the possibility of an indefinite arms race with the Soviet Union. The pervasive fear of "escalation" reflected the view that limited forms of conflict such as local wars or the arms race were inherently unstable. In an age when total war was a viable instrument of national policy, Americans tended to make all wars total. When total war became too disastrous to be an instrument of policy, Americans tended to believe that all limited conflicts would become total wars if they were not quickly terminated by agreement.

In the Cold War the Soviets were thus primarily motivated by a strong urge to win. The Americans were motivated by an urge to win tempered by an urge to agree. They held to the view that mutual compromise could produce agreements which would eliminate some of the standing issues of the Cold War. Hence they attached tremendous importance to the times when the gap narrowed between Soviet and American positions on issues such as nuclear tests or Berlin. If the only issue separating the two countries was a question of three or ten inspections per year, why not compromise the issue and make an agreement? To the Soviets, however, the issue of three or ten was a detail. The real issue was: Who will win in the long run? If a test-ban agreement seemed likely to contribute, at one stage in history, to their long-run victory, they would easily find ways of coming to agreement. That, however, would be but a tactical maneuver in a struggle, not a terminus to it. Compromises and adjustments, never ends in themselves, are accepted by the Soviet leaders only if they appear to be warranted by their pursuit of higher ends. In practice this may appear to differ little from the attitude of those nations which view such compromises in more favorable light and are prepared to consider them as ends of policy; but the significant factor is the idea of transiency that the Soviet leaders attach to any such compromise. Their conflict theory gave the Soviets considerable advantage in the Cold War. By its very nature, it validated its own assumptions and undermined those of the compromise–harmony-of-interest theory.

The conflict theory, however, also had its limitations. For one thing, it presupposed unity among communist states, and consequently did not provide a useful tool for resolving differences between them. The relatively vague American political beliefs and ideals furnished a broader framework for compromise than did the relatively systematic communist doctrinaire ideology. Ideology is intellectually unifying but can be politically divisive. The idea of "peaceful competition" or "competitive coexistence" between capitalist and communist countries can be fitted into Soviet ideology with relative ease. For the Soviets it is an appropriate description of the current phase in the struggle for world communism. The idea of competitive coexistence among communist countries, however, is alien to the ideology. Communist ideology is flexible, but it is not tolerant, and the prospect of competing orthodoxies is repugnant to the Soviet outlook. At least in part as a result of their ideology, the Soviet leadership has had greater difficulty in dealing with communist China than American leadership has had in adjusting to the new Europe. The same ideas and methods of analysis which help the Soviet Union in its Cold War with the United States become obstacles to effective dealings with allies and neutrals. The United States is ill-prepared for protracted struggle with its enemies; the Soviet Union is ill-equipped for protracted disagreement with its friends.

American assumptions of the harmony of interests and the feasibility of compromise, in fact, have helped in dealing with allies and neutrals. In the United Nations, for instance, despite the increasing number of neutral nations, American diplomacy was more effective than Soviet diplomacy at least in part because of the greater American awareness of the possibilities of compromise. Furthermore, the political beliefs of the United States are, to varying degrees, shared with its western European allies. Within this framework, solutions to individual problems can be found in political compromise rather than ideological correctness. Conflicts within the alliance can more easily be limited and isolated. In 1956, for instance, British and French interests in the Middle East came into direct conflict with American policy there. The United States administered a public humiliation to its allies. Yet within six months the alliance had been patched up again. On the Soviet side, on the other hand, ideology tends to aggravate conflicts within the bloc.

The fourth difference is that despite the shifts and turns in Soviet foreign policy in the last several decades, a persisting attribute of its long-range perspective is the sense of historical obligation to encourage the spread of communism throughout the world although preferably without excessive Soviet sacrifices. This universality of goal makes Soviet foreign policy something altogether different from czarist foreign policy, or for that matter from the rather generalized American desire to see a "free" but otherwise undefined world. (There are, however, some striking parallels between the Soviet view and the traditional American image of America as an active symbol of certain universal norms.) Admittedly, Soviet foreign policy, especially in its short-term aspects, is concerned with national security, frontiers, national power, etc.—factors which inherently introduce similarities with Russia's traditional concerns and are usually covered by the term "national interest." Quite unlike their czarist predecessors, however, the Soviet leaders' conception of their own security is inherently offensive; as long as alternative political systems exist, there is continued need to be preoccupied with security issues. Because they see themselves as part of a historical process toward a defined end, the Soviet leaders are compelled to view any effort to "stabilize" or to "normalize" the international situation as only a temporary adjustment.

Until a series of other communist states came into being, Soviet leaders did not have to face the dilemma of national versus international goals. Before that, dovetailing of national and international interests was another important ideological element; for forty years it permitted the Soviet leaders to strengthen their power without power becoming only the end of their actions. An ideology in which power is a tool as well as an end allowed the Soviet leaders to be continually concerned with making the most of their national power without letting it become an impediment to the fulfillment of ideological values. In the early 1960s China posed the new dilemma by demanding that the USSR make national sacrifices for the common interests of the communist cause. For the first time, Moscow was being pressed by a major communist state to choose communist international interests over Soviet national ones.

The traditional American approach to international politics has been more in terms of principles than of goals. A goal is the object of action; a principle is a rule guiding action. The Soviets want their policies to be directed to a goal. The test of a particular strategy or tactic is how it contributes to the worldwide victory of communism. Americans, however, have wanted their policies to be based on principles. Their traditional distaste for the flexibility of action permitted by purely goal-directed behavior is reflected in their repugnance to the idea that "the end justifies the means." To a Soviet ruler this abhorrence would be ridiculous: What else justifies means except the end? To an American, however, the choice of means is limited by moral principles which prescribe some types of action and proscribe others, quite apart from the goals to which the actions may be related. These principles may be uncodified moral standards of conduct; they may also be embodied in international law, treaties, and other more explicitly formulated codes of behavior. Thus, the concern with principles leads to a moralistic and legalistic approach to foreign policy. "It is the essence of this belief," G. F. Kennan has written, "that instead of taking the awkward conflicts of national interest and dealing with them on their merits and with a view to finding the solutions least unsettling to international life, it would be better to find some formal criteria of a juridical nature by which the permissible behavior of states could be defined."*

While the Soviets logically may employ any means to achieve their goal, Americans can employ only means which accord with their principles. Moralism and legalism make for rigidity. This rigidity also explains why Americans confuse the zigzagging of Soviet policy with alleged ideological cynicism. They fail to realize that cynicism in the choice of means is not tantamount to cynicism in commitment to ends. To Americans, the applicability of the principles is not limited by changes in time, condition, or the goals which the specific actions are designed to realize. The Soviets can become allies of bourgeois nationalists or make a treaty with Hitler not only without abandoning their goal but on the grounds that at that particular stage in history such action is necessary. American governments may also take pragmatic action when it serves their

---

* *American Diplomacy, 1900-1950* (New York, 1952), p. 94. It should be noted that Kennan criticizes American legalism from the viewpoint of American pragmatism. The alternative he poses to the legalistic approach is the thoroughly pragmatic one of dealing with problems ad hoc "on their merits." In this case, their disposition could be just as unrelated to an overriding goal as if they had been disposed of according to "formal criteria of a juridical nature."

purposes, but usually with the feeling that they sacrifice principle to expediency. In some cases, as in the Suez crisis of 1956, the sacrifice will not be made and the government will adhere to its principles, to the bafflement of its allies and the wonderment of its enemies. In other cases the sacrifice will be made, but reluctantly, over the protests of domestic opposition, and often with a guilty conscience which in turn often leads the government to take some compensatory action to "make it right" at a later date.[29]

On balance, therefore, Soviet ideology cannot be viewed merely as a liability. Ideology is not incompatible with rational behavior, once the basic assumptions are granted. While these assumptions may or may not be rational, they are at least so far removed from immediate concerns that they do not produce a conflict between the ideological commitment and a rational approach to reality. The goal of an ultimate worldwide communist society may be irrational, but it does not necessarily impose irrational conduct. Furthermore, the Soviet consciousness of change makes for greater flexibility than does the American approach, superficially flexible because of its pragmatic character but basically rigid because its vague beliefs are static rather than dynamic.

A broader aspect of this question involves the external roles of both the ideology and the beliefs. They not only affect the conduct of the foreign policy of the two countries but also tend to give them an external image which is important in relating the two countries to the rest of the world. Ideology, of course, is merely one aspect of a complex set of factors which determines the way a nation is seen by others. The fact, however, that the official doctrine of the Soviet Union has a certain appeal for the intelligentsia of some of the developing nations, and for certain alienated individuals in the more developed ones, has given the Soviet Union some initial advantages. Leaders such as Sekou Touré, or at one time Nehru or even Nasser, tend to view the Soviet system as economically and socially more rational and even just, while the economic backwardness of their own countries tends to make them view the American economic system as something quite beyond their reach. To be sure, on the whole, they reject the dogmatic and terroristic aspects of the Soviet system, but their appreciation of American democracy tends to be mitigated by an ideological bias against the American capitalist system. This bias is not threatened, furthermore, by American political beliefs, which appear to many of these leaders as merely an expression of fundamental materialism and lack of concern with issues of principle.

This is so because Marxism seems to offer a more approximate truth, in so far as social-economic and political change is concerned, than the unstructured and vague American outlook. The masses of Africa and Asia, newly awakened to politics, crave some political understanding of their past and also some insight into the future. Marxism, in an oversimplified form, provides it, and its historical phases of feudalism-capitalism-socialism-communism seem to be more directly meaningful to the contemporary experience of many millions of people than a sophisticated appreciation of the limits of the human reason's capacity to understand truly the immensely complex past, not to speak of the present or the future.

Americans tend to think themselves pragmatic and the Soviets rigid and doctrinaire. The images which other peoples have of the two systems, however, are almost exactly the reverse. The Soviet system is seen as a dynamic, adaptive society, capable of adjusting itself to changing social, economic, and international environments. The more sophisticated elite groups in other countries directly link this dynamic quality to the flexibility inherent in Soviet ideology. American politics and policy, on the other hand, are often seen as essentially static. And these qualities, in turn, are held to flow from the rigid, moralistic character of American political beliefs. These beliefs, foreign observers admit, are deeply held by large segments of the American people. This sincerity and conviction may be respected, but the resulting rigidity is viewed as a political liability. The Soviet Union, it is argued, has demonstrated a great ability to adjust to changing environments, while the United States has faced less need to adjust and its political beliefs are less susceptible to change.

Our age has been the age of ideology. Ideological commitments have tended to dominate political behavior. In the long run, however, this emphasis may fade. In western Europe, it is fading rapidly. The American pragmatism was once unique as far as the rest of the world was concerned. Perhaps it has been the destiny of America to pioneer in building a society which has not been dominated by ideology. Already, there are signs that the Soviet ideology and the Soviet system are becoming less compatible. In fact, the Soviet leaders are showing signs of apprehension that in its own terms their ideology increasingly makes the Party dictatorship in the Soviet system obsolescent. With achievement of a measure of industrial and technical know-how, strict dictatorial and ideological rule seems increasingly unnecessary. Abroad, the changes in western Europe and the development of indigenous forms of socialism in the new states also threaten the black-and-white image of the world. Diversity in the communist world has also lessened the absolutist character of the ideology and made it increasingly relative. The wave of revisionist thinking that permeated the eastern European Communists, including some of the ones actually in power, is gradually affecting Soviet thought, while the militant intensity of the Chinese is polarizing the alternatives and forcing the Soviets into ideological "revisionism." Finally, the development of new weapons has already seriously affected hitherto underlying tenets concerning future patterns of development.

This, however, does not mean the end of ideology, if by "end" is meant the conventional notion that eventually the Russian elite will become similar to its pragmatic Western counterpart. For the time being, the erosive tendencies noted above are counteracted by the persisting measures of indoctrination, by the fact that some of the basic ideological tenets have penetrated Soviet society and have become accepted by the people, and by the sense of historical momentum at home and abroad. Once an ideology is embodied in a party bureaucracy with a vested interest in its power, it can continue to exert a transforming influence on society, even if the majority of the professional Soviet Party bureaucrats (the *apparatchiki*) have lost their revolutionary fervor. In the West ideologies were associated with the traumatic struggles characteristic of the early stages of industrialization. They were the product of class conflict. The emergence of affluent, consumer-favoring economies in western Europe in the 1950s eased the class conflicts and diluted the ideologies; European political parties competed with each other in shedding the ideological chains binding them to the past in order to deal more pragmatically with the issues of the present. This decline in ideology and in class conflict, moreover, was paralleled by the weakening of nationalism and national rivalries.

In the Soviet Union, on the other hand, ideology is rooted not in the conflict of social classes but in the supremacy of the Communist Party reinforced by the vitality of Soviet nationalism. Those who talk of the erosion of ideology usually have in mind the experience of ideological movements or groups. In that sense ideologies have come and gone. But it is a different matter when an ideology becomes vested in a cohesive, bureaucratic, autonomous ruling elite. Then organizational interest breeds new ideological vitality. Today, what is novel about the communist experience is that ideology has become institutionalized both in a ruling bureaucracy and in a new society which transforms the idea into reality. Social change eventually will alter the substance of the ideology, but this in turn raises the question of what causes that change. Here the power of the vested interests, personal and bureaucratic, becomes a critical consideration. As the momentum of social engineering decreases, one is likely to see instead the emergence of more sophisticated and systematic theories of social control from above, developed on the basis of scientific insights hitherto not available. As Soviet society changes, so will Marxism-Leninism. This ideology has made its followers particularly susceptible to rational techniques of social control, and new methods of computing and guiding social behavior (see pp. 123ff.) are likely to gain favor within the elite, in keeping with its oft-proclaimed dedication to the construction of "scientific communism." Linked to real science (and not to the social pseudo-science of Lenin), Marxism-Leninism can evolve into a more effective doctrine of domestic control, while maintaining its revolutionary virtue primarily in terms of international affairs.

Perhaps the most conclusive evidence of the role that ideology will play in the Soviet future comes from the experience of the American past. The basic elements in the American political creed have remained relatively unchanged since the beginning of the nineteenth century. Lockian ideas of liberty, Jeffersonian concepts of democracy, eighteenth-century ideals of the rights of man, and laissez-faire doctrines of private property still pre-empt the American mind. In 1789 who would have thought that these ideas, adequate for a poor, small, agrarian confederation of ex-colonies, would still prevail in a crowded, urbanized, industrialized continental empire one hundred and fifty years later? Even the revolutionary changes of the first half-century of the Soviet Union fail to match this great transformation. And even if they did, Soviet ideology—as we have seen—is more flexible and adaptive than American political beliefs. The continuing vitality in America of the liberal-democratic ideas of 1800 suggests that it may be some while before the Marxist-Leninist ideology of 1900 ceases to exert its influence on the Soviet political system.

CHAPTER TWO

The Political System and the Individual

IDEOLOGICAL AND INSTRUMENTAL POLITICAL SYSTEMS

"MAN IS born free, yet everywhere he is in chains." While extreme, this famous dictum contains a truth. Every society imposes on the individual its established traditions and conventions. Every individual becomes bound by the standards of behavior of his society and often is subjected to coercive controls imposed by the political system. A political system is a complex of institutions, procedures, beliefs, and elites, through which the society is governed. A society is a web of personal and group relations which make for more or less stable collective existence. While in fact the two are inseparable—although conceptually it is possible and sometimes convenient to think of them as separate entities—the binding relationship between them differs from country to country.

In some cases, the political system merely reflects the established social patterns and is designed to protect the existing character of a society and to promote its growth along established, undisturbed paths. Such a system can be described as instrumental. In other cases, the political system antedates society. Instead of reflecting society, the system is used by political leaders to create a new society along the lines of their own beliefs and aspirations. Such a system can be described as ideological. This designation is especially applicable to revolutionary political systems, which have the twin purpose of destroying the social remnants of the old order and building a new society.

The relationship between the political system and society, however, is not quite as clear-cut as implied above. Except for phases of acute revolutionary upheaval or of initial nation-building, the political system inevitably is affected and limited by the society it governs. The more stable the society and the more established the claims (or "rights") of its citizens both as individuals and as groups, the more restricted the power of the political system in the society. With the growth of social stability, the marked dominance of a revolutionary political system tends to decrease.

71

An almost opposite tendency may be inherent in the case of a political system that a relatively stable society has established to regularize and to protect its social relations. Thus in America the growth of modern economy, rapid communications, and particularly the combination of the potential for mass well-being and the social expectation of it (because of democracy, literacy, relative affluence, and the international challenge) have produced a greater consciousness of social inadequacies which spontaneous social change cannot correct. As a result, there has developed social pressure for increased intervention by the government into societal affairs, with the consequent accumulation of power in the political system.

At the same time, however, that pressure has been matched by the emergence and consolidation of large-scale social organizations whose purpose is to protect the interests of their constituencies. Organized labor welcomed the Wagner Act but fiercely opposed the Taft-Hartley Act as unwarranted interference. Similarly, big business approved the Taft-Hartley legislation and the tariffs but violently objected to the Wagner Act and the anti-trust acts. Both cases illustrate the dynamic character of the relationship between an instrumental political system and a developed society as well as the inherent tension between pressures for social amelioration through political action and efforts to assert specific group claims.

The changes in the relationship between the Soviet political system and Russian society come from a different direction and have different reasons. Russian society is relatively underdeveloped or quasideveloped, even though it is often ranked among the developed nations because of the impressive growth of its heavy industry.* The dominant force in its political system, the Communist Party, still defines for itself major tasks of social reform involving institutional changes as well as the rearing of a new com-

---

* In the early 1960s approximately 40 per cent of the Soviet labor force was engaged in agriculture while the over-all standard of living was considerably below that of western Europe and Japan, not to speak of the United States or Canada. In 1963, out of a total Soviet population of 223 million, 108 million were rural. To the extent that communications data are an index of social integration, the United States is also a far more integrated society than the USSR. See table in Appendix.

munist man, both of which are considered prerequisites to the construction of communism. Many of these projects are dictated by the country's persisting backwardness, others by the continuing revolutionary commitment of the political elite. In part, however, the definition of these tasks may be also a reflection of the political elite's collective sense of vested interest in continuing to dominate society. Once the society itself "takes off" in social development, the social justification for an essentially ideological political system decreases, as we have seen, while such social groups as the new industrial elite or the new technical intelligentsia may begin to crave for the stability inherent in a more instrumental political system. The Soviet Union's promises of a higher standard of living, even at the price of delaying the revolutionary momentum, suggest that the system is no longer invulnerable to that kind of social pressure.

The categories "ideological" and "instrumental," however, should not be seen as mutually exclusive, since they are meant merely to underline certain dominant qualities of the two systems. Most political systems of the developed or quasideveloped societies tend to be less instrumental and less rigidly ideological than the American and the Soviet respectively. Thus in many western European countries, or in Japan, or Mexico, the impact of nationalism and nationalist wars has made political loyalty to the nation-state into the prime civic virtue, inculcated by national systems of education, while religious and doctrinal disputes have created a residual tradition which is reflected in greater emphasis on issues of principle than is the case in America. At the same time, the almost parallel development of industrial economy and technology has produced a degree of social complexity which is now reducing the appeal of purely doctrinal programs in the more developed countries and which thus favors an instrumental system. The decline of Marxism in the Social-Democratic parties of western Europe is a good example.

The lengthy isolation of America, with its relative immunity to western European doctrinal disputes, and the steady but rapid growth of the American economy favored the instrumental approach, even though Americans traditionally have tended to mask their pragmatism of action with verbal absolutes. The Russian attempt to overcome economic backwardness was the result of repeated national calamities and was directed by a political elite with an intense ideological commitment (see Chapter One). Consequently, the ideological character of the political system was intensified and the instrumental minimized. The result is a significant difference in the scope of the Soviet and American political systems. Many of the functions of governing which are performed by the government in the Soviet Union are performed in America by private "governments"—corporations, foundations, unions, churches, associations. In the Soviet Union the function of governing is almost entirely monopolized by the political system. The term "political system" hence has a considerably broader meaning there than in the United States.

The preceding considerations can be summarized briefly. (1) A stable and spontaneously developing society favors an essentially instrumental political system. Good examples are the United States and England in the nineteenth century, in both of which social dynamism made for piecemeal reform and progress without cataclysmic political interventions. In the early 1960s West Germany and Japan provided examples of rapid progress combined with political pragmatism. (2) The subsequent combination of a stable, developed society and an instrumental political system favors the gradual expansion of the latter's power, generating greater public involvement over political ends. In Sweden, the United States, and England since World War II, social welfare has become a function of government, justified by considerations of public social responsibility that were strongly attacked by conservative spokesmen. In Germany, a similar development took place even earlier, before World War I, although at the behest of the conservatives. (3) The combination of an unstable, backward society and an ideological political system favors the expansion of the latter's power through revolutionary social reconstruction. The Soviet Union under Stalin and China under Mao Tse-tung are classical cases. But even less extreme manifestations, such as the extension of Nkrumah's power in Ghana with its political and ideological stress on his special role and his doctrines, also bear out the proposition. (4) The subsequent combination of a stable, quasideveloped society and an ideological political system generates social pressure for a more instrumental approach. Thus under de Gaulle France was undergoing a political revolution to match postwar social and economic development. A new structure of administrators and technocrats was rising, and de Gaulle's regime may be seen as a transition from the old ideological politics to a more instrumental kind. A similar but more retarded development is taking place in Spain and Mexico, and was taking place in Yugoslavia until an economic-political crisis reversed the trend back to the conditions described under (3). The Soviet Union is also beginning to feel some of these social pressures, although, as will be shown later, its further development may involve quite novel political forms.

Therefore, it would be premature to conclude from the foregoing that the American political system is gradually becoming ideological or the Soviet instrumental. All that can be said is that with domestic social change, as well as with the impact of the cold war, the American system has assumed certain functions with respect to society which in the past the society had been loath to yield. At the same time, the Soviet system has lost some of its freedom to mold the society, especially since it can no longer entirely disregard the complex industrial and urban interests, which have developed considerable institutional and group cohesion. To the extent that the political system mirrors or is responsive to such social pressures, it can be said to acquire certain instrumental characteristics.

For a more precise understanding of these changing relationships it is necessary to examine specific aspects of the interaction between the system and society, particularly with reference to the individual as a citizen and to social groups as participants in the political process. The degree to which a citizen is conditioned to behave in a specific political fashion or to which social groups are satisfied, controlled, or manipulated in their behavior is bound to affect the system-society relationship. The degree of such conditioning or control, in turn, depends not only on the social-economic maturity or stage of a society but also on the actual efforts and inherent propensities of the political system.

An ideological political system is similar to such organizations as a trade union or a church in that it is militant, inclined toward action, and relatively selective and exclusive in membership. Characteristically, trade unions, churches, and other organizations of this sort insist on training their own personnel and do not consider outside, "secular" training as adequate preparation for active participation.[1] Since normally they exert great claims on individual members and demand from them a high degree of institutional commitment, they find it essential to minimize competitive allegiance and to focus all training on the organizational goal. An ideological political system is similarly concerned with commitment, although it cannot expect the same intensity of commitment from all of the members of society. There thus develops a hierarchy of organizational membership and commitment, ranging from the direct, full-time personal involvement of, for example, a high-level Party functionary to the positive loyalty of the indoctrinated citizen engaged in a nonpolitical occupation. The expectation is that by individual conditioning as well as group manipulation the political system will maintain a *relationship of control and mobilization* with society.

An instrumental political system, viewed conceptually as an "ideal type," is more limited in the demands it imposes on society. In this, it is somewhat similar to certain corporations in America which, concerned with the over-all morale of the employee, encourage his commitment to family life, local community affairs, the PTA, the church, all only indirectly relevant to the employee's organizational commitment. Such organizations recruit their personnel from outside training institutions—for example, high schools or colleges—and are satisfied with some limited subsequent in-training. An instrumental political system, such as the American, similarly stresses a certain amount of "in-training" with civics courses or military service or the more recent "anti-communist" courses to develop political commitment, but by and large it does not insist that all training be politically focused, and it is willing to recruit its personnel from non-system training institutions. It is thus more open to social pressures. They, however, need not always aim at restricting the political system's power. As pointed out earlier, social pressure may also cause an increase in political power, as can also national emergencies or economic crises. Broadly speaking, in an instrumental political system this *relationship is one of access and interaction.*

SOCIALIZATION AND POLITIZATION

Political socialization is the process by which children and adults learn to participate in the political system. In a traditional agrarian society, this process is relatively simple, although still crucially important to the survival of the system. The key factor is the loyalty of the peasant to his local landlord or provincial governor. In a modern political system, citizenship means more, and the requirements of political socialization are much more complex. At a minimum, political socialization involves the creation of public interest in: the society or political community as a whole; the political regime or form of government; political groups within the system, such as parties; the ideology and values of the system; and active participation in the system.[2] These needs are common to both the Soviet Union and the United States.

While the over-all purposes of political socialization are the same, the ways in which it takes place differ sharply in instrumental and ideological societies. In an instrumental society, responsibility for the process is dispersed among many agencies. The family is the principal agent and is supplemented by schools, secondary associations, and mass media, each acting independently. In such a society, political socialization is thus essentially an indirect process. The rationale for this approach was perhaps most cogently summed up by Burke in *Reflections on the Revolution in France:*

> We begin our public affections in our families. No cold relation is a zealous citizen. We pass on to our neighbourhoods, and our habitual provincial connections. These are inns and resting places. Such divisions of our country as have been formed by habit, and not by a sudden jerk of authority, were so many little images of the great country in which the heart found something which it would fill. The love to the whole is not extinguished by this subordinate partiality. . . . To be attached to the subdivision, to love the little platoon we belong to in society, is the first principle (the germ, as it were) of public affections. It is the first link in the series by which we proceed towards a love of our country, and of mankind.

In an instrumental political system political man is an offshoot of social man.

The other concept of political socialization, or politization, attempts to produce the desired attitudes and behavior through direct indoctrination of the individual and his direct but controlled involvement in political activity. The individual is bound to the political system not through his primary group loyalties but rather through direct subordination of his loyalties to the system. To that end, the political system maintains specialized institutions directed to the politization of the individual and to counteracting the appeals of other groups. Political man is to reflect the political system.

Politization is especially prevalent in new, revolutionary, ideological regimes. To elicit loyalty and support the regime cannot rely on the usual social institutions and groupings, whose allegiances belong to the prerevolutionary society. It must create a direct identification with itself. Once the regime becomes stabilized, however, and after the passage of sufficient time, the original need for direct politization begins to decline. In a stable instrumental system, direct politization plays only a minor supplementary role. In a revolutionary regime, it is the dominant, if not exclusive, means of socialization. In a stable ideological system, the two methods of political socialization are more evenly balanced. The regime confronts the problem: To what extent should it attempt to continue the direct politization characteristic of its revolutionary phase and to what extent should it come to rely on indirect political socialization through other entities? Social groupings usually resume some of these functions, but the system of direct politization inherited from the earlier revolutionary era still plays a dominant role.

The problem comes to a focus in the relation between the family and the other agents of socialization. The crucial importance of the family derives, of course, from the fact that "the child's political world begins to take shape well before he even enters elementary school" and that by the time he enters high school he has developed a fairly definite political outlook. During these years the family is the naturally dominant influence. In the United States this primacy is almost entirely functional to the political system, and the family is "a conserving factor in the political system." [3] The other agents of socialization are many and varied. The process through which they gradually supplant the family is slow and irregular, as the adolescent or young adult gradually affiliates with other groups. Many of these later agents may simply reinforce the political outlook already developed in family and school. In almost all instances, moreover, their claims on the individual are partial. Some are concerned primarily with patriotism and national loyalty, some with partisan allegiance, some with general ideas and beliefs, some with particular political issues. No agent, apart from the family, attempts to shape all the individual's political attitudes.

In the Soviet system, however, the Communist Party does attempt to mold all the political attitudes of the citizens. All the non-family agents of socialization, which in the United States supplement the family with diversified cross pressures, are subordinated to the Party and directed toward a single goal. The family, however, poses a special problem; it is least subject to control and yet most important. In the first years of their regime the Bolsheviks pursued a purely ideological policy of weakening the family; subsequently, they reversed themselves, stressed the importance of the family, and encouraged parents to produce the desired political attitudes and behavior in their children.

The interests of the parents in socializing their children, however, seldom if ever coincide entirely with those of the Party. The family thus can never be simply a "transmission belt" for the Party; it will always be partially a rival. Consequently, the Party must also exercise a direct politicizing influence on the children. It must rival the family when it cannot use it. Burke declared, "No cold relation is a zealous citizen." In the Soviet system, however, the claims of citizenship may put relation against relation. "In one Soviet family," a Soviet writer reported approvingly, "the father was trying to persuade the child, 'Look how badly you are behaving—you don't obey Mama and Papa. We do everything for you, we show you every concern.' 'It is not you who show concern for me,' the child answered. 'It is the Party and the government that show concern for me.' He was only five years old. But he listened to the radio and watched television." [4]

The principal agents of the Party in countering the family are the schools, youth organizations, adult political education, and mass media. Each of these is more important in political socialization in the Soviet Union than it is in the United States. Under the direction of the Party, the schools, of course, are a major force, particularly the boarding schools for children between the ages of seven and eighteen. First proposed by Khrushchev in 1956, these schools had 1.5 million pupils in 1962, and they are to have 2.5 million by 1965. There are also plans to lower the age of admission. No secret is made of the fact that these institutions are to train the future communist elite. They are to perform the function which the "public" English boarding schools did for so many years. It is quite likely that in a few decades most Soviet leaders will have had their initial training in one of these schools. Professor

S. Strumilin, the leading Soviet specialist on the future communist society, stressed the advantage of collective social upbringing, arguing that instead of "egotistic inclinations . . . all the inborn instincts and sympathies will be emphasized and brought out as a result of the newly conditioned reflexes formed in the process of daily comradely interrelationships." [5] With toys and equipment owned in common, with a vigorous twelve-hours-a-day, six-days-a-week program of training and labor, the schools will have ample opportunity to instill the desired political commitment in the future citizen.

In all schools close attention is paid to the inculcation of communist "ideals" and world perspectives. According to the most comprehensive study on Soviet education available, "political bias permeates every subject of instruction. . . . In history texts, students are informed that the American Constitution of 1787 'in effect curtailed the rights of workers,' or that with the assassination of Abraham Lincoln 'the big bourgeoisie won and from then on established its dictatorship.' . . . But political bias, present everywhere, is particularly noticeable in foreign-language courses. The English-language textbook makes reference on virtually every other page to misery, unemployment, exploitation, and racial discrimination in the United States, England, and other capitalist countries." [6] The schools also propagate atheism, while the educational process as such is characterized by a strong emphasis on discipline and subordination of the individual child's personality to the "collective."

In the United States schools play an important role in teaching children patriotic motives and national ideals. This role was particularly important for the children of immigrants whose families could not function effectively as socializing agents. More generally, the school supplements the socializing process in the family. The time consciously and exclusively devoted to political education and indoctrination, however, is less than it is in the Soviet Union. In addition, the teaching of regular academic subjects is seldom employed for such overt political purposes as in the Soviet Union.* In recent years, however, there has been a new concern about the public indifference to the communist danger. Many school systems

---

* It has been argued that 42 per cent of the average ninth to twelfth grades in the United States is devoted to political activity as compared with 27 per cent of the ninth to eleventh grades in the Soviet Union;

have established courses on the nature of communism. These courses reflect a recurring fear in the United States that indirect socialization is not enough and that direct, ideological politization is needed to instill the proper patriotic enthusiasm. The new courses, however, are often devoted primarily to exposing the evils of communism. At times this is done with a crudeness fully matching that of Soviet descriptions of the United States. "Millions of political prisoners from many nations of the world," the Boston syllabus on "Communism" declared in 1962, "including probably the United States of America, are the basis of the labor productive system of the U.S.S.R., Red China, and the other Soviet satellites." [7]

In the Soviet Union the politicizing role of the educational system has, until recently, been limited by its highly selective structure, which permits only the ablest to go on with their education. In the United States, on the other hand, general socialization through a less selective but more democratic system reaches a considerably higher proportion of the young.* The politicizing role of the schools is hence buttressed by the Komsomol (the Young Communist League, YCL) and its subsidiary, the Young Pioneers. In the initial phase of Soviet rule the Komsomol's primary task was breaking the youth's social and psychological relations with the "past" society. Young Komsomolites were encouraged to engage in anti-religious demonstrations, to smash icons, to help in coercing peasants to join collective farms, to build new industrial centers. This was the "heroic period" of the Komsomol. It was expected that in the process of such activity the young

---

these figures, however, are based on the assumption that English and history courses in American high schools are entirely "political education." This assumption is doubtful. See G. Z. F. Bereday and B. B. Stretch, "Political Education in the USA and the USSR," *Comparative Education Review,* June 1963, pp. 9-16.

* Educational statistics for the 1950s:

| | Per cent of total youth | |
	USSR	USA
Complete elementary schooling	98%	99%
Enter secondary schools	55%	85%
Complete secondary school	30%	57%

(Adapted from N. Dewitt, *Education and Professional Employees in the USSR,* Washington, D.C., 1961, p. 37.)

Komsomolites would be politicized and their commitment to the political system tested. Today, however, no such sharp dichotomy between the system and the society exists. The Komsomol, therefore, assists both in the general process of socialization—through organized leisure activity and social and physical training—and in politization of youth by cultivating in them the positive "morals" of a communist citizen and combating "alien, Western" influence. "The rearing of the new man is the foundation of the ideological work of the YCL," declared its first secretary in 1962, while elaborating the new tasks of the organization. Furthermore, some of the more active members serve in the *druzhinniki,* or special citizens' militia, whose task is to combat all public manifestations of wayward behavior.*

Komsomol organizations are also active in the institutions of higher learning. Komsomol officials participate in admission boards and encourage the selection of candidates with direct experience in productive work.** The Komsomol organization encourages student interest in the compulsory courses on Marxism-Leninism. Similarly, it has been active in implementing the Soviet decision that students in the institutions of higher learning should spend six to ten months in practical production work, a decision which was not popular, for varied reasons, with many of the students, their families, and their professors. However, the emphasis on production experience illustrates the confidence of the political system that the society itself now reflects many of the desired qualities, and that the ex-

---

* As the Komsomol first secretary, S. P. Pavlov, put it: "The YCL organizations should maintain the closest ties in these activities with the agencies of the militia, the courts, and the prosecutor's office. These organizations serve one and the same purpose—to educate people; and the success of this work depends in no small measure upon our close cooperation." (*Izvestia,* April 17, 1962.) The Komsomol is a mass youth organization with 19.4 million members in 1962, or approximately 45 per cent of the fifteen-to-twenty-six age group. It publishes approximately two hundred newspapers and magazines with a total circulation of 22.5 million copies per issue. In addition, its publishing house puts out annually approximately 23 million books and pamphlets (*ibid.*). Children below the Komsomol age bracket are organized into the Young Pioneers with a membership in 1962 of 18.5 million.

** In 1957, 28 per cent admitted to higher schools had practical job experience; in 1961, 60 per cent (*Izvestia,* April 17, 1962).

posure of the potentially—and often inherently—isolated and self-indulgent student to physical labor amid proletarians will have a politically desirable effect. Socialization as a social process is thus to reinforce politization as a goal.

The United States has no youth organization comparable to the Komsomol. Instead, many organizations with various functions and viewpoints supplement, in some degree, the family and the schools as socializing agents. The Young Democratic and Young Republican clubs perhaps have the closest superficial resemblance to the Komsomol; yet they have only about 5 per cent of its membership, and their size and activities fluctuate widely with the electoral cycle. More important in the political socialization process are groups which are not primarily political. The Boy Scouts, Girl Scouts, and Campfire Girls, for instance, have close to 10 million members and undoubtedly perform an important role in stimulating patriotism and a "Teddy Rooscvelt" type of nationalism. Religious youth organizations also help in the general process of socialization and, incidentally, to some degree in political socialization. By and large, however, the socializing roles of youth organizations are much less significant in an instrumental society such as the United States than in an ideological system.

Younger American children have an idealized image of political authorities in general and of the President in particular. The President is a "benevolent leader" possessed of all virtues: "benign, wise, helpful, concerned for the welfare of others, protective, powerful, good and honest." [8] The child transfers to public leaders attitudes originally developed toward his parents. These attitudes reflect the child's psychological need to overcome uncertainties and fears caused by his own dependent state and the lack of information about the unpleasant aspects of politics. Since these traits are universal, it seems reasonable to assume that the Soviet child has at least as benevolent an image of the First Secretary and the Communist Party. In the United States, however, the idealized image weakens as the child grows older and less dependent.* In

---

* Sixty-one per cent of the children in a second-grade sample, for instance, thought the President was the "best person in the world," but only two per cent of those in the eighth grade accorded him this accolade. Robert D. Hess and David Easton, "The Child's Changing Image of the President," *Public Opinion Quarterly*, Winter 1960, p. 637.

due course, the romantic childhood image is replaced by the dis-
illusioned, cynical, or indifferent attitude toward politics and politicians typical of the American adult. Similar tendencies toward disillusionment presumably are at work among Soviet children. The
intense indoctrination efforts in the schools and the Komsomols
are, in effect, designed to counteract this disillusionment and to
perpetuate into adulthood childhood images of the benevolent
leader and the benevolent Party. In some measure, however, this
effort is Sisyphean. The childhood image is based on need and
ignorance. The very attempts of the Soviet socializing agents to
stimulate political participation and educate the public on political
issues tend to undermine the pristine image which they wish to
preserve. In addition, by challenging the authority of the parents
over the children at an early age, the regime may also weaken the
childhood image of parental authority, of which it is a secondary
beneficiary.

For adults, political groupings such as political parties and interest groups perform the function of political socialization. Identification with a political party comes at a very early age: American
children inherit their party in much the same way and to the same
extent that they inherit their church. This inheritance, moreover,
tends to remain with the adult, although it may be eroded by upward mobility, changes in residence, or shifts in the general political
climate of the country. At the same time, the high rate of inheritance of partisanship early identifies children with a major institution in the political structure, produces a natural acceptance of the
two-party system, and thus almost forecloses a total rejection of
the political system. In the Soviet Union, on the other hand, the
people have traditionally differentiated between the regime and the
"motherland." Accordingly, the ruling party invests much effort in
identifying one with the other.

Children tend to develop a fairly coherent political viewpoint or
ideology during adolescence. By the last year in high school "the
absorption of political orientation has progressed close to its maximum level" and "even in the first year of high school, absorption
of an orientation has gone quite far." [9] In one study of American
youth, only 14 per cent of those fifteen years old or younger and
5 per cent of those nineteen or over failed to manifest a coherent
political orientation.[10] By and large, children tend to absorb the

general political attitudes of their parents, but to a lesser degree than they inherit their party allegiances. A political attitude or ideology, moreover, may soon lose its relevance as political issues change. At this point, the political party may serve as an agent as well as an object of socialization.

> No matter how well individuals were socialized in any particular ideological position in childhood, such a mode of preparation for adult politics would be inadequate. New issues continually emerge on the political scene. Certainly many of these resemble or fall within some ideological realm in which the individual had earlier been socialized. But many others would be novel, and the adult would have to face them without preparation. However, insofar as the individual has developed an abiding loyalty to some political party, it would constitute an organizing principle for these issues. The party, rather than the inherent connections between new and old issues, would define the correct position. Thus crucial to socialization as a mechanism of preparation for confronting political issues is socialization into party. . . .[11]

A political party, through either symbolic affiliation or indoctrination, can thus aid in the difficult task of defining one's relationship to the continually changing and often hard to grasp reality. Once loyalty, and hence receptivity to the party, has been established, public utterances by the party leader can quickly define the individual's own attitudes to some new political, social, or international phenomenon.

In the Soviet Union, loyalty to the ruling Communist Party provides that sense of direction and self-assurance. The absence of any competitive organization capable of doing this on the society scale (as contrasted with more limited professional organizations) means further that the alternative is frequently a frustrating and fearful sense of isolation and a purely negative rejection of the system. Trust in the Party and dedication to it help to resolve some of the dilemmas and uncertainties which are inherent in modern life and in the dangerous world situation, in a way not unlike that in which some religious institutions have provided the faithful with psychological relief and stability in the face of pestilence, poverty, and other ills.

In the Soviet Union the Party attempts to monopolize this role. In the United States the individual obtains his policy guidance from a variety of groups. The political party apparently plays a significant role in shaping the attitudes of its followers on foreign-policy issues.[12] In addition, the President as a national institution, and not as a partisan leader, has in recent years performed a crucial educational role in this area. In domestic affairs, the attitudes of the public are shaped by more diverse sources. The National Association of Manufacturers (NAM) or a trade union can have much to do in influencing the individual's thinking on the farm problem, medicare, or tariffs. In recent years some business corporations and other organizations have undertaken programs of political indoctrination, usually of an anti-communist variety. In the diversified context of American society, programs of this sort do not arouse much interest unless they are focused on issues of direct social or economic concern to specific groups. No single organization monopolizes the shaping of attitudes toward any one issue, and very few attempt to shape attitudes on all issues.

Another means of politization employed by the Communist Party, and virtually unknown in the United States, is political education for adults. Agitation and propaganda among the populace have always been major responsibilities of Party members. The techniques employed have varied through time. In the early 1960s, many local Party committees set up special "ideological commissions" so as "to embrace with political influence every Soviet man." [13] Working closely with the established Agitprop sections, their purpose is to draw the Soviet intelligentsia into Party work by coordinating all aspects of political indoctrination. The composition of the "ideological commission" varies; in one cited case it was composed of eleven people, including the regional Party secretary, the commission chairman, the head of the Party Agitprop, the editors of local newspapers, the head of the local cultural administration, the local head of the Society for the Dissemination of Political and Scientific Knowledge, the local radio-television chief, and the Komsomol secretary. In another case, the commission included as many as eighty people since it also embraced the local teachers, theater personnel, library staff, and the like. The varied composition depends on local needs, but its purpose remains the same: to coordinate and activate the often scattered but usually extensive political education.

Many leisure activities are also linked to the politization process.

For instance, a Soviet spokesman estimated late in 1961 "that 200 million persons visit clubs, palaces of culture, and other cultural-enlightenment institutions each month," adding that "the activity of the cultural-enlightenment institutions is at present directed toward propagandizing the resolutions and documents of the XXII Party Congress." [14] In addition, all towns and districts in larger cities have their own centers of political education. In Orenburg (population approximately 300,000), the local House for Political Education provided special refresher courses, organizational co-ordination, and diversified training for some 40,000 Agitprop activists working in Orenburg province or oblast (population approximately 2,000,000).*

---

* B. Sherbarshov, "Dom politicheskogo prosveshchenia—agitatoram" (The House of Political Education—to the Agitators), *Agitator,* May 1961. Other examples could be cited from a 398-page book entitled (in English translation) *In Close Touch with Life* ("From the Experience of Propaganda and Mass-Political Work of Leningrad Party Organizations in Leningrad Province"), which explains how the Leningraders allegedly achieved striking successes in stimulating the political self-education of Communists, ideologically educating the intelligentsia and students, and setting up seminars for various responsible cadres in industry and agriculture. Sherbarshov's account, as revealing as it is typical, can be summarized as follows:

The Orenburg party organization has about 40,000 agitators, and the House of Political Education's main task is to teach them the art of agitation, arm them with necessary data for political work among the masses, and generalize and propagate their experiences.

Every third or fourth agitator is a leading factory or "sovkhoz" worker, kolkhoznik milkmaid, swineherd, or participant in the Communist labor movement; in agit collectives there are more than 2000 Party and Soviet workers, almost 8000 agricultural and industrial production specialists, almost 7000 teachers; almost two-thirds have higher, unfinished higher and secondary education.

At HPE, an agitator receives all the basic data on the nationwide, oblast, city, and individual-enterprise seven-year plan, familiarizes himself with the results of oblast economic development for two years of the seven-year plan, and with the tasks of the third year learns the names and the outstanding feats of our luminaries, members of brigades, shifts, collectives, and shock workers of Communist Labor. These are formulated on poster stands, folders, reference sheets, albums, bulletins, etc.; e.g., for elections there is an exhibition, "Leaders

In both America and Russia mass media of communications, particularly the press, also play a major role in political socialization. The editorial attitude, the slanting of news, the emphases in presentation, as well as the degree to which the citizen is exposed to diverse opinions have a direct impact on the formation of the citizen's political outlook. Even a cursory comparison of Soviet and American publications illustrates the difference stated earlier between direct ideological politization and indirect political socialization. The table on page 89 illustrates the choice available in the two countries to a politically minded citizen who happens to be preoccupied with more than the local news or sports. Although Americans read more newspapers than the Soviet people (see Appendix), the data suggest two basic contrasts: the Soviet publications are more politically focused and all represent the outlook of the ruling Party, unlike the diversity of opinion represented by the American equivalents; the relatively lower circulation of the American political-ideological journals reflects the American citizen's somewhat lesser scale of involvement in political matters and, by the same token, fewer demands put on him by the system.

In addition to such mass media, most major American interests publish their own materials and distribute them among individuals or newspapers. The NAM puts out press-releases to some 7500 weekly newspapers, as well as a special release, "Farm and Indus-

---

of Production are Candidates for Oblast Soviet Deputies," with biographical information and short descriptions of their award-winning work methods.

In response to the January 1961 Plenum of the CC of the CPSU on ideological work, they carried out a three-week course for managers and a five-week seminar for instructors, in gorkom and raikon departments of agitation and propaganda in which problems of economics and advanced techniques in sovkhozy and kolkhozy were studied. Courses for department managers were on the basis of the Orenburg Agricultural Institute. The program was twenty-nine hours of general political problems and the experience of party organizations in organizational work, twenty-six hours in problems of mechanization and electrification of agriculture, plus live issues (in the problems) in agronomy, zootechnology, and veterinary science. Courses were conducted in auditoriums, laboratories, in fields and on farms by leading scientists and teachers from agricultural and research institutes, specialists in oblast administration of agriculture, by Party and soviet workers, leaders, and leading workers in kolkhozy and sovkhozy.

try," directed at about 35,000 farm leaders. This is a particularly important vehicle for influencing public opinion, and can have special political significance at times when controversial issues are debated by Congress. No parallel or even analogy to this is remotely present in the Soviet Union; the Soviet citizen has access only to official sources of information, designed to elicit from him the desirable political reaction.

TABLE 1

CIRCULATION OF PERIODICAL LITERATURE

USSR (1961)		USA (1962)	
Major newspapers			
Pravda	6,300,000	New York Times	776,100
Izvestia	2,300,000	(Sunday)	1,347,500
Literaturnaia Gazeta	750,000	New York Herald	
Trud	888,000	Tribune	400,000
Komsomolskaia Pravda	3,400,000	Christian Science	
Pionerskaia Pravda	3,000,000	Monitor	194,400
		Wall Street Journal	774,000
Ideological-political magazines			
Kommunist	573,500*	National Review	35,810
Partiinaia Zhizn'	507,800*	Reporter	170,150
Politicheskoe		Nation	25,100
Samoobrazovanie	293,000	New Republic	40,280
Agitator	571,000*	Commentary	25,400
Voprosy Istorii KPSS	52,000*	America	63,000
Voprosy Filosofii	14,500*	Commonweal	21,700
Voprosy Istorii	18,700*	Foreign Affairs	45,500
Molodoi Kommunist	120,500*	American Political	
		Science Review	7,020
		Saturday Review	266,500

* 1962 figures.

The intense efforts by the Party to indoctrinate adults and children could conceivably become self-defeating. The strong rule by the father in German families tends to produce more systematic rebellion by German youth than do the more consensual patterns of decision-making in American families. Similarly, young American voters whose parents exercised normal control over them as children tend to deviate from the parents' political opinions least frequently; deviation is more frequent among those over whom parental control was weak, but most frequent for those whose parents were most strict.[15] If a similar relation exists between strict Party control and deviance in the Soviet Union, some of the regime's problems with *stilyagi, dzhentelmen,* and other "antisocial" types may well be of its own making.

In both countries, also, nationalism plays a key role in developing interest in the political community. Increasingly, in the Soviet Union, politization is complemented by patriotic appeals. Nationalism—and for the first time Soviet nationalism on a mass scale (not the more traditional and ethnically restricted Russian, Byelo-Russian, Kazakh nationalism)—develops an intense commitment to the political system. Here, the regime can tap the deep-seated feelings of ambivalence, insecurity, and inferiority-superiority which have characterized past Russian attitudes to the West. Recent Soviet space achievements, as well as the Soviet victory over Germany and the possibility that the Soviet Union might equal the United States in industrial production, have given the Soviet man a deep and unprecedented sense of pride in his country. The political system has not been loath to take full credit for these achievements, and its appropriation of the appeals of science and technology as well as its identification with nationalism reinforce its politization process. In both the Soviet Union and the United States compulsory military service, with its intense overtones of patriotic duty, involves the use of nationalism in creating loyalty to the political system. In the United States, religious sentiments also assist in generating support for the political community. Children, it appears, have difficulty distinguishing between God and country; patriotic rituals elicit responses similar to religious rituals; and "religious affect . . . is . . . displaced upon political object. . . ."[16] The cumulative effect of such conditioning is to prepare the Soviet and the American citizen for his respective modes of participation in the political system.

POLITICAL PARTICIPATION AND CONTROL

Among the many ways in which a modern polity differs from a traditional one is the degree of popular participation in the political system. In the past, the vast majority of the people lived apart from politics. Occasionally their lives were interrupted by wars or foreign invasions, and they were impressed into feudal or royal armies. Otherwise, leaving taxes or duties apart, politics had no meaning for them. The cumulative and interdependent impact of industrialization, nationalism, and literacy in our age, however, has made all modern political systems dependent on mass support and mass participation. The masses legitimize and sustain the power of the leadership. Participation satisfies their need for a sense of belonging and direction. In totalitarian states as well as democracies, the "good citizen" participates in public affairs. In the Soviet Union as well as the United States leaders point with pride to high rates of citizen participation and deplore apathy and indifference.

Political participation, however, has no necessary connection with self-government. An ideological system has much of the former, little of the latter. An instrumental political system represents the claims and aspirations of the great variety of groups that make up a modern society, and it is therefore so structured that there is access to political power at all levels of society. At the very bottom, the exercise of popular suffrage either sanctions the existing political leadership or changes it. On higher levels of the social pyramid, access to political power is through the medium of organized social and economic influence and interests, as well as through the interchangeability of social and political elites (see Chapter Three). In that respect, an instrumental political system is indeed that of an open society, although the overall level of political participation may still be low.

Although both American and Soviet citizens participate widely in politics, their participation differs in its scope, its forms, and the functions which it performs in the political system. Apart from the decisive fact that the American electorate does directly choose its leaders from alternative slates presented before it while the Soviet population does not, American popular participation differs from the Soviet by being indirect, segmented, and pluralist, while the Soviet is direct, hierarchical, and centralized. Soviet leaders, dedicated to the creation of a communist society, must stimulate active participation by the citizens in their programs of social reconstruction. "The greater the changes in the structure of the society or organization that a governing group is attempting to introduce, the more likely the leadership is to desire and even require a high level of participation by its citizens or members." [17]

For the Soviets, it is extremely important that political participation be intense and almost all-embracing because it facilitates continued direct politization even as it creates the impression of popular consent for the political system and for the social changes effected by it.

Most Soviet citizens, however, like most people elsewhere, are not interested primarily in politics. Consequently, the government must actively stimulate participation. Some participation is undoubtedly directly compelled by the government, and consequently is not comparable to voluntary American participation. It would be a mistake, however, to assume that the immense amount of political activity that takes place in the Soviet Union is exclusively or even primarily a product of coercion. Most of it is induced by the twin forces of direct politization and pressures of social conformity.

In the United States participation is valued, but it is not the goal of a vast, centrally controlled system of indoctrination. Participation is an opportunity and a right, but only voting is generally viewed as an obligation. Many Americans believe they have a responsibility to vote and tend to feel guilty if they do not. They do not, however, feel an obligation to engage in other, more intense forms of political participation. In addition, the relative stability of the social system means that only rarely is there a sense of mass involvement in political issues. Many citizens find an outlet in less directly political activity, conducted with highly segmented semipolitical associations, and most neither participate nor associate politically. Indeed, for most Americans politics has something of a spectator-sport quality—it is to be watched on television but it is not a matter of direct personal involvement.

Political participation in the United States also helps establish reciprocal controls between citizens and political leadership. Through electoral participation and civic associations the citizen exercises some control over his leaders. At the same time, these activities induce thought patterns which establish a binding link between the citizen and the political system. This form of indirect social control establishes certain norms of political behavior, usually backed by social conformity and, particularly in America, by the social conservatism of a stable and relatively affluent society.

The Soviet regime increasingly uses political participation to control its people. The more terroristic controls are no longer employed as they were during Stalin's days. This is not to say that secret police intimidation has altogether disappeared; there is persistent evidence of politically motivated arrests, involving even such "crimes" as possession of unauthorized Western literature or disseminating politically undesirable information.[18] But in addition, political control now takes advantage of social conformity, the result of greater stability in the social system. However, to the extent that this conformity is utilized to limit the range of political dissent and is imbued with a direct political content, it is appropriately seen as a politically induced and organized social orthodoxy rather than as analogous to the more spontaneous conformity of the American society. The controls produced by political participation flow in one direction only.

Both Soviet and American citizens belong to political organizations, but the scope and significance of this membership varies considerably. In the Soviet Union, of course, the single most important form of political participation is membership in the Communist Party. In 1962 the Party had 10,400,000 members, roughly 7 per cent of the adult population. These were the primary political activists in Soviet society. As Party members they had special opportunities, special responsibilities, and special obligations for political work. The Party is the general leader of society, and its members participate in virtually all forms of political action. The more important leadership functions are performed only by Party members. Other functions are discharged through the mass participation of both members and nonmembers.

The United States has no core of *general* political activists comparable to the Party members in the Soviet Union. The most significant form of mass political participation in the United States is the election, and electoral activity is cyclical. Organized about the electoral process, however, are political organizations ("machines") which do maintain a continuing existence. Just how many Americans participate in these is hard to estimate. In 1956, 3 per cent of a national sample, representing about 3 million people, said that they belonged to a political club or political organization. To the extent that these organizations were concerned with electoral activity, their hard core consisted of 250,000 precinct leaders in the two major parties.[19] Thus, the organizations which do exist in the United States and are more specifically concerned with the electoral process include a smaller fraction of the total adult population than does the Soviet Communist Party.

Although the ballot is the simplest but symbolically most significant and most common form of political participation in the modern state, the functions of American and Soviet elections could hardly be more different. American elections are designed to select leaders. The Soviet elections, on the other hand, as has been noted, are designed to express popular approval for the leaders' policies. "The question is sometimes raised," Cyril Black has remarked, "as to why the Party bothers with elections and a parliament. It bothers with them because they are essential instruments of Party control. The electoral process gives the average voter a sense of participation in the political process, and indeed it may in some subtle psychological fashion commit him to sharing responsibility for the Party's directives." [20]

American elections are a means of popular control over government, yet in the 1960 presidential election, only 68,839,000 persons voted, roughly 64 per cent of the estimated 107,949,000 potential voters. In off-year congressional elections, the turnout drops to about 40 per cent. On the other hand, the percentage of participation in recent elections in western Europe has been: Italy, 93.7; West Germany, 87.7; France, 72.07; Norway, 79.1; Great Britain, 78.7; Switzerland, 68.5. All these percentages, of course, pale before those achieved in communist states, where the function of the election is to control the populace rather than the government. In the Soviet elections of 1962, 99.95 per cent of the registered voters went to the polls.

Voting is only the final and most common form of electoral participation, and in both the Soviet Union and the United States large numbers of people engage in related electoral activities. In the Soviet Union, the final decisions on who should be nominated are made by the appropriate Party groups, but an impressive number of citizens are still drawn into the nominating process. In 1957, for instance, 1,200,000 Soviet citizens (not all Party members) served on electoral commissions to help select over 1,500,000 candidates (not all Party members) for national, republic, and local soviets. In the United States, the electoral campaign is, of course, the high point of political participation among citizens. The forms and extent of this participation are suggested by following results from a national poll after the 1956 election: 28 per cent conversed on behalf of a party or candidate; 10 per cent contributed money to a party or candidate; 7 per cent attended political meetings; 3 per cent worked in the campaign; and 3 per cent belonged to a political organization.[21] Fourteen per cent of the adult population, or about 14 million people, engaged in some form of political activity beyond voting and talking for their side.* In presidential elections, two-thirds of the funds raised at the national level and one-third at the state and local level come from gifts of $500 or more. Yet 8 million people contributed at least some money to the 1956 campaigns, and about 10 million contributed in 1960.[22]

From the foregoing data it would seem that more people participate actively in American electoral campaigns than in the cut-and-dried Soviet elections. On the other hand, citizen participation in part-time governmental activities undoubtedly is much greater in the Soviet Union. In the United States there are approximately 525,000 elected officials, many of whom, on the state and local levels, serve on a part-time basis. A total of 810,700 people work part-time in local government. In 1962 in the Soviet Union, on the other hand, 1,823,500 citizens served as deputies to national, republican, or local soviets. And reportedly some 20 million citizens participated in the work of the soviets by serving on commissions and in other ways. The Soviet leaders also make conscious efforts to insure that those people drawn into this work are a broad cross section of the public.

Citizen participation in government serves two crucial functions in the Soviet system. In the first place, it involves a substantial segment of the people, including large numbers of non-Party members, in the workings of the system and thereby increases their identification with the regime and their feeling of responsi-

---

* A roughly parallel poll in Norway found 22 per cent of the Norwegian population engaging in such activity. Stein Rokkan and Angus Campbell, "Citizen Participation in Political Life: Norway and the United States of America," *International Social Science Journal*, No. 1, 1960, p. 78.

bility for its success or failure. Since the basic decisions are made in the Party organs, widespread participation in government is no real threat to the Party. Conversely, it furnishes the Party with an important "transmission belt" through which policies are brought back to and explained to the people. Secondly, citizen participation also serves as a check on the inertia, inefficiency, and abuses which inevitably exist in a highly bureaucratic system. The complexity of modern society is such that the job of centrally directing that society impairs the functioning of the political system, even if it has the most up-to-date means of coordination, planning, rapid communications, and pervasive coercion. The 1957 devolution of certain economic planning and administrative responsibilities to new regional economic councils (*sovnarkhozy*), although subsequently reversed in part, reflected an effort to bring administration closer to society and to tap the increased technological knowledge and political loyalty of that society.

In keeping with the increased emphasis on popular control, the factory permanent productivity councils, established in 1958, have been used to stimulate the introduction of new techniques and to supervise current operations. According to an unusually detailed Italian communist report,[23] by 1961 there were 112,000 such councils comprising 4.5 million members. Generally, each council would contain at most 20 per cent ex-officio members (directing personnel, Party, trade union, Komsomol), and the rest would be recruited from among the workers, but with technicians and engineers playing an important role. In larger factories, there would also be departmental councils. While only elected council members could legislate, any employee could attend, and during the first half of 1961 some 15 million workers were reported to have done so. The productivity council could not revise production plans or interfere with the administration, but it could recommend improvements and criticize performance. It thus fits the current effort to encourage popular participation without political power and popular responsibility without policy-making authority.

The average citizen has also been encouraged to assist in local administration. The Party program adopted by the 22nd CPSU Congress declares: "An effort should be made to insure that the salaried government staffs are reduced, that ever larger sections of the people learn to take part in administration, and thus that work on government staffs eventually ceases to constitute a profession." What this means is illustrated by an account from the town of Vyburg (population approximately 50,000), where the public was said to have taken an active hand in civic affairs: citizens' militia, 1700 members; apartment-house committee, 103; public sections and councils attached to executive committees and institutions, 165; sanitation *aktif,* 912; public inspectors of trade and public catering enterprises, 288; volunteer fire brigade, 484; "green patrol," 575; parents' committees, 236; pensioners' club, 500; total, 5070 individuals.[24] According to the account, the civic bureaucracy was substantially reduced, while public control insured orderly development as well as a sense of direct civic participation.

Although the Soviet leadership maintains central coordination from above, even to the point of issuing minute instructions guiding the conduct of deputies to the local soviet,[25] the elite views the assumption of these subsidiary functions as demonstrations that the state is indeed withering away. The assumption of social-security operations by the trade unions and the creation of a non-governmental union of sport societies are seen as part of the process of society's assuming greater self-government, now that its values and organizational forms no longer conflict with those of the political system. Even Party members have been encouraged to interest themselves more actively in Party management, and the suppression of criticism by middle-range Party officials has been condemned through negative publicity.

Furthermore, citizens in general discuss politics in both the United States and the Soviet Union, but again the functions and the context of the discussion differ significantly. Americans normally discuss politics with those who have similar views, and most of the discussion tends to reinforce existing opinions. Although political awareness is stimulated during presidential campaigns, and conflicting views gain circulation through the mass media, the American discussion is largely spontaneous, personal, and unstructured. In the Soviet Union, public discussion is organized and highly focused. Thus, according to Soviet claims, some 40,820,000 people "debated" the industrial reorganization plans of 1957, and some 82,000,000 people participated in discussions concerning the new Party program presented in 1961. These organized discussions focus public attention on specific problems which the Party wishes to have aired. Under Stalin, they also pre-empted all public discussion; Soviet citizens simply did not discuss politics among themselves. Since Stalin's death, there is evidence that political subjects have gradually begun to intrude into informal discussions, but the tradition of personal self-restraint and caution is still deeply ingrained. While the Soviet government would like to stimulate more public criticism of performance, it is still unwilling to allow public criticism of policy. To an average citizen this distinction is tenuous, and there are too many risks involved in confusing the former with the latter.

The contrasts in the nature and functions of American and Soviet participation are also reflected in distinctive forms of political participation: the social-mobilization organization in the Soviet Union and the civic-action association in the United States. The roles which these play are directly related to the social dynamics of political participation in modern societies. In all societies, people of higher social-economic status participate more than those of lower status. The gap between participation levels of the higher and lower strata in the United States, however, is particularly great.* Those in the United States with higher incomes and more education participate in politics in roughly the same way as their European counterparts do. The American lower classes, however, participate significantly less than European lower classes. The major reason for this lies, paradoxically, in the greater social mobility and, in a sense, "classlessness" in American society. In the words of Lipset: "the more open the class structure of any society, the more politically apathetic its working class should be;

---

* Typical American figures are the following for the 1952 election:

SOCIAL CLASS	PER CENT VOTING
Upper middle	88.9
Lower middle	80.5
Upper lower	76.0
Lower lower	54.6
Farmers	67.7

Source: Morris Janowitz and Dwaine Marvick, *Competitive Pressure and Democratic Consent* (University of Michigan, Michigan Governmental Studies, No. 32, 1956), p. 26.

and, conversely, the more rigidly stratified a society, the more likely that its lower classes will develop their own strong forms of political activity."

The United States thus has an open society and low working-class participation in politics. Western European countries have more stratified societies and more working-class political activity. Which course has the Soviet Union followed? The Soviets, it would appear, are attempting to eat their cake and have it too. Soviet society is relatively unstratified and offers multiple opportunities for social mobility. In this respect it is like the United States. So also, political participation, as measured by membership in the Communist Party, is probably distributed among social classes in about the same ratio as political participation in the United States (see Table 2). The Soviets, however, cannot accept this situation with equanimity. Ideologically and traditionally, the Party is supposed to be proletarian. The leaders must engage in a continual struggle against one of the consequences of the "class-lessness" of Soviet society. They have to make recurring efforts to increase the proportion of "workers and peasants" in the Party and otherwise to counteract the natural tendencies for those of higher social-economic standing to participate more than those of lower standing.

Soviet efforts to recruit lower-class elements into the Party in large part reflect a realistic appreciation of what those elements actually are. By and large, in Western democracies those of lower social-economic standing tend to be less tolerant, more authoritarian, more anti-intellectual, more given to ethnic prejudices and hates, less favorable toward democratic institutions, more favorable toward strong leadership, and less concerned about civil liberties than those of higher social-economic standing.[26] Presumably similar tendencies toward working-class orthodoxy exist in the Soviet Union. There they are exploited by the regime. By mobilizing the masses into social control organizations the regime attempts to limit and suppress deviant behavior among other groups in the population. In the pre-Soviet period, groups in opposition to the czarist regime were handicapped by the passivity of the politically unconscious masses. The contemporary Soviet system, in a curious parallel, also undermines the effectiveness of individual or group dissent, but by pre-empting mass support. It does

Table 2

SOCIAL STATUS AND CPSU MEMBERSHIP 1961*

ADULTS	USSR	PER CENT OF EMPLOYED BY OCCUPATION	CPSU	PER CENT OF PARTY BY OCCUPATION	PER CENT OF PARTY MEMBERS IN EACH OCCUPATION
Gainfully employed in national economy	107,600,000	100.0	10,000,000	100.0	9.3
Workers	49,700,000	47.3	3,450,000	34.5	6.9
Peasants	34,300,000	32.0	1,750,000	17.5	5.1
Employees (mental workers, intelligentsia):	22,250,000	20.7	4,800,000	48.0	21.6
Heads of organizations, institutions, enterprises, construction projects, *sovkhozy*, RTS, and their subdivisions	1,400,000	1.3	490,000	4.9	35.0
Engineers, technicians, agricultural specialists, architects, economists	4,700,000	4.7	1,400,000	14.0	30.0
Personnel in science, education, public health, literature and art	5,200,000	5.1	1,030,000	10.3	20.0

Source: *Partiinaia Zhizn'*, 1962, #1, pp. 44-54: *SSSR v Tsifrakh-1961*, Moscow, 1962, pp. 32-60.
In 1960 28.4 per cent of the 8,784,000 specialists working in the national economy belonged to the Party, and in 1961, 34.2 per cent of the 3,800,000 Soviet citizens who had completed higher education were in the Party. See also p. 169.
* Employment figures are adjusted, based on 1959 census.

so by mobilizing mass social orthodoxy, especially of the first-generation urban dwellers, in order to suppress any deviant behavior. The regime's use of anti-Semitism should be seen in the light of the foregoing. By appealing to and subtly exploiting the anti-Semitic prejudices of the Russian masses, the Party both mobilizes mass support and isolates the alleged "social deviants."

Such mass organizations as the *druzhinniki* or volunteer teams of trade-union members and young Komsomolites, over the age of eighteen wearing red arm bands, have been widely used in towns and villages to assist the law-enforcement agencies in combating crime and hooliganism. They enjoy the right of detaining individuals for deviant behavior. In addition, the druzhinniki, who by 1962 numbered about 3 million, have been active in suppressing such social deviations as excessively Western styles of dress, hairdos, or dancing, in addition to combating speculation and black-marketeering. Detailed instructions have been published to guide their conduct, to assist in their organization, and to instruct their commanders.[27] Citizens are obliged to respect their authority. The Soviet press has published accounts of frequent cases of abuse of authority by the druzhinniki, of excessive exuberance in the pursuit of their duties, and of simple-minded interpretation of what constitutes a departure from the communist code of social behavior.

An even more extreme form of coercive mass orthodoxy and self-sustaining social control involves the comrades' courts and the public assemblies. Popular justice usually tends to be quite severe (soldiers, for instance, generally prefer to be tried in courts-martial by officers rather than by their peers) and by invoking it the system assures itself both severity and the semblance of democracy.* The comrades' courts, set up in collectives of over fifty workers, have been empowered to judge all forms of social misbehavior, to make their decisions by majority vote, and to

---

* The general increase in severity has been justified on the grounds that the higher the socialist morality of the workers the more they demand that "moral principles" be enforced. (V. Tenenbaum, "The Interaction of Communist Morality and Soviet Law," *Politicheskoe Samoobrazovaniie,* No. 6, June 1961.) It is symptomatic that the Soviet press frequently concludes its trial reports by stating that the sentence of death meted out to some accused was applauded by the public present.

impose fines or refer the case to the regular courts. Judging by Soviet accounts, their purpose is to subject the offender to public pressure and to contribute to his re-education. Furthermore, all the republics have authorized the formation of the so-called public assemblies, gatherings of a minimum of one hundred people to judge "parasites" and to impose on them sentences of exile with corrective labor for two to five years. This is nothing less than the institutionalization of social control by reliance on mass orthodoxy for punitive sanctions.

There is a striking parallel here between the purposeful efforts of the Soviet political system to take advantage of "lower-class" intolerance (during the 1956-1957 intellectual ferment Khrushchev openly threatened to call out the workers against the intellectuals) and McCarthyism in the United States. In the United States, however, the same social facts have very different political implications. Not only do those of higher social-economic status participate more actively in politics than those of lower status, but they are also more "liberal" in their outlook than the rank and file. While there are greater differences in power between leaders and populace in the Soviet Union, there may well be greater differences in attitude between leaders and populace in the United States. The Soviet regime mobilizes the masses against dissenters or deviants from the Party line. In the United States, dissenters from the liberal consensus attempt to mobilize the anti-liberal but normally apolitical masses against established leaders and institutions. In both, however, the passivity of the masses encourages the preservation of the political status quo.

The social-mobilization organization typifies participation in Soviet society. Somewhat similarly, the civic-action association typifies participation in the pluralistic American democracy. Ever since Tocqueville, much has been made of the role of private associations in American life. In actual fact, however, one-third to two-thirds of the American people belong to no voluntary association other than a church, and membership in such associations appears to be no more widespread in the United States than in most other western European democracies, with the possible exception of France. What is different in the United States is the important role of civic and welfare associations devoted primarily or exclusively to promoting what their members believe to be improvements in community life. The Rotary Clubs, PTA, League of Women Voters, and Red Cross are only the most obvious examples. It is precisely the prevalence of this type of association, moreover, which impressed Tocqueville:

> Americans . . . have not only commercial and manufacturing companies, in which all take part, but associations of a thousand other kinds, religious, moral, serious, futile, general or restricted, enormous or diminutive. The Americans make associations to give entertainment, to found seminaries, to build inns, to construct churches, to diffuse books, to send missionaries to the antipodes; in this manner they found hospitals, prisons, and schools. If it is proposed to inculcate some truth or to foster some feeling by the encouragement of a great example, they form a society. Wherever at the head of some new undertaking you see the government in France, or a man of rank in England, in the United States you will be sure to find an association.

His comments highlight the principal functions of such associations: to generate proposals for reform, to arouse support for these proposals, and thus to stimulate governmental or community action to put the proposals into effect. "Nearly every 'cause,' " Lord Bryce noted fifty years after Tocqueville, "philanthropic, economic, or social, has something of the kind." Such associations, he added, "rouse attention, excite discussion, formulate principles, submit plans," and thus nourish "young causes and unpopular doctrines into self-confident aggressiveness."

Membership in civic associations is widespread. In the late 1940s 31 per cent of the American public belonged to organizations which sometimes took stands on housing, better government, school problems, or other public issues.[28] Other studies have found the memberships of Americans concentrated in unions, religious and church-affiliated organizations, fraternal societies, and business, civic service, and improvement associations. Such groups are far more important in American public life than in that of other democracies. Germans, for instance, join organizations just as often as Americans do, but they join leisure ones more frequently and occupational associations, special-interest organizations, and "organizations with a political or social-action program" less frequently.[29] In other countries ideological political parties pre-empt the ground which in America is occupied by the more segmental, pragmatic, and reform-minded civic associations.

The civic association is thus a peculiarly American form of political participation. Its roots, as Tocqueville pointed out, lie in the absence of an aristocratic class whose members could easily and naturally assume the role of propagating new opinions. It was further stimulated by frontier needs for cooperation and collective self-help. It is, however, a form of participation peculiarly characteristic of the upper middle class. Upper-class, lower-middle-class, and lower-class organizations tend to eschew politics and public affairs. It is in the upper middle class that "civic mindedness has a flowering." [30] Thus, in the United States civic associations are a means through which those of higher social-economic standing participate in and limit the political system. In the Soviet Union, on the other hand, social mobilization encourages lower-class participation to strengthen the political system.

ALIENATION AND DISSENT

No political system ever achieves total compliance and total commitment from its citizens. In one way or another, with varying degrees of intensity, dissent makes itself felt, thereby once again showing that there is no fully satisfactory mold capable of encompassing the complexity of the human condition. In an ideological system dissent can take either an instrumental or an ideological form. The first involves efforts to lift ideological controls on the grounds that their removal will actually benefit both society and the political system; the second tries to provide an ideological alternative to the system. The first is orthodox dissent, the second unorthodox. In an instrumental system, on the other hand, dissent tends to be primarily ideological, for instrumental criticism (how to do something better) is accepted as long as it is justified pragmatically. Instrumental dissent is not really dissent at all but part of the accepted game of politics.

Thus in the Soviet Union orthodox dissent is instrumental, and unorthodox dissent is ideological. In the United States, however, all political dissent is ideological, and orthodox dissent differs from unorthodox only in terms of the values and principles which it invokes. If these values are generally within the American pantheon of principles, the dissent is orthodox. If the dissent invokes principles which are not accepted as legitimate by substantial elements of American opinion, it is unorthodox. Most

Americans would see some legitimacy in the values invoked by both white southerners (states' rights, property rights) and Negro leaders (human rights, equality). Both forms of dissent are orthodox. Unorthodox dissent involves a rejection of the varied but traditional American values and an appeal to principles and values which have no sympathetic support in the American tradition. The Communist Party would be one example; the American Nazi Party of George Lincoln Rockwell would be another.

Finally, the condition of alienation is common to both ideological and instrumental systems and involves a purely negative rejection of the political system. However, in an ideological system, individual alienation is in itself seen as politically pernicious because of the demands of the political system on the individual. In an instrumental system, individual alienation becomes politically significant only when it becomes crystallized into radical movements of dissent.

In the Soviet Union social alienation or deviation from socialist morality can be documented by published Soviet sources. The January 1960 resolution of the Central Committee of the CPSU, entitled "On the Tasks of Party Propaganda in Present-Day Conditions," condemned the persistence of such "capitalist survivals" as nationalism among the various nationalities, cosmopolitanism, persistence of religious views, and gross violations of labor discipline, and demanded the intensification of all propaganda efforts. There are frequent complaints that the level of political awareness of the average Soviet worker is very low and that there is a general lack of interest in ideological-political matters (a point corroborated by Western interviews with former Soviet citizens). Party workers, furthermore, often seem to adopt a "formalistic" attitude toward mass political education. This condition has been complicated in recent years by increased contacts with the West. "It is no secret that the education of the man of the future is taking place in a difficult and acute struggle with the influence of corrupt bourgeois ideology and morality, with harmful ideas entering from outside the border." [31] The increased contacts and exchanges with the West, the presence of foreign students in the USSR, and even the new diversity prevailing in the communist camp mean greater exposure of Soviet youth to foreign views and styles.

A closely related aspect has involved the tendency, especially marked among some of the new technical intelligentsia, to "emigrate internally"—to find escape in their own activity and to see in it the fulfillment of their social tasks. Soviet leaders and press have frequently attacked this inclination, seeing in it "apoliticality" and an antisocial attitude. In part, this attitude may involve a conscious effort to evade the time-consuming and generally unrewarding political obligations which the system expects everyone voluntarily to assume. In part, however, it is also an inescapable consequence of the production demands put on every Soviet citizen by the government as well as of the pressures for specialization and expertise which any modern, technological society generates. To the extent that the political system fails to perceive this, it creates an insoluble dilemma for itself as well as acute tensions for its citizens.

A broader social problem facing the regime is the gradual erosion of "revolutionary" mores, or perhaps merely the gradual shedding of external forms in reality never fully absorbed by society but adopted by it because of political terror. There is considerable evidence to suggest that portions of the Soviet youth, especially in the larger cities, and of the managerial-intelligentsia class (on the basis of census data, the latter would amount to approximately 10 per cent of the youth) have been succumbing to a fascination with various forms of leisure usually associated in the West with "modern mass culture." Similarly, probably because of the rapid urbanization, with its disturbing impact on established rural tradition, and the consequent inadequate housing, with its negative effects on family life, there appears to be a serious delinquency problem. Both represent challenges to the Komsomol conception of Soviet youth.

That the political elite has also deviated from communist morals has been openly admitted. In the words of the first secretary of the Armenian Communist Party:

> How can we explain the fact that for many years now Comrade Zadoyan, chairman of the Aykavan village collective farm, has been unable to complete the construction of the public bath and club building in the village, while in the meantime, and a short time, he has built a wonderful house for himself? It is simple. It is explained by the fact that he has paid more attention to his personal welfare than to the welfare of members of the collective farm. And here is a case of Comrade Shaginyan, regional chief

of the militia, who, although the owner of a communal house, has built a private two-story house in two years' time. We do not speak of how he found the means to build such a house, but the campaign against crimes and to consolidate the public order is poorly organized in the rayon. These cases show that tendencies to petit bourgeois ownership *are still firmly established in the consciousness of our leading communist workers.*[32]

If the secretary's generalization is correct, it may be assumed that such tendencies are even more widespread among the rank and file of the Party and the nonmembers. The absence of terror has encouraged a certain amount of illegal economic activity, while the increased material rewards but continued shortages in consumer supplies have created considerable opportunities for graft. That corruption, black-marketeering, and appropriation of state property have become a serious economic and social problem is not denied by the state, and in the one year from May 1961 to May 1962 the death penalty was extended in more than two hundred cases for these offenses. The following is a typical account:

In the city of Pyatigorsk, the Russian Republic Supreme Court heard the case of a criminal group that for a long time had been stealing wheat and other grain products in especially large amounts at the Mineralnye Vodi Grain Receiving Depot by cheating collective and state farms when they delivered grain: short-weighing, overstating moisture content, and undergrading. . . . It was headed by Maly, previously tried for abuse of his office. Having obtained, through his connections, the post of official in charge of grain receiving at a mill, he created large surpluses of grain products and sold the stolen goods. In Maly's home alone, about 50,000 rubles in cash in the new price scale, more than 22,000 rubles in saving bank deposits, 3-per-cent loan bonds in the amount of 9100 rubles and more than 3000 rubles' worth of various valuables obtained through theft were discovered and confiscated. The Russian Republic Supreme Court, in view of the special danger of the crimes committed by Maly and on the basis of the May 5, 1961 decree of the Presidium of the USSR Supreme Soviet "On Intensifying the Struggle against Especially Dangerous Crimes," sentenced M. I. Maly to death by shooting with confiscation of his property. Maly filed a petition for clemency. The Presidium of the Russian Republic Supreme Soviet considered this petition and denied it.[33]

(To think of an American counterpart, one has to imagine Billie Sol Estes getting the electric chair for his alleged operations.)

The extreme severity of the punishment presumably is a good measure of the political-economic gravity and of the social scope of the problem.

The political leaders explained the above as "aberrations" or lags from the pre-socialist era. It is indeed difficult for the political system to account for these social deviations from its norms, since any systematic explanation would involve both some embarrassing disclosures and an implicit refutation of the system's basic doctrinal assumptions concerning the role of social-economic environment in shaping human consciousness. In the United States, delinquency and similar social misdeeds can be blamed on family shortcomings, or immigrant maladjustment, or poor housing, and so on. In the Soviet Union, open discussion is inhibited, and the tendency is to blame either foreign influence or "lags in social consciousness," both of which have certain ideological overtones and inhibit remedial measures. In any case, these deviations impede efforts of the political system to construct a new society.

Soviet ideology endows social deviation with political significance. Corruption, delinquency, withdrawal, indifference to politics, and fascination with "bourgeois" mores thus indicate that the individual has become alienated from the political system. In the United States, similar behavior does not have the same implications. The American political system does not impose a single code of morality on society: moral standards are more complex, flexible, and numerous. Beatnik behavior, which may be proscribed in the Soviet Union, is viewed as desirable by some Americans, as distasteful by others, and with indifference by the vast majority, including the organs of government. In some cases, deviant behavior passes the limits of legality, but even so it is not commonly the product of alienation from the political system. For this reason, attempts to discuss with the Soviets the common problems of industrialized societies, such as juvenile delinquency, are unfruitful. Where deviant forms of behavior are illegal in the United States, as with some forms of corruption and delinquency, the stigma attaches not to the underlying motive but to the means employed to satisfy it. Billie Sol Estes was punished not for his motive (to get rich quick) but for his methods. Marijuana-smoking adolescents are taken in tow not because they seek exotic personal pleasures but because of the means they employ to satisfy those desires. In the Soviet Union, however, not only the methods but also the motives of those who engage in deviant behavior are a challenge to the political system. Personal wealth or pleasures should be subordinated to the collective efforts to build communism.

In the West, and particularly in the United States, the term "alienation" normally means a state in which the individual, dissatisfied with himself and his environment, attempts to escape from both through participation in a radical protest movement. The alienated American attempts to escape *into* just exactly what the alienated Soviet citizen attempts to escape *from*. Alienation is usually the consequence of rapid social change, the break-up of the traditional order, rapid industrialization and urbanization, or other major discontinuities in social life. Alienation typically involves a rejection of the existing political system and may lead to a commitment to direct and fundamental changes in it. The alienated individual sees the political system as a façade hiding the machinations of conspiratorial groups. Alienation is linked to feelings of political futility and a low sense of personal accomplishment.[34] One study of Boston, for instance, revealed that

> a large proportion of the electorate feels politically powerless because it believes that the community is controlled by a small group of powerful and selfish individuals who use public office for personal gain. Many voters assume that this power elite is irresponsible and unaffected by the outcome of elections. Those who embrace this view feel that voting is meaningless because they see the candidates as undesirable and the electoral process as a sham. We suggest the term "political alienation" to refer to these attitudes.[35]

Mass attitudes such as these are a sword over the head of American democracy. Where they exist without political action, the apathy of the alienated cannot be distinguished from the apathy of the satisfied. In times of turmoil and upheaval, however, the alienated can be swiftly mobilized and "people who have previously rejected politics turn out in large numbers to support demagogic attacks on the existing political system."[36] Because the government monopolizes political mobilization in the Soviet Union, alienation can be expressed only in terms of individual deviation. In the United States, however, it becomes politically relevant when

of relativity was without foundation. . . . It seems to me that our philosophers make such erroneous generalizations not only in physics but in biology as well." Kapitsa ended by pleading for a more experimental approach.* His argument was an overt plea to expand the scope of the instrumental and narrow down the ideological.

Writing on another occasion, Kapitsa went even further, almost crossing the invisible line between orthodox and unorthodox dissent by suggesting that social organization ought to be based not only on I. P. Pavlov's teachings concerning the human personality but also on Sigmund Freud's.[37] To this the ideologues could not remain indifferent. The official ideological organ of the Central Committee of the Party, *Kommunist,* charged in an unsigned (therefore even more official) article that Kapitsa's comments on science had neglected to mention that cooperation between the Soviet scientists and "philosophers" had saved the former from slipping into "the positions of idealism." It added that his comments on Freud did not deserve a serious refutation.[38] The reply was included appropriately in a longer polemic on "Peaceful Coexistence and Ideological Struggle."

This dispute, as well as the literary debates, illustrates the difficulty of determining the limits of orthodox dissent, especially in an ideological political system. What is more, a spontaneous expression of even limited social dissatisfaction tends to be interpreted politically as unorthodox dissent. For instance, in 1962 a series of strikes broke out in many parts of the USSR, sparked in part by the governmental increase in food prices. The strikes were suppressed, but in some places the suppression prompted resistance, inevitably with strong anti-governmental overtones. Workers cannot strike against "a workers' state," the ruling bureaucracy explained. In the United States, similar types of behavior do not have the same political implications. At first, strikes were often brutally suppressed, but usually directly by the economic interests involved,

---

* P. Kapitsa, "Theory, Experiment, Practice," *Ekonomicheskaia Gazeta,* March 26, 1962. That Kapitsa had the ideologues in mind is made clear by his reference to biology (the Lysenko controversy) and by his citation of a negative definition of cybernetics which appeared earlier in the philosophical dictionary, a highly ideological organ.

with the government adopting the stance of benevolent neutrality (in favor of the economic interests). In time, the sympathies of the political system shifted and strikes gained legal protection, but are still seen by and large as an activity outside the political process.

Under Stalin a highly coordinated, monistic, and insecure political system was ruling a backward society whose values and social organization were alien to the system. It inevitably tolerated a narrower margin than the more secure Soviet system now governing a society whose values and organization increasingly reflect the ideology of the system. At the same time, the new society itself may find useful a greater margin for dissent, while within the political system there may be uncertainty as to what is tolerable. This was true, for instance, in the case of the anti-Stalin and anti-concentration-camp literature which began to appear in the early sixties, and, more generally, in the case of the more assertive, nonideological style adopted by many Soviet writers. Late in 1962, after much internal hesitation, the Party leaders reached the conclusion that orthodox dissent had gone too far, and in March 1963 Khrushchev execrated "anti-Party" trends among the intellectuals, including even such orthodox dissenters as Yevtushenko and Ehrenburg, and warned that violation of the principle of *partiinost** is a step toward "counterrevolution." Their condemnation showed that in an ideological system even orthodox dissent eventually tends to become unorthodox. It is noteworthy that Khrushchev's remarks, crude and often vulgar, were also designed to stir up the anti-intellectual prejudices of the masses. Suppressed from above, isolated from below, uncertain of the limits of official toleration, the Soviet orthodox dissenter tends to be a lonely and politically insecure figure.

In an ideological system, orthodox dissent means instrumental criticism; in an instrumental system, ideological criticism is still tolerated as orthodox dissent. Thus in the Soviet Union orthodox dissent pits pragmatic needs against ideological orthodoxy. In the United States the nature of the political process produces almost exactly the reverse relationship. The orthodox dissenters in the United States are those who point to the gap between American ideals and American reality.

---

* *Partiinost:* literally "party-ness," the principle of subordination of one's activity to the desires of the Party.

Soviet ideology furnishes the motive, the rationale, and the guide for manipulating social change. Instrumental needs may moderate or temper social change, but they do not determine its direction and course. Unorthodox dissent—the rejection of communism in favor of another ideology—plays only a marginal and politically insignificant role in Soviet society because the political system suppresses it. In contrast, in western Europe ideological pluralism has meant that both fundamental changes in society and the opposition to fundamental changes have been motivated and rationalized in ideological terms. Socialism and Marxism, on the one hand, have opposed liberalism and conservatism, on the other. In the United States, a third pattern has prevailed. Political controversy at any given time typically involves three groups: (1) radical dissenters, who invoke some fundamental American values to justify major changes in the social system or governmental policy; (2) conservative dissenters, who invoke other fundamental American values to object to the current trends and proposed changes; and (3) the pragmatic middle, which is willing to support small, incremental changes in the direction desired by the radical dissenters, where it can be convincingly demonstrated that such changes are "really necessary."

American politics differs from European and Soviet politics in that ideology plays only a minor role in bringing about change. To some degree the radical dissenters prepare the way intellectually and morally for the moderate changes of the pragmatic middle. But the changes adopted by the middle invariably undermine the appeal of the more sweeping reforms desired by the radicals. The changes which the middle does bring about, in turn, are *almost never* justified on the ideological grounds advanced by the radicals. Instead they are advanced in terms of immediate, practical needs; they are abstracted from an ideological context; and their adoption is often urged on the grounds that it will head off the necessity for any fundamental changes. These moderate changes, however, are usually opposed primarily on ideological grounds. Those groups which see themselves threatened by the course of change appeal to fundamental values and also frequently develop at least a primitive ideology to resist such change.

The interplay of ideological *avant-garde,* pragmatic middle, and ideological conservative opposition can be seen in most of the great American political controversies. In the struggle over the ratification of the Constitution a small ideological minority (represented by Hamilton) wanted a highly centralized system of government. A much larger conservative group (the anti-federalists) developed an ideological opposition to a strong national government and an ideological rationale for states' rights. The pragmatic middle went along with the sweeping changes embodied in the Constitution (which was, after all, a revolutionary step) not on ideological grounds but because they seemed necessary in terms of the immediate practical needs of law and order, economic development, and defense against foreign threats. Similarly, between 1831 and the Civil War the abolitionists constituted an ideological *avant-garde* denouncing slavery in terms of some fundamental American values. Their attacks gave rise to counterattack from the South, which was, indeed, politically much stronger and ideologically much more sophisticated than the radical abolitionists. The actual course of change, on the other hand, was shaped by the pragmatic middle through a variety of legislative enactments each embodying a response to some immediate need. Eventually the political and ideological interests of the South led it to choose secession rather than face further pragmatic changes in the direction to which it was opposed. The North fought the Civil War, however, not on behalf of abolitionist principles but to preserve the Union, and the end of slavery in 1863 was justified not on moral principles but as a military necessity.

The drive for Negro rights in the twentieth century has followed a similar course. The civil-rights groups appealed to basic American values of liberty and equality to justify federal action. Southern and conservative groups invoked states' and property rights (as well as constitutional doctrines of "interposition") in opposition to federal intervention. The leaders of Kennedy's Administration (unlike those of Eisenhower's) sympathized much more strongly with the values of the civil-rights groups than with those of the Southerners. Yet throughout 1961 and 1962 the Kennedy Administration did little on civil rights. It responded only when the situation began to get out of hand in the spring of 1963, and its proposals were then justified largely on the pragmatic need "to get the conflict out of the street and into the courts."

Historically the most important form of orthodox dissent in

American politics has been the "protest movement." It normally feeds on elements alienated from the status quo or the existing course of events. It typically involves charismatic or demagogic leadership, a primitive ideology or other theoretical formulation of grievances, a definite target in some institution or group which is held responsible for the grievances, a nebulous set of demands, and the mobilization of normally apolitical elements of the population into the political arena. Since in the United States political change occurs either slowly or not at all, many of the most significant protest movements in American history have been fundamentally protests against new conditions and the measures which the government has taken to adapt society to them. The Anti-Masonic, Free Soil, and Know-Nothing movements enlivened the political scene before the Civil War with their protests against free trade, the extension of slavery, and immigration. The surge of industrialization after the Civil War produced a new wave of protest movements in the Grangers, the Greenbackers, and Populists. These groups were a negative reaction to industrialization. "The utopia of the Populists was in the past, not the future." They wished to return to a simple, rural, pre-industrial America. So also after the turn of the century the Progressive movement was an "effort to restore a type of economic individualism and political democracy that was widely believed to have existed earlier in America and to have been destroyed by the great corporation and the corrupt political machine. . . ." [39] In a similar manner, the McCarthyist and Radical Right movements of the 1950s protested against the new involvement of the United States in world affairs. Other protest movements have been more radical—protesting an unchanging status quo and promulgating goals or remedies to improve conditions. During the depression, the Townsendite, EPIC, Share the Wealth, and Social Justice movements capitalized on the appalling economic conditions to advance a variety of nostrums and panaceas. Both reactionary and radical protest movements usually have short lives. They flare up, dominate the political scene for a brief while, and then disappear, undercut by the processes of gradual change.

Unorthodox dissent was much more widespread in the Soviet Union during the initial phases of political takeover and social-economic revolution. But the Soviet leaders forcibly eliminated all opposition and even possible opposition (for example, by the massacre of the intelligentsia of the various nationalities including also of the Jewish minority). Dissent thus differs from outright resistance or subversion. Active political resistance no longer seems to be a major factor in the society-system relationship. Even disputes within the top Party leadership, as after Stalin's death, are no longer represented as efforts to overthrow the communist system, as was still the case with Stalin's liquidation of his opponents. Unorthodox dissent involves primarily the intellectual rejection of the system and occasional efforts to develop an ideological alternative to it. However, this is limited by the fact that without access to the complex planning machinery of the state it is impossible to develop a meaningful alternative. The political elite thus enjoys the advantage of being able to force its opposition into a stance of opposition to society as a whole—that is, total rejection. This "dilemma of the one alternative" paralyzes much of the resistance. To the extent that it is practiced by isolated members of the new intelligentsia, it seems to confirm "the general proposition that the more isolated the intellectuals from their society, the more revolutionary and messianic their outlook." [40]

The poetry of the young Russian writer Alexander S. Yesenin-Volpin conveys the spirit of the unorthodox dissenter. Unlike Yevtushenko, he has not had his poetry published in the Soviet Union; he has not been allowed to travel abroad; and late in 1959 he was imprisoned. By his request his poetry was published abroad. His is a poetry of political rejection.*

---

* There Is No Freedom

"There is no freedom, never was."
Joke on, my son: I press your hand:
Smite down their power! These jokes amuse
And horrify a father's mind. . . .
Big children do not fear the whip,
And adults lock them up in prison;
But this has no effect at all;
They just don't care, who still are children,
Joke on, my son! Mere sound and fury, yet
I love your fresh and caustic wit,
Though the foe will ridicule your pranks

That Yesenin-Volpin's is not an isolated case was demonstrated by the ideological and political ferment precipitated by the events of 1956 in Hungary and Poland. The student unrest, their open demands for the "true" story of October 1956, the university wall-newspapers "slandering" official policy,[41] gradually took the form of more serious searching and questioning. Inspired in large part by the Marxist writings of such Yugoslavs as Kardelj and Djilas, the Hungarian philosopher Lukacs, the Polish philosopher Kola-kowski, and even Adam Schaff (who by Polish communist stand-ards is an orthodox Marxist-Leninist), the Soviet discontent took on the shape of "revisionism," as it has been labeled by the official Soviet ideologues. Although revisionism, as the name suggests, in-volves an effort to revise the existing ideological system, and not to destroy it, revisionist writings in eastern Europe made it clear that a political system based on its principles would differ most profoundly from the existing Soviet one. To be sure, the formal structure of the social-economic organization would not be altered fundamentally (although both the Yugoslav and the Polish experi-ences point to the possibility of major structural and even substan-tive reforms, such as in agriculture), but the internal ideologi-cal component of the political system would be deprived of its dogmatic quality and the Party of its monopoly on many aspects of life, especially the creative-intellectual. Revisionism is thus the extension and generalization into an over-all political-ideological alternative of many specific aspects of orthodox dissent. It is this generalization which makes it offensive to the political system.

> As for friends, they've ceased to care
> For what they cannot justify:
> The anger of an adult babe!

A. S. Yesenin-Volpin, *A Leaf of Spring,* New York, 1961, translated by G. Reavy. To the critic who might say that his poetry cannot be compared to Yevtushenko's, the retort is: Was he arrested for bad poetry? Other examples of the Soviet literature of political rejection are A. Tertz's two volumes, *On Socialist Realism* and *The Trial Begins;* I. Ivanov, *Est-li Zhizn' na Marse;* N. Arzak, *Govorit Moskva,* all smug-gled abroad from Russia and published by Instytut Literacki in Paris. They are characterized by their stress on the cynicism and corruption of the present political system, and particularly of its bureaucratic elite.

Unlike that of Yugoslavia and Poland, however, revisionism in the Soviet Union has no forum, no open spokesman, and no proclaimed supporters. Yet even the official organs of the government make it clear—through their attacks, warnings, and accusations—that it represents the most pervasive, the most serious, and the most socially constructive form of unorthodox dissent. Revisionism relates itself to the present Soviet environment; it aims not to destroy but to reconstruct it. It draws on many of the socialist principles which the system has succeeded in inculcating among the people. Finally, it claims to be based on the humanist traditions of Marxism, and it challenges therefore the Marxist orthodoxy of the present Soviet regime's Leninist-Stalinist tradition. Judging from Soviet attacks, revisionism has made inroads primarily among the Soviet-trained intelligentsia, thus also paralleling the experience of the eastern European countries, where revisionism was a post-communist phenomenon (and not the standard of the pre- and anti-communist generation). As the system becomes more invulnerable to anti-communist opposition, it becomes more vulnerable to communist-led opposition.

Another form of unorthodox dissent is posed by the persistence of religious beliefs among some sectors of the population. This is confirmed by frequent Soviet press attacks, by the continued activity of such mass atheist-propaganda organizations as the All-Union Society for the Dissemination of Political and Scientific Knowledge, by the trials of members of certain sects, and by the state's forcible separation of children from religiously devoted parents.[42] The traditional Russian Orthodox religion and the Islam of the large Moslem minority, both more widespread among the rural population than in the larger cities, have in recent years been overshadowed by the activity of certain proselytizing sects such as the Baptists and the Jehovah's Witnesses. The Soviet government has responded with particular brutality. However, none of the above provide a systematic social, political, and economic alternative to the existing system in the way that is posed by the unorthodox dissent of revisionism. This fact makes it easy for the political system, which can take advantage of its monopoly on all positive planning and development, to isolate and crush such opposition.

In the United States the distinction between orthodox and unorthodox dissent is seldom clear-cut. Almost all groups (including the Communist Party) attempt to find some element in the American tradition to which they can appeal. As one historian of American dissent has noted, "the line between useful and valid criticism of any society and a destructive alienation from its essential values is not easy to draw. Some men, and indeed some political movements, seem to live close to that line and to swing back and forth across it more than once in their lives." [43] Traditionally, two criteria have been applied to dissenting movements in the effort to draw this line. First, to what extent do the goals of the movement conflict with those fundamental principles embodied in the Declaration of Independence, the Constitution, and the Bill of Rights? Second, to what extent does the movement resort to illegal, nondemocratic, or violent means to achieve its goals? In the Negro movement of the 1960s, for instance, the NAACP generally pursued orthodox goals through orthodox means (persuasion, voting, legal action). The Student Non-Violent Coordinating Committee pursued the same goals through the unorthodox or semi-orthodox means of mass demonstrations and direct nonviolent, but illegal, action. But both these Negro organizations appealed to values accepted as legitimate by millions of Americans and by the national government. Other Negro organizations, however, rejected the American political system and its principles to support the supremacy of the Negro race and the creation of a separate Negro nation. At times these nationalist groups appeared ready to resort to unorthodox means to achieve their unorthodox goals.

In an ideological system such as the Soviet Union, unorthodox dissent is necessarily illegal. In an instrumental system, this is not so. In the Soviet Union the Party leadership draws the line between legal, orthodox dissent and illegal, unorthodox dissent on ideological grounds. In the United States unorthodox dissent traditionally becomes illegal only when it becomes a danger; the test is pragmatic rather than ideological. All sorts of radical and fanatic movements are tolerated—despite their rejection of American values—as long as they do not constitute a menace to the political system. The decisions on what dissent is dangerous and what is not are made through a variety of legislative, executive, and judicial bodies, among which the Supreme Court usually has the final word. In the classic formulation made by that Court, unorthodox dissent becomes illegal when it constitutes "a clear and present danger." This doctrine has had a varied history, but it embodies perfectly the prevailing American approach to the problem. Hence the legality of dissent can change over time. A Soviet-controlled United States Communist Party could be permitted much more freedom of action in the 1920s and 1930s when the Soviet Union was not a major rival of the United States than it could in the Cold War of the 1950s. The liberal dissenters of the 1950s, however, refuse to accept this difference and argue that to abandon the standards of the thirties is to surrender to the police state. The ideological critics of the New Deal, on the other hand, retroactively excoriate the left-wing dissent of the thirties by the standards of the Cold War.

Unorthodox dissent has had little appeal in the United States. The American consensus has been too varied, too overpowering, and too all-encompassing to allow it much scope. Unorthodox dissent (and some extreme orthodox dissent) can, however, play an important negative role in American politics. In particular, the proponents of limited, pragmatic reforms are always in danger of being linked to extremist, unorthodox dissenting groups which supposedly have similar goals. Thus, the devotees of free enterprise (orthodox reactionary dissenters) attempted to identify the New Deal (pragmatic reformers) with the Communist Party (radical, unorthodox dissenters). In a similar vein, liberals and other reformers have at times attempted to identify opposition to their reforms with extreme right-wing, unorthodox dissenters such as the John Birch Society. As a result, endorsement of a proposed reform or a political candidate by an extremist group can be the "kiss of death." Much of the art of politics in America is devoted to making one's opponents appear ideologically more extreme than they actually are, at the same time divorcing oneself from any identification with ideology.

SCIENCE AND SOCIAL MANIPULATION

In both America and Russia the scientific and technological revolution is increasing the importance of technical experts and the predominance of bureaucratic specialization and hierarchy. Inevitably these developments affect relations among the political leadership, the new scientific-managerial-technical elite, and the masses.

Each political system has attempted to respond to this change with-out altering the basic patterns of control and mobilization on the one hand and those of access and interaction on the other.

In the decade after the death of Stalin several major changes took place in the relation between the Soviet political system and society. Under Stalin the Party *apparat* (professional bureaucratic staff) had been reduced to the status of only one of several institu-tions and hierarchies at the control of the dictator. Khrushchev's victory in the succession struggle and his elimination of Beria, Malenkov, and Zhukov re-established the political supremacy of the apparat. This was reinforced by the industrial reorganization of 1957. No other elite groups are now in a position to challenge that supremacy. Concurrent with the assertion of Party supremacy went a relaxation of the scope and intensity of the ideological con-trols on literary, intellectual, and scientific activity. Ideology re-mained a universalist creed and a guideline for social relations, but no longer served as a standard by which to judge scientific and technical issues.* The various technical elites were assured that some degree of autonomy, however imprecise and changeable, would be recognized in their work on scientific matters. Although fraught with uncertainty, such a policy obviously would be pre-ferred by them to one based on the omniscience of dialectical materialism.

At the same time, however, the Party stressed the need to break down the division between political and technical specialists. The Party realizes that in our age technical skills are both important and highly regarded, and it therefore insists that efficiency and know-how, as well as ideological commitment, are the trademarks of the new man. In the armed forces the distinction between politi-cal officers and professional commanders was de-emphasized; "in-terchangeability" between the two roles became the new goal. Efforts were made "to make professional commanders and staff officers more interested in Party-political work, and at the same

---

* To emphasize this point, the Central Committee took the unusual step of publicizing a medical dispute concerning a cancer cure, in which the parties concerned appealed to the Party Presidium for a ruling and to which the Presidium responded by stating that the Party was not an "arbiter" for medical matters. *New York Times,* August 2, 1962.

time to make the political officers and Party units better grounded in military affairs and thus more responsive to the real interests and needs of the professionals." [44] Unity of command was again stressed. Similarly, the division of the Party hierarchy into industrial and agricultural branches in the fall of 1962 was in part designed to encourage the apparatchiki to become technically skilled in one area of economic activity or the other.

Through these means the Party attempted to ease tension and promote cooperation between the political leaders and technical elite. These developments did not, however, reflect any significant change in goals, for they rested upon prior acceptance of Party supremacy. The aim of the Party remained to control and mobilize the population for the task of building communism. The new technical orientation of the Party led it to appreciate new means of control and direction. At times Western observers have stressed the inherent conflict between technical rationality and ideological irrationality. The Soviet leaders, however, stress the compatibility of technological means and ideological ends. The new Soviet interest in cybernetics, for instance, stems precisely from its potentiality as a means of social control. Cybernetics, in the words of the most authoritative Soviet expert, is "a science of control by complex dynamic systems based on a mathematical foundation and on the use of modern electronic instruments." He pointedly quoted Lenin as having foreseen the social-political significance of cybernetics when he said, "We, the Bolshevik Party, have conquered Russia. We have won Russia from the rich for the poor, from the exploiters for the working class. We must now control Russia. All of the distinctiveness of the time in which we are living and all of its difficulty lie in understanding the characteristics of transition from the main task of convincing people and military suppression of exploiters to the task of control." [45]

It is striking to note that the Soviet presentation of this new science of control in many respects resembles the Soviet political system itself. This science is said to have four basic features: (1) the most general and abstract approach to control; (2) simple systems and dynamic laws; (3) control through the utilization of information; (4) unity of control and optimization.[46] It thus parallels the principles of the ideology, the expansion of control, the absorption of values by the people, and the growing importance of social feedback in central policy-making. The basic principles for constructing a control system, namely "the feedback principle and the principle of hierarchy (multistage nature) of control," seem especially applicable to the Soviet system:

> Feedback from the motor stages to the control organs is essential for monitoring the operation of the system and for taking into consideration the influence of environmental factors. The principle of hierarchy of control assures economy of the structure and stability of function of the system. It consists of the construction of a many-tiered system, in which direct control of motor stages is carried out by lower-level organs, which are monitored by second-level organs, which themselves are monitored by a third-level organ, and others.[47]

Certainly, the parallel between these remarks and the recent efforts to combine rational decision-making from above with social control from below is suggestive; it is strengthened by the observation of the Soviet author that "these principles of feedback and hierarchy of control are also utilized in the . . . organization of control processes in social life."

It seems reasonable to assume that a political elite which has an inherent propensity toward and a vested interest in social planning is not likely to yield its power monopoly at a time when the scientific computing facilities for social control are becoming increasingly available. Furthermore, the new techniques are likely to result in greater rationality in planning. They will make the elite's control more palatable and more enduring, thereby also legitimizing its power position. In the United States, social inhibitions and pluralistic institutions obstruct the overt political use of the control science. In the Soviet Union the discovery of new or more sophisticated means of control is likely to be followed by their utilization. The 22nd CPSU Congress in 1961 called for "the extensive application of cybernetics," and it is now regarded as reinforcing the dialectic-materialist viewpoint. Its new ideological legitimacy has obvious political implications, even though the limits of social control are still unknown. In addition, new developments in control sciences, particularly linear programming and input-output analysis, mean that centralized economies can be "rationally" directed. This is enormously important for the Soviet Union, as it removes the earlier incompatibility between a high level of complex development and the rational allocation of resources. Thus, technological change in the Soviet Union can be used to forge a closer partnership between the political leadership and technical specialists, and it furnishes new means of strengthening the control of the Party.

In the United States the Oppenheimer controversy was evidence enough that the new role of scientific and technical experts in public affairs has caused at least some problems. In general, however, the American political system functions reasonably well in assimilating new groups to positions of political leadership. Vertical mobility and lateral entry ease the adjustment between professional politicians and technical experts. In America the main problems caused by the scientific and technological revolutions have been the increasing prevalence of bureaucracy, hierarchy, and large organizations on the public scene. The development of great organizations was one of the single most important changes in American society in the first half of the twentieth century. The rise of national corporations, labor unions, government agencies, universities, and foundations was indeed, as Kenneth Boulding has argued, an "organizational revolution." The development of these organizations created new responsibilities for the politician as the mediator or broker among them. It also created new problems in terms of relations between the new bureaucratic institutions and the unorganized mass public. Before the development of the big organizations a closer relation existed between publics and political leaders. The leaders of the large organization, however, were bureaucratic not popular leaders. They had to develop new techniques of political persuasion.

The resulting shift in political style was noted by Charles Merriam in 1933 when he commented upon the decline of the older system of direct, personal lobbying and the rise of the new lobby which relied on "the employment of professional press agents, public relations counsels and propagandists" and "organized educational campaigns on an elaborate scale." [48] Public relations developed as a direct response to the attacks of the muckrakers and others on the "trusts" in the first two decades of the twentieth century. These opponents thought that trusts were dangerous aggregations of power such as had not occurred previously in American life. Public relations was a defensive reaction against public suspicion. The public-relations counsel became the mediator between the large institutions and the mass public. Ivy Lee, indeed, described himself as a "Physician to Corporate Bodies." Business public relations, it has been observed, reflects "an ideology of defense." [49] Public relations techniques were first systematically applied to politics when the Democratic Party, after its defeat in 1928, established its Publicity Bureau under the direction of Charles Michelson. Two decades later the Republican Party, also out of power, brought the political use of public relations to a new height in the 1952 campaign.

The mass media created the opportunity and bureaucratic organizations the need for a new link between institutional leaders and the public. Significantly, public relations developed more slowly in politics than in most other areas. The reason, of course, was that politics was the least bureaucratized of the major areas of public life. The politician had his own means of maintaining contact with his public. Public relations was superfluous: What could FDR learn from BBD&O? In the 1950s, however, politicians were eager to learn from the successes of business, and weaker organizations or candidates turned to public relations as a means of mobilizing new strength. The declining effectiveness of the political machines, the growing tendencies toward independent voting, and the greater flexibility and lack of partisan commitment by interest groups all gave public relations a new relevance to politics. The contrast between the old and the new politics was most dramatic, perhaps, in the Maryland 1950 Senate campaign, where a political unknown with an out-of-state campaign manager defeated the strongly entrenched Democratic incumbent, Millard Tydings. While many factors contributed to the outcome, the most notable was the skill of the Republicans at "mass communication politics" contrasted with the reliance of the Democrats on more traditional methods.[50] The lessons of that campaign were not lost on the politicians of either party in the following decade. By the early 1960s political leaders were evaluated largely in terms of their current "images" among the voters.

The increased role of public relations in issue politics and electoral politics was one way in which the political system reacted to social change. As in the Soviet Union, however, these adjustments perpetuated and perhaps even strengthened the existing basic characteristics of the system and its relation to society as a whole. The

Soviet leaders reacted to technological change by attempting to forge a closer relationship between the political and technical hierarchies for the purpose of social control. In the United States the tremendous proliferation of the machinery and techniques of persuasion was in large part an outgrowth of the intensely competitive nature of the American political economy. In a pluralistic order, control is impossible without persuasion, and persuasion is inevitably a competitive process. Consequently, it led to an increased sensitivity (reflected in the development of public-opinion polling) to the views of the unorganized populace and the multiplication of linkages between the elite, political and nonpolitical, on the one hand, and the mass public on the other. In both societies the social consequences of technological change were mediated through the political system. In the ideological Soviet system, technology was harnessed to the purposes of control and manipulation; in the instrumental American system, it was harnessed to the purposes of stimulation and persuasion.

CHAPTER THREE

Political Leadership

POLITICAL leadership in modern industrialized societies differs significantly from that in pre-modern agrarian societies. In the latter, typically, the functions of political and nonpolitical leadership are exercised by the same people. The primary distinction is between the elite or ruling class or aristocracy and the mass of the people. The political leaders of society are also its military, economic, cultural, and religious leaders. Certain individuals, of course, may spend more of their lives in politics, or in the army, or in the church, but they are all recruited from the same relatively limited social class, and in many cases the same individuals are leaders in more than one field of endeavor.

The principal political impact of industrialization is to diversify the pre-modern agrarian ruling class. The functions and institutions of military, educational, economic, religious, and political leadership become more specialized. Mass armies develop, commanded by professional officer corps. Specialized economic institutions—corporations or trusts—are created by private entrepreneurs or government and, in due course, give birth to a new class of industrial managers. Scientific and technical knowledge multiplies, giving rise to a variety of experts. The ability of any individual to be a Renaissance (or Enlightenment) man diminishes, as does the ability of any social group to monopolize positions of leadership within society. A complex society, containing many specialists and subgroups, requires someone to coordinate and integrate their activities. This is the function of political leadership. To perform it the political leader requires some degree of power over others in society. Hence, unlike other individuals who may exercise power, he is formally invested with the authority to exercise it. He is the general manager of the modern state.

The differentiation of society also gives rise to specialized political institutions. The state bureaucracy expands and is rationalized; cabinets and legislatures develop and acquire more distinctive roles; and, most importantly, the political party emerges as the key institution for the representation and integration of competing interests

129

and for the recruitment of political leaders. Politics, as Weber said, becomes a vocation. The professional politicians who make it one specialize in the control of people. They operate the party system and operate through the party system to achieve leadership in the state. Not all professional politicians, however, become political leaders, and not all political leaders are necessarily professional politicians. The pattern in each society is different. A comparison of Soviet and American political leaderships suggests the range of difference which is possible.

ACCESS TO LEADERSHIP

In both the United States and the Soviet Union it is claimed that leading political positions are open to all groups of the population: the log-cabin myth in the United States is paralleled by the proletarian myth of the Soviet Union. In fact, the principal political offices in these two systems are probably more generally open to individuals of diverse social backgrounds than those in any other major political system. In western Europe, the son of working-class parents may well become the leader of a working-class party and thus prime minister in his government, but similar positions in conservative or traditionalist parties are likely to be closed to him. In the United States, a son of poor parents is not barred from the leadership of either the Republican or the Democratic parties, and in the Soviet Union he certainly is not barred from leadership in the Communist Party. Nonetheless, not all political offices are necessarily equally open to individuals from different backgrounds. Political leaders are made, not born, but in both societies some individuals at birth are more likely to become leaders than others. Among the factors involved are race, nationality, and social origin.

Both the Soviet and American populations are diverse. The Soviet population, however, is made up of various nationalities, while the American is composed of people of various national origins. In 1959 the Soviet population included 108 national groups, of which 22 had a population of 1 million or more. The Russians were the largest single group, accounting for 115 million or 55 per cent of the total population of 209 million. The remaining 45 per cent included 37 million Ukrainians, 8 million Byelorussians, 6 million Uzbeks, 5 million Tatars, and 38 million others. The mosaic of Soviet society is the result of the Slavic Russians' expansion from Muscovy eastward into Siberia and central Asia, westward toward the Baltic, and southward to the Black Sea. The non-Russian people were submerged first in the Russian-dominated czarist empire and then in the "federal" Soviet Union. Each of the non Russian peoples, however, remains identified with a particular territory, and most strive to maintain their own cultures, traditions, and languages. Nationality divisions are thus an inherent and permanent feature of the Soviet scene.

In terms of nationality, the American people in 1960 were much more homogeneous than the Soviet population. Only their historical origins bore comparison to current Soviet diversity. Between 1820 and 1961 over 40 million immigrants entered the United States. These included 6.7 million from Germany, 4.9 million from Italy, 4.6 million from Ireland, about 3 million from Poland, 3.8 million from Great Britain, 3.6 million from Canada and Newfoundland, and 3.3 million from territories now in the Soviet Union. After World War I, however, immigration declined markedly. In 1960 88 per cent of the American population of 179,323,000 was white; 83 per cent was native-born white; and 70 per cent was native-born white of native-born parents. The most important division in American society was not between nationalities but between the white majority and the 18-million Negro minority.

In Russia the big break in the Russian monopoly of ruling positions came with the Bolshevik Revolution and the subsequent creation of the Soviet Union. The national republics were led largely by native Communists, some of whom participated in the Union leadership. This pattern, however, was reversed during the great purges which almost entirely destroyed the non-Russian Bolshevik leadership. Subsequently, only in certain nonpolitical occupations did non-Russians appear to enjoy a definite advantage. Armenians and Georgians seem to play a disproportionate role in trade, although no specific data are available; Jews, who number 2.3 million or 1.1 per cent of the total population, according to Soviet data, account for 15.7 per cent of all doctors, 11 per cent of higher scientific specialists, 10.4 per cent of all jurists, and 8.5 per cent of journalists and other writers.[1] This may be due to their relatively limited access to political or military careers. Significantly, ethnic minorities are overrepresented in the "dignified" institutions of the Soviet political system, such as the Supreme Soviet. In the "efficient" political institutions, on the other hand, the closer one comes to the top the more striking is the dominance of the "SRAPPs"—the Slavic-stock Russian-born apparatchiki. At the peak of the system the predominance of the Russians has tended to increase as the cosmopolitan participants in the Revolution have disappeared from the scene. In 1962 Russians made up 55 per cent of the Soviet population, but 75 per cent of the Presidium and Secretariat.

TABLE 1

NATIONAL ORIGIN AND ACCESS TO POLIT

1962	POPULATION		SUPREME SOVIET		CPSU	
	Number (millions)	Per cent of USSR	Members	Per cent of total	Members (thousands)	Per cent of total
Russians	114.6	54.6	626	43.4	6,100	63.5
Ukrainians	37.0	17.8	211	14.6	1,400	14.6
Byelorussians	7.8	3.8	54	3.7	287	3.0
Uzbeks	6.0	2.9	43	3.0	143	1.5
Tatars	5.0	2.4	No data		No data	
Kazakhs	3.6	1.7	33	2.3	149	1.5
Azerbaijanis	2.9	1.4	45	3.1	106	1.1
Armenians	2.8	1.3	40	2.8	161	1.7
Georgians	2.7	1.3	46	3.2	170	1.8
Lithuanians	2.3	1.1	30	2.1	43	.4
Jews	2.3	1.1	No data		No data	
Moldavians	2.2	1.1	19	1.3	27	.3
Latvians	1.4	.7	21	1.5	34	.35
Finns	0.1	.05	No data		No data	

* S. V. Kosior is considered Polish, even though he held high posts in the

Throughout the nineteenth century the overwhelming majority of American leaders in society and politics were native-born Americans of native-born parents, of northern European (usually Anglo-Saxon) ethnic stock, Protestant, and white. Foreign-born citizens, second-generation Americans, those of Irish, southern European, eastern European, or Asian background, Catholics, Jews, and Negroes were, by and large, underrepresented in the elite. Slowly but steadily, however, the "WASP" (white Anglo-Saxon Protestant) monopoly of political office was broken. Successive immigrant groups fought their way up the political ladder, electing first congressmen and mayors, then governors and senators. Where many nationalities competed with one another, as in the older cities of the east, complex patterns of ethnic ticket-balancing developed in local and state politics. At the national level, however, no established practice of ethnic representation has emerged either in the selection

ICAL LEADERSHIP IN THE SOVIET UNION

POLITBURO-PRESIDIUM AND SECRETARIAT* 1919-1962		1919-1933		NEW MEMBERS 1934-1962		PRESIDIUM AND SECRETARIAT, 1962	
Members	Per cent of total	Members	Per cent of total	Members	Per cent of total	Members	Per cent of total
61	75	20	66.7	41	82	12	75
5*	8	0	0	5	10	2	12.5
0	0	0	0	0	0	0	0
1	1.6	0	0	1	2	0	0
0	0	0	0	0	0	0	0
0	0	0	0	0	0	0	0
1	1.6	0	0	1	2	1	6.3
3	5	2	6.6	1	2	0	0
0	0	0	0	0	0	0	0
6	10	6	20	0	0	0	0
0	0	0	0	0	0	0	0
2	3.2	2	6.6	0	0	0	0
1	1.6	0	0	1	2	1	6.3

Ukraine.

of presidential candidates or in the appointment of cabinet or other executive officials. All presidential and vice-presidential nominees except two have been of northern European Protestant background. The overwhelming percentage of cabinet members have also been "WASPs." The cabinet is supposed to have geographical balance, but to date no practice of ethnic balance has developed. The cabinets of Democratic Presidents, however, have tended to have at least one Catholic and one Jew, and Kennedy's appointments of

Anthony Celebrezze and John A. Gronouski to the Cabinet reflected the rising importance of the Italo-Americans and Polish-Americans.

The single most significant factor restricting eligibility for positions of political leadership is race. In 1960 Negroes constituted over 10 per cent of the American population, yet less than 1 per cent of the House of Representatives was Negro. There has been no Negro senator since Reconstruction, when Mississippi was represented by two. In 1963 no Negro had ever been a member of the President's cabinet. Few Negroes had served in the higher ranks of the civil service or officer corps. Unlike nationality differences, racial ones do not disappear over time. Unlike religious differences, they are neither invisible nor considered irrelevant to political choice. At least as late as the early 1960s the absence of the Negroes from positions of political leadership was the closest parallel in the United States to the absence of the central Asian nationalities from the top positions in the Soviet Union. Nonetheless, the growing political awareness of the Negro, the emergence of a significant Negro middle class, and the rise of Negro voting participation in both the North and the South stimulated an increasing role for Negroes in American politics. Each election brought fresh gains for middle-class Negro leaders: while there was one Negro in Congress in 1945, there were five in 1963. Thus, while the dominance of the "SRAPPs" in Soviet political leadership has been constant or increasing, the dominance of American political leadership by "WASPs" is slowly subsiding.

The social origins of the national political leaders in the two systems differ significantly. Soviet political leaders come primarily from proletarian or peasant backgrounds. American political leaders come primarily from upper-middle-class or upper-class backgrounds.

In the United States both Administration leaders and congressmen are the products of comfortable circumstances. In recent years about 60 per cent of the fathers of both categories have been professional men, business executives, or business owners. The other most important occupation among the fathers of governmental leaders is farming, and, significantly, the percentage of farmers among the fathers of congressmen is about twice as high as the percentage among the fathers of Administration officials. Less than

10 per cent of the senators and representatives have fathers who were low-salaried workers or wage earners, and only 15 per cent of national politically appointed executives have fathers who were laborers. Business and professional men appear among the fathers of senators four to five times as often as they would in a random distribution of occupations and about six or seven times as often among fathers of politically appointed executives. Lower-status occupations are correspondingly underrepresented.[2] A poor man's son may make his way to the top of the political ladder, but the odds are against him. At state and local levels of government the preponderance of individuals of upper-middle- and upper-class origin undoubtedly is somewhat less. In small and medium-sized cities, indeed, the "economic dominants" often withdraw from politics, leaving the local political offices to individuals of lower-middle-class and working-class origin. The son of a laborer may well be elected to the city council or even to the state legislature but is unlikely to appear in statewide office or in Congress.

In contrast to the American pattern, the top Soviet political leaders in the past decade have come overwhelmingly from working-class or peasant families. Khrushchev himself is apparently the son of a peasant who also worked as a coal miner. In the 1930s and 1940s, most of the party leaders in the Ukrainian apparat seemed "to be men of humble origin and little schooling."[3] The ten members of the Presidium in December 1957 who were also Central Committee Secretaries all came from peasant or worker families. From the information available on the occupations of the fathers of 148 of the 175 members of the Central Committee elected in 1961, it appears that half of the fathers (49.3 per cent) were peasants, and a third were manual workers or factory workers. Altogether 128 of the fathers (or 86.5 per cent of the total) had essentially working-class occupations. Of the remaining 20, 11 were civil servants, 4 were teachers, 2 had other white-collar occupations, and 1 was a cattle trader. Only two of the fathers (a physician and a scientist) were in the higher occupational strata.[4]

Apparently American national political leaders have been recruited primarily from the upper-middle and upper classes since colonial times. From 1789 to 1934, 58 per cent of the Presidents, Vice Presidents, and Cabinet members had fathers who were businessmen or professional men. Thirty-eight per cent had fathers who were farmers. Only 5 per cent had fathers who were wage earners or low-salaried workers.[5] Similarly, in a separate study of the 513 men who held the position of President, Vice President, Speaker of the House, Cabinet member, or Supreme Court Justice between 1789 and 1953, C. Wright Mills found the following percentages of family background:[6] upper class, 28; upper middle class, 30; middle class, 24; lower class (small business or small farms), 13; working class or destitute, 5. Neither the "American Revolution" nor the "Jeffersonian Revolution" nor the "Jacksonian Revolution" broke the pattern of upper-middle-class dominance.

The Soviet pattern differs from the American not only because its current leaders come from humble backgrounds but also because the origins of its political leaders have changed drastically in recent history. The leaders of czarist Russia came from the gentry and the aristocracy. They were overthrown in a revolution led by middle-class intellectuals. Before and immediately after the 1917 Revolution the leaders of the Communist Party came primarily from the middle class. Over half the delegates to the 6th Party Congress in the summer of 1917 were intellectuals; 94 of 171 delegates on whom information is available had received a secondary or higher education, a reliable indication at that time of middle-class origins.[7] Four of the five members of the Politburo elected in 1919 came from middle-class families, and six of the nine persons elected to the Politburo before 1925 had similar backgrounds. Only with Stalin's consolidation of his power after 1929 and during the great purges of the 1930s did a majority of the top leaders of the Communist Party come from proletarian and especially peasant origins. The party of revolutionary intellectuals thus became the party of peasant bureaucrats.

In both the United States and the Soviet Union political leaders tend to have lower social origins than other key elite groups in society. The difference in the United States, however, is quite small. Business leaders are more likely than political officials to have businessmen fathers, and on the average they have slightly higher social backgrounds than political leaders. United States senators seem to come from somewhat less affluent environments than do the presidents of the largest industrial corporations.[8] The basic pattern of upper-middle-class and upper-class dominance, however, remains the same. The more specialized leadership groups in the national government, such as the military and the foreign service, come from similar backgrounds.

In the Soviet Union, on the other hand, there is a much greater gap in origins between the top leaders of the Party and leaders in other walks of life. Precise recent data, unfortunately, are lacking. However, interviews with former Soviet citizens showed that those of middle-class background were more likely to fulfill career ambitions than those of humbler origins. This inescapably made a political career seem more attractive as an avenue to rapid social promotion, and many saw it as an opportunity not unlike that which the priesthood held out to young peasant boys in a traditional society.

Similarly, there is some evidence that in the 1930s the son of a worker or peasant had an almost equal chance with the son of middle-class parents to become the director of a factory.[9] By contrast, in all other management positions in industry the sons of middle-class parents had an overwhelming advantage. During these years, factory directors were recruited largely from party workers; they were essentially political figures appointed to insure that the technical specialists in industry adhered to party directives. Thus the gap between the factory directors and the occupants of other industrial positions in itself is some measure of the difference in

TABLE 2

PER CENT IN SOVIET UNION WHO FULFILLED ASPIRATION TO WHITE-COLLAR JOBS AMONG MEN 21-40: BY FATHER'S OCCUPATION*

FATHER'S OCCUPATION

	Arts and Professional-Administrative	*Semiprofessional and White Collar*	*Worker*	*Peasant*
Arts	58	31	20	11
Professional-administrative	82	45	29	29
Semiprofessional and white collar	100	93	82	68

* Source: A. Inkeles and R. Bauer, *The Soviet Citizen* (Cambridge, 1959), p. 92.

social origins between party leaders and industrial managers. Many department superintendents in Soviet factories of 1936 must have since risen to top management positions in Soviet industry. It thus seems probable that the social origins of the Soviet industrial manager today are considerably higher than those of the Soviet political leader.

The origins of other groups of Soviet leaders are difficult to discern. In general, origins of the top military leaders probably resemble rather closely those of the top political leaders. In the late 1940s the two dozen top marshals were about equally divided in origins between workers and peasants. Among the several hundred top generals the largest group came from peasant backgrounds, the next largest from the working class, and the smallest from the intelligentsia.[10] In most industrial societies, military careers have relatively little appeal for the sons of the urban middle class. Consequently, it seems likely that proletarian and peasant origins will continue to predominate among Soviet military leaders. At the other extreme, however, the intelligentsia and middle-class professional groups probably furnish the bulk of the intellectual, scientific, technical, artistic, and professional leaders in the Soviet Union.

In the United States political and nonpolitical leaders come from essentially similar upper-middle-class environments. In the Soviet Union, political leaders have lower-class backgrounds; nonpolitical leaders tend to have middle-class backgrounds. The American pattern promotes harmony and understanding between the leaders of society and those of the polity. It is one more factor minimizing the cleavages between the two and facilitating the movement of individuals between positions of political and nonpolitical leadership. On the Soviet side, the differences in background contribute to the tensions between the Party apparatchiki and other elite groups, particularly the "middle-class" intellectuals. A major question on the Soviet side is the extent to which the next generation of Soviet leaders will be drawn from sources similar to those of the present one. Already there is some evidence of a gap between the older, tough, earthy, mobile, poorly educated top leaders in Soviet politics, and the younger, better educated sons of the new Soviet middle class who appear to be on the verge of replacing them. It would not be surprising if the current ruling elite provided its own offspring with special opportunities for advancement within the bureaucracy.

Other factors, however, may counterbalance the tendencies toward political leaders of middle-class origins. Under Khrushchev major efforts have been made to recruit more proletarians and collective farmers into the Party. In addition, there may be considerable "selection out" among the sons of the urban middle-class intelligentsia. Some evidence exists that Party work does not have high prestige in the Soviet Union.[11] A career as an apparatchik requires a fairly complete personal, ideological, and organizational commitment. The well-educated sons of reasonably well-off Soviet parents, including the apparatchiki themselves, may not want to pay that price. They may well prefer to become scientists, doctors, intellectuals, academicians, technical specialists, engineers, or industrial managers. Thus, the conscious policy of the Party leadership plus the natural dynamics of social mobility help to maintain the distinctive character of the apparatchik career and to attract to it able and ambitious children of workers and peasants. The price of success in this policy, in turn, is a continued division between political leadership of humble background and nonpolitical leadership from the middle class.

The relatively humble social origin of the Soviet political elite and the middle-class origin of the American have an impact on their respective political styles. Just as in America the upper-middle-class origin of the top political and business elite has spawned a certain implicit code of behavior and values, quite noticeable in the "Establishment," so in the Soviet Union the leadership style is the product not only of the Communist ideology and organization or national tradition but also of social origin. In general, American political leaders are men marked by moderation, restraint, and a belief in the superiority of compromise solutions. Bargaining is their basic mode of settling problems. The business experience and middle-class origin of American leaders also induce a pragmatic attitude toward challenges as well as an inclination to focus on short-range, concrete objectives. As a result, they are suspicious of grand designs and reject systematic, longer-range conceptions of historical change as dogmatic, irrational, and overly intellectual "cubby-holes." American leaders often tend to assume that other elites elsewhere do likewise and hence that any conflicting issue can be resolved in a manner tested and found true in the American social-economic context.

The peasant-worker origin of the Soviet elite has left an imprint on its behavior and mores. It is certainly reflected in the directness, roughness, even occasional crudeness of official expression, both domestically and in relation to those foreigners whom the Soviet leaders view with hostility. It also stimulates a marked tendency, common among the less educated masses, to simplify issues and reduce them to black and white categories. To the extent that this facilitates mass indoctrination, it may be done consciously, but there is also ample evidence indicating that Stalin, Khrushchev, and others reason in fairly simple, dichotomic categories. In this respect, Marxism-Leninism provides conveniently simple perspectives, reinforcing intellectually an inherent predisposition. On the level of behavior, there is a curious combination of earthy ruthlessness with joviality, quite typical of rural life, and without the sadistic hatred characteristic of the Nazi leaders. The taking of life is accepted as necessary and politically normal. Very often problems are resolved by eliminating those responsible for them. The dogged and single-minded determination of the leadership in pursuing their long-range objectives also cannot be explained in purely ideological terms. By now certainly the new elite has some vested interest in promoting goals that justify their power. But they also have an element of self-assertion which combines both nationalism and the ambitious drive of the socially newly risen. Hence the Soviet leaders, to a much greater extent than their American counterparts, display the characteristics, psychological and otherwise, of self-made men "who have risen to power from one suspender": expansive self-confidence tempered by gnawing insecurity, and the driving ability to succeed combined with the burning desire to be accepted.

PROFESSIONAL POLITICIANS: ELECTORAL AND BUREAUCRATIC

In America, the old colonial-Federalist ruling class declined during the nineteenth century and was replaced by a more diversified social-economic elite which included new frontier wealth, new merchants, and new industrialists. Its decline was also marked by the development of the party system, the extension of suffrage, the multiplication of elective offices, and the emergence of the American-style professional politicians. Confronted with an almost infinite variety of elective offices in local, state, and national governments, the American politician made his career by campaigning for elected offices of successively bigger constituencies and broader responsibilities. The key decisions in such a career were frequently matters of selection and timing: which office to run for in which year. The American thus differed significantly from his British counterpart, whose election interests were simply to get into the Commons and to stay there. The American professional was an electoral politician, the British professional a parliamentary one.

In Russia the ruling class first declined and then was overthrown by an organization of professional revolutionaries. The resulting vacuum in political leadership was filled by the rapid expansion of the party apparatus and the transformation of Lenin's organization of professional revolutionaries into Stalin's organization of professional rulers. In the United States the professional politician is the product of democratization of the government. In the Soviet Union he is the product of bureaucratization of the Party.

As professional politicians the Soviet apparatchik and the American electoral politician have some similarities. To some degree each may develop expertise in a particular set of policy problems important to his constituency or oblast. But the distinctive character of each is that he is a generalist—an expert in dealing simultaneously with a variety of issues and pressures, balancing one against another, attempting to resolve problems at the least cost to the greatest number of interests. In addition, the politician in both systems must be flexible in viewpoint, adaptable in outlook, and contingent in loyalties. He must reward his friends and punish his enemies, but he must also be aware that today's friends may be tomorrow's enemies and vice versa. He must be able to adapt to a variety of circumstances and responsibilities. He must be a mobile individual, committed wholeheartedly to the position or institution he is in at the moment but also able to move quickly on to a different position in a different institutional context. The higher authorities in the Soviet Union shift the promising apparatchik every few years from one oblast and one type of responsibility to another. The vagaries of the voters and the variety of opportunities in the American political system require a comparable degree of mobility on the part of the politician.

Apart from these generic characteristics, the Soviet apparatchik and the American electoral politician are rather different political animals with different habits and habitats. They differ especially in their degree of political professionalization and their commitment to politics as a career. The typical American politician is really only a semi-pro: he usually combines his public career with the simultaneous pursuit of a private career in law, business, education, or journalism. If circumstances or the voters retire him from his public career, he can pursue his private one with little loss and perhaps with considerable benefit. His commitment to politics is thus not nearly as profound as that of his Soviet counterpart. Even for the professional, politics in America is in many respects an avocation rather than a vocation. Only 5 of 513 top political leaders in the United States from 1789 to 1953 had no career other than politics.[12] Indeed, the professional politician may well make a public career out of politics with the thought that its primary benefits will be in other fields, that the political ladder may be used to scale nonpolitical heights in business and society. For his Soviet counterpart, on the other hand, a political career is normally a more-than-full-time lifetime commitment. He enters upon it as an American might enter the priesthood or the Army. He becomes engulfed in the life of the apparatus. Lacking a private career upon which to fall back, he would find escape difficult even if it were conceivable. His life is more focused, his loyalties more exclusive, his commitment more intense.

The apparatchik's career itself is also highly professionalized. The apparat is a sort of cross between the Hague political machine in New Jersey and the United States Army. The apparatchik's career resembles that of the military officer in many ways. Certain minimum educational attainments are usually required. Like the normal successful officer the successful apparatchik starts at the bottom of the ladder and moves up to posts of broader and broader responsibility—raion or oblast or krai to union republic or to major party organizations such as those of Moscow and Leningrad and eventually to the Central Committee Secretariat. The apparatchik can also move upward in the type of responsibility at each level: from second secretary in one oblast to first secretary in another. At various points in his career he will be "seconded" to positions in the state or industrial bureaucracies. He will be expected regularly to improve his education through correspondence courses. Like the Army officer who goes to a staff school or war college, he may also be sent for a four-year course at the Party School in his union republic or to the Higher Party School of the Central Committee in Moscow. The schools were founded in 1946, and during the first decade of their activity some 55,000 individuals were trained in the local Party Schools and 9000 by the Higher Party School. Party officials under the age of thirty-five and with a good record of Party work are nominated for the four-year course at the Inter-Oblast Schools; more senior officials under the age of forty may be assigned for two years to the Higher Party School, which also includes courses by correspondence. (In 1956, 200 officials were in attendance at the Higher Party School and 3000 more were studying by correspondence.) Several of the younger top Party leaders, such as Polyansky, Mazurov, and Furtseva, have received their training there.

The Party official assigned to such advanced studies will receive intensive training designed to improve his political and ideological knowledge as well as his adeptness at handling economic and technical-managerial issues. Of the 3200 hours prescribed in 1957 in a typical curriculum of a four-year Inter-Oblast Party School, 41.5 per cent were assigned to strictly political subjects such as *diamat* (dialectical materialism) and history of the CPSU; 15 per cent to economics, economic organization, and planning; and 43.5 per cent to such varied specialties as industrial technology, agriculture, regional planning, and statistics (see Table 3). The training is obviously designed *to develop professional political leaders of society,* capable of providing expert social-economic direction within the framework of the ideological goals and political vested interests of the ruling Party. After "graduation" the rising Party official keeps in touch with the latest organizational guidelines and techniques by receiving the regular Party journals and through various "handbooks" issued by the Central Committee, containing detailed instructions on how to act in various contingencies. This emphasis on organizational control over the training of the Soviet political elite is an extension of the emphasis on *exclusive* politization noted in Chapter Two.

"Alternation of intensive training with practical experience," one scholar has observed, "is a basic principle of the process of moulding the apparatus official." [13] While he may hold some jobs longer, his normal tour of duty, like that in the United States Army, is three or four years. If he develops a reputation as troubleshooter in industrial, agricultural, or construction projects, he may well be shifted from one trouble spot to a similar but worse one. Even so, if he demonstrates his ability he will eventually take on jobs with more varied responsibilities. He may also serve in the political staff supervising the military. His success depends on his political and administrative abilities and his affiliations with more powerful patrons who can speed his way up the apparat hierarchy. If he does not succeed at the oblast level he will be shunted off to a low-level secondary post.

Contrast this highly professionalized career pattern with that of the "professional" American politician. The American may or may not start on the bottom rung in politics: the higher his social-economic status before entering politics the higher will be the first office for which he runs. If he starts with some local office —city council, district attorney—he may move on to the state legislature, from there to statewide office or House of Representatives, and then to governor or senator. If he is elected governor in a small state, he will probably eventually run for senator; if he is elected senator in New York or California, he may run for governor. He may also be content to rest on a lower rung of the complex ladder of American politics and to make his career within his city government, the state legislature, or Congress. If, after a creditable service in lower elective office, he runs for a higher one and loses, he can be reasonably assured of appointment to executive or judicial position in some government. No higher power consciously shapes his career. It is up to him to make the most of what the political system offers.

Engineering provides the most frequent professional background for Soviet bureaucratic politicians. More than 40 per cent of the Central Committee members elected in 1961 had engineering training, with heavy industry the most frequent specialization. The second largest group in terms of professional training, the agri-

TABLE 3

CURRICULUM OF THE FOUR-YEAR PARTY SCHOOL

SUBJECTS	INSTRUCTION HOURS
History of the Communist Party of the USSR	250
Dialectical and historical materialism	200
Political economy	300
History of international workers' and national liberation movements	180
History of the USSR	150
Party and government affairs and procedures	150
Foundations of Soviet jurisprudence (civil, labor, and collective farm law)	100
Economic geography of the USSR and foreign countries	100
Economics, organization and planning in industry, construction and transport	200
Economic organization and planning in agricultural enterprises	180
Power resources in industry	80
Industrial technology (in major branches of industry)	270
Industrial and civil construction	100
General agriculture, plant cultivation, and agrochemistry	240
Animal breeding	140
Mechanization and electrification of agriculture	160
Regional planning of local industry and cultural services	80
Trade, finance, and banking	80
Accounting and auditing techniques	60
Statistics	80
Mathematics	100
Industrial practice	2 months*
Total	3200
Optionally:	
Foreign language	200
Russian language	150
Automotive and driving instruction	120

Students who have completed the curriculum take state examinations in the history of the CPSU, dialectical and historical materialism, political economy and national economy (of the USSR).

Source: V. A. Malin, ed., *Spravochnik Partiinogo Rabotnika,* Moscow, 1959, pp. 414-415.
* Not included in total.

cultural experts, accounted for only 10 per cent, or a little more than the military.* The engineering background of the Soviet apparatchik is supplemented by intense and continuing political training and many years of direct occupational experience in politics. Political experience and engineering background combine to give Soviet leaders a highly focused, direct, down-to-earth, problem-solving approach, without concern for legal niceties and with little tendency toward compromise solutions. Indeed, the engineering background, with its concentration on meeting issues head-on, and the ideological background, with its militant style of work, combine many of the political methods and technical skills necessary for leading a developing country and for directing a radical social and political reconstruction of society.

In contrast, American electoral politicians are more often lawyers than anything else. Two-thirds of the top leaders of the national government, a majority of congressmen and senators, a majority of state governors, and one-quarter to one-half of state legislators have regularly been lawyers.[14] No institutions of political education compete with those of legal education; as a result, legal styles, legal concepts, legal ways of thought and behavior permeate politics. The dominant role of the lawyer in electoral politics derives from the relative ease with which a law practice can be pursued on a part-time or intermittent basis, the extent to which the skills of the lawyer in articulation and interpersonal relations are also those of the politician, and, most importantly, the close historical linkage of law and politics. In the Anglo-American tradition, legislatures themselves were originally thought of as courts, and the political function of law-making was closely allied to the legal functions of law interpretation and adjudication. The pre-eminence of lawyers as politicians reflects the pervasiveness of law in politics. In the Soviet Union, in contrast, law plays a purely instrumental role, and legal training and experience have no special relevance to a political career.

---

* These figures on professional training should not be confused with those on primary occupations given in Table 4. The Central Committee member typically has the training of an engineer but does the work of a bureaucratic politician. See S. Bialer, "Comparative Communist Elites" (Ph.D. Thesis, Columbia University, 1964).

Bureaucratic politics and electoral politics impose different requirements upon the ambitious young politician. To get off to a fast start in the Soviet Union it is necessary to attract the attention of some upper-level political leader and become his protégé. Malenkov, for instance, attracted Stalin's attention and became a secretary in the Central Committee apparat at the age of twenty-four. When he became operating head of the Personnel Department of the Central Committee at the age of thirty-two he was in an excellent position to build up his own clique. Khrushchev was in his early thirties when he attached himself to Kaganovich. Apart from the Old Bolsheviks (who were leaders before they were bureaucrats) every major political leader in the Soviet Union has risen to power under the aegis of a patron and as a member of a clique. In the United States the ambitious politician is not as directly dependent upon the patronage of established political leaders. Indeed, the quickest way to make his name is not to become identified with an important leader but rather to challenge him. The youngster who defeats an established political figure is off to a fast start in politics. He can do this because of the relative ease with which other resources may be transferred into political ones. Patron-protégé relationships are not unknown in American politics, but they play a strikingly small role. Political popularity and voting appeal tend to be untransferrable. Furthermore, a great deal of prestige accrues to the "young reformer" in American politics, a form of institutionalized rebellion.

The struggle for advancement in Soviet politics thus has an inherently conservative influence and tends to perpetuate the mores and outlook of the leaders at the top. The struggle for power in America, on the other hand, tends to challenge and disrupt the "inner core" of the political system. The system is continually adjusted and modified by the lateral entrance of leaders in other fields directly into positions of political leadership or from the overthrow of established politicians by newer generations embodying new interests and perspective (the warhawks of 1810, the Jacksonians of 1828, the "sons of the wild jackass" of 1922, the New Dealers of 1932). In a bureaucratic hierarchy a demonstrated ability and will to adjust to the leadership's mode of behavior is necessary to advancement. In an electoral system, advancement often requires open refusal to adjust to the leaders' mores.

In bureaucratic structures the hierarchy of positions is relatively clearly defined, and almost all the positions are on a single ladder. The achievement of high office is a step to still higher office. In the American system of the separation of powers, however, leadership in one branch of government may preclude leadership in another branch. This is particularly true of Congress and the executive. After a short while as a representative or senator, a man usually has to decide whether to build his career within or beyond Congress. Representatives confront a "fourth-term crisis." If they stay four or more terms in the House, they have, with rare exceptions, chosen the House as their career. They build up an investment in seniority which they become loath to sacrifice. In addition, they act more and more like "House men" and find increasingly difficult the adjustments necessary to become a successful governor or senator. To a lesser extent, the same is true in the Senate. The members of the "inner club" are usually those who view with disdain the prospect of being anything but a United States senator. Men of power in Congress seldom run for other office and can seldom be persuaded to accept appointive office. This promotes institutional strains between Congress and the executive, but at the same time it multiplies the avenues of political advancement and thereby reduces tensions in the political struggle.

The intensity of conflict in the American political system is further reduced by the extent to which most participants have both political and nonpolitical careers. The victors in an electoral contest can at least envy the vanquished their income. In the Soviet Union, on the other hand, political defeat during the Stalin regime often meant physical death. More recently the consequences of defeat in Soviet politics have not differed significantly from those in other bureaucratic systems. Those who lose out may be demoted, publicly castigated and denounced, exiled to undesirable posts, expelled entirely from the bureaucracy, or put on the shelf in honorific but inconsequential posts.

In contrast, the American political system also provides many more opportunities to withdraw from the political competition. A Soviet apparatchik can choose between a career in the Party apparat or in the state bureaucracy. The former is pregnant with opportunity but also carries the risks inherent in the almost unavoidable factional conflicts. The latter is safer, can lead to a reasonably high status and even rewards (for example, the directors' bonuses for plan overfulfillment) but can *never* lead to the apex of the political power pyramid. In America, politicians can withdraw to private life or to specialized plateaus within the framework of government, such as the judiciary. A majority of American electoral politicians are lawyers, and appointment or election to the bench is often a satisfactory conclusion to a political career when the opportunities of advancement to higher legislative or executive office seem remote. Indeed, the status and prestige of judges is considerably higher than that of legislators and often higher than that of executives. The attractiveness of the judiciary may even, in some respects, harm the political system as a whole by luring able political leaders away from higher political office.* The judiciary is a place where tired politicians can retreat, defeated politicians can be taken care of, and obstreperous politicians can be retired to. Until recently, the Soviet Union had nothing quite comparable. The appointments of Molotov, Pervukhin, Ponomarenko, Aristov, and others to ambassadorships suggest that diplomatic service may play a similar role in the Soviet Union. If it does, it would be for much the same reason. American higher-court judges are barred by the ethos of the bench from playing an active role in party politics. Soviet diplomats would be similarly barred by the fact of distance.

The Soviet professional politician thus functions exclusively in a bureaucratic environment. Since the Party apparat is the most important bureaucracy in Soviet society, the power of the apparatchik depends upon his position in the Party bureaucratic structure. Organizational positions are to him what votes are to the American politician. The immediate environment of the latter is, indeed, one of the least bureaucratized segments of American society. The United States has industrial, administrative, military, and educational bureaucracies, but it does not have a political one. Hence, the skills which are required of the Soviet politician

---

* Cf. *New York Times* headline: "Vanishing Candidates: Many Promising Democrats Have Fled Turmoil of Politics for Quiet of Bench." June 4, 1962, p. 21.

differ considerably from those of the American. The apparatchik requires executive traits: the hard-driving, promoting, bulldozing abilities of the old-style American entrepreneur, plus the flexibility to trim his sails and blend with his environment of the organization man. He must also be adept at bureaucratic in-fighting, anticipating changes in the Party line and Party priorities, identifying the rising apparat stars and the falling ones, and choosing the right side of the crucial issue while maneuvering his opponents onto the wrong side. For success he needs not necessarily the support of large numbers of people but rather the backing of the right man at the right time.

The American politician needs to sense public rather than Presidium opinion, to articulate common symbols which have wide appeal, to avoid commitment on issues where his constituency is divided, and to negotiate satisfying compromises among the interests making demands upon him. He must be expert in the strategy of the forum, whereas the apparatchik is expert in the strategy of the closet. In campaigns and legislatures the American politician functions in an egalitarian environment where the ability to help and harm operates both ways. The Soviet apparatchik, however, works in a more asymmetrical bureaucratic environment. Power never flows exclusively in one direction, but he is still largely at the mercy of his superiors while he exercises extensive controls over his followers. The American politician must persuade equals; the apparatchik must please superiors and prod subordinates. When confronted with another politician, the American asks himself, "What's he got to offer?" while the Soviet thinks, "Who is to be master?"

CINCINNATUS AND THE APPARATCHIK:
THE RELATION BETWEEN POLITICAL
AND SOCIAL LEADERSHIP

In the Soviet Union the apparatchiki furnish the leader for the system, are a majority in the Presidium and the Central Committee, often fill the top posts in the state bureaucracies, and monopolize the Central Committee Secretariat and the Party apparat. In the United States, the electoral politician shares the positions of political leadership with many other types. The professionals occupy many posts in state and local government and usually dominate legislatures at all levels. They may also fill the Presidency. With that exception, however, they are infrequently found elsewhere in the Administration or in the governmental bureaucracies or in the private bureaucracies of the "Establishment." The governmental and private bureaucracies are usually led by their own products, and Administration leaders are in large part recruited from those products. In addition, even the professional electoral politician, of course, usually combines public and private careers. The model political leader in the Soviet Union, in short, is the apparatchik who has devoted his life to the Party. The model political leader in the United States is the Cincinnatus-like distinguished citizen who lays aside other responsibilities to devote himself temporarily to the public service.

On the national level, professional politicians always occupy the top political position in the Soviet Union and they usually occupy it in the United States. Lenin was a professional revolutionary, Stalin and Khrushchev both apparatchiki. Of their four principal rivals for power—Trotsky, Kirov, Malenkov, and Molotov—the first was a professional revolutionary and the other three apparatchiki. Of the nine American presidents since 1917, six had almost exclusively political careers; one moved from education into electoral politics; one moved from business into Administration positions; and one spent most of his life in the Army. At the next levels the difference in the roles of the professional politicians becomes more apparent. Forty-five men and one woman were on the Politburo or Presidium as full members between 1919 and 1963. At the time of their appointments, five had served most of their careers as underground professional revolutionaries; seven combined revolutionary experience with work in the party apparat; five combined revolutionary experience with work in the state bureaucracy; one combined revolutionary experience with work in the military establishment; twenty had worked primarily within the party apparat; six had worked primarily as officials in the state bureaucracy; one was primarily an economist; one was a military officer. Similarly, of the hundred and seventy-five members of the Central Committee elected in 1961, sixty-six had spent their careers almost exclusively in party positions, forty-two combined experience in party and government, thirty-three were in industry or commerce, and thirty-four were specialists in other branches of governmental or technical work.[15]

Unfortunately for the social scientist, the United States has no Central Committee. One social scientist, however, attempted to identify one by asking knowledgeable people to name the "top leaders in the development of policies affecting the nation." This method is not beyond dispute, for the result is an arbitrary sample of national leaders; but it is probably as reliable a sample as any other means would produce.[16] In 1958 these hundred leaders were strewn across the commanding peaks of politics, government, business, and the professions. Forty-three were in the national government and two others were ex-Presidents. The only state governor (Harriman) had previously occupied important positions in the national government. Thirty-nine were in business, twenty-six of whom were in industry. The remainder included five editors and publishers, two lawyers, four educators, three labor leaders, and one cardinal. Table 4 compares the primary occupations of the Central Committee members of 1961 with those of these top American leaders of 1958.

These samples dramatically suggest the expertise required to run a modern society. With a few minor variations, the same skills and experiences are present in each elite.* Approximately one-fifth of each elite consists of individuals with primary careers outside politics, civil government, commerce, and industry. The representation of some of these careers is remarkably similar. Professional military officers, for instance, constitute 7 to 8 per cent of each elite. Each group also includes three or four scientists and educators, three trade unionists, and one (USSR) or a few (USA) who have followed exclusively legal careers.**

---

* The Central Committee includes no religious leader. The American sample does not include any professional diplomats; while possibly significant, this omission may also reflect a primary concern with domestic policy. The two factory workers and two *kolkhozniki* in the Central Committee were undoubtedly more "dignified" than "efficient" members. The less efficient and more dignified Supreme Soviet contains a much higher proportion of rank-and-file workers.

** Lawyers are generally presumed to play a major role in American politics, and hence the small number of individuals who had law as a primary occupation requires some comment. Twenty-two of the

TABLE 4

PRIMARY OCCUPATIONS OF TOP
POLITICAL LEADERS

	USSR 1961 N-175	USA 1958 N-100
	Per cent	
Total politics and government	61.7	37.0
Politics (party bureaucracy: USSR; electoral politics: USA)	37.7	19.0
Private career and politics	—	8.0
Politics and government bureaucracy	24.0	1.0
Private career and government bureaucracy	—	9.0
Total commerce and industry	18.8	40.0
Total other occupations	19.5	23.0
Military (including 1 military and business: USA)	8.2	7.0
Journalism, mass media, writing	3.4	4.0
Education and sciences	1.7	4.0
Labor organizations	1.7	3.0
Law	.6	3.0
Diplomacy	1.7	—
Religion	—	1.0
Farming	1.1	1.0
Factory worker	1.1	—
Total	100.0	100.0

The great difference in the elite composition concerns the balance between politics and government on the one hand and commerce and industry on the other. Thirty-seven per cent of the Soviet leaders were professional party politicians, compared to 19 per cent of the American leaders whose careers had been

---

American elite had law degrees or were members of the bar. The primary career of half of these, however, was in politics; three were principally businessmen; two combined law and politics; two combined law and government service; and only three devoted the bulk of their career to the law. Apparently, it is precisely because law is such a good stepping stone to leadership positions that so few political leaders have worked for long at the legal profession. On the legal background of electoral politicians, see page 146.

primarily in electoral politics. The careers of almost two-thirds (61.7 per cent) of the Soviet leaders were primarily political and governmental, compared with somewhat more than one-third (37 per cent) of the American leaders whose careers included extensive governmental and political service. Only one-fifth (20 per cent) of the American leaders had careers devoted exclusively to politics or civil government. Of these twenty individuals in 1958, fifteen were in Congress, three in the executive branch, one on the Supreme Court, and one (Harry Truman) was an elder statesman. Forty per cent of the American leaders, on the other hand, had primary careers in commerce and business and 11 per cent more combined a career in business with one in either politics or government. In contrast, less than 19 per cent of the Soviet leaders had careers primarily in industry.

Two possible qualifications should be mentioned in connection with these figures. First, many Soviet party and governmental bureaucrats spent much of their careers dealing with industrial problems. When a party bureaucrat dealt with industry, however, it was usually as one activity in a city, region, or union republic for which he as secretary had responsibility. Industrial problems might demand much of his time, but his responsibility was an overall political one. Second, on the American side, it could be argued that many of the individuals whose primary occupations were in business and industry also held at times important posts in government. In all cases, however, these governmental responsibilities were either brief (say, three or four years in the subcabinet and thirty-five or forty in business) or in addition to their principal business activities (for example, service on a presidential commission). Thus, the broad tendencies suggested by the figures are valid.* One-fifth of each leadership sample is composed of representatives from the more specialized elite groups present in the modern state. In the Soviet Union the other top political leaders consist overwhelmingly of professional party politicians and gov-

---

* As is noted later, the top leaders of the Kennedy Administration at the outset had more experience in politics (although not in running for electoral office) than the top leaders in either the Truman or Eisenhower Administrations. This small change in the Administration, however, would not have altered significantly the ratio between businessmen and politicians in the national leadership as a whole.

ernmental bureaucrats. In the United States half the remainder is composed of business executives, and the rest is divided between electoral politicians and individuals with mixed private and government careers.

The more important the office in the Soviet system, the more likely it is to be occupied by an apparatchik. At the 22nd Party Congress, for instance, 26 per cent of the delegates occupied positions in the party apparatus. Forty-nine per cent of the Central Committee elected by that Congress, however, consisted of party office holders. At the very top, 81 per cent of the members of the Presidium and Secretariat were apparatchiki. In the American system, apart from the Presidency, the situation is almost exactly the reverse. The more important the post the less likely it is to be filled by an electoral politician. Only 19 per cent of the hundred top leaders were electoral politicians and fourteen of these were in Congress. Only three held office in the Administration. At the state and local levels the proportion of electoral politicians in key jobs—elected and appointed—is much higher. Less than 10 per cent of the governors elected between 1870 and 1950, for instance, had held no previous public office, and over 50 per cent had served in the state legislature. Over 30 per cent had served in elected or appointed law-enforcement offices, 20 per cent in local elective office, 19 per cent in statewide elective office, and 14 per cent in federal elective office.[17] The low status of state and local government compared to national government is both a cause and a consequence of the prominent role which the electoral politician plays in those governments.

During the forty-five years after 1917 the role of the apparatchiki in the Soviet political system tended to increase in importance. In terms of sheer size the apparat kept pace with the growth of Party membership. In 1922 there were 15,325 responsible officials in the Party, approximately 4 per cent of the Party membership. In 1962 the number of professional paid Party workers numbered about 150,000 to 200,000, or somewhat less than 4 per cent of the membership.[18] The number of apparatchiki, however, was much larger since many held temporary assignments in the government and specialized bureaucracies. Much more significant than simple numerical growth was the movement of the apparatchiki into most of the key positions of leadership in the Soviet political system. During Stalin's struggle for power in the 1920s the idealistic revolutionaries and intellectuals were gradually eliminated from the leading party bodies and replaced by Stalin's adherents from the apparat.

While the role of the Soviet apparatchik has increased in importance, that of the American electoral politician has tended to decline. In 1888 Bryce could argue that a distinctive aspect of American politics was the large class of professional politicians who dominated the public affairs of the country.[19] His observations, however, applied primarily to the state and local level. The emergence of the professional politicians was accompanied by a decline in the political experience of leaders at the national level. Prior to the Civil War the top leaders of the national government (President, Vice President, Cabinet member, Speaker of the House, Supreme Court Justice) spent more of their careers in politics than in other pursuits, the peak being the generation of 1801-1825, which devoted 65 per cent of its working life to politics. Since the Civil War the top members of the national government have usually spent more of their working life in nonpolitical occupations. Between 1901 and 1921, for instance, only 28 per cent of the careers of these national political leaders was devoted to politics. A similar decline has taken place in the proportion of top national leaders who have risen primarily or in part through elective office, the percentage who have held state or local office, and the percentage who have served in state legislatures.[20]

The same factors responsible for the rise of the apparatchik were also responsible for the decline of the traditional American electoral politician. The fundamental cause was the bureaucratization of modern society. The electoral politician is at home in the state legislature or Congress but sadly out of place in an administrative, industrial, or military bureaucracy. The skills of the bureaucrat are not those of the electoral politician. Few men in recent American politics have been able to perform successfully in both worlds. Averell Harriman demonstrated a sustained ability in a variety of national government posts: NRA administrator, presidential adviser, ambassador, Cabinet member, foreign-aid director, Assistant Secretary of State; but he conspicuously failed to achieve the same level of success as governor of New York. Those who follow electoral careers must identify themselves with a single constituency or state. Those identified with national institutions find it difficult to sink the local roots necessary for an electoral career. In many cases they see little reason to do so. "Although they were policy makers," Floyd Hunter remarks of the business-men among his hundred top national leaders, "with rare excep-tions they did not wish to run for public office, and they held themselves superior to the men who seek office." [21]

In the United States the gap between electoral and Administra-tion politics produces a gap between the individuals whom a presidential candidate depends upon to win office and those whom the President depends upon to discharge his office. The first group includes the political leaders and bosses in key states and cities: governors, mayors, state and county chairmen, and perhaps United States senators. They are professional electoral politicians whose national functions are limited to nominating the presidential candi-date (they appear in full glory at the conventions), and then electing him to office. They are the Daleys, the Lawrences, the Crottys: local satraps who emerge for a few months every four years to try to shape the course of the nation. Once the candidate is elected, however, they can be of little help or hindrance to him. To capture the Presidency the only resources needed are those which can be translated directly into votes. To govern the country, much else is required. The success of the President de-pends, in part, on the leaders of Congress, who, because they are leaders in Congress, are usually not the dominant political figures in their parties at home. The President's success, however, also depends on the cooperation of the leaders of the "Establish-ment" and his ability to mobilize political and technical expertise in a wide variety of fields. This need leads him to segments of American life which he may never have penetrated in his electoral career. Even someone as well connected as John F. Kennedy, it is reliably reported,

> suddenly discovered he didn't know "the right people." During his campaigning he had, of course, met practically every poli-tician in the country. But as far as picking a cabinet was con-cerned, his large circle of acquaintances seemed inadequate. The strength of these remarks, made matter-of-factly and with no

suggestion of regret, was subsequently borne out when Mr. Kennedy appointed men not previously known to him to several key posts in his administration.[22]

"Nine strangers and a brother" did not quite accurately describe Kennedy's Cabinet, but it did acutely suggest the problem which faces an incoming President.

TABLE 5

PRIMARY OCCUPATIONS
OF ADMINISTRATION LEADERS*

	TRUMAN 1949 N-65	EISENHOWER 1953 N-68	KENNEDY 1961 N-75
		Per cent	
Electoral politics	5	6	14
Government bureaucracy	48	23	21
Civil	35	10	12
Military	13	13	9
Private	39	53	41
Business	15	28	11
Law	14	13	11
Education	3	6	16
Other	6	6	4
Mixed	8	17	23
Private—electoral	5	7	10
Private—government bureaucracy	3	10	13
Total	100	100	100

* For 1949, 1953, and 1961, respectively, Administration leaders were distributed as follows: Executive Office of the President (including President and Vice President): 14, 14, 14; heads of executive departments: 9, 10, 10; State Department officials: 4, 6, 9; Defense Department officials (including JCS): 11, 11, 12; subcabinet officials in other departments: 8, 9, 10; heads of noncabinet agencies: 19, 18, 20.

As the figures in Table 5 suggest, the President's principal subordinates can come from the most diverse backgrounds. Each administration embodies a slightly different combination of interests. Almost half the top personnel in the Truman Administration in 1949 had pursued careers in the civil or military administrative branches of the national government, a proportion twice that of either the Eisenhower or Kennedy Administrations. As successor to a President who had held office for twelve years, Truman recruited his top subordinates from among the middle-aged bureaucrats who as bright young men fresh out of college or law school had flocked into Washington in 1933. "The most noticeable difference between the present Administration and the New Deal," John Fischer perceptively observed, "is about eighty pounds, comfortably larded around the bureaucratic paunch." [23] The Truman Administration was also able to call upon the large numbers of senior military officers who had demonstrated their abilities during the war. The Truman Administration thus reflected extensive governmental if not electoral experience. In European terms, it was a "government of technicians." Yet this was also an indication of its political weakness. It did not recruit substantial numbers of individuals who had made careers in business, law, education, and other private pursuits. In effect, it was divorced from the principal nongovernmental sources of power and influence.

The Eisenhower Administration placed little reliance on professional government administrators. Over half of its top leaders in 1953 had private careers and well over a quarter had spent most of their lives in business. The proportion of professional businessmen in the Eisenhower Administration in 1953 was almost twice the proportion in the Truman Administration in 1949 and two and a half times that in the Kennedy Administration in 1961. "We're here in the saddle," Ike's Secretary of the Interior said, "as an Administration representing business and industry." He was right.

The Kennedy Administration in its first year assumed a still different pattern. Unlike the earlier administrations, no single source of leaders predominated. Three types of leaders, however, were present in much higher proportions than they had been under either Truman or Eisenhower. Many members of the Kennedy Administration combined private and governmental careers. In large part this reflected the extent to which Kennedy was able to draw upon the experience of the Democratic Administration eight years before: twenty-nine of his top seventy-five leaders had served under Truman. Secondly, Kennedy's was, in one sense, a more political Administration than its predecessors. Fourteen per cent of its leaders had careers in electoral politics, more than twice the proportion in the Administration of either Truman or Eisenhower. The higher proportion of specialists in electoral politics in the Kennedy Administration reflected not so much a return of the old-style electoral politician as the presence within the Administration of the new-style campaign assistant and political manager, of whom the President's brother was the archetype. A third distinguishing characteristic of the Kennedy Administration was the high proportion of professors and educators. While businessmen were two and a half times as prevalent under Eisenhower as under Kennedy, the proportion of educators in the Kennedy Administration was two and a half times that under Eisenhower and five times that of the handful under Truman. The "Irish Mafia" and "Harvard" were statistics as well as stereotypes.

No other major country draws its political executives from such diverse sources. And in no other major country do individuals move back and forth so often between positions of leadership in the executive branch of the government and in the great institutions of society. In eighteenth-century societies, the social-economic leader, the aristocratic landowner, might also because of his status command a regiment in the army and a seat in the government. In the late nineteenth century, Americans reluctantly abandoned this reliance on amateurs in their army. In the late twentieth century, they still continue it in politics.

In the Soviet Union, on the other hand, whatever inner feuds may rack it, the Party Presidium, in terms of shared experience, is in a real sense a team. The same is true of the British Cabinet. When a party comes to power the choices that its leader can make for inclusion or exclusion in the Cabinet are relatively limited. With a few exceptions its members are in the Commons; rarely have they been there for less than a decade, and most of them have functioned together for several years as a "shadow cabinet." In contrast to the Soviet Presidium and the British Ministry, the American Administration is a completely ad-hoc body. As a group, its members share no previous experience. A President must honor his political debts and achieve some balance of interests, but within these limits he can appoint almost any individual whom he can persuade to accept office. In contrast to the heterogeneity of the American leadership, Soviet political leaders come up through the common channel of the Party apparat. Their political homogeneity is illustrated by the data in Table 6.

TABLE 6

PRIMARY INSTITUTIONAL CONNECTION OF TOP SOVIET LEADERS: PARTY PRESIDIUM AND SECRETARIAT COMBINED

	STALIN 1949 N-15	MALENKOV 1953 N-18	BULGANIN-KHRU-SHCHEV 1956 N-21	KHRUSHCHEV 1962 N-21
	Per cent			
Party apparat	54	61	67	81
(Ideologue)	(7)	(11)	(14)	(20)
State bureaucracy	33	28	23	19
(Industrial)	(20)	(17)	(14)	(5)
Police and military	13	11	9	—
	Educational Background			
Higher	40	56	71	76
(Technical-Scientific Institute)	(33)	(45)	(53)	(52)
(Economics, Marxism-Leninism, and humanities)	(6)	(11)	(18)	(24)
Incomplete higher and secondary	34	21	14	19
(Seminary)	(13)	(5)	(5)	(5)
(Technical)	(13)	(11)	(5)	(10)
Primary	13	11	5	5
Less	13	11	9	—

The data warrant some qualification and a few further observations. First of all, it must be stressed once again that the division of the top leadership echelons into Party or state bureaucracy is quite arbitrary. Most of those who are listed as owing their primary institutional connection to the state bureaucracy were or still are high Party officials—for example, Beria or Mikoyan. However, they were assigned to the category whenever it could be assumed that their responsibilities were such that they concentrated primarily on some specific operation of the state machinery and were not directly involved in internal Party affairs.

The table graphically illustrates the steady growth in the preponderance of the apparatchiki. It is noteworthy, however, that this increase was achieved entirely by the enlargement of the Presidium and Secretariat, and by the disappearance from the scene of military and secret police "representation." (In 1949 and 1953 there was one of each; in 1956 there were two individuals with military association, although it may be assumed that Voroshilov's links with the military were tenuous in all three cases; in 1962 there were none, although Shelepin, an apparatchik who for a while headed the secret police, may be in charge of supervising security affairs.) The absolute number of individuals associated with the state bureaucracy remained constant, suggesting that their number was considered functionally desirable.

Noteworthy also is the steady increase in the number of professional ideologues in the top leadership, an indirect reflection of the new emphasis on social indoctrination and perhaps even of concern over recent challenges to the ideology. Furthermore, in some respects the later phases of Stalinism were marked by the absence of social-economic innovation, and static orthodoxy requires fewer ideological interpreters than a period marked by considerable experimentation. The definition of goals and the choice of new means is also an ideological issue. In 1949 there was only one such professional ideologue in the top ranks; in 1953 there were two; in 1956, three, including one now in the Presidium; in 1962, four, with two in the Presidium. Their institutional origin and educational background can serve to offset any excessive tendency toward a purely "pragmatic" or technical attitude. Their increase can be contrasted with the gradual fading of the industrial bureaucrats, although the importance of this decline should not be overrated. Many of the top apparatchiki have industrial experience, more than half have had technical-scientific training, and some have had occasional industrial assignments (for example, Brezhnev supervised the industrial bureaucracy's reorganization in 1957-1958). More important still, some of the others may promote industrial interests either for ideological reasons or because they see in industrial development the basis for the Party's continued primacy.

The table supports the view that the trend in the Soviet leadership is toward greater predominance by the professional apparatchiki assisted on the one hand by the professional ideologues and on the other by the experts. For an American analogy, one would have to imagine an Administration dominated by a combination of the old-time city-machine bosses and high civil servants, with Senator McCarthy or General Walker setting the ideological tone on the one side, and a group of industrial executives providing the technical counsel on the other. The educational data (in several cases quite arbitrary classifications were made because of the imprecision of available information) also support the view that the composition of the leadership is becoming increasingly undifferentiated. Stalin's Politburo of 1949 involved a variety of institutional backgrounds and educational levels, with one-fourth of the Politburo lacking any formal education (the self-made men). Khrushchev's Presidium of early 1962 was four-fifths apparatchiki and almost four-fifths higher educated. In that, too, its composition was in keeping with the trends in modern professional bureaucracy.

The Presidium and the Secretariat do not strive to "represent" the various institutional segments of the Soviet system or the varied geographical and national interests of the society, and some (as, for instance, the military) are currently altogether unrepresented. But the members perforce do specialize in particular functions and in that sense may be said to reflect indirectly certain specific considerations. Furthermore, an effort is usually made to have two or three non-Russians in the top Party organs. However, it is always important to bear in mind that the organizational tradition and discipline of the Party inhibit the formation of a narrow, specialized outlook among the Presidium and Secretariat members. Like the cardinals on the Vatican Curia, they are predominantly professional politicians, sharing a common organizational outlook, common interests, and increasingly a common background.

The career histories of two Soviet officials, both of whom represent the new apparatchiki, are good illustrations in point. They illustrate graphically the generalizations made above.

PANTELEIMON K. PONOMARENKO	LEONID I. BREZHNEV
Born 1902.	Born 1906.
Joined CPSU in 1925.	Joined CPSU in 1931.
1918-1931, various posts in the Red Army and oil and railway industries, Komsomol and Party posts.	1927-1930, land surveyor in Kursk. 1930-1935, in raion and then oblast land departments in Urals.
1932, finished studies at the Moscow Institute of Transport Engineers.	
1932-1935, in the political apparat of the Red Army.	1935, graduated from the Dneprodzerzhinsk Metallurgical Institute.
1935-1937, engineer and group leader at All-Union Electrotechnical Institute.	1935-1937, engineer at Dzerzhinsky Metallurgical Plant.
1938, joined the CC apparat and then became First Secretary of the Byelorussian Republic— until 1947.	1938, Department Chief in Dnepropetrovsk Oblast Party Committee.
1939, was elected to the CPSU Central Committee.	1939, became Propaganda Secretary in the same oblast.
	1941-1945, served as a political commissar for the 18th Army, part of the 4th Ukrainian Front, rising to rank of major-general.
	1946-1947, First Secretary of Zaporozhe Oblast Party Committee and member of Ukrainian CC.
1948-1953, Secretary of the CC of the CPSU and from 1950-1952 Minister of Procurement.	1948-1950, First Secretary of Dnepropetrovsk Oblast.

(PONOMARENKO)

(BREZHNEV)

1950-1952, First Secretary of the Moldavian Republic CC.

October 1952–March 1953, member of the Presidium of the CPSU CC as well as Secretary.

October 1952–March 1953, Secretary and Candidate member of CPSU CC.

1953-1954, Minister of Culture.

1953-1954, head of the Political Administration of the Navy.

February 1954, appointed First Secretary of Kazakhstan Republic CC, an agriculturally critical area, which proved to be his undoing; also identified with Malenkov; after the latter's resignation as Premier in 1955, was appointed to increasingly less significant ambassadorial posts.

February 1954, appointed Second Secretary of the Kazakhstan Republic CC, under Ponomarenko.

August 1955–February 1956, became First Secretary of the Kazakhstan CC, replacing Ponomarenko.

February 1956, Secretary of the CPSU CC and candidate member of the Presidium.

1957, was elected full member in reward for supporting Khrushchev during June 1957 crisis.

1957-1958, trouble-shooter in charge of industrial reorganization.

1961, dropped from membership in the CPSU Central Committee.

1960, was elected Chairman of the USSR Presidium of the Supreme Soviet (nominal Head of State) and left the Secretariat of the CPSU CC.

June 1963, returned to Secretariat of the CPSU CC—the man to watch.

These two similar and highly professionalized career patterns may be contrasted with those of two representative American political leaders, one an electoral politician who, like Brezhnev, was in 1963 a man to watch, and the other a leading Cincinnatus-style executive, who, like Ponomarenko, had faded from the scene.

Lewis L. Strauss	Lyndon B. Johnson
Born 1896 in Richmond, Virginia, son of shoe-company executive.	Born 1908 in Johnson City, Texas, son of farmer, school teacher, local politician.
1912, graduated from high school.	1924, graduated from high school.
1912-1916, worked as traveling salesman for father's company.	1924-1927, worked as laborer.
1917, volunteered for staff of Herbert Hoover, served as assistant to Hoover in Food Administration relief work.	1927-1930, attended Southwest Texas State Teachers College.
1919, joined Kuhn, Loeb, & Co., Wall Street banking house, at invitation of partner, Mortimer Schiff.	1930-1931, taught in Houston public schools, helped Kleberg in campaign for Congress.
1929-1946, partner in Kuhn, Loeb.	1931, went to Washington as secretary to Representative Kleberg, wealthy conservative Texas Democrat.
	1935, was appointed Texas director, National Youth Administration, youngest state director in country.
	1937, elected to Congress on strong New Deal platform, became favorite of Roosevelt.

(STRAUSS)

(JOHNSON)

1941, called to active service as Lieutenant Commander, USNR.

1937-1949, Representative from Texas.

1941-1945, naval service in Ordnance Bureau, then assistant to James Forrestal, Under Secretary of Navy, and Secretary of Navy, promoted to rear admiral.

1941, lost close race for Senate to isolationist Pappy Lee O'Daniel.

1946, was appointed by Truman as Republican member of Atomic Energy Commission.

1941-1942, served in Navy in Pacific.

1946-1950, as AEC member, pushed development of detection system and hydrogen bomb.

1948, won Democratic nomination for Senate, 494,191 to 494,104.

1950-1953, returned to private life, consultant and financial adviser to Rockefellers.

1949-1961, United States Senator from Texas.

1953, was appointed Chairman of AEC by Eisenhower.

1951, elected Senate Democratic whip.

1953-1955, involved in controversies over Oppenheimer security case and Dixon-Yates electric power contract.

1953, elected Senate Democratic leader, youngest man ever named floor leader by either major party.

1958, retired as AEC Chairman, was given recess appointment as Secretary of Commerce.

1955-1961, majority leader, United States Senate, played constructive role in handling Eisenhower legislation.

1959, Senate by vote of 49 to 46 refused to confirm Commerce appointment.

1960, candidate for Democratic presidential nomination; selected by Kennedy as Vice Presidential nominee.

1961, Vice President of the United States.

The American and Soviet leadership systems thus differ in terms of their relationship to society as a whole. American political leadership overlaps and interacts with the social-economic leadership, because of the pluralistic character of American society and its many sources of personal and group power. The possibility of lateral access to American political leadership by nonpolitical leaders means that the political leadership in its values and procedures and personnel tends to reflect middle-class America. But, unlike the American groups, whose intermediate structure helps to maintain social access to the political system precisely because the groups are independent of it, those in the Soviet Union make possible social mobilization by the leadership because they are controlled by the Party.[24] By controlling promotions within the nonpolitical groups and by training its members for service in them, the Party prevents other social groups from developing their own standards of operation and promotion. In addition, by stressing the interchangeability of roles among the professional apparatchiki, and by offering sizable financial inducements upon promotion, the Party further enhances its capacity to control and diminishes the sense of specific group identity, or at least limits it to smaller and therefore less powerful units.

For example, the conventional counterpoise of the Party leaders versus the managers is quite illusory. One might ask: What managers? All of them? Can they act as a group? And do all of them really have certain common interests in relation to the Party? Is it not more likely that conflict among them (heavy industry versus light, steels versus alloys and plastics, coal versus electric energy) will be arbitrated by the top Party leadership, thus preventing a "managerial" alliance against the leaders? Furthermore, increasingly the Party is absorbing the new Soviet intelligentsia and technical personnel. Of the 8,784,000 specialists working in the national economy as of December 1960, 2,495,000 were CPSU members. Of the administrative-management personnel, which in 1956 numbered 4,403,000 people, 1,230,000 were CPSU members. Approximately 500,000 of these were directors of various administrative or economic institutions.* Of the approximately 3.8 million Soviet citizens who had completed their higher education as of 1961, 1.3 million were CPSU members.[25]

---

* To get a comparative sense of the high percentage, it may be noted that in 1958 there were in the United States 700,000 corporation presidents.

These figures have political and social significance. The Party itself becomes more aware of certain economic and administrative requirements, and in that sense the bureaucratic-managerial interests are represented by the Party leadership and within the Party leadership.

TABLE 7

EDUCATION AND PARTY MEMBERSHIP: SOVIET UNION

	USSR POPULATION (1959)	CPSU MEMBERS (1961)	RATIO
	In millions		*Per cent*
Complete higher education	3.8	1.3	34.2
Incomplete higher and secondary	10.6	2.9	27.4
Specialized secondary	7.9	1.8	23.0
Incomplete secondary	35.4	2.8	8.2
Primary or less	151.1	.8	.5
Total	208.8	9.6	4.6

The Party thus includes both the professional politicians and a substantial proportion of all other elite groups. In effect, it is the only all-national political organization which siphons off the ablest and best trained elements, embraces them with its organizational outlook, subjects them to its discipline, and gives them a vested interest in maintaining the Party's monopoly of power. The differences in social origins and institutional interests between the apparatchiki and other elite groups are in some degree moderated by the common bond of Party membership. This common membership makes the Party leaders more sensitive to the needs of the other groups but at the same time makes these groups more susceptible to control by the Party professionals.

There is, of course, the danger that the Party gradually will be turned into a club for professional engineers and managers, with the concomitant changes in style and attitudes. To prevent this, new ideological campaigns have been undertaken and much stress put on political training. Furthermore, it is unavoidable that on the upper levels of the Party hierarchy political problems will continue to dominate over purely technical (and therefore narrower, more specific) concerns. Hence there will be a continuing need for politically motivated leaders. The 1962 split of the Party into two parallel hierarchies (the industrial and agricultural) also means that the possible effects of the permeation of lower Party staffs with technicians will be offset by the concentration of political power at higher levels of the bureaucracy. Integration of policy will henceforth be above the regional level, and there the professional "generalist" apparatchiki continue to hold sway.

The absence of a corps of professional bureaucratic politicians is the most important feature distinguishing political leadership in the United States from that in the Soviet Union. The top leader in the Soviet Union is a politician and a bureaucrat. The top leader in the United States is either a politician or a bureaucrat. Kennedy had fourteen years in politics but none in bureaucracy. Eisenhower had thirty-five years in bureaucracy but none in domestic politics. Khrushchev combines the experience of both. Here is the crucial problem of political leadership in the United States. The modern society is a bureaucratized society: it needs bureaucratic politicians. In the United States the traditional type of professional politician is retiring into the legislatures. To what extent is the United States likely to develop a type of professional bureaucratic politician to replace the declining electoral politician? Can the nonpolitical leader from the "Establishment" become a successful bureaucratic politician and political leader in government? He is probably more likely to succeed in Administration posts, apart from the Presidency, than is the electoral politician.* But if his career has been primarily or exclusively in industry, banking, education, law, or the military, is he likely to bring into government the principal skills and experience required there? To some extent, of course, all bureaucratic organizations are similar, and the skills required to lead them are the same. The successful military commander can transform himself—not entirely painlessly—into a suc-

---

* "By and large, the members of President Kennedy's Cabinet who have held elective office seemed to have had more difficulty in adjusting themselves to their Cabinet roles than did those previously associated with big business, big labor, or big foundations." E. W. Kenworthy, *New York Times,* July 16, 1962, p. 16.

cessful corporation executive officer. But adjusting to shifts from one specialized bureaucracy to another may well be easier than shifting from any one specialized bureaucracy to leadership in the Administration. Within a specialized bureaucracy, advancement is normally a product of influence, contacts, "pull," on the one hand, and ability judged by fairly objective standards of technical knowledge and achievement, on the other.

In a political bureaucracy such as the Communist Party of the Soviet Union or any American Administration, these two grounds become both more general and less distinguishable. Access and contacts are, in a sense, technical criteria for judging politicians. Achievement on the job is measured in terms of social, political, and ideological values which, unlike the standards in the specialized bureaucracy, are diverse, subjective, and controversial. The Cabinet officer who is a success to a conservative may be a dismal failure to a liberal. Thus the factors which may bring a man to the top of a specialized bureaucracy do not necessarily prepare him for the wide-open competition in a political bureaucracy. Not having made a career of the struggle for governmental office and power, he may well have problems in adjusting successfully to that struggle. In general, the more technical and specialized his experience in private life the more difficulty he will have in government: hence the common observation that Wall Street bankers seem to do better in Washington than Midwest industrialists. Inherent in the American amateur tradition has been the assumption that men who are leaders in one area can also be leaders in another, that leadership consists of certain traits which some may develop while others do not. Leadership abilities, however, are not universal but specific to particular situations: the leader in one environment may be most inadequate in another.

Successful political leaders thus are likely to be those with experience in political bureaucracy. The immense expansion of the federal bureaucracy has multiplied the number of "political offices" at its top. It is not inconceivable that a new type of American professional bureaucratic politician may be emerging. This would be an individual who probably gets his start in one of the private institutions of the "Establishment" but then moves into a junior position in government at a still relatively early age and works himself up to a top position in the Administration. Apart from the normal risks of politics, the key problem in such a career is that no Administration lasts longer than eight years. Hence, a career as an Administration political executive is not likely to last a lifetime.

Three alternative patterns are possible. First, if one Administration is succeeded by another of the same party, undoubtedly many of the bureaucratic politicians in the first will also find places in the second. Second, even if the other party comes to power, a few individuals may still continue their governmental careers. (They would, under Galbraith's definition, be the true "Establishment men.") Or, third, if the other party does come to power, many of the political bureaucrats from the previous Administration may temporarily return to private institutions and come back to government when the parties change once again. That the United States may be developing such a corps of "ministrables" is suggested by the fact that 13 per cent of the leaders in the Kennedy Administration had mixed governmental-private careers, as compared to 10 per cent under Eisenhower and 3 per cent under Truman. The fact that almost 40 per cent of the Kennedy leaders had held some post in the Truman Administration also suggests that the future pattern may be one in which a party recruits the elite of one Administration from the sub-elite of its previous Administration. Extensive governmental service interlaced with some private experience may be the pattern for the new American "apparatchik."

The emergence of a professional political elite would be a novel development in America. The predominance of the apparatchik in Russia reflects historical continuity. The Soviet apparatchik continues the long tradition of centralized and powerful Russian state bureaucracy, composed of individuals with little class identification but characterized primarily by a devotion to the state and representing its interests. The absence of this tradition in America means therefore that it is unlikely that the new American professionalism will bring about a type of leadership similar to the Soviet kind. The more ideological Soviet system also requires more selectivity in recruitment and far greater emphasis on personal commitment to a particular and overt outlook than can be justified by the purely functional requirements of a political system in an advanced industrialized society. But since that selectivity and commitment are vital to the elite's hold on power, it is likely that the ruling elite will continue to stress them, using the device of party membership to draw the politically ambitious elements of society into its own professional bureaucratic network. Lateral entry into political leadership from nonpolitical posts of high responsibility will continue to be viewed as dangerous to the homogeneity of the leadership and hence to its power. In fact, it would be an important clue to change in the Soviet Union if at the political apex significant numbers of individuals should appear whose careers had been associated primarily with a nonpolitical profession. Until this happens, the exercise of power and the making of policy in the Soviet Union, unlike those in America, will remain a matter of bureaucratic professionalism and ideological commitment.

CIRCULATION OF LEADERS

The rate of turnover of leaders in top positions and the nature of the mechanisms for producing turnover are significant for two reasons. First, within any political system differences in tenure among leaders affect differences in power. Power may be limited in terms of scope, and also in terms of tenure. The scope of the President's power is far greater than that of any congressman or bureaucrat, but the latter may confront the President as equals in a given area simply because they can outwait him. From the point of view of the system as a whole, a regular but not rapid turnover generally produces better results. The most appropriate rate will, of course, vary from one system to another. But quite obviously neither extreme is desirable: a system in which no office changed except when its incumbent died would be just as fragile as one in which every office changed every year.

Second, the rate of turnover in office also affects the way in which office holders are prepared for their jobs. In collegial offices especially a slow, steady turnover means that each newcomer to the body is absorbed into an on-going system and can learn its ways and values. Such a system tends to protect the institution against powerful but transient external influences. This is a rationale behind staggering the terms of independent regulatory commissioners and United States senators. A slow rate of turnover for an individual office or a collegial office may also allow greater preparation if individuals become candidates some time before they assume office. Candidates may be selected by the institution itself—for example, candidate members of the Presidium or the Central Committee—or they may be self-selected—for example, candidates for the Presidency. In each case, however, candidacy imposes upon the individual a pattern of behavior more closely approximating that of the office to which he aspires than would otherwise be the case.

Within any single American Administration a fairly rapid and regular turnover occurs in most offices. In the early 1950s the average tenure in office of 1650 high-level federal executives was thirty-nine months; for deputy and assistant agency heads it was only twenty-three months.[26] The two- or three-year tenure reflects both lateral movement in and out of government and shifts in posts within the Administration. The most distinctive feature of the turnover of leadership in the American executive branch, however, is the complete change in personnel which takes place with a change in Administration. In 1953, several thousand policy-making jobs changed hands. Eight of sixty-four top civilian officials in the Eisenhower Administration in 1953 had held top posts in the Truman Administration in 1952. Four of these, however, were holdovers in the independent regulatory commissions, where statutory restrictions did not permit quick change. They were all replaced by the end of 1954. The "New Look" broom also produced a complete change in the membership of the Joint Chiefs of Staff before the end of 1953. Seven other officials, including Eisenhower himself, had held subordinate positions during the last year of the Truman Administration. Thus, about 6 per cent of the top leaders in Eisenhower's Administration had been top leaders in Truman's, and an additional 10 per cent of those in Eisenhower's had held subordinate positions in Truman's.

This pattern was repeated in 1961. Of the seventy top civilian leaders of the Kennedy Administration, seven had held top posts in 1960 under Eisenhower. Three of these, however, were holdovers who were replaced before Kennedy had been in office eighteen months. Three other leaders of Kennedy's Administration had held subordinate posts at the end of Eisenhower's. Thus, about 6 per cent of the top leaders under Kennedy had also been at the top under Eisenhower, and an additional 5 per cent had held second-level jobs under Eisenhower. Like Eisenhower, Kennedy also wanted his own military advisers: by the summer of 1962 four of the five Joint Chiefs had been replaced.

The change of Administration also means a significant change in the total national structure of leadership. The top leadership of the Kennedy Administration, for instance, was almost completely unrepresented in the list of one hundred leaders compiled by Professor Hunter in 1958. Not one of the 1961 Cabinet secretaries was, according to this test, a top national leader in 1958. Only five of the hundred leaders in 1958 occupied high positions in the Kennedy Administration in 1961: Johnson, Harriman, McCloy, Stevenson, and General Taylor. Not even the President in 1961 had made the grade as a top national leader in 1958.

The average tenure for all Administration officials is much less than that of Congressional leaders. Fifty-one of eighty-two Congressional leaders in 1953, for instance, had also been leaders in 1949.* Thirty-six of ninety-one Congressional leaders in 1961 had been in congressional leadership positions eight years earlier in 1953, and twenty-five had occupied such positions since 1949. Thus, between 1949 and 1953, there was no change in 63 per cent of the leaders of Congress. Between 1953 and 1961, there was no change in 40 per cent. The more important leaders, moreover, spend much longer periods in both Congress and leadership positions. In 1961 the nine top leaders of the House averaged nineteen years in leadership positions and thirty-one in Congress. Top Senate leaders averaged nine years as leaders and twenty in the Senate.** Elected officials, Robert Michels once argued, tend to stay in office longer than appointed ones.[27] Corroborating this thesis,

---

* Congressional leaders include: (1) President Pro Tem, Speaker, majority and minority leaders, majority and minority whips, in both houses. (2) Chairman, Vice Chairman, and ranking minority members from both houses of joint committees. (3) The members of the House Rules Committee. (4) The chairman and ranking minority member of the standing committees of both houses. These totaled ninety-six positions in 1949 and 1953 and one hundred and three in 1961. Eighty-two individuals occupied these positions in 1949 and 1953, ninety-one in 1961.
** Top House leaders include Speaker, majority and minority leaders, chairmen and ranking minority members of Rules, Appropriations, and Ways and Means Committees. Top Senate leaders include President Pro Tem, majority and minority leaders, and chairmen and ranking minority members of Foreign Relations, Appropriations, and Finance Committees.

the average tenure of the biennially elected leaders of the United States House of Representatives far exceeds that of any other group of officials in either Soviet or American government.

The leadership of Congress, moreover, unlike the Administration, is always bipartisan. Changes in the control of Congress alter

TABLE 8

LEADERSHIP TENURE IN CONGRESS

	AVERAGE TENURE IN YEARS		
Top Leaders	*1949*	*1953*	*1961*
In House	29	27	31
As House leader	16	15	19
In Senate	17	17	20
As Senate leader	9	7	9
All Leaders			
In House	19	19	20
As House leader	8	8	9
In Senate	12	13	16
As Senate leader	6	5	7

the relative importance of the top leaders, but normally all the top leaders remain in Congress. In virtually all committees and even on the floors of both houses, seniority is a far more reliable index to influence than is partisan identification. Turnover in congressional leadership is thus slower and more regular than it is in the Administration, and individuals who become congressional leaders usually have many years of congressional experience behind them.

Turnover in Soviet political leadership is more regular than it is in the American Administration and somewhat faster than it is in Congress. Thirty-five full members went on and off the Politburo or Presidium between 1919 and 1961. They averaged 9.3 years as full members. Six of the thirty-five served three years or less; six also served twenty years or more. The tenure of the remaining twenty-three—two-thirds of the total—ranged from four to eleven years, terms of office which might be presumed to be close to an optimum length. More significant than length of tenure, however, is the regularity of turnover. At no point in Soviet history except during World War II has the full membership of the Presidium remained unchanged for more than two years. On the other hand, only once has there been a major upheaval in Presidium membership. New full members with only a few years of service have normally been a minority. From 1931 through 1938 a majority of the Politburo members served at least five years as full members; from 1939 through 1956 a majority served at least nine. The only major break in continuity was the upheaval of 1957. At that time Presidium membership was expanded from eleven to fifteen; six members were dropped, ten were added. In 1956 a majority of the Presidium had served ten years on the Presidium; at the end of 1957 a majority had served less than a year. This abrupt break, unique in Soviet history, was comparable to the drastic change in top-level leadership which takes place each time a new Administration comes to power in the United States. This change, in effect, marked the beginning of the "Khrushchev Administration," after he had crushed the Presidium majority's attempted coup d'état against him.

While the Soviet turnover is, in general, fairly regular, it does speed up during succession struggles. Twenty-four of the forty-one additions to the Presidium and fifteen of the thirty-five losses after 1919 occurred during the succession struggles of the 1920s and the 1950s—that is, during one-fourth of the last forty-four years. During a succession struggle the Presidium tends to expand in membership; gains exceed losses as the victor in the struggle establishes his majority in the Presidium. In the years of consolidation and purge after the succession struggle, on the other hand, turnover subsides, and the losses tend to exceed gains as the victor weeds out early supporters no longer needed or now viewed as potentially dangerous. As Table 9 shows, the pattern applies also to candidate members and the Party Secretariat.

Similarly, change is continuous and relatively regular on the Central Committee, although more rapid than on the national leadership level. The size of the Central Committee has grown steadily, as indeed it should, given the growth in party membership (from 430,000 in 1920 to about 9,000,000 in 1960, or twenty times). It is noteworthy, however, that the most substantial increases in the size of the Central Committee (leaving aside the thirteen-year gap between 1939 and 1952) took place during struggles for power, thereby allowing significant changes in the composition of the Central Committee, but without a total upheaval in the membership of the outgoing Committee. One-half of the 1956 membership was still re-elected to Khrushchev's 1961 Central Committee, but within it they amounted to only 37 per cent. Casualties among Central Committee members were the highest during

TABLE 9

CHANGES IN CPSU POLITBURO-PRESIDIUM AND CC SECRETARIAT, 1919-1961

Dates	Number of Years	POLITBURO-PRESIDIUM*		SECRETARIAT		Character of Period
		Gains	Losses	Gains	Losses	
1919	1	7	0	1**	0	Establishment of Politburo and Secretariat
1920-1923	4	5	2	8	6	Lenin's last years
1924-1930	7	17	14	12	10	Succession struggle
1931-1933	3	1	1	0	1	Consolidation
1934-1939	6	8	10	5	5	Purge
1940-1945	6	3	1	3	2	World War II
1946-1952	7	7	5	4	4	Stalin's last years
1953-1957	5	19	11	14	9	Succession struggle
1958-1961	4	6	13	6	7	Consolidation
Totals	43	73	57	53	44	

* Full and Candidate members.
** In 1919 the Secretariat consisted of one responsible secretary—a member of the Orgburo—and five technical secretaries.

Sources: Leonard Schapiro, *The Communist Party of the Soviet Union.* New York, 1960.

R. Conquest, *Power and Policy in the USSR.* New York, 1961.

Merle Fainsod, *The 22nd Party Congress,* Special Supplement to *Problems of Communism,* V. 10, no. 6, 1961.

——, *How Russia Is Ruled.* Cambridge, Mass., rev. ed. 1963.

VKP(b) v Rezoliutsiiakh i Resheniiakh S'ezdov, Konferentsii i Plenumov TsK, 2 vols., 5th ed., Moscow, 1936.

Bolshaia Sovetskaia Entsiklopediya, 2nd edition.

Michael T. Florinsky, ed., *Encyclopedia of Russia and the Soviet Union.* New York, 1961.

the post-succession purge period of 1934-1939 as well as in the course of Khrushchev's consolidation of power. During this period, the turnover among the middle-upper ranks of Soviet state and Party bureaucrats was also high. In 1962, some 70.5 per cent of

TABLE 10

TURNOVER IN CENTRAL COMMITTEE
MEMBERSHIP, 1917-1961

Party Congresses	Number of CC Members Elected	Number Who Had Served on Previous CC (Per cent)	Per Cent of CC Members Re-elected to Subsequent CC
6th—August 1917	21	— —	61.9
7th—March 1918	15	13 (86.7)	80.0
8th—March 1919	19	12 (63.2)	68.4
9th—March 1920	19	13 (68.4)	78.9
10th—March 1921	24	15 (62.5)	83.3
11th—March 1922	27	20 (74.1)	88.9
12th—April 1923	40	24 (60.0)	92.5
13th—May 1924	53	37 (69.8)	92.5
14th—December 1925	63	49 (77.7)	82.5
15th—December 1927	71	52 (73.2)	80.3
16th—June 1930	71	57 (80.3)	78.9
17th—February 1934	71	56 (78.9)	22.5
18th—March 1939	71	16 (22.5)	46.5
19th—October 1952	125	33 (26.4)	64.0
20th—February 1956	133	80 (60.2)	49.6
22nd—October 1961	175	66 (37.7)	

Sources: Zbigniew Brzezinski, *The Permanent Purge,* Cambridge, Mass., 1956, p. 104.
Pravda, March 22, 1939.
Leo Gruliow, *Current Soviet Policies,* vols. I-IV.

the obkom, kraikom, and republic first secretaries had held their jobs for less than three years; only 12.8 per cent had been in office for more than five years.[28]

In general, turnover is gradual and tenure long among American congressional leaders. For the top Soviet leadership, turnover is gradual and tenure moderate. For American Administrations, turnover is abrupt and tenure moderate, while for higher Soviet and

American administrators and for Soviet Central Committee members, turnover is gradual and tenure short.

Political commentators frequently deplore the relatively short tenure of executives in particular jobs within the Administration. The disadvantages of a rapid turnover are marked, however, only when individuals move in and out of the Administration and Washington experience is exchanged for political innocence. A fast game of musical chairs within the Administration, however, may benefit the Administration by broadening the experience and knowledge of its executives, developing loyalties to the Administration and its programs rather than to particular departments, and stimulating morale and interest through prospects of rapid advancement. The more serious problems of continuity in the executive branch concern not the turnover of officials within an Administration but rather the turnover of Administrations themselves.

Communist one-party systems and European multi-party systems, such as those of the Third and Fourth French Republics, both seem to provide a relatively measured, regular turnover in the top national leadership. Changes in two-party systems tend to be more abrupt. Changes in party control in the United States, moreover, produce much more drastic changes in leadership than they do in British-style parliamentary systems. In the first place, the gap between new and old leaders is greater. In the parliamentary system both the Cabinet and the shadow cabinet exist in Parliament. The members of the latter are the recognized leaders of their party; they play an active role in the legislature; they are close observers of and even, at times, participants in the great decisions of state. In the American system, on the other hand, the leaders of the incoming Administration are a diverse group, most of whom have been recently preoccupied with either political campaigning or private occupations. By and large they have been far removed from the top echelons of government. Secondly, the change in the American system is more drastic because it reaches much farther down into the administrative hierarchy. A new government in Great Britain means a change of leadership in probably less than a hundred positions. A new Administration in the United States means a change in at least a thousand top positions, and conceivably, as in 1953, in thousands of secondary ones. It is, in a sense, a peaceful revolution as the new elite moves into Washington. No other stable government—parliamentary or Communist—regularly goes through such a tremendous upheaval.

The results for the operation of the government are far-reaching. The new leaders have to spend a year or more simply establishing themselves in office, getting to know one another, learning the ropes of their individual offices, familiarizing themselves with the complexities of Washington politics if they are new to government, and developing a common outlook, a common set of policy priorities, and a common political style. All new Administrations share many problems and many characteristics as they scramble about discovering themselves. The members of the Administration are equally new to each other as an Administration, and often equally new to Washington. As a result, instead of adjusting to an established style and set of attitudes—as is the case, say, of those who aspire to leadership in Congress or in the apparat of the CPSU—they have to develop a method of governance on their own. They have to learn what the previous Administration learned four or eight years earlier.

This is a wasteful procedure, but it does have the virtues of its vices. It does not guarantee new policies, but it makes them possible. Every Administration begins with a "new look." To be sure, the expectations of a fundamental overhaul in policy common at the start of every Administration are seldom realized. After it has been in power three or four years commentators will argue that its policies differ little from those of its predecessor. Changes, nonetheless, do take place, and new priorities are assigned to different areas of policy.

In that respect, the Soviet system tends to be more rigid. Until the adoption in 1961 of a new CPSU statute, providing for a periodic renewal of the Party Presidium by one-quarter at every Party Congress, removal from the Presidium was tantamount to political disgrace. Given the bureaucratic character of Soviet politics, this was bound to have a conservative effect on policy, inhibiting individual initiative. The adoption of formal provisions for a regular turnover at the top of the Soviet leadership will reduce some of the stigma attached to removal and, therefore, is likely to have a revitalizing effect, while the actual rate of change will not be much increased since past turnover was as high as provided by the new rules.

Under the 1961 rules, turnover in lower echelons is to be even more rapid, although here too the actual change will be not in the rate (since there has always been a steady turnover) but in its effect on policy initiatives. The membership of territorial and regional committees and of union republics is to be renewed by one-third; that of lower bureaus and committees by one-half. However, "particular Party workers . . . by virtue of their generally recognized authority and high political and organizational and other abilities" will be exempt; hence the position of the actual leader is not likely to be affected.

The new Party rules also make explicit the previous patterns of less turnover on higher levels and thereby formally consolidate the power of those at the top and minimize it at the bottom. In the American system, on the other hand, differences in tenure enhance the power of bureaucratic and congressional leaders and reduce that of the Administration. As the Administration has become the initiator of policy, the ability of the other leaders to outlast the Administration in effect gives them a veto on policy. Thus, the turnover rates in the Soviet and American systems tend to reflect the more pervasive aspects of those systems: the concentration of power at the top on the one hand and the separation of powers on the other.

THE PROBLEM OF SUCCESSION

Two key differences between the Soviet and American political systems concern the tenure of the top leader and the way in which the top leadership is filled when a vacancy occurs.

The United States has a regular procedure for replacing its top political leader at least once every eight years and possibly every four years. The Soviet Union lacks any such system. This is one of the most important ways in which the American political system is more stable and effective than that of the Soviet Union. Eight American Presidents have died in office. This is not an inconsiderable number, but it is still less than one in four. In the Soviet system the top leader, like the Czar, always dies in office. The 22nd Amendment limits a President to a maximum of eight years. The tenure of a Soviet leader depends on his age and health. Lenin was leader for six years, Stalin for twenty-four; Khrushchev, in 1963, had been the effective leader for six. At the age of sixty-nine and with various reported ailments, it seems probable that his tenure in office will be less than fifteen years.

In terms of the needs of the modern state the American system of limited tenure and regular turnover in the chief office has many

TABLE 11

TURNOVER AT THE TOP, 1917-1964

	USSR	USA
1917	Lenin	Wilson
1921	"	Harding
1923	Zinoviev-Stalin-Rykov	Coolidge
1929	Stalin	Hoover
1933	"	Roosevelt
1945	"	Truman
1953	Malenkov-Molotov-Khrushchev	Eisenhower
1957	Khrushchev	"
1961	"	Kennedy
1964	"	Johnson

advantages over the Soviet system, quite apart from easing the succession problem. In particular, it ensures a new President, a new Administration, and new policies every eight years. The 22nd Amendment, whatever the motives behind it, does have the desirable effect of compelling frequent, but not too frequent, changes in leadership at a time in history when political, international, social, and military change is the rule. It affords some protection against the President's growing old, stale, and tired in office. To be sure, even without the two-term limit, a President could always be thrown out of office every four years, but the electorate may not be the best judge of when change is necessary. An incumbent President has a tremendous advantage in running for re-election, and a popular President conceivably could be re-elected several times because the voters liked him as a "human being" even if his policies failed to keep up with the times.

In addition, every Administration tends to become the prisoner of its initial successes and failures. What has worked is repeated; what has failed is avoided. In minor degree, tendencies in this direction existed in both the Truman and Eisenhower Administrations. They pale, however, before those of Stalin. The last eight years of Stalin's twenty-four-year rule saw a general stagnation and rigidification in Soviet policy. Completely new challenges, of course, such as war, may reinvigorate a Presidency or a leadership, but less serious challenges are unlikely to break an established pattern.

Succession struggles take place in both the United States and the Soviet Union. In both countries they may last for some time: one or two years in the United States, four to six in the Soviet Union. In both, the struggle at the outset may involve about a half-dozen aspirants. In both, the fate of the aspirants may be determined by the deals which they can make with other powerful figures, the king-makers and king-vetoers, who are not themselves contenders for the crown. During the struggle the candidates are gradually tested and eliminated until only one remains. The crucial differences in the two systems are that the American succession struggle occurs before the office is vacant, much of it takes place outside the operating components of the political system, and it has a formal conclusion with a regularized transfer of power. The Soviet struggle, in contrast, occurs after the office is vacant, even if it begins beforehand; it pervades the political system; and it has no formal conclusion. In addition, when a President dies the American system provides an automatic constitutional heir and thereby precludes any succession struggle. In this respect, the American system differs not only from the Soviet one but also from most parliamentary systems, where the death of a premier normally unleashes a competitive scramble among his would-be successors.

Furthermore, the American system of prevacancy selection provides for a clear-cut transfer of leadership responsibilities, accepted as legitimate by the entire political structure and society and executed literally in the light of day, in full view of the public. In the Soviet Union, there is no such clarity. A succession struggle involves prolonged periods of confusion. Table 11 indicates that periodically the Soviet political system changes drastically from a one-man dictatorship to an oligarchical "collective leadership." But when does collective leadership end and the personal one begin? This Soviet citizens and—what from the standpoint of the political system is even worse—Soviet officials have no clear-cut way of knowing. The transfer of Soviet executive power is determined by informal processes. Unlike the American citizen or official who can watch the inauguration on television and be quite certain who the President is, the Soviet citizen and official has to search for informal clues that indicate the end of the collective leadership and the beginning of a new phase of personal dictatorship.

He thus must watch carefully the composition of the ruling party bodies, particularly the Party Presidium and Secretariat. He must assess the significance of changes in it and try to guess whose supporters the new members might be. Stalin gradually weeded out his opponents while consolidating his position. But precisely because of that, Khrushchev was unable to effect any significant changes until after he had crushed his opponents on the Presidium in 1957, and only then did he effect a sweeping purge. (See Table 10, page 179.) Thus the absence of a gradual change may also indicate that the conflict is being fought out elsewhere. Needless to add, the Soviet observer will attach considerable significance to the post of First Secretary, considering both Stalin's and Khrushchev's experience. He will carefully scan the newspapers for clues to preeminence; even the sudden capitalization of a title may be a clue.[29] Similarly, the frequency with which a Soviet leader is pictured in the press is a good indication that the transfer of power is being effected, as Table 12 illustrates. The attribution to a particular Soviet leader of special merit in ideological creativity is also an important indication of power, in view of the system's emphasis on its ideological foundations. Lastly, the Soviet observer will try to

TABLE 12

NUMBER OF PICTURES OF TOP SOVIET LEADERS IN *IZVESTIA* AND *PRAVDA* DURING VARIOUS PHASES OF THE TRANSFER OF POWER

| | JANUARY-FEBRUARY 1955 | | JANUARY-FEBRUARY 1957 | | JANUARY-FEBRUARY 1959 | |
	Pravda	Izves-tia	Pravda	Izves-tia	Pravda	Izves-tia
Khrushchev	3	3	23	19	23	22
Malenkov	3	3	9	8	0	0
Molotov	2	2	12	9	0	0
Bulganin	3	3	26	19	0	0
Suslov	2	2	7	7	4	5
Brezhnev	0	0	5	5	3	3

assess the distribution of political offices among the Soviet leaders: the fact that Khrushchev for several years has been the only Soviet leader to combine membership in the Party Presidium with a secretaryship of the Central Committee, the Chairmanship of the Bureau for the Russian Socialist Federal Soviet Republic of the CC, and the Premiership* may serve as the conclusive bit of evidence that he has become the dictator. From the standpoint of the system, this is a cumbersome, prolonged, and confusing procedure. It leaves many bureaucrats in doubt and often contributes to conflicts between professional loyalty and personal career.

One conceivable solution to the Soviet problem would be for the dictator to designate his successor. Lenin did not try to do this; he simply hinted that he did not think Stalin was qualified for the job. Stalin also did not formally designate a successor, but he did place Malenkov in a position where the latter was certainly the second most powerful man in the political system. Khrushchev has kept power fairly evenly divided among his chief subordinates. Judged by the experience of Lenin and Stalin and others elsewhere, a dictator cannot determine who will inherit his position. In this respect, his power may be less than that of the American President, who usually chooses his vice-presidential running mate. A retiring President also can often control and certainly at least veto the nomination by his own party and can exercise, if he wishes and has prestige, strong influence on the election of his successor. The power of the dictator, however, goes to the grave with him. If prior to his death he gives his designated successor too much power, he will no longer be dictator. Hence, in addition to designating an heir-apparent, he may also build up a "counter-heir" as a rival to maintain his own power.[30] During the dictator's life his power thus limits that of the successor. After his death his power cannot help the designated successor.

The only way to resolve this dilemma would be for the dictator to abdicate while he was still alive and transfer power to his successor. In this case the most powerful man in the system and the second most powerful man would be cooperating in a common purpose. Between them they could presumably carry off the trans-

* Each of the other Presidium members has only one additional post, with the exception of Polyansky and Brezhnev, who have two.

fer. But such a transfer would leave the new leader in a much weaker position than if he had achieved power through a succession struggle. One function of the latter is to make the power of the victor more secure by eliminating his most capable rivals. Presumably a successor who acquired power by abdication and transfer would find it in his interest to achieve a similar result by quickly purging his potential rivals. In that he would require the support of his promoter, since the victims would appeal to him, and thus it would still mean that his power was conditioned on his sponsor's cooperation. In fact, to achieve real power he would finally have to purge his sponsor—which may explain why such a transfer has not yet been effected.

Prevacancy choice of a successor thus seems unlikely in the Soviet system. The question then becomes: to what extent can the disruptive effects of a postvacancy succession struggle be minimized? One reason the two succession struggles in the Soviet Union have been so intense and prolonged is that the office at stake has no formal legitimacy within the political system. In theory the leadership organs of the Communist Party—the Presidium, Secretariat, Central Committee—are all collective. The role of leader, nonetheless, is a real one. Under Stalin and Khrushchev it was associated with the position of General Secretary or First Secretary of the Central Committee, but in both cases also it was not the occupancy of the office but the uses to which it was put which made Stalin and Khrushchev the leaders. Each had held the top position in the Secretariat for several years before he emerged victorious.

The leader in the Soviet system is thus like the traditional city boss in the United States. He may control a government effectively while occupying several important offices or almost none at all. As in the struggles for power following the death of a city boss, the victory of his successor can be legitimized only by the disappearance or acquiescence of his rivals.

Other bureaucratic and highly centralized power systems have solved problems similar to that of the Soviet leaders because they have formally recognized and accepted the concentration of power —but not its arbitrary exercise—in a particular office. An American corporation, for instance, may be completely dominated by its president, but if the president dies the board of directors is available to select a successor. Even more in point is the practice of what may be the second most powerful bureaucratic organization .in the world next to the CPSU. When a Pope dies, a succession struggle ensues, but in recent centuries at least the struggle has always been reasonably quickly resolved by the College of Cardinals. The cardinals can do this, however, only because the office of Pope is formally recognized, while the electors (the College of Cardinals) are generally the senior statesmen of the Church, whose own position and personal security are not likely to be altered drastically by the election's outcome.

One alternative solution might involve fixing a specific time limit of the First Secretaryship of the CPSU and the Premiership. This would have the advantage of regulating what is now a purely personal power and of turning it into formal authority. However, this solution (assuming it was not circumvented by the dictator's assumption of a new post and title, both created purposefully to evade the above reform) would mean a significant change in the character of the system. A fixed-time dictatorship would begin to resemble some of the existing strong presidential systems, and would probably bring in its wake more regularized forms of selection of the First Secretary, probably by the Central Committee. Yet the very limitation on his tenure would impose strict limits on his power—of both a practical and a psychological character—while the role of the Central Committee as the electoral college would serve to transform the dictatorship into an oligarchy.

Indeed, even if the tenure was not limited but selection institutionalized in the Central Committee, it is likely that the character of the system would be altered. It would be in the interest of the Central Committee to avoid selecting "strong men" who might threaten, through the use of their power, the individual and collective interests of the Central Committee. The French National Assembly of the Third Republic gave ample demonstration of this inclination. To wield arbitrary power, it is necessary to win it arbitrarily.

A prolonged postvacancy succession struggle creates difficulty for any political system. In the Soviet system there is the additional danger that the struggle may involve a succession crisis, that is, a major institutional upheaval which conceivably could have revolutionary effects upon the system. The death of any strong leader (Franklin Roosevelt, Sam Rayburn) disrupts the existing equilibrium within his political arena and tends to produce a dispersion of power. As long as this dispersion is kept within the Communist Party apparat, the struggle among the competing factions does not threaten the system as a whole. The results of the struggle could transform the system, however, if the contenders directly involved the other institutions of power in the battle and if the state bureaucracy, the police, or the Army were able to subordinate the Party apparatus.

The extent to which nonparty institutions are drawn into the struggle depends largely upon the institutional structure of power at the death of the dictator. Reduction of the Party apparat, such as happened in the last years of Stalin, to almost a position of equality with the police and state bureaucracies enhances the probability that the latter will be drawn into the struggle. Whether the struggle becomes a constitutional crisis thus depends on what happens before the death of the dictator. Although a dictator cannot select his successor, he can to a large extent determine the institutions which will play a role in making that selection. If the primacy of the apparat is preserved under the dictator, the succession struggle may be intense, but it is also likely to be brief and to be resolved largely within the apparat. Accordingly, in the post-Khrushchev struggle, the role of the police and the high state bureaucrats may be much less important than was their role after the death of Stalin.

The Soviet postvacancy succession struggle means, in effect, that there are *two* Soviet political systems: one in which power is concentrated in a single leader and one in which power is dispersed among several aspirants for leadership. The former is a dictatorship; the latter is an oligarchy. Between 1917 and 1963 the Soviet Union was ruled by a dictator for about thirty-five years and by an oligarchy for about eleven; in the decade after Stalin's death, five years were dominated by the power struggle within the oligarchy.

In the United States, there may be an informal dispersion of power during the last year's tenure of a "lame-duck" president. But the formal structure of power is never broken; the President still rules. In the Soviet Union the struggle to be dictator occurs within a dictatorless system at unpredictable intervals and for unpredictable duration. The succession struggle in the United States may play a key role in politics and policy-making (as it did in

1959 and 1960), but it does not completely absorb the political system as the struggle of 1953-1957 absorbed Soviet politics to the point even of drawing into it the various institutions of government. Equilibrium in the American system means divided power. Equilibrium in the Soviet system means concentrated power in a single leader. Concentrated power may be undesirable, but few things are worse for a political system than an *unstable* division of power. Yet unstable oligarchy is what appears in the Soviet Union when the dictator dies.

CHAPTER FOUR

Power and Policy

THE RELATION BETWEEN POWER AND POLICY

A KEY feature of any political system in the relation between the processes of policy-making and those of acquiring power. In general, it would seem that the correspondence between these processes is less in the United States than in Great Britain and considerably less in both than in the Soviet Union. In the Soviet system no real distinction exists between the processes. The predominance of the professional politician in the Soviet system means that the former process tends to be subordinated to the latter: that policies—foreign and domestic—are major weapons in the struggle for power within the system. Hence it is not surprising that while Americans have written much about their own policy-making processes they have written very little about those in the Soviet Union. The reason is not simply lack of information. It is rather that policy-making in the Soviet Union is not nearly as distinct and identifiable as it is in the United States. Instead, it is one aspect of the struggle for power and is absorbed into it.

In every political system power depends in part on the control of office, and in part on the control of other resources. At the national level in the United States, control of office is of primary importance. Some Presidents are, to be sure, stronger than others, but they all share an underlying pattern of power since one set of institutions specializes in filling offices, another in making policy. The election of candidates to public office is virtually monopolized by the political parties. The parties, however, have considerably less influence on policy. On the national level it is the policy-making institutions—the President, the Congress, the bureaucratic agencies, and various interest groups—that dominate the scene. But, at the same time, they play only a secondary role in electing national policymakers. In the Soviet Union, on the other hand, the Communist bureaucracy is concerned both with filling offices and with making policy.

In addition, the processes of office-seeking and of policy-making in the United States tend to be separate in time. Elections and hence campaigns are arbitrarily fixed by the calendar. At some point in the summer or early fall of even-numbered years the process of policy-making symbolically comes to a halt with the adjournment of Congress and that of office-seeking gets under way in earnest. Policy-making resumes the center of the stage with the assembly of the new Congress in January. In the Soviet Union the key policy-making bodies never adjourn and the campaign for office never ends. Policy proposals are forever directly involved in (even if not always motivated by) the struggle for or the consolidation of personal power.

In the United States the distinction between "campaigning" (that is, office-acquiring) and policy-making is a fairly clear one in the minds of political figures. The two influence each other but are nonetheless distinct. Policy proposals made during a campaign have a very different status from those made outside one. Like party platforms, they are recognized as directed primarily to producing votes—and hence office—rather than policy. Policy proposals during a campaign may or may not be taken seriously by the voters; they usually are not treated very seriously by other policy makers. As many American political scientists have regularly deplored, the relation between action in the policy-making process and in the electoral process is frequently very tenuous. Party affiliations, traditions, personalities, situational conditions (economic ups and downs, peace and war) only partially within the control of the policy-maker in office often play a decisive role in elections. The results of the elections, correspondingly, have some but not a decisive influence on policy-making.

In the United States, differences in policy proposals between two parties or candidates are likely to decrease during the struggle for office. The need to appeal to the same important blocs of voters compels each contestant to moderate his views. Differences which are highlighted in a campaign often concern dramatic but unimportant issues where one contestant has been maneuvered into taking an extreme or vulnerable position. Once a candidate is elected, his policies in office often have little relation to those which both he and his opponent advocated when they were campaigning for office. Important differences in policy often tend to reflect differences between the "ins" and the "outs" rather than between Republicans and Democrats, or between liberals and conservatives. Two parties or politicians are more alike in their policies when they are both campaigning for the same office. They differ more when one is securely in office and the other is definitely out.

In the Soviet Union, on the other hand, during a succession crisis or other serious struggle for power, each leadership faction appeals for support to different institutional groups; each attempts to endow its policy with ideological legitimacy; and each strives to demonstrate the opponents' "deviationism." Once one group emerges victorious, however, it not infrequently reverses itself and adopts the policies which had been advocated by its opponent (Stalin versus Trotsky in the 1920s; Khrushchev versus Malenkov in 1955). The power take-over is accompanied by a policy take-over. The reasons for this inhere in the system: having achieved power, in part with the support of one set of interests, the victorious leader and group minimize their dependence upon those interests by winning the support of others which originally had backed their opponent. The shift in viewpoint is part and parcel of the struggle for power, and policy consistency is the victim of that struggle. Competition for power in the Soviet Union tends to magnify policy differences between the contestants; in the United States it tends to moderate them. The conquest of power by one contestant in the United States tends to produce policies different from those which both contestants supported during the campaign but similar to those which probably would have been adopted by the other contestant if he had achieved office.

BARGAINING AND DECIDING

In the American system the focus of policy-making is the inter-action between the President and his Administration on the one hand, and the leadership of Congress, the governmental bureaucracies, industry, labor, and agriculture on the other. Here are the principal bargaining relationships. In the Soviet Union, in contrast, the relations between the central political leadership and these other elite groups is more one of control and manipulation than of bargaining.

The implications of these generalities can be easily seen in a comparison of the scope and limits of the power of the President of the United States and the First Secretary in the Soviet Union.

The power of each is limited, not only by the inherent limits on the time, energy, and intelligence of a single man, but also by the workings of the system. In the United States, however, the limits are concrete, visible, and institutionalized. The President controls a greater variety of resources relevant to the political struggle than any other participant. But all the other major participants also control autonomous resources which can be used in that struggle. Hence they are in a position to bargain, more or less effectively, with the President. The power of the President, as President Truman said, is the power to persuade, the power to mobilize the resources at his disposal and use them in such manner as most efficiently and economically to induce other participants to do what he would like them to do. The President starts with many advantages, but in specific cases the resources controlled by other participants may be exactly those which the President needs to achieve his goal. The diffusion of resources stimulates "arm's length" bargaining, explicit and implicit, between the President, on the one hand, and Cabinet officers, bureau chiefs, congressional figures, leaders of industry, labor, and agriculture, and interest-group spokesmen. The Presidency is a lonely office because its perspective and needs differ significantly from those of all other officials and institutional leaders. The latter have their own interests, constituencies, and resources which they can deploy to achieve their ends. They control votes in the electorate, strategic positions in Congress, talent, expertise, prestige, money, political machines, productive facilities, corporation hierarchies, university campuses, the media of communication. The President's job is to win their support for what he wants to do, and what he wants to do necessarily differs from what any one of them wants to do. The gap between his objectives and theirs may be relatively narrow (as would normally be the case with the members of the President's Cabinet), or it may be vast and almost unbridgeable, as is often the case with congressional committee chairmen and the leaders of interest groups. It is hardly surprising that bargaining has been identified as the pervasive means of making political decisions in the American system.[1]

In the Soviet Union, in contrast, the resources which can be employed in the political struggle are much more limited and dependent. Industrial authority, scientific knowledge, military expertise, national popularity, personal wealth, ethnic-group support, are neither autonomous nor deployable on the plains of politics in the same manner. The political system is monolithic not because few people participate in it, but because the resources which can be employed in the political struggle are very limited. The key resource is control of the party organization. The division of power in the United States stems from the variety of resources which can be employed in politics and the degrees of control which various groups have over them. In the Soviet Union, the division of power means the sharing of a single resource: control over the party organization. By its very nature this resource can be shared only at the top. Thus, insofar as there are limits on the power of the top leader in the Soviet Union, they stem from his sharing control of the apparat with a small number of colleagues. The rivals of the President are distant, institutionalized, formal, and diffused in the sense that they have different resources and goals. The rivals to the top leader in the Soviet Union are his colleagues on the Presidium; the rivalry is close, personal, informal, and focused in that both the goals of the contestants and the resources at their disposal are very similar. The principal limits on the power of the President are outside the White House; the principal limits on the power of the Soviet leader are inside the Kremlin.

This is not to say that the Soviet political leadership operates in a social vacuum, immune to social pressures. The very fact of Soviet economic development imposes a limit on the power of the leader. The combination of a vested interest in the efficiency of the Soviet economy and the sheer scale of integrating policy for more than 200,000 industrial enterprises, more than 100,000 construction projects, and more than 40,000 large-scale farms, all subject to central control, introduce limits of size and complexity which were not present during Stalin's earlier days and which are still not present in communist China. Thus the political leadership has to be responsive to the needs of an increasingly complex, and hence also differentiated, society.

In that society bargaining and deciding take place in a hierarchical context composed of three types of groups. At the very bottom are *amorphous social forces,* with certain inherent aspirations but little opportunity for direct articulation. They include the peasants, the workers, the "white-collar" workers, and technical intelligentsia, or what is sometimes called the new Soviet middle class. They exercise pressure which over a long period of time cannot be altogether ignored but which is not capable of direct political expression. A more assertive role is played by the *specific interest groups,* such as the intellectual community, the scientists, or certain minorities, such as the Jews. They have specific, narrow interests which, broadly speaking, are "defensive"—that is to say, they are concerned with a certain measure of autonomy and object to political interference or suppression. Groups whose scope of activity is directly dependent on the allocation of national resources and which are directly affected by any shift in the institutional distribution of power (for example, the 1957 economic and administrative reorganization) come the closest to participating in the policy-making process, as both claimants and advisers. The military, the heavy-industry and light-industry managers, the agricultural experts, and finally the state bureaucrats may be called the *policy groups.* They advocate to the political leadership certain courses of action; they have their own professional or specialized newspapers which, at times and subject to over-all Party control, can become important vehicles for expressing specific points of view; but for their own sake they are careful not to cross the shadowy line between advocacy and pressure. Many abrupt dismissals of high non-Party executives reflect the vagueness of that distinction as well as the Party apparat's sensitivity to any challenge of its policy-making monopoly.

Since the structure of Soviet society was determined by a revolution from above directed by the political elite, it does not permit the existence of autonomous groups whose overt participation in the political struggle is an accepted part of the political game. In that, the Soviet society differs from the American, where social and economic interests can: (1) control some policy-makers directly, through fiscal means or electoral representations; (2) manipulate some policy-makers, either by obstructing their goals and thus forcing them to compromise or by stimulating public opinion through the mass media, often directly owned by such interests; (3) enjoy access to policy-makers, either in the institutionalized form of lobbies or simply because the policy-makers themselves seek their support, given the cross-checking nature of the American political system. In the United States, public opinion helps to shape policy because it is crystallized by and into specific interest groups, which can exert direct and continual pressure on policy-makers.

In the Soviet Union such crystallization does not take place. Communication and organization are the first steps to political influence, and both are denied to public opinion. Presumably the apparatchiki strive to anticipate the reactions of groups, and in that sense the latter do share in the formation of policy. But, unlike those in the United States, the groups concerned lack the means for independent articulation of their desires and for autonomous existence. Indirect social pressure is therefore a better term than public opinion for describing the influence that society can bring to bear on the policy-making process. In the Soviet Union, only one group—the political professionals of the Party apparat— can be said to "control" the policy-makers, in the sense that the policy-makers are recruited from them and wield power through them. Manipulation, a more subtle process and hence more difficult to isolate, presumably takes place when there is political weakness at the top. At such times, certain groups, especially those with institutional cohesion such as the Army, may be in a position to obstruct or promote policies, but certainly only *within* the political system, without any external public appeal. Only with respect to access is there greater similarity to the American case: in the CPSU Central Committee and even in the Presidium there is a form of representation for the differentiated occupations and professions that exist in any complex society. This representation, however, lacks the capacity to translate its specific expertises, or even economic or social powers, into political power, because of the control over appointments and promotions (the *nomenklatura*) wielded by the Central Committee's Secretariat, and the permeation of such groups with leaders drawn from the Party apparat. In the Soviet Union economic or social power is not an autonomous political resource.*

---

* In this connection it is still too early to tell whether the division of the CPSU into two parallel hierarchies, industrial and agricultural, promulgated late in 1962, will have the effect of creating two distinct groups of Party officials, with specific interests and autonomous political resources. If that were to come about, it would represent a fundamental change in the political configuration of policy-making.

The roles of different groups in the Soviet policy-making process during a succession struggle necessarily differ from their roles when a single leader is clearly dominant. It almost goes without saying that during a struggle for power Soviet policy-makers become more responsive to the demands or aspirations of groups; for example, Khrushchev not only rallied certain policy groups to his side but through his agricultural and (after 1957) his housing policies he was acknowledging broader social pressures. If Party leaders are more or less evenly divided in the struggle for power, the support of key policy groups can significantly affect the outcome.

Nonetheless, the political weakness of nonpolitical groups is well documented by the history of the Soviet Army. Of all the possible groups outside the Party, the Army comes closest to having internal cohesion, defined membership, specific interests, and its own leadership. Yet not once has this group challenged the political monopoly of the Party, or even effectively protected its own personnel against physical or political destruction. The ease with which Khrushchev was able to purge Zhukov suggests that the military leadership will be careful not to cross the line between offering expert advice and actively intervening in the policy-making process. If that is the case with the armed forces, it is even more so with less cohesive groups. Furthermore, conflicts and antipathies among and within groups enhance the position of the apparat as the mediator, and it may be assumed that the Party consciously fans and exploits such divisions. Thus in 1962 the Party press published several attacks by the military leaders on intellectuals.[2]

It follows that the principal locus of significant political bargaining in the Soviet Union is among the central leaders within the Presidium and the Secretariat. Direct evidence on the nature of this process is virtually unobtainable. It is possible, however, to make some inferences about the probable nature of the process and to draw some contrasts with the more open institutionalized American bargaining relationships.

Whereas in the American system the political power of the participants in national politics is differentiated, institutionalized, and hence relatively stable, among the top Soviet leaders (and particularly the top officials on the Presidium and Secretariat) power depends upon clique loyalties, factional alliances, influence with the top leader, and organizational affiliations. All these are highly personal and subject to rapid change. The struggle for power goes on concurrently with the struggles over policy. Agreements reached one day may be invalidated the next as a result of drastic changes in the power relationships.

In the American system the principal bargainers usually have relatively little in common: they have different institutional loyalties, different careers, different political resources at their command. As a result, the values and goals of the participants in the American system may differ widely. Quite apart from the more specialized interests active in politics, the major bargainers may be spread across a political spectrum from Ross Barnett and Barry Goldwater to Martin Luther King and Walter Reuther. In the Soviet system, on the other hand, the principal bargainers are very much alike. They are all (or almost all) products of the Party apparat; they have shared many of the same experiences; a majority have probably been associated on the Presidium or Secretariat for many years. Hence there should be a high degree of consensus among them. Those policy differences which do exist, however, are likely to intensify because they become directly involved in the struggle for power.

In the United States the incentive to reach an agreement is often asymmetrical. The President may be eager to reach agreement on a policy and another group (for example, the leaders of a congressional committee) may have no interest whatsoever in coming to terms with the President. Institutional autonomy encourages political intractability. In the Soviet system, however, the members of the Presidium have a common interest in reaching agreement among themselves. This interest derives in part from the ideological emphasis on the monolithic unity of the party, but in part also from the natural pressures at work in a small cohesive group. Only one of the top bargainers in the American system has the Presidential perspective. All, or almost all, of the top bargainers in the Soviet system have "the Presidial perspective." Furthermore, in the Soviet Union, defeat often means the end of the participant's political career. This has the double effect of inhibiting disagreement and intensifying the contest once disagreement has broken out.

Decision-making bodies of the size and character of the Presidium usually act unanimously; formal votes become a rarity; controversial issues are avoided; informal procedures of consensus-building become the established means of resolving questions.[3] Fragmentary evidence suggests that these tendencies are not unknown in the Presidium.* American committees similar in size if not in power to the Presidium have developed a variety of means of reaching agreement among themselves. They eschew controversial issues, engage in compromise and logrolling, express policies in vague generalities representing the "lowest common denominator" of agreement, and base agreements on unrealistic assumptions. Presumably these techniques are not unknown to the Presidium, but they are probably employed there less frequently than in many American decision-making bodies. This could be due either to the superior power of the top leader to induce acquiescence from his colleagues or to the greater frequency of initial agreement among the leaders on policy questions. One major function of an American leader is to mediate between the claims of the "extremists" within his constituency and other claims in the body politic. Presumably the top Soviet leaders are not under the same pressures, and are freer to reach agreements among themselves.

In the American system an agreement is enforcible only when it is public. Bargaining takes place in a fishbowl. Victories and defeats, supine concessions and petty triumphs, are available for all to see. In some instances, such as presidential bargaining with Congress, score is kept of the proportion of legislative requests which the President has been able to induce Congress to approve. More often than not publicity compels the bargainers to increase their opening demands and to stick to their guns when the going gets tough. In contrast, bargaining in the Soviet system goes on

---

* "Meetings of the Presidium are regularly held at least once a week, and according to both Khrushchev and Mikoyan most decisions are unanimous. Mikoyan has further elaborated by stating that if a consensus were unobtainable, the Presidium would adjourn, sleep on the matter, and return for further discussion until unanimity was achieved." Vernon V. Aspaturian, "Soviet Foreign Policy," in Roy C. Macridis, ed., *Foreign Policy in World Politics* (Englewood Cliffs, N. J., 2nd ed., 1962), p. 159.

behind the closed doors of the Kremlin. It would appear that even those Soviet leaders just below the top are often in the dark as to the line-ups in the Presidium and Secretariat. Such secrecy has its benefits. The participants can bargain more easily and more quickly come to agreement without loss of face. Secrecy not only preserves the façade of unity but also facilitates the achievement of it.

Substantial agreement among its members is a prerequisite for the effective operation of a small decision-making body such as the CPSU Presidium. If agreement among the members becomes impossible, the only recourse is to change the membership. The United States President fights an unending cold war with his opponents. Within the Presidium peaceful coexistence is an organizational necessity. Not all changes in the membership of the Presidium are necessarily indications of insoluble differences, but certainly all insoluble differences must shortly produce changes in membership.

Agreement within the CPSU Presidium is also facilitated by the specialization of its members in various aspects of external or domestic policy. This means that on some issues certain members carry more weight than others, with the exception of the top leader himself, whose responsibility is to integrate all policies. For example, in the early 1960s matters of diplomacy and security would involve Brezhnev, Mikoyan, Kosygin; international communist affairs, Suslov, Kuusinen, Kozlov (until his illness), Mikoyan; domestic Party affairs, Kozlov, Brezhnev, Podgorny; industry, Kosygin, Polyansky, Grishin; agriculture, Voronov, Podgorny, Polyansky, Yefremov. Division of responsibility and specialization should contribute to a diminution of internal tensions and bickering. Significantly, however, it appears that critical and urgent policy decisions tend to be a responsibility of a still more select group within the Presidium. For example, during the Cuban crisis of 1962, when every decision involved matters of life and death, Khrushchev did not call in for consultation all the Presidium members present in Moscow, nor did he summon to Moscow those who were absent. He apparently consulted mainly with Mikoyan, Brezhnev, Kozlov, Suslov, and Kosygin, and it was this inner group which made the decision to withdraw the missiles.[4] The size of the group bore a striking resemblance to President

Kennedy's inner circle which formulated American policy during the crisis. The restriction of the decision-making to such a very small and cohesive group promotes both speed and agreement.

THE POLICY-MAKING PROCESS

While the essence of political leadership is the art of formulating and implementing policy, the character of the policy-making process differs from one political system to another. In the Soviet Union policy-making has two aspects. The political aspect pertains particularly to the relations among the top Party leaders, either in the struggle for power during a succession or in manipulation and/or accommodation during periods of stability. The operational aspect expresses the organizational vested interests of the ruling Party, including also its ideological purposes, in relation to the needs of the society as a whole. Thus while bureaucratic efficiency, economic productivity, and social well-being are high on the priority list of the Soviet policy-makers, they are not always the determining ends of policy-making. During periods of stability, operational considerations dominate; in crises, political ones do. In the United States, the pluralism of autonomous economic interests and the pluralism of political institutions participating in the policy-making process fuzzes the line between the operational and the political aspects of the process.

For purposes of analysis, the policy-making process can be divided into four phases. *Initiation* embodies the first response to a new need or problem and the first formulation of a proposal to deal with it. *Persuasion* involves efforts to build up support for the proposal among a larger number of groups. In this phase opposition develops, alternatives and amendments are suggested, and the original proposal is modified so as to win broader support. In the *decision* phase the modified proposal is either approved or vetoed by those who have the effective and legitimate authority to do so within the political system. The number of people who must approve the proposal so that it becomes "policy" or who can prevent it from becoming policy varies greatly from one political system to another and within any system often from one issue to another. Finally, in the *execution* phase, the policy which has now been blessed with legitimacy is presumably carried out. In actual fact, however, the policy-making process continues, and those groups which execute policy are able to remake it. In some instances they have to change it significantly to achieve the principal goals of the policy-deciders. In other instances, they may change it significantly to frustrate those goals.⁵ This phase hence is often characterized by adaptation or distortion.

The processes of policy-making in the United States and the Soviet Union can be analyzed in terms of these phases. Similar groups (for example, military chiefs or party leaders) do not necessarily play similar roles in the processes in the two systems. Nor do the roles of groups in either system necessarily remain constant over a period of time. The processes change with changes in the issues of policy and the structure of power. In the American system, secular changes during this century have seen an increasing role for executive agencies in the initiation, persuasion, decision, and execution of military policy. Similarly, in the Soviet Union the very fact of the growth of Soviet industrial and military power enhanced the policy importance of managerial and military groups.

Initiation: Bubble Up and Trickle Down. Identifying precisely the sources of policy is a difficult task for the scholar in almost any political system. It is out of the question for the student of Soviet policy-making. It is possible, however, to attempt some comparative generalizations about the extent to which the top political leadership initiates policy, and the extent to which private groups, social forces, and lower-ranking governmental agencies share in initiating. A distinctive feature in the United States appears to be the extent to which the top political leadership does *not* play a major role in the generation of specific policy proposals. It is now a commonplace that, though Congress may approve, veto, amend, or postpone legislation, it rarely originates it. Much the same is true of the top leadership in the executive branch: the initiating role of the "Indians" or middle-level officials has become proverbial in Washington. A Cabinet officer, such as Defense Secretary Robert S. McNamara, who insists on playing an initiating role, is viewed as a strange phenomenon. In general, in the American system, initiation is a less important function for the top political leader than either decision or persuasion. To be sure, the position of the top leader gives him the "strategic opportunity" to initiate policy, but the option is rarely exercised.⁶ The

idea that " 'policy' originates at the top and is passed down," Dean
Acheson has said, is a misleading bit of folklore. It should be
"clear to anyone with experience in government," he added, that
"the springs of policy bubble up; they do not trickle down." [7]

This may well be clearer, however, to those with experience in
American government than to those experienced in other governments. In NATO headquarters, for instance, American and continental styles of policy-making apparently differed markedly.* From
what we know about the Soviet process, it would seem that their
top leaders play an active role in policy generation. Undoubtedly
ideas and proposals do drift up the party and governmental hierarchies. But the initiative in formulating most important policy
measures probably rests with the Central Committee Secretaries
and the departments of the central apparat. Each top leader must
also have his own brain trust and personal staff which feeds ideas
to him. Certainly the first formal proposal of a new policy is usually
made by one of the top leaders. Policy may be initiated by an
informal memorandum (*zapiska*) circulated by the First Secretary
among his Presidium colleagues. Khrushchev, for instance, revealed in April 1963 that after visiting a number of major enterprises of the chemical industry he drafted a *zapiska* "concerning
the further acceleration of the development of the chemical industry." This was subsequently discussed by the Presidium, and
in December a Central Committee Plenum adopted a formal decision to launch a major development drive in the chemical industry.

---

* American staff officers felt that "French and other European officers
were too reluctant to conclude their studies with firm and precise
proposals for action . . . and too quick to go to their superiors for
advice on policy premises or on the way in which the problem should
be formulated." French officers, on the other hand, regarded the
American "bubble-up" procedure as rather peculiar. "Here one rarely
receives higher guidance regarding the position to adopt," one French
officer warned his successor. "Ideas do not circulate from top to
bottom but from bottom to top." Laurence I. Radway, "Military Behavior in International Organization—NATO's Defense College," in
Samuel P. Huntington, ed., *Changing Patterns of Military Politics*
(New York, 1962), p. 109. Administratively speaking, the French
staff officers apparently would be more at home at Warsaw Pact headquarters than in American-shaped SHAPE.

In the post-Stalin period, policy-making on key issues in agriculture, industry, education, and other fields often followed similar patterns. Typically, the policy-making phase was preceded by a fairly prolonged period of difficulties and deficiencies, during which the problem to be dealt with became increasingly worse. During this period some public discussion might take place with respect to the problem and also some limited ad-hoc remedies might be initiated by the Party leadership. Much depends, however, on the political circumstances involved. During periods of stability there is an orderly development of the problem, with a certain measure of participation from below in the formulation of the new policy. During a succession struggle, the initiatives tend to come from above, abruptly, with an element of surprise, designed in part to put one's rivals on the defensive.

The problems of bureaucracy, waste, ministerial autarchy, overcentralization, and absence of machinery for regional planning plagued Soviet industry for many years prior to the industrial reorganization of 1957. But while the reorganization "followed upon a period, dating roughly from Stalin's death, of sustained and critical public discussion of shortcomings in the planning and direction of industry and their ill effects on industry's performance and its structural, locational, and technological evolution," [8] Khrushchev's initiative to that end in February 1957 involved a sudden attempt to reverse remedies adopted only a few months earlier, in December 1956. At that time, the State Economic Commission (*Gosekonomkomissiia*) was endowed with new powers and staffed almost entirely with professional economic administrators; irrespective of its economic merits, this inherently weakened the relative position of the First Secretary. Similarly, his February attack on "ministerialism" and overcentralization, apart from its actual administrative justification, was bound to strengthen the political position of the head of the Party, since the Party would remain the only centralized political institution. Presumably both political and operational motives were also involved in Molotov's objections to the scheme, submitted by him in writing to members of the Presidium at three a.m. on the morning of the Central Committee session to which Khrushchev made his proposal, and in Malenkov's and Kaganovich's charges that the proposal would lead to anarchy.[9]

This first prolonged phase of "the development of the problem" thus ended with Khrushchev's open denunciation of the alleged evils and his proposals for drastic decentralization. The new policy was gestating but the struggle was far from over. At stake now was the power of the First Secretary. It is useful to compare this to the circumstances involved in the educational reform, launched by Khrushchev a year later, when his power had been more firmly consolidated. As in the case of the economy, from 1953 on the crisis in Soviet education steadily worsened as the ten-year schools turned out increasing numbers of graduates who were not prepared for productive labor and for whom there was no room in the higher educational institutions. The Party press repeatedly began to suggest that manual labor was as good as intellectual activity and the 20th Party Congress stressed the importance of technical training. Finally, in April 1958 Khrushchev openly criticized the "existing separation of the school from life." As in the case with his February 1957 speech on economic administration, his criticism suggested possible remedies in only the vaguest terms, but in the case of the educational reform there was no sudden reversal of a recently instituted policy, nor were there any high political stakes. Khrushchev's speech, furthermore, was an outgrowth of earlier views.

Each speech, nonetheless, marked the beginning of the process of policy initiation. Each served notice on Soviet society that major overhauls were under consideration, and each stimulated a small amount of public debate concerning the existing evils and the ways in which they might be remedied. In each case, also, after an interval, the top leadership came forward with a formal policy proposal. The plans for industrial reorganization were embodied in Khrushchev's theses of March 30, 1957. The outlines of the educational reform were advanced in Khrushchev's memorandum of September 21, 1958, and in the theses jointly proposed by the Central Committee and the Council of Ministers on November 17, 1958. In this case Khrushchev apparently consulted with the regional Party secretaries and other officials about their dissatisfaction with the educational system. He then formulated his proposals for dealing with them. "The top decision-making leadership played the initiating role in the education reform, after having secured from the Party apparatus, as well as from government

agencies, information concerning the problems of education." [10]
In both instances the policy proposals of the top leaders embodied
the basic ideas of the reforms which were eventually adopted. The
pattern was thus: (1) several years of growing difficulties and discontent during which the specific groups directly involved presumably tried to make their complaints heard; (2) a formal denunciation of current evils by a top Party leader or leadership, with
the timing and manner much influenced by the specific power
relations within that leadership; (3) an interval of several weeks
or months during which presumably the top leadership formulated and agreed to its basic proposals for dealing with the evils;
and (4) the official announcement of these proposals in the form
of a "memorandum" or "theses" from a top leader or top Party
body. Clearly, in these and similar cases, policy initiation is the
prerogative of the top leadership.

The exception to this pattern involves the relatively rare cases
when the leader's initiative has been nipped in the bud, or at least
delayed, by the combined opposition of most of the other top
leaders and the most important policy groups in the country or
simply by his own hesitations and ambivalence. Even as late as
the mid-thirties Stalin failed to gain the support of his colleagues
for his proposal to arrest and try his former rivals. Obviously, the
implications of this initiative were clear to the other Politburo
members, the Party apparat, and the top officials of other bodies.
Similarly, in 1961 Khrushchev did not succeed in reducing relatively the resources committed to heavy industry; a number of
Presidium members, as well as the Army and the heavy-industry
spokesmen were against it. Both leaders, however, were later able
to return to their schemes.

The reasons behind the different patterns of leadership in policy
initiation must involve differences between the United States
on the one hand, and the Soviet Union and western Europe on
the other. Four hypotheses suggest themselves.

First, society and politics in America are more egalitarian in
character than those in Russia and Europe. This difference has
been noted by European observers since Tocqueville. Presumably
it affects policy-making even in hierarchical organizations. American social scientists have stressed the two-way flow of authority
and influence in American governmental institutions.[11] One form

which this egalitarianism may take is the limitation of the top
leadership primarily to the decision function and domination of
policy initiatives by lower-ranking groups in the power structure.
In this way, a separation of functions contributes to a balance of
power between various administrative levels.

A second explanation might derive from the legalistic flavor of
American politics and the dominant role which lawyers play in
both legislative and executive policy-making. This too distinguishes the American scene from Russia and western Europe. The
"bubble-up" concept of policy generation implies an essentially
judicial role for the political leader. Acheson, indeed, explicitly
stressed what he termed "the judicial element in the function of
headship." The chief of a government department, he argued,
"must from time to time familiarize himself with the whole record;
he must consider opposing views, put forward as ably as possible.
He must examine proponents vigorously and convince them that
he knows the record. . . ." These are lawyers' words, and the
prominent role of lawyers in American politics may be responsible
for the prevalence of this judicial definition of the role of the
political leader. Certainly, this concept describes the way in which
many congressmen define their job: viewing themselves as essentially judges or arbitrators who in semi-judicial hearings listen to
the testimony of all sides and then attempt to formulate an equitable resolution of differences.

A third and related explanation may be differing attitudes *toward*
government and political leaders. If the principal end of government is thought to be response to the felt needs of society, obviously policy proposals should originate with groups in society
rather than with political leaders. The policy-initiation role of the
leaders should be restricted not only vis-à-vis bureaucratic subordinates in the name of egalitarianism but also vis-à-vis private
groups in the name of limited government. Generation of policy
proposals by the political leaders presumably would mean the
subordination of policy to power rather than vice versa. Certainly
Soviet political leaders, particularly during the succession struggle
of 1953-1957, did initiate policies as tactical maneuvers to advance their own positions. The policy-generating role of the top
political leadership in America thus may be limited not only because the leadership is top but also because it is political. The

traditions of continental Europe and of both czarist and Soviet Russia, on the other hand, certainly accord top governmental leadership a much more important role in generating policy proposals.

The fourth follows from the preceding and involves differing attitudes *of* government and political leaders. A leadership imbued with over-all goals derived from ideologically affected long-term perspectives has inherently a different conception of its role from that of a leadership that is guided by a tradition of pragmatic day-to-day reaction to events seen basically as part of a spontaneously unfolding reality. In the former case, to shape reality initiative must be monopolized by the leaders; in the latter case, initiative can impose itself on the leaders.

Persuasion: Consensus-Building and Mobilization. Persuasion is the development of support for a policy proposal beyond its original initiators. Generally it is necessary to obtain the support of a much larger number of groups in the United States than in the Soviet Union. As a result, there are significant differences in the processes of persuasion in the two systems. Persuasion in the United States can perhaps best be described as "consensus-building." [12] It is usually a competitive process between conflicting coalitions of interests, and many groups and institutions share in it. Persuasion, moreover, usually precedes decision. In the Soviet Union, on the other hand, persuasion can best be described as the "mobilization" of support. It is monopolized by the party, and it normally occurs not before but after the decision phase.

In the American system persuasion differs in domestic policy and in foreign policy. Important new domestic policies usually involve the passage of a bill through Congress and its approval by the President. The lead in the early stages of persuasion is taken by the leaders of the private group or governmental agency which has generated the policy proposal. They approach other groups and agencies who may have similar interests. They explore ideas with sympathetic senators and congressmen, and endeavor to enlist an active and committed core of congressmen, preferably situated in the relevant congressional committee. Throughout this process the broadening of the base of support for the proposal is accompanied by the modification of its contents as objections are met and concessions made. If the initiators of the proposal are astute they leave considerable leeway in their original proposal so that they can purchase the support of other groups without sacrificing their primary objectives. Frequently, and particularly with respect to major new policies, the supporters may organize an ad-hoc coordinating committee made up of representatives of continuing interest groups (labor, business, farm, veterans, and so on) who share a common interest in that particular piece of legislation.

While the proponents of the proposal are thus at work on a variety of fronts, the opposition is also usually stirring. Their job is easier. They have on their side not only inertia but also the structure of the legislative process. The proponents of the policy have to mobilize sufficient support to get their proposal past a number of possible "veto points." The opponents only have to hold the line at one of these. Like the defending forces in a military campaign they can concentrate their strength where the lay of the land is most favorable. Inevitably, both proponents and opponents are drawn into the competitive mobilization of political allies and into a struggle to shift the locus of decision to the most favorable arena. This latter involves questions of both timing—when to bring the issue to the fore—and institutional strategy—in which house of Congress, for instance, to bring it up first.

As the process of consensus-building broadens, the leadership in recommendation shifts to individuals and groups of greater prestige and authority. If the proponents are successful, key committee chairmen or other influential figures take the lead in recommending it within the legislature. Outside Congress, respected public figures—ex-Presidents, ex-generals, elder statesmen—are brought forward to appeal to wider and wider publics. From the executive branch, the Cabinet official primarily concerned usually takes over as the principal campaign manager for the proposal. At some point, the President himself comes to play an active role in the process of persuasion, usually toward the end rather than at the beginning of the process. Usually also, his hand is first felt behind the scenes—in the private persuasion, for instance, of other key figures—before it is shown openly. In many cases, the degree of presidential support determines the fate of the measure in Congress. Congress at times passes bills which the President does not want, but it rarely passes a major bill which he does want unless he demonstrates his concern by actively deploying and employing the prestige, powers, and persuasions of his office on behalf of the measure.

With respect to foreign-policy measures the process of persuasion is somewhat different. Here presumably the proposal is generated somewhere in the governmental bureaucracy. It is advanced within its originating department and circulated for comments and endorsement to other interested agencies. It may be taken up through the National Security Council or other interdepartmental committees, functioning, in effect, as small-scale executive legislatures. The leadership in recommendation continues to rest primarily with the officials of the originating department and eventually with the head of it. If serious opposition develops within the executive branch, it is up to those officials to mobilize the support necessary to persuade the President. At times, this search for support leads them outside the executive branch to Congress, sympathetic journalists, outside consultants, and what Paul Nitze has called "distinguished citizens' committees." On some issues of foreign and military policy, the presidential decision will be final. On other issues formal congressional approval is required, and the recommendation process here resembles the later stages in the process for domestic policy. On foreign-policy measures recommended to Congress, however, the President and his top subordinates are normally active at a much earlier stage in the process than they are on domestic issues. It is often in the President's interest to allow other groups to take the initiative in recommending a domestic measure to Congress. On foreign-policy measures, there are few other groups, and he must play an active role from the start in pushing the legislation through Congress.

In the Soviet Union the character of the persuasion phase is shaped by the close connection between policy initiation and policy decision. Most important policy proposals originate with the top leadership. This leadership also possesses the power of decision. Hence the step from generation to decision can be a very short one, certainly much shorter than it usually is in the United States. A Presidium member or Central Committee Secretary who advances a policy proposal has to win the support of only a dozen other men to secure its approval. In some cases he may have to win the support of only one other man. Where policies affect key policy groups—the military, economic planners, the agricultural bureaucracy—presumably the leaders of these groups are also consulted. In most instances, however, the institutional and other divisions which exist among the leaders of any particular policy group preclude their maintaining a united front against a proposal favored by the dominant faction in the top Party leadership. Thus, for much, if not most, of Soviet policy—and certainly for all foreign and military policy—only the leaders and those at the peaks of the relevant government bureaucracies become involved in the persuasion phase.

On some major issues, however, persuasion encompasses a much wider range of groups. Once the basic principles of a policy have been agreed upon, an intensive effort may be made to mobilize the interest and support of other groups outside the top leadership. The "theses" promulgated by the leaders may be discussed extensively in the press and in meetings throughout the country. In some instances these discussions (as with the 1961 discussion of the CPSU's draft program) may produce only minor modifications in detail. In other instances, however, they may produce some fairly significant changes. During the Stalinist period such discussions and mobilization efforts were relatively rare. Fear and coercion rather than persuasion made the policies adopted by the top leadership acceptable to other groups. Since Stalin's death, however, the leadership has found it desirable to stimulate, under appropriate conditions, discussion of its policy decisions and thereby to persuade the groups affected to accept them. Thereby, it can also discover where the shoe pinches and modify its policy or inaugurate new policies accordingly.

Debates of this sort occurred in connection with the pensions law of 1956, the educational reform and the abolition of the Machine Tractor Stations in 1958, and the Party program of 1961. In these cases, the predominant issues were operational, not power-political. The public debate over the educational reforms lasted about six weeks (November 17 to December 25, 1958). Representatives of many more or less formally organized specific interest groups participated: the Academy of Pedagogical Sciences, the Administration of Labor Reserves, secondary school administrators and principals, university officials, spokesmen for nationality groups (interested in preserving instruction in their language). The measure approved by the Supreme Soviet differed in many important respects from the proposals originally advanced by Khrushchev and the Central Committee. The idea of special schools for gifted children was dropped; the full-time secondary day schools were reinstated; the absolute requirement of full-time work before entering a higher educational institution was changed to "priority" for those with full-time work. All-in-all, important concessions were made to the academic experts, intelligentsia, and educational administrators who had urged the importance of academic education against that of productive labor.[13]

It is revealing to contrast the foregoing with the much more politically charged debate on the industrial reorganization proposed by Khrushchev in February 1957 and opposed by a Presidium group that subsequently attempted the unsuccessful "anti-Party" coup against Khrushchev in June 1957. Between the publication of Khrushchev's theses on March 30, 1957, and the approval by the Supreme Soviet on May 9 an extensive debate took place. Khrushchev and his supporters actively campaigned for the proposal, claiming that it would "strengthen the Leninist principle of democratic centralism" and taking oblique swipes at Molotov by suggesting that his Ministry of State Control must be "radically reconstructed." The opponents of the reform in the top leadership, who not accidentally were also Khrushchev's rivals —notably Molotov, Kaganovich, Bulganin, and the two top Party leaders specializing in economic affairs, Pervukhin and Saburov (both of whom had been active in adopting the December 1956 measures)—were ostentatiously silent. Nonetheless, *Pravda* and *Izvestia* published more than eight hundred letters commenting on the proposed reform, suggesting various adjustments. Some demanded even more decentralization and workers' control; some factory managers demanded more authority. In the process of developing support, Khrushchev made several significant changes. In order to win the approval of some key policy groups, the Ministry of Defense Industry, the Ministry of Aviation Industry, and six other important industrial ministries were exempted from the decentralization plan. Other groups were not as successful. Ten all-union ministries and fifteen union-republican ministries

the Soviet Union, these outspoken attacks in the United States can produce modifications of policy in practice. They certainly shape the Administration's anticipations of the reactions to its next decision in the same area and thereby also presumably affect the content of that decision. Anticipated reaction is thus a restraint in both the British and American cases; it is of much less significance in the Soviet Union, except during succession struggles.

Decision: Approval and Veto. In every political system there are formal loci of authoritative decision. In the Soviet Union the one crucial locus is the central apparat of the Party. By generating a policy proposal the Party leadership also approves and legitimizes it. On some issues this approval may be followed by considerable public debate of particular aspects of the proposal. At the close of this public debate the proposal, with some modifications, is then approved and legitimized again by the national legislature. This action by the Supreme Soviet, however, is only the culminating formal ratification of the policy-making process which has preceded it. By the time the Supreme Soviet considers a proposal all the key decisions have been made. Indeed, the two or three days' debate within the Supreme Soviet on such measures as industrial reorganization and education reform was stylized and empty compared to the relatively vigorous six weeks of public debate which had gone before. The effective decisions on what modifications to make in the original proposal as a result of the public debate were made by the Party leadership, not by the legislature.

In the American political system, decision is usually the result of consensus-building. The latter is the indispensable prerequisite to the former. The power of decision is dispersed among many different institutions in the United States. The diffusion of the power of decision compensates for the diffusion of the power to generate policy proposals. Ease of proposal is counterbalanced by ease of veto. In the American policy process, many are called but few are chosen. In the Soviet Union, few are called but all are chosen.

The mechanisms of decision reflect the sources of legitimacy. In the Soviet Union, the "correct" policy is that which is supported by the ideology. Authority to decide whether policy is in accord with ideology is monopolized by the central Party leadership. In the United States, on the other hand, policy is, in general, legitimate if it is widely approved—that is, if it rests on popular consent. That consent, however, can come only from the acquiescence of a number of governmental institutions reflecting various publics and interests. The road leads from a theory of popular government through the mechanism of multiple approvals to the harsh fact of minority veto. In addition, the process of decision is usually a continuing one through time. Approval takes place by accretion. In one sense, no single decision is ever final, and approval in one arena can be countered by disapproval in another. In the Soviet Union the decision phase—the authoritative legitimization of a proposal—is brief and unitary. In the United States it is time-consuming and segmented.

This does not mean that policy proposals in the Soviet Union do not require the approval of a number of people. But those who must approve are usually all part of a single, fairly small institutional complex: the Central Committee apparat. A policy proposal in any particular area of policy (e.g., agriculture, heavy industry, education) presumably benefits in the extent to which it receives, in reverse order of importance, the approval of: (1) the top officials of the government agency primarily concerned with the area; (2) the officials in the Central Committee department most directly concerned; (3) the Central Committee Secretary with primary responsibility for the area; (4) the Presidium member or members (if different from number 3) specializing in the area; (5) a majority of the Presidium; and (6) the top leader (Stalin, Khrushchev), if there is one. Depending upon the structure of power at the very top of the Soviet system, one or more of these six groups may be able to exercise a veto. By definition, the top leader always can. So also can a majority of the Presidium, although a political crisis would ensue if the top leader and a Presidium majority were irreconcilably opposed on an important issue. Vigorous disagreement with a policy proposal by any one of numbers 1 through 4, on the other hand, would presumably be handled by removing the dissenting official or officials. Obviously, a Presidium majority or top leader could not do this on every issue where a Cabinet minister or Central Committee secretary dissented. And hence on some measures undoubtedly the indi-

of an aggravating international situation. This was also the case with the Soviet resumption of nuclear tests in September 1961. In addition, stimuli or triggers may also occur within the political system. Policy proposals and policy-making are closely related to the struggle for power. Hence, changes in the distribution of power are much more likely to stimulate policy proposals and decisions than they are in the United States. Zigzags in policy are often closely correlated with the changing fortunes of Party hierarchs. The whole strange pattern of the de-Stalinization campaign illustrates this: from its abrupt initiation in February 1956, through the subsequent partial "restoration" of Stalin in December 1956, through new attacks at the 21st and 22nd Party Congresses, and again a limited "rehabilitation" in late winter 1963. In each instance, new policies followed but in each the trigger was a shift in the internal power of the leader.

Execution: Amendment and Sabotage. Those who execute policy can also make it. They can do so by interpreting the words of the top decision-makers, by applying those words to unanticipated conditions, and by choosing which goals of the policy deciders will receive primary emphasis and which of conflicting goals will be given preference. The executors thus can amend policy to further the goals of the policy-makers, or can sabotage policy to frustrate them. The post-decision struggle over policy may be less visible than that which precedes decision, but it is no less real. In the long run, it is often more important.

In the American political system the execution phase in policy-making is delimited in time and in institutional responsibility. Formal approval of a policy proposal by President and Congress marks the beginning of the process of execution. The policy is passed into the hands of the appropriate administrators. Of crucial importance here is the role which these administrators have played in shaping the policy in the recommendation phase. If a new administrative agency is created to execute the new policy, it will probably be staffed initially by individuals who were its more ardent proponents before decision. Very possibly the attitudes of the administrators will more closely resemble those of the original generators of the proposal than they will the more moderate views of the coalition eventually responsible for its approval. At the other extreme, a policy may be assigned for execution to an existing agency which is already heavily committed to competing or even contradictory purposes. In this case the policy in execution may be even further removed from the goals of the generators than the one which was formally approved. Usually little leeway exists as to who must approve a proposal in order to give it authoritative sanction. There is greater leeway, however, as to who gets the responsibility for its execution.

In the Soviet Union initiation and decision are closely linked. So also are persuasion and execution. These functions are not assigned to different, specialized institutions in the same degree to which they are in the United States. Once a policy is approved in the United States the policy-deciding agencies often lose control over it. An act passed by Congress can be at the mercy of its administrators and the courts. A decade may pass before the courts have delimited its scope, defined its content, and removed all doubts concerning its constitutionality. The members of the relevant congressional committee and of the appropriations subcommittees can continue to play a major role in its execution, but groups not represented on these bodies can exercise little leverage. So also, the President can wield direct control over the execution of only a few policies at a time. Administrative agencies often administer a policy in their own way in the face of presidential indifference and even, at times, of presidential opposition. In the Soviet Union, on the other hand, the pressure on the executors to adapt or distort policy is greater, but so also are the means by which the policy deciders can limit the executors' independent action. The executors of policies are normally government agencies. The Party apparat, however, functions both as a generator of policy and as a supervisor of its execution. The apparat is continually available to the Party chiefs to check up on the execution of policy, to spur on government administrators, to stimulate one hierarchy through the competition of another. At times, policies may also, as in the case of the virginlands campaign of 1954, be directly administered through Party agencies as well as through governmental bureaus. Checking up on the execution of policy, insuring the proper "follow through" on top decisions, is a perennial problem in the American executive branch. American policy-deciders have tried to devise means (such as the legislative veto) to increase their control over the execution of policy. The Soviet system attempts to solve this problem by making the generator of policy the supervisor of its execution.

The Soviet policy-maker, however, faces a problem of scale that is qualitatively different from that faced by his American counterpart. The fact that all significant aspects of economic and social life in the Soviet Union are state-controlled creates a state bureaucracy with enormous problems of coordination. Soviet spokesmen themselves admit that the Soviet bureaucracy suffers from chronic inefficiency, poor organization, overplanning, and overstaffing. Conflicting instructions from the top, frequent plan changes (in one oblast the construction plan for 1962 was altered five hundred times! [16]), all affect the execution of policy. That is why so much effort is perennially put into the organization of effective control machinery, on both state and Party levels. The frequent changes in that organization suggest that the problem is far from being resolved.

Any policy involves both the definition of goals and the allocation of resources. The extent to which the top-level deciders of policy attempt to do either of these, however, may vary considerably. In general, where resources are scarce, leaders put more emphasis upon the definition of goals. The executors of policy then have to take responsibility for securing the resources to achieve those goals. Thus, in the Soviet Union economic production targets are set by the top agencies of the Party and government. Theoretically, resources are also allocated by these agencies. But to achieve the goals of the economic plan individual factory administrators often may have to engage in semilegitimate or illegitimate practices. In a more affluent system such as the United States, top leadership decisions often take the form of an allocation of resources, and the definition of goals is more widely shared with policy-executing agencies than it is in the Soviet Union. In defining goals these agencies also generate new policy proposals which may eventually "bubble up" and be given official sanction.

The gap between the goals defined in Soviet policies and the resources which are allocated to achieve them gives rise to the phenomenon of "family circles." Local officials have a common interest in moderating goals, procuring resources, and collaborating with one another across governmental and party lines. The attempt to maintain a system of checks and balances in the execution of policy has the same effect in the Soviet system as in the formation of policy in the United States. Individuals and groups in theoretically competitive organizations get together to agree on the rules of peaceful coexistence. In the United States, bureaucrats, congressmen, and interest-group representatives collaborate to minimize the influence of the Administration and various outside groups in the policy-making process. In the Soviet system, lower-ranking bureaucrats in party and government collaborate to protect themselves against the spurs and prods of their superiors. From the communist viewpoint, the "family circles" which reduce competition and promote compromise in the execution of policy are just as evil as the "factions" which promote competition and disrupt harmony in the higher-level formulation of it. But they often have to be tolerated, since they may contribute to the execution of policy. With many goals set in an unrealistic manner at the top these informal circles stimulate a more effective distribution of limited resources on the working level. As a result, most prosecutions take place only when such circles fail in this informal function.

In the American system, the executors of a policy can expect to get considerable support from those groups primarily responsible for its official sanction during the first few years after it has been approved. After a while, however, the coalition of interests originally responsible for the policy dissolves. The number of groups directly concerned with it declines. The policy arena may come to be dominated by groups whose objectives differ considerably from those of the coalition responsible for the policy. The executive agency, as it is said, has "to come to terms" with the congressional committee responsible for its budget or the industry with which it has regular contact. This shift in objectives is particularly noticeable in the case of policies affecting powerful economic interests and administered by independent regulatory commissions. Gradually the goals of the commissions come to resemble those of the groups which they were created to regulate. In the Soviet Union, on the other hand, the Central Committee apparat always remains an important element in the constituency of an executive agency. While the pressures to modify a policy may be more diverse and immediate, the pressures to uphold its original conception are also more concrete and permanent.

THE DIMENSIONS OF POLICY-MAKING

Three key questions are relevant to the analysis of any policy-making process. To what extent does the process produce clear-cut alternatives and facilitate choice between them? To what extent does the process facilitate the integration of policies in different areas of subject matter? To what extent does the process facilitate major innovations in policy?

These questions, it should be noted, are analytical, not evaluative. Analysis of a policy-making process may show that it fudges policy alternatives and obstructs major innovations. Whether these characteristics are good or bad, however, depends on whether one favors clear-cut choices and radical changes. An ardent reformer presumably would do just this; a defender of the status quo might well prefer very different characteristics.

Selection. For many years American scholars have debated how policy *ought* to be made. Should grand alternatives be formulated in sweeping, clear-cut fashion, and a decisive choice made between them? Or should policy develop through a series of small-scale adjustments to immediate needs? One scholar argues eloquently for "The Necessity for Choice"; another persuasively defends "The Science of 'Muddling Through.' " [17] However much they may disagree over how policy should be made, however, almost all agree on how it actually is made in the United States. Policy is the product of muddling through: it is the result of incremental, ad-hoc decisions, in which issues and values, ends and means are hopelessly confused. As a result, it lacks coherence, consistency, and rationality.

A pervasive characteristic of the American political system is the extent to which it frustrates choice between well-defined policy alternatives. American political parties are heterogeneous coalitions of interest groups and viewpoints. Both contain liberals and conservatives, isolationists and internationalists. Party heterogeneity also contributes to the fudging of issues in Congress. The process of recommendation in the national legislature results in moderation. Congressional procedures facilitate amendment in committee and on the floor. At times a bill may be so amended that its original proponents turn against it. The bill which emerges from Congress is usually a compound of many viewpoints and influences woven together through compromise and logrolling. Within the executive branch policy issues similarly tend to be compromised and obscured. Just as the compromise and fudging of issues in elections and in Congress stimulated demands for party responsibility and congressional reorganization, so also the same phenomena in the executive branch stimulated demands for drastic reforms there: abolition of committees, stronger presidential leadership, presentation of policy alternatives at the top levels of government.

Thus, in the American system, the structure of the parties often denies the voters a clear-cut choice in the electoral process; the complex and segmented character of congressional procedures often denies the congressmen a clear-cut choice in the legislative process; and the pressures for agreement among subordinate officials deny the President a clear-cut choice in the executive formulation of policy. The alternatives open to a policy-maker usually involve only marginal differences. The policy-maker himself, moreover, attempts to limit the consequences of his own choice; he tries to make the minimal choice so as to enhance his future freedom of action; he wants "to decide without actually choosing." [18] The groups backing the policy may have opposing goals; agreement on means often exists without agreement on ends. The consensus underlying any one policy, moreover, usually differs from that underlying other policies. Majorities are transient. Enemies on one issue are allies on the next. The emphasis is on the short-run perspective, the pragmatic compromise. The grand choices are made more by accretion than by selection.

These characteristics of policy-making in American national government are also found in state and local governments, business corporations, and other institutions. They may well inhere in any complex policy-making process. The question here is: To what extent do they exist in the Soviet Union? If incremental, ad-hoc, short-range policy-making also prevails there, this would be fairly conclusive evidence that it is a universal characteristic of complex decision-making structures. If it is much less prevalent in the Soviet system, this would suggest that the ad-hoc method is typical of a particular type of political culture. On the whole, it can probably be said that Soviet history offers more examples of clear-cut selection, both domestically and in foreign policy. Both the Stalin period and the post-Stalin phase have been punctuated by dramatic new programs and reforms. The collectivization, the Stalin-Hitler pact, the Party-state reorganization of 1962, and the "peaceful coexistence" doctrine all involved sharp turns. It is, however, likely that gradually, with the Soviet Union becoming a more developed society, it will become more difficult for the leaders to change course abruptly, at least in domestic affairs, without causing major economic and social dislocations. While the lack of resources has in some important areas forced a piecemeal approach (this has been most evident in Soviet agriculture), it is also paradoxically a fact that the availability of resources inhibits their sudden concentration on a specific goal simply because more interests become involved in not suddenly altering the status quo. To the extent that the Soviet picture is a mixed one, the difference from the United States appears to be one of considerable degree but not of kind.

Integration. The modern state—communist or democratic—makes policy in many areas. Foreign affairs, military affairs, labor, industry, agriculture, finance, commerce, education, natural resources, welfare—all demand its attention to at least some degree. Each area of policy and policy-making is in part autonomous and in part interrelated with the other areas. The degree to which policy in one area is integrated with policy in another depends upon the power which the central policy-making institutions have vis-à-vis the specialized ones in each area.

In the American system each policy area has a high degree of autonomy. American government, Ernest Griffith has said, is "government by whirlpools." [19] Congressmen, executives, bureaucrats, interest groups, local party leaders, technical experts, even newspapermen, tend to specialize in one or a few areas. The interaction among the specialists in an area tends to be much more frequent and intense than that among individuals in the same institution in different areas. To reverse an old truth: two congressmen, one of whom is an agricultural specialist, may have less in common than two agricultural specialists, one of whom is a congressman. In every whirlpool, of course, there are some individuals and institutions concerned with policy in other areas. But the ability of these general policy-making groups to influence policy in any one area is normally weak. Moreover, the connecting institutions themselves tend to fragment. Over the years many of Congress's policy-making activities have devolved to specialized committees, each concerned with one policy area and jealously guarding its prerogatives against invasion. The Appropriations Committee, which conceivably might play an integrating role, is divided into autonomous subcommittees, each responsible for one major supply bill. Among congressmen generally an informal specialization develops. Policy expertise is accorded deference and carries political weight. But the congressman who may be worth fifty or sixty votes on an antitrust measure is usually worth nothing on a foreign-policy issue. In most political systems the final power over policy is concentrated in the hands of less than a score of individuals, the cabinet in parliamentary democracies, the Presidium in the Soviet Union. The same is true of the United States, except that there are many cabinets and presidia. Except for the President, an individual in one is seldom found in another.

In the Soviet Union, on the other hand, the more explicit goals of the political leadership as well as greater scarcity of resources compel more conscious coordination of policy. In the United States little coordination is required between, for instance, agricultural and military policy. The individuals principally concerned with the formulation of the one are normally different (except for the President) from those concerned with the other. In the Soviet system, the two are directly related. Two major goals of the political leaders are increased agricultural production and strong military forces. The achievement of either requires large capital expenditures. Capital invested in one area is denied to another. As a result, the Presidium, the Secretariat, and the Central Committee have to maintain close control over both agricultural and military policy. In the United States, the absence of competition between the two areas enhances the power of the specialized interest groups and bureaucracies and reduces the control of the President in both fields. While American policy is made in many separate whirlpools, Soviet policy is boiled in a single caldron.

Both the instrumental American system and the ideological Soviet system contain certain biases in the distribution of power among different policy areas. In the Soviet Union, heavy industry has traditionally been in a favored position. The priority which the political leadership consciously gave it during the industrialization drive of the 1930s cannot now easily be removed by the political leadership—even in a totalitarian system. Time and again some

Soviet leaders have spoken of the desirability of shifting resources into light industry, consumer goods, and agriculture. But in practice heavy industry has not suffered. In the Soviet Union, as well as in the United States, the redistribution of resources is easier by economic expansion than by conscious reallocation. Similarly, in the United States the political system is skewed in favor of private control of resources and the production of consumer goods. The difficulty which a Soviet leader faces in de-emphasizing heavy industry is comparable to the difficulty which an American leader faces in raising taxes.

The ability of the central institutions to coordinate policy also reflects differences in their nature. One of Khrushchev's charges against Stalin was that he reduced the importance of the Politburo by dividing it into committees concerned with particular policy areas. In effect, Stalin himself took over the function of integrating policy and compelled Politburo members to become primarily policy specialists. In the post-Stalin era, Presidium members have still specialized in particular areas, but apparently they have shared to a greater degree in the formulation of important policies. The integration of policy is one of their primary responsibilities as Presidium members. In the United States, on the other hand, only the President, with the aid of his staff, such as the White House assistants and the Budget Bureau, has the power and the right to coordinate. But inevitably his policy-integrating capacities are limited. Usually he must focus his attention on one or two key areas, such as foreign policy. Coordination in other areas is largely by default.

Innovation. A system incapable of innovation in the long run is incapable of survival. Policy innovation necessarily partakes of the general characteristics of the policy-formulation process. In the United States, the pressures for change tend to bubble up continually. At times there are periods of intense innovation as in domestic policy in the mid-1930s and in foreign policy in the late 1940s. But in general great leaps forward are rare. Change is slow and piecemeal. The growth of policy is similar to the growth of the common law. Once an innovation is made, however, it is seldom reversed. Congress rarely repeals a major statute; only slightly more frequently does the Supreme Court reverse itself on a major issue. Policies are changed through the slow process of amendment, formal and informal, and are often supplemented by new policies with different and perhaps conflicting objectives. They may become outdated, but almost never are sufficient interests adversely affected by a major policy to procure its repeal. The price of innovation is high; but, once bought, change is permanent.

In the Soviet Union, in contrast, innovation tends to have a stop-and-start, trial-and-error quality. Major changes are initiated from the top. More of them take place when a new leader is attempting to consolidate his power. The first response to a new need often comes later than it would in the United States. Here, at least in part, the problem is rooted in the bureaucratic character of the Soviet leadership. "In the formally structured group, the idea man is doubly dangerous. He endangers the established distribution of power and status, and he is a competitive threat to his peers. Consequently, he tends to be suppressed." [20] While the same is true in the United States, as both Nelson Rockefeller and Chester Bowles might confirm, it is still possible for the "idea man" to generate support on the outside. In the Soviet Union he must do it inside the political system, and his task is doubly difficult because the Soviet bureaucracy is not only bureaucratically conservative, as most are, but also dogmatically conservative.

Innovation is easier in times of trouble and crisis. Success breeds its own conservatism, often represented by special interests and institutions. This is true of both the Soviet Union and the United States. In the United States recent years have seen a deepening chasm between the executive branch, representing more often the forces of change and innovation, and Congress, a conservative institution reflecting more frequently both the traditions and the interests of the past. In the Soviet Union the ability of the Soviet system to survive the difficult days of Stalinism and of the war created its own brand of conservatism, represented by the Party and state bureaucracy, permeated with individuals with a strong pro-industrial bias. The dramatic contrast between Kennedy calling for a New Frontier and for civil rights while Congress defended the old limits on federal power has had its counterpart in the Soviet Union, with Khrushchev seeking new welfare for the Soviet people while the apparat—out of both inertia and prejudice—quietly strove to reduce the impact of his proposals.

Once the top Soviet leadership determines that change is necessary, however, innovation can proceed expeditiously. All the energies of the regime are devoted to the recommendation and execution of the new policy. After Khrushchev obtained the approval of the Presidium for industrial reorganization in 1957, for instance, he insisted that this fundamental overhaul of Soviet industrial structure be carried out in two or three months. The gap between Khrushchev's first memorandum on expanding the chemical industry and the decision to rush headlong into a vast expansion program was similarly a matter of only a few months (see page 204). This pattern reflects the concentration of the policy initiation and decision functions in the top leadership. It also may reflect the role of ideology, which may retard the initial decision to innovate but also may accelerate the innovation process once that decision is made. Innovation in the American system is often leisurely; in the Soviet system it is almost always undertaken in a spirit of crisis. Politically and psychologically, the Party seems to need and thrive upon crusades and crash programs. Its energies are mobilized and directed to the achievement first of one goal and then of another. This pattern appears to be typical of communist regimes generally. At times this seems to produce a trial-and-error approach to the solution of major policy problems. First one innovation is launched. If it does not solve the problem quickly, it is canceled, and another approach is tried. In areas of chronic trouble, such as agriculture, Soviet policy zigzags vigorously, first on one tack, then on another, and then off on a third. Such responses may be characteristic of any regime when it is faced with serious and continuing problems. Much of the atmosphere surrounding Soviet policy-making in an area like agriculture, for instance, seems similar to that of the New Deal in the early 1930s. "Bold, persistent experimentation" was Roosevelt's slogan; and like the Soviets the New Dealers did not hesitate to drop one policy if it did not work and to try another. Trial-and-error innovations thus appear on the American scene during periods of severe crisis, but they seem to be a permanent feature of the Soviet system. Hence policies once innovated are often reversed.

Whereas the slow process of piecemeal amendment typically alters major policies in the United States, in the Soviet Union policy reversals are often far-reaching, dramatic, and highly visible. They are caused by power struggles or critical shortages in resources.

TABLE 1

MAJOR POLICY INNOVATIONS, 1945-1963

USSR	USA

Foreign-Military Policy

USSR	USA
U.N. Membership, 1945-	Creation of and leadership in United Nations, 1945-
"Two-camp theory" and the rejection of the Marshall Plan, Council for Economic Mutual Assistance, Warsaw Pact, 1947-1952	Containment: reconstruction and defense of Europe (Marshall Plan, NATO, Truman Doctrine, troops to Europe), 1947-1951
Development of Nuclear Strategy, 1953-	Military rearmament, 1950-1952
Space programs, 1953(?)-	Development of nuclear weapons and deterrent strategy, 1949-1955
Foreign Aid Programs for "neutral" states, 1955-	Economic and technical assistance to non-European countries, 1949-
"Peaceful Coexistence" and noninevitability of war, 1956-	Military assistance programs and military alliances with non-European countries, 1951-
Courtship of Yugoslavia and acceptance of autonomy within the Soviet camp, 1956-	Space program, 1955-
Berlin crisis and missiles to Cuba, 1959-1962	Alliance for Progress, 1961
Public rejection of China, 1963	Trade Expansion Act, 1962-
Nuclear test ban treaty, 1963	Nuclear test ban treaty, 1963-

Domestic Policy

USSR	USA
Consolidation of collective farms, 1951	Taft-Hartley Act, 1947
Virgin-lands development, 1954	Urban renewal, 1949-
De-Stalinization, 1956-	Internal Security programs, 1950-
Industrial reorganization, 1957	Desegregation of public facilities, 1954-
Abolition of Machine Tractor Stations, 1958	
Education Reform, 1958	
Party-state administration reorganization, and economic recentralization, 1962	

They usually involve a drastic decline in reputation of the sponsor of the original policy and the purging of his followers. Statements from the Party leaders abruptly terminate the ideological legitimacy of the old policy and hail the new one as the correct Marxist-Leninist solution.

In any political system centralized power makes innovation more possible although not necessarily more probable. During the last years of his rule Stalin created an atmosphere hostile to innovation. His successors, however, initiated rapid changes in many areas of Soviet policy. The diffusion of power in the American system, on the other hand, provides many channels through which changes may be initiated. If one channel is blocked, action may still be possible through another. During Reconstruction the initiative was with Congress; in the early twentieth century state governments took the lead in introducing female suffrage and welfare legislation; before World War II the President had the initiative in domestic policy and after the war he had it in foreign policy; the most important domestic-policy innovation of the 1950s, however, was made by the Supreme Court when it ordered the desegregation of the public schools.

In the years after World War II both the Soviet and the American political systems produced major innovations in policy. Their styles and methods, however, differed greatly. Whether these innovations were adequate is a question which cannot be answered here. At the least, it can be said that each system was able to make some major innovations in response to some major changes in its environment. Many political systems lack the capacity to innovate and to adjust to new challenges. Such was the case with neither the United States nor the Soviet Union. Neither lacked flexibility. Neither was frozen in *immobilisme.*

PART II

The Dynamics of Power:
Responses to Common Crises

CHAPTER FIVE

The Struggle for Power

" I N POLITICS two plus two does not make four" gloated Nikita Khrushchev in 1957 after crushing the majority of the Party Presidium who had unsuccessfully tried to unseat him. However, he was more right about Soviet politics than American. In the Soviet political system the struggle for power is entirely an informal process; officially it never takes place. In the United States, it combines both formal and informal aspects, and in the formal process there are decisive moments, such as the nomination and the election, when two and two do make four, and a numerical majority gives both victory and legitimacy. But in both systems the gaining of power requires a skillful manipulation of issues and appeals, systematic generation of political support, and effective denigration of principal rivals. Both Khrushchev and Kennedy gained the leadership of their countries because they proved themselves extremely adept in the struggle for power.

The struggle for power in a political system may be moderated by procedures, such as drawing of lots and family inheritance, for automatically assigning positions of authority. It may also be reduced by formal or informal agreements for sharing office among competitive groups. Neither the Soviet nor the American political system, however, makes much use of these devices. The only significant exception is seniority in the American Congress. Apart from congressional leadership positions, almost all authoritative offices in both systems are filled through a highly competitive struggle.

Individuals compete in this struggle, but normally they are organized into groups. In the American electoral system, the groups include the political parties and the more informal personal cliques and groupings within them. In the Soviet system, the Communist Party simply provides the framework for the struggle for power; it is not a competitor for power. The competitive groups in the Soviet system are factions. The faction is the Soviet bureaucratic equivalent of the American electoral party. Both the faction and the party are groups of politicians bound together by a common interest in acquiring power or in preventing someone from getting it. They are the dynamic elements in the political system. Political parties in democratic systems are the outgrowth of the concentration of power in popularly elected bodies and the expansion of the electorate. They are the descendants of the uninstitutionalized factions of eighteenth-century politics. Their function is to contest elections, and the regularity of elections compels them to become more or less permanent organizations. A faction, on the other hand, is a transient body. Factional politics are less institutionalized than party politics, and hence are more likely to involve the bureaucratic institutions of the state in the struggle for power. In America the formal character of the electoral contest keeps the struggle for power apart from the administrative process.

The personal faction has its origins in personal associations and its cement in personal loyalties. Officials participating in a common line of work early in their careers may develop ties which will have an important influence on their later careers. An association develops in which patrons and protégés arc bound together by reciprocal bonds of personal loyalty. A major political leader normally has a solid base in some territorial party organization—Leningrad, Moscow, the Ukraine, Georgia, Azerbaijan. When he becomes a national figure he attempts to move his regional subordinates into key positions in the central government and Party organizations. Zhdanov brought many Leningraders into key spots in the central apparat. Georgia was the source of Beria supporters who were given important posts in the police and other bureaucracies. Khrushchev's victory in the succession struggle was marked by the rapid upward movement of many of his former Ukrainian associates.[1] The rising political leader may also establish alliances with individuals and groups in other bureaucracies with whom he has been closely associated or has some common interests. On the other hand, the death or defeat of a top political leader, as in the cases of Zhdanov and Beria, usually has drastic consequences for his protégés.

A coalition faction usually has even briefer existence than a personal one. It is typically composed of the leaders of several personal factions who share a temporary common purpose. Thus, after Lenin's death, Stalin, Zinoviev, and Kamenev joined together to oppose Trotsky; two years later, Stalin, Bukharin, Rykov, and Tomsky joined against Zinoviev and Kamenev; later Kamenev,

Zinoviev, and Trotsky cooperated against Stalin; and in the final stages of the struggle for power, Stalin turned against his erstwhile allies, Bukharin, Rykov, and Tomsky. Coalition factions thus have prominent roles during a succession struggle when the top position is vacant. When a top leader is in power, presumably second- and third-ranking leaders engage in comparable, if less visible, coalitions and maneuvers in order to enhance their own position within the limits permitted.

In the Soviet Union the struggle for the top position automatically occurs when the position becomes vacant and involves the top Party leaders. Whatever his subjective, personal desires, a Soviet leader who is in the Party Presidium cannot escape the struggle for power. He must either compete for the position himself or identify himself with someone who is competing. Whatever his choice, his political and perhaps personal future is at stake. He cannot stand aside or retreat into neutrality. Having reached the top of the political ladder, he must engage in a Hobbesian war of all against all until a new Leviathan has emerged.

In the United States, in contrast, eligibility for the struggle is established by both objective and subjective factors. In general a presidential candidate must be reasonably well known and preferably should have demonstrated some vote-getting ability. He must have a political base within his own party, that is, some concentrated and influential geographical or institutional source of support. He should be a political moderate. He should not have antagonized any single important interest group or voting bloc, and he should not be identified too closely with any single interest group or bloc. He should also have the appropriate personal qualifications and appeal: an appropriate age, a distinguished appearance, an attractive family, a white skin, and, at least until 1960, a Protestant religion. These general characteristics make an individual politically, as well as constitutionally, eligible for the Presidency.

The extent to which these qualities are developed or exploited depends in large part on the candidate himself. No single ladder of achievement leads directly to the top. The last four Presidents to enter the office through nomination and election—Hoover, Roosevelt, Eisenhower, and Kennedy—held no office in common except the Presidency. Hoover rose to Presidential eligibility through national appointive office and the Cabinet, Roosevelt through state politics, Eisenhower through the Army and wartime generalship, Kennedy through Congress. When he became available for the Presidency in 1958, Kennedy, in terms of formal position, was only one of ninety-six senators, and a fairly junior one at that. It was not his position which made him eligible, but the other qualities which he developed, making use of his position.

STAGES OF CONFLICT

In both the United States and the Soviet Union the struggle of the eligible candidates for the top position goes through distinct phases. In the Soviet case, these involve first the acquisition of power in a "free-for-all" competition and then the consolidation of power in the struggle of "one against all." In Khrushchev's case, the first lasted roughly from the death of Stalin in March 1953 to the demotion of Malenkov in February 1955; the second from 1955 to the collapse of the "anti-Party group" in June 1957 (including in its aftermath the purge of Marshal Zhukov in October of that year). From then on, Khrushchev had effective control at the top level. During the first phase there was a sharing of power among peers, all former close associates of Stalin. This was the period of real collective leadership: there was no *primus,* all were *pares.* The several leaders adopted conflicting policy initiatives and varying ideological postures. Moreover, some had independent institutional sources of power. Khrushchev's primary task during the phase of acquisition was to undermine and gradually subvert the power of his peers. During the next phase of consolidation Khrushchev was clearly *primus inter pares:* he dominated the political scene, monopolized both political and ideological initiatives, but was still faced by powerful opponents within the top leadership, and his power was not secure. His task was thus to complete their subordination, and in 1957 he eliminated his peers from the top leadership.

From then on he was the *primus* but there were no longer any *pares.* His colleagues were no longer his peers but his subordinates, in large measure appointed by him.* These younger leaders may

---

* This change is reflected even by comparative age statistics: in 1953 Khrushchev, the new Party Secretary, was fifty-nine and the average age of the entire Party Presidium was fifty-six; in 1956 he was sixty-

occasionally oppose the top leader, but their opposition is hardly the same thing as the rivalry of peers. Only Mikoyan and Suslov could perhaps be seen as Khrushchev's peers in terms of stature, but both of them are specialists and could hardly qualify for the position of the leader-generalist. Finally, Khrushchev was the *only* Soviet leader to hold posts in the four key institutions of power: Party Presidium, CC Secretariat, CC Bureau for the Russian Republic, and the Council of Ministers. This concentration of power compensated for the lack of legitimacy and constitutional security vested in the United States Presidency.

In the United States, unlike the Soviet Union, there are formally prescribed procedures and phases for winning the top position: first nomination by a major party, secondly victory in the presidential election. These form a constant framework within which the struggle takes place. The character of the struggle, however, is also shaped by political conditions and circumstances. An incumbent first-term President who has avoided disaster can always be renominated. He monopolizes presidential eligibility in his party. Since the odds favor presidential re-election, the number of contenders for the out-party nomination is usually limited. When, at the end of a second term, the President cannot run again, the competition broadens. The in-party may well have two or more heirs apparent. The out-party nomination, in turn, is more promising and attracts more candidates. This was the situation in 1960.

In these circumstances Kennedy's struggle for the Democratic nomination went through two phases similar to those which Khrushchev went through. In the first, from the middle of 1959 to the West Virginia primary on May 10, 1960, the struggle was relatively open and equal among the five candidates seeking the nomination: Kennedy; Lyndon Johnson, Senate majority leader; Adlai Stevenson, Democratic presidential nominee in 1952 and 1956; Stuart Symington, Senator from Missouri; and Hubert Humphrey, Senator from Minnesota. During the second phase, from May 10 to his nomination on the first ballot at the Democratic convention on July 13, Kennedy was *primus inter pares*. He had

---

two while the top leadership averaged fifty-six; in 1959, the undisputed leader, both First Secretary and Prime Minister, he was sixty-five while his associates averaged fifty-seven.

established his leadership and he now struggled successfully to consolidate it, winning the support of state party leaders and others, while his opponents unsuccessfully attempted to band together to stop him. Having achieved nomination by his party, however, Kennedy still had to defeat his Republican opponent. In this two-person struggle the acquisition and consolidation phases were merged, and, unlike the case in the Soviet Union, control of the top position was simultaneously acquired and consolidated on election day. The uses which Kennedy could make of presidential power, however, would depend on his political skill and ability to get what he wanted by negotiating with autonomous institutions and interests and by mobilizing broad popular support for his policies.

Acquisition and consolidation thus involved a struggle for power, although under differing conditions and with differing objectives in each. After them came the exercise of power. There was, clearly, some overlapping between the phases, and because of the fluid and informal character of the Soviet pattern of the seizure of power they cannot be sharply compartmentalized. This is also true of the United States, although the fact that the process is at least in part a formal one, based on both the Constitution and gradually evolving tradition, makes it somewhat easier to define the steps to power. Furthermore, precisely because the American process is regular, it takes less time than the Soviet; a semiformal schedule for advancing one's candidacy, for entering the primaries, and for clashing at the nominating conventions determines the duration of the initial contest. The schedule is explicitly formalized in the case of the election itself. Also, quite unlike the Soviet system, the most intense contest in America takes place among leaders out of power; the President usually can determine the candidate of the party in power. In the Soviet Union, to compete for power, the politician has to be already close to the seat of it.

KHRUSHCHEV'S STRUGGLE

When Stalin died, the first concern of his successors was to make certain that no one would become dominant. That is why Malenkov, whom Stalin had clearly designated as his heir, within a week was prevailed upon to yield one of the two positions he had quickly assumed on the old tyrant's death, the Prime Ministership and the Party Secretaryship. Malenkov apparently chose the Prime Minister's post, calculating that this would be a more secure position, since during Stalin's later days the state bureaucracy had emerged as the dominant force on the Soviet scene. Khrushchev was selected by the leaders to be the Secretary; he was no longer young; he had shown himself in the past to be a loyal Party apparatchik; he seemed too crude and too preoccupied with operational matters to be a threat. Beria retained the secret police, Molotov foreign affairs, Kaganovich heavy industry. Power seemed neatly balanced.

Stalin, however, left behind not only a power vacuum but a series of policy dilemmas. As the new leaders began to take their stand on them, their power positions came into play, and the neat balance gave way to quickly shifting alignments. In the first clash, Beria was physically eliminated in June 1953, a mere four months after Stalin's death. Beria's liquidation, and even more important the subsequent annihilation of much of the top-secret police leadership, had the vital consequence of removing from the power struggle the element of physical violence. No contender could now advance his cause by a sudden arrest and personal liquidation of his rival. The struggle had to take a political form, and the question now was who had the better resources, the better tactics, and the better issues.

By the time of Malenkov's resignation in 1955, Khrushchev's rivals had learned that he was the better politician. Unlike them, he succeeded in identifying himself with *both* a defense of the interests of the communist regime and social reform designed to revitalize it. He made skillful use of certain key issues of vital importance to the Communist Party bureaucracy; he made compromises with other important groups in order to build up his personal appeal; he engaged in institutional manipulation in order to change the structure of power; and he projected an image of himself designed primarily to win the support of the apparatchiki. He skillfully made use of the powers vested in his position as head of the Party Secretariat and built up a core of supporters. His choice of issues is a case in point. In 1953-1955 he concentrated on three: the need for reform and new initiatives in agriculture, the defense of the traditional priority for heavy industry in Soviet economic development, and the maintenance of a hard theoretical position in foreign affairs. Each in its own way helped Khrushchev to isolate his rivals, to undermine Malenkov, who initially emerged as the heir apparent, and to prevent a hostile coalition from forming against him.

His concentration on the agricultural issue was particularly apt. First of all, more than any other top leader he actually knew a great deal about this subject and so approached it with a secure sense of personal expertise. He could point to his experience in the Ukraine and to his various proposals during Stalin's life to establish his credentials as the only top leader capable of tackling a problem affecting every Soviet citizen, and critically important politically and ideologically to every Communist dedicated to the construction of a new communist society. Second, the agricultural sector was *the* sector of the Party's weakness. A disproportionately small percentage of Party members lived in the rural areas, and in 1953 the majority of collective farms did not even have a Party cell. Efforts to improve the Party's control of agriculture also provided Khrushchev with an opportunity to criticize the performance of the state administration. This immediately gained him the support of hard-pressed, inadequately backed, and often unfairly blamed regional Party secretaries, who heretofore had shouldered much of the responsibility for the inadequate economic performance of their regions.[2] At the same time, in the name of improved performance Khrushchev was able to initiate personnel change in the agricultural sector which gradually led to the reimposition of the Party's supremacy over the state bureaucrats, thereby contributing to his own power as First Secretary. Third, his concern for agricultural production did gain him some popularity, particularly in the agricultural sector of the country but also in the cities, since in 1952 there had actually occurred some serious food shortages in parts of the Soviet Union. Although at this stage popularity was not an important political resource, his peers could hardly object to his efforts since they too realized that the food problem had become critical (for a fuller discussion, see Chapter Seven). Fourth, Khrushchev's explicit denunciations of the critical situation in the countryside contrasted sharply with the glowing report given on that very subject by Malenkov to the 19th Party Congress in October 1952 (when Stalin was still alive), and they accordingly reflected obliquely on Malenkov's own position.

Because of these considerations Khrushchev moved boldly. As early as September 1953 he made a scathing denunciation of the conditions prevailing in rural areas and particularly did not spare in his criticisms the inadequate performance of the state planning and administrative officials. A series of measures was adopted to lighten the burden of the collective farms in the hope of spurring them to higher productivity. In February 1954 Khrushchev followed this with the highly controversial initiative to develop the "virgin lands" of north Kazakhstan and southern Siberia, in order to create some 13 million additional hectares of arable land. The program required a major commitment of resources and many new appointments; it was at this time that Brezhnev, a close associate of Khrushchev, went to Kazakhstan as Second Secretary. As far as is known, some Soviet leaders opposed this venture as too risky; others, however, including apparently Malenkov, whose close associate, Ponomarenko, was chosen to be the First Secretary in Kazakhstan, conceded the necessity of drastic action.[3] Thus after much debate Khrushchev was allowed to proceed with his initiative, and later he was able to capitalize on it and charge his rivals with a lack of concern for the stomachs of the Soviet people, in the meantime having gained much additional patronage for the Party's apparat.

On the subject of heavy industry, Khrushchev was able to appear in the guise of the dedicated Leninist-Stalinist, defending its primacy in Soviet economic development and thereby gaining the grateful loyalty of the heavy industrial cadres and (presumably) the military leaders, like Marshal Zhukov, interested primarily in further defense production. This issue marked Malenkov's second major miscalculation, his choice of the Prime Ministership being the first. In a desire to improve the lot of the Soviet man, Malenkov committed himself shortly after Stalin's death to an increase in production of consumer goods. In a major address a month before Khrushchev's September 1953 speech Malenkov stated that "the Soviet people has the right to demand from us . . . durable, well-finished, high-class goods," and he promised "to raise the targets for the production of goods for the masses very considerably," noting significantly that the Soviet Union already possessed a modern industry. Khrushchev sprang to the defense of the established priorities (and interests), loudly proclaiming that some "pseudo-theoreticians try to claim that at some state of socialist construction the development of heavy industry ceases to be the main task and that light industry can and should overtake all other branches of industry. This is profoundly incorrect reasoning, alien to the spirit of Marxism-Leninism —nothing but slander to our Party. This is a belching of the rightist deviation, a regurgitation of views hostile to Leninism, views which Rykov, Bukharin, and their ilk once preached." It may be safely assumed that on this score he was backed by Molotov and Kaganovich, thus effectively isolating Malenkov, his chief rival at this time.

On foreign policy, Khrushchev was also aligned with the more conservative position, allowing Malenkov to expose himself on behalf of a more moderate course (logically necessitated by Malenkov's consumer-goods policies). He explicitly differed with Malenkov when the latter warned against the dangers of a nuclear war, rejecting the proposition that such a war would mean the end of humanity. The First Secretary insisted that it would mean only the end of capitalism and here, again, by stressing the further importance of defense development, he presumably earned the gratitude of the military leaders. The differences between him and Malenkov became so extreme that in the middle of the summer of 1954 one of Khrushchev's more bellicose speeches, delivered in Prague, was simply censored by *Pravda*.[4]

Skillful choice of key issues thus enabled Khrushchev during this early stage of the struggle for power to identify himself with the three key power groups in the Soviet political system: the Party's apparat, including its regional leadership (especially in rural areas) and the Agitprop, both smarting under the impositions of the state bureaucracy which had been elevated in power and prestige in Stalin's later days; the industrial management, fearful of Malenkov's reforms; and the military leadership, now somewhat more important after the liquidation of the secret police. This identification Khrushchev was able to buttress by using his power of political patronage as First Secretary and by institutional manipulation, designed to restore the pre-eminence of the Party. He thus promptly effected changes in the leadership of the two most important regional Party organizations, those of the Ukraine and of Leningrad (in June and November 1953 respectively), and this was followed by extensive changes in the other republics. The consolidation of the Party Presidium immediately after Stalin's death into a smaller, more effective body (from twenty-five members to ten) in itself did much to re-establish the primacy of the Party's top governing board at the cost of the Council of Ministers, and Khrushchev gained additional powers for his Secretariat by investing it with responsibilities for the agricultural reforms.

Throughout this period he represented himself, above all else, as a loyal Party servant, a true Leninist dedicated to collective leadership and democratic centralism, "a faithful disciple of Lenin and a comrade in arms of Stalin," who defended the vital priorities of the communist regime, in contrast to Malenkov whose policies seemed dangerously "revisionist." By early 1955 Khrushchev so succeeded in isolating and discrediting Malenkov that Stalin's erstwhile heir apparent "resigned" as Prime Minister, significantly confessing most serious errors in the field of agriculture, Khrushchev's forte. ("I see with particular clarity my guilt and responsibility for the unsatisfactory state of affairs in agriculture. . . .") His demission was apparently backed by Khrushchev's subsequent opponents, Molotov and Kaganovich—clear testimony to Khrushchev's success in effecting a split among his rivals. Even in 1955 his peers apparently saw him as a lesser threat. A "neutral" candidate, Marshal N. A. Bulganin, an affable but ineffective bureaucrat, was chosen to be the new Prime Minister. Very revealing of the new political reality, however, was the new Prime Minister's immediate declaration acknowledging the government's subordination to the leadership of the Party. This stood in sharp contrast to Malenkov's earlier thesis that "after the victory of the proletarian revolution" there necessarily had to be "the primacy of state organs over Party." [5]

This change marked the beginning of Khrushchev's domination of the Soviet political scene. Although his peers could oppose, obstruct, even partially impose (as in December 1956, when the position of state economic planners was strengthened at the cost of the Party), and plot (as in June 1957), none of them singly could come out with independent initiatives and ideological positions. From then on Khrushchev alone as the First Secretary had the prerogative of innovating and postulating. However, he had to move cautiously lest the other leaders charge him with trying to become another Stalin. The fear that another tyrant might emerge was the dominating psychological bond uniting even most diverse attitudes within the top leadership, and Khrushchev, who skillfully identified himself with the "centrist" position, did not want to provide the "softs" (Malenkov's group) and the "hards" (Molotov's) with a joint cause. At this stage, the principle of "collective leadership" was still an active force, and Khrushchev could not deprive his peers of their posts. Instead, he proceeded gradually to introduce his supporters into the top leadership (in July 1955 A. I. Kirichenko, the First Secretary in the Ukraine, and M. A. Suslov, Khrushchev's second in the Secretariat, were added to the Party Presidium), while continuing to discredit his peers.

The widespread and persisting discussion of agricultural inadequacies kept up a steady barrage of charges against the state administration, and it was more and more explicitly (but not entirely correctly) asserted that in Stalin's time Malenkov had been responsible for it. In March 1955, three additional First Deputy Chairmen of the Council of Ministers were appointed—Mikoyan, Pervukhin, and Saburov—and their established expertise in industrial matters meant that Kaganovich's sphere of influence was being sharply reduced.[6] In September Molotov was forced to publish in *Kommunist,* the Party's ideological organ, an odd admission of ideological error: apparently in a speech he had stated that the foundations of socialism had been laid in the Soviet Union, instead of claiming that socialism had been built in the Soviet Union. His public recantation of "theoretically erroneous and politically harmful" views did not contribute to his political prestige.

During this phase of the struggle, Khrushchev focused consecutively on three interdependent issues: foreign policy, the problem of Stalinism, and the question of economic reorganization. Agriculture, of course, remained a bone of contention throughout the post-Stalin era. In foreign policy, Khrushchev now moved against the "hards" and began to associate himself with a policy of détente insofar as the West was concerned and reform insofar as the Soviet bloc was concerned. In both instances, the opportunity to appear on the international scene and share the ceremonial functions with Bulganin enhanced his personal status. This was particularly the case during the Geneva 1955 meeting with Eisenhower and Eden. The greatest controversy within the leadership was produced by Khrushchev's efforts to improve relations with Yugoslavia (in the hope of creating a healthier climate within the bloc), a policy violently opposed by Molotov, who saw in it a repudiation of Stalin's and his own foreign policy. In July 1955, presumably with the support of the "softs," Khrushchev gained the endorsement of the Party leadership for this initiative.

The question of Stalinism came out into the open during the 20th Party Congress in February 1956. Although the circumstances surrounding Khrushchev's sudden attack on Stalin are still far from clear, the net effect of the speech was to identify Khrushchev as the leader of a powerful current desiring a general break with the Stalinist past. The attack, furthermore, also had from his point of view the desirable effect of seeming to reassure the Party cadres that he was not another Stalin. By destroying the Stalinist myth, he was rejecting Stalin's mantle. That gained him additional support within the upper ranks of the apparat. At the same time, his highly selective "historical" treatment of Stalinism was neatly calculated to implicate his peers in Stalin's "errors and aberrations" (an extensive discussion of Stalin's "crimes" came only in 1961), thus identifying them with the vilified past. In the struggle for Stalin's succession, most of the peers had equal claims and some, like Molotov, even better than others; by turning the contest into an issue of anti-Stalinism and seizing the initiative in it, Khrushchev gained the field for himself.

The Congress also provided Khrushchev with the opportunity to announce several important ideological innovations, thereby for the first time establishing his stature as ideologue. Second, it marked his first major effort to appeal for support outside the narrow confines of the political "establishment," associating him more directly with all the various groups in Soviet society—the experts, the intellectuals, the military, and the people in general— which wanted a complete break with the terror, the concentration camps, the fear, the suspicion that characterized Soviet life. Presumably the message which the several thousand delegates took back with them was that Khrushchev stood for change. Although shocked and bewildered by the sudden denunciation of Stalin, they then helped to create the groundswell of support for Khrushchev.

But most important of all, the Congress provided Khrushchev with the vital opportunity to improve his position within the top leadership by introducing new supporters into it. According to one close student of Soviet leadership, the Central Committee elected by the Congress included 76 officials with close career connections to Khrushchev out of the 133 full members.[7] He also improved his position within the Presidium and the Secretariat: five new candidate members were added to the Presidium and five new secretaries to the Secretariat. All were Khrushchev's protégés, although later two of them, Zhukov and Shepilov, were purged by him. In an institutional innovation, a special Bureau of the Central Committee to handle Party matters in the Russian Republic (by far the largest) was also created, with Khrushchev at its head. Although, as the events of 1957 showed, his power was far from secure, he now had a very solid base within the entire structure of leadership and could be challenged only by a coalition of *all* his peers. The consolidation of Khrushchev's power was shortly afterward reflected by the further weakening in the positions of his rivals: in June Molotov was removed as Foreign Minister, and in September Kaganovich was assigned to the relatively modest post of Minister of Construction Materials Industry. Both, however, retained their posts on the Party Presidium, and together with Malenkov probably brooded over Khrushchev's meteoric rise. Their past differences were becoming secondary to their common misery.

But, as in the case of Stalin, Khrushchev's rivals came together too late. Khrushchev had effectively seized the middle ground, and the "left" and the "right," even when directly opposing him, were always closer to his position than to that of the other extreme. They came together only because Khrushchev's success reduced their policy differences to a matter of secondary importance; their own positions were clearly at stake. Their combined opposition made its first major move in December 1956. At the time, Khrushchev's prestige was at a low point. His de-Stalinization had produced considerable ferment within the USSR itself, and the regime was forced to suppress dissenting students. In Poland it brought to power a new leadership of seemingly uncertain loyalty to the USSR; while in Hungary the suppression of the revolution by the Soviet Army gained the Soviet Union the opprobrium of world opinion. Khrushchev himself conceded that he had gone too far in denouncing Stalin and by the end of 1956 was saying, "I am proud that we are Stalinists." In December a session of the

Central Committee was called to discuss problems of economic organization, and its proceedings and resolution reflected Khrushchev's reduced prestige. He did not speak at the session; his recent appointee Shepilov was dropped from the Party Secretariat; and the decisions taken to improve economic planning and operations laid primary stress on the role of state organs. The State Economic Commission, buttressed by the appointment of several top government bureaucrats, was endowed with special powers, making it in effect the economic government of the Soviet Union.

The political consequence of this measure was twofold: it inevitably somewhat weakened Khrushchev's over-all power, although it left his control over the Party essentially unchanged; second, it strengthened the position of the state and, therefore, the personal position of Bulganin as Prime Minister. It would appear from the foregoing that even as late as the end of 1956 Khrushchev's peers could agree only on blocking him; they could not agree on a substitute leadership and could settle only on a "neutral" alternative such as Bulganin. This, however, gave Khrushchev time to recoup. His counterattack came in February. Addressing himself this time personally to the continuing difficulties in the industrial sector, the First Secretary used the opportunity of a new Central Committee plenum to launch his important proposal for the decentralization of the entire state economic machinery. Despite vigorous, even bitter, opposition among his colleagues on the Party Presidium (see p. 205), Khrushchev was able in March and April to generate enough support throughout the Party machinery to ram his proposal through. The reason for that is almost self-evident from the nature of the proposal. Its net effect was to leave the Party apparat as the only source of political integration for the entire state and society. The entrenched bureaucrats in the ministries, in the central industrial complexes, even in the top government were to be dispersed to the provinces, and the Party machinery was to assume over-all coordination. In addition to the apparat's support, Khrushchev was able to count on the sympathy of the military leaders. In the course of the discussion of the proposals, he exempted defense industries from their application, and he apparently convinced the military leaders that Party leadership was a lesser threat to defense interest than the direction by managers, who in the end might be more likely to adopt Malenkov's earlier policies. Underscoring the apparat's involvement in the reform was the appointment of Khrushchev's close collaborator in the Secretariat, L. Brezhnev (see his biography on pp. 164-165), to supervise the execution of the reform.

At the same time, Khrushchev renewed his campaign for mass support. Such support, although not a direct political resource, meant that the apparatchiki were reassured that under Khrushchev's leadership their vested interests were more secure. The Party press extolled his wartime achievements, portraying him even as the architect of the Stalingrad victory, while Khrushchev himself used the theme of peace and the widespread popular fear of war to create for himself the image of a statesman dedicated to "peaceful coexistence." By implication, his opponents were made to appear as proponents of risks and conflicts. The First Secretary was not even above making wild promises to the masses. In May he outraged his rivals by delivering a public speech, apparently without prior Presidium clearance, in which he promised the Soviet people that by 1960 their per-capita consumption of meat would be higher than the American. "That's an adventure," complained Molotov.* The political effect was to strengthen the conviction of the regional Party apparatchiki, more likely to be in tune with mass sentiments, that their future was well served by the First Secretary's leadership.

His enemies now reached the conclusion that their only salvation was Khrushchev's removal. From scattered evidence, it is clear that discussions within the Presidium became increasingly acrimonious and that Khrushchev's peers accused him of trying to become another Stalin.[8] The decentralization reform demanded by Khrushchev was so precipitous that it consolidated a coalition of rivals, including even Bulganin and Shepilov (who apparently calculated that their careers would be advanced if they were to back Khrushchev's enemies) in addition to the original rivals. They carefully prepared a coup, and had they succeeded history

---

* By 1962 the promise had been quietly expunged from Khrushchev's published speeches, while not only was Soviet meat consumption still lower but the price of meat had risen by a third.

would have probably judged that Khrushchev erred in pushing through such drastic changes. In any case, upon return from an official trip to Finland in June 1957, Khrushchev suddenly found himself confronted by a Presidium majority (of seven to four) demanding his resignation. Against him were his old enemies Molotov, Malenkov, and Kaganovich, now joined also by Bulganin, Voroshilov, Pervukhin, and Saburov. It may be assumed that Bulganin joined for essentially opportunistic motives; Voroshilov probably because of Khrushchev's attacks on Stalin, which, by more than implication, reflected also on Voroshilov; the last two because they opposed Khrushchev's economic reorganization. The First Secretary was backed only by Kirichenko, Mikoyan, and Suslov.

Khrushchev, however, astounded his rivals by simply refusing to equate mathematics with politics. He refused to resign on the technical grounds that he had been elected by the Central Committee, and his enemies, no longer being able simply to rely on the mechanism of violence as Stalin could have done, were at a loss. During the 22nd Party Congress in 1961 many colorful details of these dramatic moments came to light: Khrushchev's supporters among the candidate members to the Presidium (of the six, only Shepilov was against him and—quite crucial to the outcome—Marshal Zhukov was strongly for him) and the Central Committee tried to gain entrance to the Kremlin proceedings and were locked out by Bulganin's guard; the majority tried to prevent Khrushchev from communicating with his supporters; there were bitter exchanges; and so on.[9] But the important political fact was that the majority had simply assumed that Khrushchev would bow, as Malenkov had done in 1955. They had neither assumed nor prepared for the contingency that he might defy the Party's highest decision-making body. But defy he did. With the support of Zhukov and some younger leaders such as Polyansky, he managed to call together a Central Committee session. His very defiance shattered the confidence and the ranks of the majority. By the time the Central Committee had assembled on June 22, four days after the initial move within the Presidium against Khrushchev, several of the initial opponents had already shifted sides. With the overwhelming support of the assembled apparatchiki, Khrushchev emerged victorious, while Molotov, Malenkov, Kaganovich, and Shepilov were stripped of their posts and expelled from the Central Committee. Pervukhin and Saburov were demoted but not immediately exorcised; the first became an alternate member of the Presidium, while the second, dropped from the Presidium, retained his Central Committee membership. Bulganin and Voroshilov were not affected for the time being, which suggests that they had been the first to switch back to Khrushchev. Nine new members, all Krushchev's supporters, were brought into the reconstructed Party Presidium, increased to fifteen. Khrushchev's monopoly of power had begun.

But since in the Soviet Union power rests neither on an institution nor on the legitimacy associated with holding it, it was still important for Khrushchev to strengthen his position. Two categories of leaders were yet to be purged: those who had opposed him in June, even though they later switched sides, and those whose support of Khrushchev had been *too important* to his success. In the period which followed, Bulganin was eased out of office in March 1958, and Khrushchev also assumed the post of Prime Minister. Later Bulganin was explicitly implicated in the attempted coup, as were Voroshilov, Pervukhin, and Saburov. All had to engage in public self-criticism and were dropped from the ruling Party bodies. In the second category was Marshal Zhukov, whose support according to some reports was instrumental in the quick convening of the Central Committee. In October of 1957 he was suddenly removed from office while abroad on an official trip (see Chapter Eight). In February 1959, at the 21st Party Congress, Khrushchev launched the slogan of rejuvenation of Party cadres, and extensive changes were made in the Central Committee and the top leadership. Instead of lieutenants to whom the leader might be indebted for support, Khrushchev was increasingly surrounded by lieutenants indebted to him for their promotion. Mikoyan and Suslov remained as the only more senior partners, but their high specialization (as well as proven loyalty to Khrushchev) meant that they could not threaten the top leader. Broad campaigns were launched in the Party and among the masses, designed to portray Khrushchev as the initiator of all positive reforms, world statesman, creative contributor to Marxism-Leninism.

KENNEDY'S STRUGGLE

John F. Kennedy had established his availability for the Presidency by the end of 1958. His national fame dated from the 1956 Democratic Convention, where he nominated Adlai Stevenson for the Presidency and then came within a few votes of winning the vice-presidential nomination in an intense, dramatic struggle with Estes Kefauver. He had accepted his defeat gracefully and campaigned vigorously for the Democratic ticket. The following year he supplemented his martial appeal as a war hero with a literary appeal as a winner of the Pulitzer Prize for biography. In 1958 he had conclusively demonstrated his ability as a vote-getter by winning re-election to the Senate from Massachusetts with 73 per cent of the vote. This victory gave Kennedy a secure personal political position in the Senate for six years (and would present him with a dilemma in 1964, if he did not become President in 1960). He also had a well-organized political base in Massachusetts. In 1956 he and his followers had seized control of the state Democratic Party from Representative John McCormack; he had close ties with Democratic Party leaders elsewhere in New England; and through his wealthy family's connections and the contacts he had made on the national scene, he could look forward to the support of other key figures in politics, journalism, and business scattered across the country.

In his years in Congress Kennedy had established himself as a moderate. He had worked hard for economic and social-welfare legislation, but he had never become identified as an ideological liberal. He had demonstrated a keen sense of political realism and practicality and great skill at compromise. He was acceptable to both Southern conservatives and Northern labor. In 1957 and 1958 he had gone on record in favor of aid to education, extension of minimum wage, raising unemployment benefits and extending coverage, loosening immigration quotas, elimination of labor-union racketeering, economic aid for Poland, and stronger national defenses. He had also played a major role in implementing the recommendations of the Second Hoover Commission and in pushing more businesslike and efficient procedures in governmental budgeting and administration. The only interest which he had seriously antagonized was agriculture, and in 1958 and 1959 he was slowly modifying his views on that matter. Thus, in terms of his policy interests and positions, he was thoroughly qualified. Finally, he had many of the personal characteristics desirable in a presidential candidate: good looks, a distinguished war record, a charming wife and daughter, education, brains, and money.

Three things, however, detracted from his availability. First and least important, he was a senator, and it was a hundred years since the Democratic Party had nominated a senator for the Presidency. Second, he was young: he would be only forty-three in 1960, and he looked even younger. Third and most important, he was a Catholic. The legacy of 1928 still lay heavy on the Democratic Party. Could a Catholic be elected President? Would a Catholic candidacy seriously divide the party and the country? Despite the high percentage of Catholics in the northeastern industrial states, many if not most political leaders—including the Catholic Democratic bosses in the northeast—remained convinced that Kennedy's religion would be a major handicap. For these reasons, many politicians found it difficult to take Kennedy seriously as a presidential candidate. Just as Khrushchev's peasant style and earthy approach seemed to disqualify him as a serious contender in the succession struggle, Kennedy's youth and religion seemed to disqualify him. In each case, these more obvious and superficial qualities obscured the more relevant abilities and resources which the two contenders brought to the struggle.

In Soviet politics the single most important political resource is control of the Party machinery. Capitalizing on his position as First Secretary, Khrushchev single-mindedly devoted himself to moving his supporters into key positions in the Party organization. In American politics, the ultimate tests are votes at a national convention and in a presidential election. The search for votes goes on through various means. To acquire political power a candidate must mobilize a variety of resources and then transform them into votes at the proper time and place. Success requires a single-minded pursuit of this goal. Each of Kennedy's opponents, however, wanted to win the nomination on his own terms and without sacrificing other roles which he considered important. Kennedy simply wanted to win the nomination. He did not think that it would come to him because he was titular leader, Senate leader, border-state moderate, or fighting liberal. For eighteen months before the Democratic Convention the struggle for the nomination dominated Kennedy's activities.* In the end, he won the nomination mainly because he invested more resources in pursuing it than did either Stevenson, Johnson, Symington, or Humphrey.

Four resources were key to the Kennedy victory. The first was people. Each participant in the Soviet succession struggle had an institutional or geographical home base upon which he drew for support; Khrushchev's rise to power was accompanied by the rise and diffusion of the members of the Ukrainian apparat throughout the Soviet political system. So also in American politics. Each of the major candidates had a geographical home base, from which campaign workers were deployed across the countryside. Kennedy mobilized and employed more workers in the preconvention campaign than did any of his rivals. From Massachusetts he recruited many able and energetic political operatives to further his cause across the country. In the early phases of the campaign the country was divided into areas, each assigned to a relative or close associate of the candidate. The area men then recruited others to take the lead for Kennedy within each state. For the primaries, Kennedy friends from prep school, college, and the Navy were recruited, and the senator's own staff was brought in from Washington. As a result, Kennedy was able to staff eight of the ten congressional districts in Wisconsin with superior personnel, while Humphrey could staff only two. Humphrey had to rely on the support, which was not always forthcoming, of the

---

* One index is Senate attendance. Kennedy did not hesitate to abandon Capitol Hill for the precincts and state capitals which would control the convention. Symington, Humphrey, and Johnson spent more time on their senatorial jobs and lost the nomination.

PARTICIPATION IN SENATE ROLL CALL VOTES—PERCENTAGE

	1959	1960	1959-1960
Kennedy	77	35	56
Humphrey	81	49	65
Symington	89	58	74
Johnson	95	95	95

Source: *Congressional Quarterly Almanac,* Vol. XV, 1959, p. 105, Vol. XVI, 1960, p. 103.

local unions and Democratic Party leaders; Kennedy depended primarily on his own men. Similarly, in West Virginia, Humphrey brought in ten top volunteer assistants; Kennedy brought in fifty to staff eight main headquarters and eight subheadquarters. On primary day Kennedy had nine thousand volunteers working for him. At the same time that he had one campaign staff working in West Virginia, he had additional staffs preparing for the primaries in Maryland, Indiana, and Oregon.[10] This ability of a new group of young men to create their own political organization, move in on and take over a major political party, and nominate and elect their man President is fascinating testimony to the permeability of the American political system.

People are useful, however, only if they are well organized. Kennedy's brother Robert had closely observed Stevenson's 1956 campaign; from his experience and from Kennedy's own experience in Massachusetts, the leaders of the Kennedy campaign developed a sophisticated set of organizational techniques and political tactics. Between 1956 and 1960 they had built up extensive files on the politics of every state, so that they knew who hated whom, who controlled whom, who was going up, and who was going down. Special attention was given to the states where there might be primary contests: in West Virginia the first organizations were created early in 1959. In the contest for the nomination all the chief assistants of the candidate had carefully defined responsibilities: press relations, organization, speeches and policy statements, finance, public-opinion polling, travel, and logistics. Kennedy thus welded the people he mobilized into an effective organization.

Campaigns cost money, and the evidence indicates that Kennedy spent far more than any of his opponents in his quest for the nomination. According to one analysis, the campaigns of Johnson, Humphrey, and Stevenson each cost about $250,000; Symington reportedly spent $350,000; Kennedy, however, spent $912,000.[11] Other estimates place his spending still higher. In any event, it seems likely that Kennedy invested three to four times as much money as did any one of his opponents. Contributions to the Kennedy preconvention campaign totaled $693,939, of which $150,000 came from the candidate and his family. In addition, the members of his family banded together to buy a $385,000 airplane, which was leased to Kennedy.[12] His primary opponent, Hubert Humphrey, had the most difficult time of all the contenders in raising money. Humphrey reportedly had to spend as much time raising it as he spent in actually canvassing for votes. Although Humphrey apparently spent about the same amount of money as Kennedy did in the Wisconsin primary he had to cut his staff in half for the West Virginia primary, and reportedly spent only about $23,000 there. Three weeks before the primary one of his top aides declared flatly, "We're broke!" Kennedy spent $100,000 in West Virginia, $34,000 of which went for television time alone.[13]

Kennedy's fourth major resource was his general popularity and a favorable public image. From the middle of 1958 until the end of 1959, he and Stevenson had been at the top of the public-opinion polls as the leading contenders for the Democratic nomination. In 1960 Kennedy pulled ahead in the polls, and at the opening of the Democratic convention in July, Kennedy was the preference of 41 per cent of the country's Democrats with Stevenson getting the backing of 25 per cent, Johnson of 16 per cent, and Symington of 7 per cent. Kennedy's many inherited and inherent qualities, the opportunities which had opened to him and which he had seized, and the fact that he was different—rich, young, and a Catholic—made Kennedy better known than most of his opponents. His popularity and attractive image were of tremendous value to him. In addition, he worked hard to become better known. "Between 1956 and 1960 no Democrat, not even Adlai Stevenson, spoke in more states, addressed more Jefferson-Jackson Day dinners, participated in more local and mayoralty campaigns of deserving Democrats, than did John F. Kennedy." [14]

Each candidate not only had to mobilize resources; he also had to determine how, when, and where they would be employed. He had to fashion a strategy which would win him the 761 convention votes needed for the nomination. Each candidate started with a reasonably secure bloc of votes from his political base. With Humphrey and Symington, this base really amounted for certain to no more than the 31 votes of Minnesota and the 39 of Missouri. Stevenson lacked even that, having little or no support from the Illinois delegation and having to rely, as his base, on the strong support which he had in California. Johnson and Kennedy, in contrast, not only started out with the votes of their own states, but expanded their state bases into regional ones with little difficulty. Johnson easily lined up 300 votes in the South; Kennedy acquired the 114 votes of New England. From these starting points, each candidate then had to decide what routes to follow to achieve the majority needed at the convention. Three roads were open. The candidate could enter *primary contests* and attempt to win delegates and convention votes by appealing to the people. Primaries would be held in sixteen states casting 584 votes at the convention. Winning a substantial proportion of these votes would be important in itself; it would also be important in gaining the support of party leaders in other states. A second method would be through *factional struggles,* capitalizing upon the divisions within a state party and organizing a group to control the state convention or other means of selecting delegates. The third means would be direct negotiations between the candidate and the state party leadership, thereby winning the state's votes through a *leadership decision.*

The tragedy of Stevenson's campaign was that he refused to choose any one of these strategies. He stayed out of primaries and did not become involved in factional struggles; thus he had little to trade on in negotiating with state leaders. In contrast, Humphrey had little choice but to pour his resources into primary contests. He had to demonstrate his vote-getting ability in the primaries before he could hope to gain additional votes through factional struggles or leadership decisions. Symington and Johnson avoided primaries. They devoted some effort, but not a lot, to winning votes through factional struggles, Johnson in the mountain states and Symington in the border states. Primarily, however, they relied on negotiations with and decisions by the state party bosses. In the last analysis they felt that the convention would be deadlocked and that the final choice of a candidate would be made by perhaps a dozen top state party leaders in a Los Angeles hotel room. In such a situation Johnson could trade upon past and current favors he had performed in Congress; Symington could trade on his acceptability to all major groups in the party.

In contrast to the other candidates, Kennedy pursued the nomination through all three routes. He entered seven primaries and won them all, for a total of 134 convention votes. By winning the West Virginia primary, he demonstrated his ability to carry a heavily Protestant area and eliminated Humphrey as a candidate for the nomination. At the same time, the Kennedy organizers and supporters were also working to capitalize on splits within the Democratic Party in other states and, where possible, to take over the party leadership in these states. In New York, for instance, the state chairman, Michael Prendergast, and the Tammany leader, Carmine De Sapio, both wanted to take an uncommitted delegation to the convention. Kennedy's supporters, however, won over the up-state party leaders for Kennedy, got the support of the Bronx and Queens County leaders, appealed to the reform groups in the party, and thus undermined the Prendergast–De Sapio leadership. As a result of this shrewd, tough political in-fighting, Kennedy got 104½ of New York's 114 convention votes. Similar struggles in other states produced perhaps 100 more votes. The state party leaders in New Mexico, Arizona, and Colorado, for instance, were all inclined toward Johnson. The Kennedy lieutenants, however, built up support in the local party organizations and walked off with all of Arizona's votes, a majority of Colorado's, and a substantial share of New Mexico's, for a total of 34½.

Finally, in those states with strong party leadership, Kennedy dealt directly with the leaders. He won the support of the governor of Ohio (and 64 votes), for instance, and the neutrality of the governor of California (and 33½ votes) by threatening to enter the primaries in those states. After demonstrating his vote-getting abilities in West Virginia, he got the support of the Michigan party leadership (42½ votes). As the convention opened, Mayor Richard J. Daley of Chicago came out for Kennedy, bringing with him 61½ Illinois votes, and the following day Governor David Lawrence of Pennsylvania came across with 68 more. Kennedy's three strategies thus interacted with and reinforced one another. And in the end this combination of strategies produced some votes for Kennedy in every non-southern state except four (New Jersey, Delaware, Minnesota, Missouri) and a narrow but clear-cut victory on the first ballot at the convention: Kennedy, 806; Johnson, 409; Symington, 86; Stevenson, 79½; others, 140½; total, 1521.

Winning the struggle "all against one" within his party gave Khrushchev effective control of the Soviet political scene. Winning the Democratic nomination, however, was only the first stage in Kennedy's race for the Presidency. It was still necessary to defeat Nixon and the Republicans. In this contest, moreover, inherited allegiances and voting patterns would play a far greater role than they had in the nomination. Party conflict is institutionalized in a way in which the free-wheeling conflict among candidates and factions within the party is not. As a result, the impact of the candidate's strategy and resources would be proportionately less. He would be more a prisoner of events and institutions.

Kennedy's first need was to reunite his party behind him. This received top priority during the two or three weeks after his nomination. The first step was taken at the convention itself. Kennedy's selection of Johnson as his vice-presidential nominee was an effective bid for southern support; during the campaign it enabled Kennedy to concentrate his energies on the northern and western industrial states. The week after the convention Kennedy's brother—his campaign manager—went to New York in an effort to heal the wounds there and bring the reformers, Kennedy leaders, and state leaders together in a working electoral alliance. The candidate himself consulted with Stevenson and appointed him a foreign-policy adviser. The first week in August Kennedy talked with former President Truman and persuaded him to campaign for the ticket. He also visited Hyde Park and successfully appealed to Mrs. Roosevelt for her support. He thus followed through in the consolidation of his power within the party by uniting behind him both its liberal and its conservative factions. These efforts to unite the party were made easier by the intense dislike of Nixon shared by all segments of the Democratic Party.

As leader of the out-party Kennedy also had to take the offensive in defining the issues. In late August and the first half of September Kennedy outlined his views on agriculture, labor, social welfare, and foreign policy. Yet the role of policy issues during the campaign was relatively minor and the differences on policy between Kennedy and Nixon were small. Kennedy, it has been calculated, made some 220 specific policy commitments during the course of the campaign.[15] Some of these undoubtedly influenced some votes, but far more important than stands on particular issues were the image and the general appeal which the candidate projected. Kennedy's appeal was designed to transform his youth (a handicap) into vigor (an advantage): he stressed over and over the need "to get the country moving again." While Nixon appealed primarily in terms of "experience," Kennedy appealed primarily in terms of "movement." [16]

The one issue which was critically important in the campaign involved not policy but prejudice. That was religion. In a sense, Kennedy handled it in a manner similar to that in which Khrushchev handled the industrial reorganization. In the winter of 1956-1957 Khrushchev had been thrown on the defensive by the reorganization of economic planning approved by the Central Committee in December. In February, however, he counterattacked in the same area by bringing forth his proposals for industrial decentralization. In effect, he took the initiative away from his opponents, brought the issue out in the open for extensive public discussion, and in due course turned it to his advantage. Kennedy's handling of the religious issue in both the nomination and election campaigns was similar. Here too he was initially on the defensive. As long as the issue operated beneath the surface, moreover, it could do so only to his disadvantage. This was particularly true in West Virginia, where the population was 95 per cent Protestant and suspicious of him as a Catholic. To dispel this suspicion he had to meet the question head-on. He brought the issue up in successive speeches and attempted to turn it to his advantage by defining the question as one of tolerance versus intolerance.

In the campaign against Nixon, he acted similarly. Early in the campaign, on September 12, he confronted three hundred Protestant ministers in Houston, Texas, with a clear-cut and definite statement of his belief in the separation of church and state which played a major role in quieting Protestant fears through the remainder of the campaign. In the end, religion, unlike industrial reorganization for Khrushchev, did Kennedy more harm than good. While he attracted back to the Democratic Party many Catholics (and others) who had supported Eisenhower, Kennedy also lost many normally Democratic voters in the southern and border states and the midwest. By meeting the issue head-on, however, Kennedy undoubtedly minimized his losses on that score.

The most dramatic innovation in the 1960 presidential campaign was the series of four television debates between the two candidates. Less well known than Nixon and laboring against the alleged handicaps of youth and inexperience, Kennedy had everything to gain from these debates. Just why Nixon agreed to them is uncertain, but apparently he was simply confident of himself as a debater. The debates, however, were a major Kennedy triumph. Without them, Kennedy probably would not have won the election. The debates placed Kennedy on a footing of equality with Nixon and gave him the opportunity to demonstrate visually and dramatically that he was just as well informed and mature as the Vice President. They, in effect, undermined Nixon's campaign based on his appeal of "experience." Opinion surveys reveal that Nixon outpointed Kennedy on the issues but that Kennedy led in terms of appearance and "image," and "the debates were more effective in presenting the candidates than the issues." From 50 million to 75 million people watched each debate. Some 3 million voters reportedly decided how to vote on the basis of the debates, and a substantial majority of them voted for Kennedy.[17]

To win a majority in the electoral college Kennedy had to win the large northeastern and midwestern industrial states, where the Democratic machines were strong, labor unions well organized, and Catholics numerous. The Kennedy organization identified nine large states which accounted for 237 of the 269 electoral votes necessary to win: Massachusetts, New York, New Jersey, Pennsylvania, Ohio, Michigan, Illinois, Texas, and California. In terms of actual campaigning Kennedy concentrated his effort in these states, particularly those in the northeast. It was in these areas also that the Democrats made the biggest efforts to increase registration and voting participation. As the party of the low-income groups and the less well educated, the Democrats presumably benefit from a large vote. Their efforts in this line also paid off. Public interest in the candidates, the television debates, and the registration drives produced a vote of 68,832,000, 6 million more than in 1956.

The election was fantastically close. Kennedy received 49.7 per cent of the popular vote, Nixon 49.6 per cent. Kennedy won 303 electoral votes, Nixon 219. Kennedy's strategy of concentrating on the northeast and the midwest paid off, but the margin was razor thin. In New England and the middle Atlantic states, he won 134 electoral votes to Nixon's 12. He also carried the south and the border states by substantial majorities, 81 to 33 and 30 to 17, respectively. The candidates split the midwest, 50 votes for Nixon,

47 for Kennedy. In the twenty-one non-southern states west of the Mississippi, on the other hand, Nixon overwhelmed Kennedy, 114 votes to 34. Of his nine key states, Kennedy carried seven, losing only Ohio and California. In terms of the division of the popular vote between the major parties, it was the closest election since 1888.

POLICIES, APPEALS, AND POWER

Kennedy's and Khrushchev's respective strategies in the struggle for power had several important similarities. First, both Kennedy and Khrushchev combined appeals to the party organization and professional party workers with more general appeals to the people at large. To acquire power in the Soviet Union Khrushchev first had to capture the support of the Party apparat; to consolidate it he also courted the masses. To win the Democratic nomination, Kennedy first had to capture the imagination of the people through the primaries; to consolidate his lead he then had to win the support of the state and local party organizations. Khrushchev's appeal to the people was in terms of greater liberalization, de-Stalinization, and more food and consumer goods. Kennedy appealed in terms of his dynamic youthfulness, directness, and political moderation. For both Kennedy and Khrushchev, however, the key elite group was that of the professional party leaders. These were the men who would dominate the Central Committee on the one hand and the national convention on the other. Their opponents, in contrast, looked for support elsewhere. Beria drew his support from the secret police, Malenkov and Kaganovich from the governmental bureaucrats and economic planners. Similarly, Stevenson's support came largely from liberal groups and citizen groups on the fringes of the Democratic Party, while Johnson appealed to the Democratic members of Congress. Khrushchev, however, went after *obkom* secretaries and republic Party organizations, who held the key to political power, and, as insurance, the military who would be the arbiter if politics failed. Kennedy went after mayors, governors, state chairmen, county leaders—the electoral apparatchiki of American politics. He was seen as the leading candidate by Democratic state chairmen as early as 1958. The Soviet apparatchiki wanted to enhance their power vis-à-vis the governmental bureaucrats. Khrushchev won them by holding out the promise of a more influential Party apparat. The Democratic state and local leaders wanted to enhance their power within their party and vis-à-vis the Republicans. Kennedy won them with the prospect of winning more Democratic votes than any of his opponents.

Both leaders used their "home bases" to advantage as staging areas, sources of recruitment, and points of departure. Khrushchev's career is intimately related to his experience as Party leader in the Ukraine and as the political commissar of the wartime front there. This gave him direct contact with many Party and military leaders, and he could use these connections to combat the "Leningrad" group and to staff the apparat with loyal and tested protégés and supporters. Similarly, Kennedy took advantage of New England as the take-off point for his national campaign. Bailey, the loyal Connecticut strategist, and Kirichenko, the devoted Ukrainian Party boss, played similar key roles in the success of their leaders.

The Kennedy and Khrushchev campaigns also were similar in that both took the offensive early and consistently maintained it. In the initial, free-for-all phase of the struggle, neither Kennedy nor Khrushchev was the obvious winner, but by his efforts each established himself as *primus inter pares.* Khrushchev's ouster of Malenkov in February 1955 was comparable to Kennedy's defeat of Humphrey in the West Virginia primary. After these victories, Khrushchev and Kennedy became the men to beat. As a result, their opponents attempted to take advantage of changing conditions: the unrest in the satellites in 1956 adversely affected Khrushchev just as the U-2 incident and the break-up of the Paris summit conference adversely affected Kennedy. Khrushchev was charged with responsibility for the former, Kennedy with insufficient maturity to deal with the consequences of the latter. In this second phase, the only hope for their opponents lay in a strategy of "all against one." Despite differences in policy and ideology, they had to cooperate to head off the complete conquest of power. Thus, the "softs" (led by Malenkov) and the "hards" (led by Molotov) joined together in the anti-Party group. Similarly, Johnson, Symington, and Stevenson hoped to prevent Kennedy from getting a majority on the first ballot at the convention. In such circumstances, the position and power of lesser political leaders is also suddenly enhanced. Pervukhin and Saburov, for instance, helped form the Presidium majority against Khrushchev; among the candidate members, Shepilov and Zhukov played crucial roles on opposing sides. In the American case, the state leaders such as Lawrence, Daley, Crotty, and Williams, and favorite-son candidates such as Loveless, Docking, Smathers, and Meyner briefly found themselves in the position to shape the course of events. In the more circumscribed environment of the Soviet Presidium, the "anti-*primus*" coalition was able to hold together sufficiently to defeat Khrushchev temporarily until it was reversed in the larger Central Committee. In the American case, many of the older leaders of the Democratic Party —Truman, Rayburn, Mrs. Roosevelt, Stevenson himself—were opposed to Kennedy's nomination. If the Democratic Party had had a Presidium, it probably would have been dominated by such people, who could have blocked Kennedy's advance. But as it was, the issue went directly to the convention, and in that locale Kennedy (like Khrushchev in the Central Committee) was able to muster a majority from the regional party leaders. In both cases, however, the victory was close.

In their campaigns for the top position, both Kennedy and Khrushchev strove to pre-empt the "centrist" position, thereby stamping their opponents with the label of extremism. Kennedy is reported to have been immensely impressed in the course of the campaign with the conservatism of the American voter, and his appeal was designed to create the image of a vigorous but statesmanlike and *moderate* leader. This moderation of the American middle class had its counterpart in the "Don't rock the boat" outlook of the Soviet apparat. They resented Malenkov's early reforms, and in Khrushchev they found an effective protagonist of their interests. Desiring neither Malenkov's concessions to the public nor the dangerously antiquated Stalinism of Molotov and Kaganovich, they backed the vigorous yet "moderate" Khrushchev. And in that sense, both Kennedy and Khrushchev duplicated the earlier stratagems of Eisenhower and Stalin.

The struggles for power also revealed significant differences in the two political systems. Kennedy's support came initially from groups outside the system. His campaign was devoted essentially to converting this support and appeal into strength within it: strength at the Democratic convention in July, strength in the voting booths in November. Both Kennedy and his rivals, of course, made efforts to undercut one another's sources of support. More importantly, however, each attempted to broaden his own source of support, to widen his appeal to encompass more groups, and to mobilize the apathetic, the indifferent, the ambivalent. This was true during both the preconvention campaign and the electoral campaign.

Khrushchev won by eliminating from the competition those political forces which might challenge the Party bureaucracy. Each stage in the build-up of his power was marked by the contracting of other power bases: the execution of Beria and the subsequent weakening of the secret police; the ouster of Malenkov and the subsequent industrial reorganization, breaking up the governmental economic bureaucracy; the firing of Zhukov and the reimposition of strict political controls on the military. The dynamics of the Soviet system make it impossible for the Party apparat to tolerate potentially autonomous institutions. Nor can the top leader tolerate potentially autonomous political figures. Lacking a secure office and clear-cut legitimacy, Khrushchev had to weed out all those who might be in a position to oppose him. He won by crushing competitive groups; Kennedy won by generating and absorbing sympathetic ones.

Kennedy's victories in the nomination and election struggles did not eliminate from politics those who had opposed him. They kept their positions and much of their influence. They had not staked all or nothing in the struggle for power. Instead, after gaining the nomination of his party, Kennedy had to pacify the leaders of the opposing factions and win their support for the election. Johnson, Stevenson, and large numbers of their adherents subsequently held high office in the Kennedy Administration. Similarly, after winning his narrow electoral victory, Kennedy appealed for Republican support, took steps to identify himself with key Republican leaders, and appointed important Republicans such as Dillon, McCloy, and Clay to posts in his Administration. In the Soviet case, the consolidation of power meant the elimination of potential opponents; in the American case, it meant their conciliation. Zhukov, who supported Khrushchev's bid for power, was purged; Johnson, who opposed Kennedy's bid, became Vice President.

In the Soviet Union the struggle for power took place within the ruling circles of the government. In the United States it occurred outside the government. As a result, policy issues played a major role in the Soviet struggle, while political appeals dominated the American contest. As key figures in the government, Khrushchev and his competitors were immediately concerned with the making of policy as well as the struggle for power. The test of an individual's power was his ability, first, to get his policy adopted by his colleagues, and, second, to insure that the policy would be a success in practice, at least during the struggle. (Both the virgin lands and the economic decentralization backfired, but too late to be of any help to Khrushchev's enemies.) Victories and defeats in the struggle for power were directly reflected in the direction of governmental policy. To win support Khrushchev had to make major innovations in policy, on the one hand, and to bargain over policy issues with institutional interests, such as the Army and the agricultural apparatchiki, on the other. Between 1953 and 1955 Khrushchev conducted his struggle for power by pushing agricultural reform, heavy industry, and a "hard" line on foreign policy. Between 1955 and 1957, he shifted his tactics and his policy views and backed de-Stalinization, industrial reorganization, and co-existence with the West. All these policy stands were directly related to winning the support of key groups in the struggle for power. Khrushchev's ouster of Malenkov with the aid of the military and heavy industry groups, for instance, was immediately followed by an increase in the defense budget. Similarly, his daring but successful innovations in policy—the virgin lands, rapprochement with Yugoslavia, de-Stalinization, industrial reorganization— registered the expansion of his power and won him additional support from key groups in the political system.

The struggle between Kennedy and his competitors, in contrast, was divorced from a policy-making context. Khrushchev had to win the support of Party and bureaucratic leaders directly concerned with the specific content and substance of governmental policy. Kennedy and Nixon, however, had to win the support of large masses of voters, who, unlike institutional leaders, were moved not by specific commitments but by general appeals. While real issues of policy were at stake in the Soviet struggle, the differences between Kennedy and his opponents on policy issues were marginal at best. To find an American counterpart to Khrushchev's proposals for de-Stalinization or industrial reorganization it would be necessary to imagine Nixon endorsing socialism or Kennedy advocating the abolition of state governments. The Soviet struggle took place within the closed confines of the higher Party bureaucracy, and everything was at stake in terms of both individual power and governmental policy. The American struggle took place in the open; it involved many more participants, and its implications for both policy and individual power were correspondingly limited.

CHAPTER SIX

The Ambivalence of Power

IN ANY political system rare is the policy that enjoys unanimous support. Most policies are backed by some groups, opposed by others, and viewed with indifference by still others. In the exercise of power a leader must calculate the cost to his power of a commitment to a particular program, and must estimate the likely consequences for his other policies. Even when a policy is acknowledged to be socially or nationally desirable and the leader is able to adopt it, he must still make the subjective judgment of whether the policy is politically expedient.

The Soviet leader and the American President are both generalists: they must look at problems in broad perspective and integrate increasingly complex structures of political power. In certain conditions, the policy choices facing them may be ambivalent, and, confronted with conflicting advice and clashing interests, they may prefer to probe and explore rather than to initiate directly a policy and commit their power on its behalf.

In the United States the choice that the leader makes is complicated by the fact that he operates under strict constitutional limits on his power. To act he must bargain. In addition, the political tradition of the country precludes reliance on coercion if substantial minority opposition exists. Instead, it is necessary to rely on persuasion, compromise, delay. Determined opposition to a policy enjoys an automatic advantage over equally determined support. The opponents can take refuge in states' rights, in local autonomy, in Congressional jealousy of executive power, in cross-checking interests, in the generally conservative outlook of the American people. As a result, it is often politically advantageous to avoid controversial measures since the very controversy could paralyze all policy-making. Postponement of action (however desirable that action may be) thus can be seen as more constructive than provoking the anticipated destructive consequences of conflict. National unanimity on behalf of action is generated in the face of a sudden foreign threat to national survival. Otherwise, national consensus is built gradually, through accretion, and eventually the country perceives the dangers of inaction. The United States President thus faces external limits to his power, and these in turn may be fortified by his own personal, politically motivated constraints.

In the Soviet Union the ever-present unanimity of support for the leader's actions shields the restraints which affect his power. Although free of the formal and external limits that are so important in the American case, the Soviet leader often must anticipate the reactions of his followers. He finds it desirable to avoid policies the execution of which would compromise his ability to pursue other aspects of his program. He too must weigh risks and costs of action against the consequences of inaction. During periods of the struggle for succession, the Soviet leader's calculation becomes even more complex—any initiative is likely to create a coalition of rivals and opponents; but any temporizing is likely to yield the advantage of political initiative to the competitor. In these circumstances, as we have seen, abrupt changes of policy are frequent, and policy becomes the means to power. This was eminently the case with the decentralization scheme of 1957: Khrushchev's success in having it adopted was a key factor in his political victory.

In stable dictatorial conditions, however, the leader may sometimes exercise power in matters which do not affect the security of his position. Then, as with the education reform of 1958, he can tolerate substantial amendments to his original proposal. In other cases, the secure leader applies his power to the full and overrides even well-entrenched opposition, either because failure would have a negative feedback effect on his power or because there is sufficient backing within the ruling bureaucracy for the specific measure. The reorganization of the CPSU and the food-prices increase of 1962 were thus adopted with the leader's full and evident commitment on behalf of these policies. Finally, even the secure Soviet leader may be uncertain of the costs of a particular policy, he may be unwilling to pay the political price of overriding the opposition it would enkindle, and he may be too preoccupied with other concerns to commit himself fully on behalf of its adoption.

The Kennedy Administration's attitude on civil rights during 1961-1962 and Khrushchev's attitude toward the production of consumer goods in 1960-1961 reflected this ambivalence of power. Substantively these two issues were very different. Politically, however, they posed similar problems for the top leadership. They are hence more comparable examples of the limits on power than, say, a comparison of Soviet discrimination against the Jews with the American civil rights problem. The Jews in the Soviet Union did not have powerful proponents in the government; in recent years, the Soviet leaders have not tried—against entrenched political opposition—to improve the lot of the Soviet Jew. A small minority (only about 1.5 per cent of the population), the Jews could not command mass support. No Soviet leader was inclined to stake his position on a policy of improving their lot. Neither his power and political popularity nor the domestic tranquillity of the country depended on it, as to an extent they were involved in the consumer-goods debate. And both political power and civic order were certainly heavily involved in the case of civil rights in America.

For both Kennedy and Khrushchev, political means and political ends were out of joint. Yet in the two countries there was urgent need for political action. A hundred years after the Civil War one-tenth of the American people were living in conditions of social and political discrimination. A large portion of this minority was denied even the elementary constitutional right to vote. Negro children in most southern states were attending segregated schools, and a similar condition existed *de facto* for the Negroes residing in the north. Due process of law was often violated in the southern states in cases involving Negroes. There was rampant discrimination in hiring and employment; the Negroes were also the first to feel the impact of unemployment. Social discrimination was openly proclaimed to be "the way of life" in the southern states: the Negroes could not eat in the same restaurants or lunch counters as whites, sleep in the same hotels, attend the same churches or theaters, play on the same athletic teams, swim in the same swimming pools, or marry with whites. The structure of political power in the South rested on the principle of white supremacy. Because of the seniority system in Congress, it was effectively defended within the central government.

In the Soviet Union thirty-five years after the Bolshevik revolution the standard of living was still below the levels attained in 1928, the year in which "the socialist reconstruction" of Soviet society was commenced. The people lived in a state of relative poverty, and this poverty was the proclaimed policy of the government. The official theory of the rulers was that during the construction of socialism popular demand should exceed supply, and this formula justified coerced social exploitation in order to develop most rapidly a heavy industrial base. As a result, housing stagnated,* consumer goods were short in supply and of extraordinarily poor quality, agricultural production slumped, and by the early fifties there were widespread food shortages. The World War had wrought enormous devastation, which further helped to keep the standard of living low. The regime, however, associated the building of socialism-communism with the development of heavy industry, and did little for the Soviet consumer. The leading Soviet Party cadres were accordingly permeated by men to whom heavy industry and building communism were inseparable.

KHRUSHCHEV AND THE CONSUMER-GOODS "DEBATE," 1960-1961

Power not only corrupts; it also educates. It is striking how Kennedy and Khrushchev became more and more preoccupied with the political implications of social inadequacy as they climbed higher and higher on the ladder of power. Khrushchev at first even opposed Malenkov's efforts, initiated immediately after Stalin's death, to improve the lot of the Soviet consumer. Both Malenkov and Khrushchev were guided by opportunistic motives: Malenkov, the chief Party apparatchik, was courting popular support; Khrushchev opposed Malenkov and thereby gained the support of the Party apparat, the military, and the heavy industrial bureaucracy. By 1957, however, the roles of the two men had been almost reversed: Khrushchev, firmly in charge of the Party machinery, was campaigning for popular support and was promising the Soviet people higher standards of living. His views were ridiculed by his opponents, who were now joined by Malenkov.

By 1960 Khrushchev had been firmly in power for three years.

---

* For example, by 1961, after an intensive housing-construction drive, the average living space per Soviet inhabitant was approximately 8 square meters. (The minimum sanitary standard recommended by the United States Bureau of Prisons is 9 square meters.)

He had had time to shape his longer-range strategy and to take stock of his domestic situation. It appears that he became convinced that in the context of mutual nuclear deterrence the internal character of Soviet society would play a greater role than ever before in determining the effectiveness of communist appeal abroad. His travels to the United States and to western Europe also must have made him more conscious of the backwardness of Soviet society. At the same time, the relaxation in domestic terror made the Soviet citizens more inclined to voice their dissatisfaction with living conditions. Some even complained (the Party press reported disapprovingly) that too much emphasis was being put on the construction of space rockets and too little on a decent pair of shoes. The relative improvement in the standard of living after Stalin's death, resulting in an annual 6.3-per-cent increase in average real wages, had whetted public appetites. With Khrushchev's power more secure, the problem of consumption was no longer the object of merely political manipulation; it could now be examined in the perspective of broad public policy.

Early in 1959, in outlining the seven-year plan for 1959-1965, Khrushchev proclaimed that one of the principal Soviet tasks is "to attain the world's highest living standard. In this stage of the competition, the Soviet Union intends to surpass the United States economically." But in spite of his promise, the plan subscribed explicitly to the traditional formula stressing "the preponderant development of heavy industry," and the projected rates of growth reflected the old bias for producer over consumer goods. If the lot of the Soviet consumer were to improve, changes both in doctrine and in practice had yet to come. The first hint that they might actually be coming was given the Soviet public in the late summer of 1960 when *Izvestia* published (on August 4) an "esoteric" criticism of Stalin's "law" which had postulated that during the building of socialism-communism demand should exceed supply. The critic, the Deputy Minister for Trade of the RSFSR, M. Denisov, suggested instead almost the opposite formulation: that sales determine the output of consumer goods. Later that year, the December session of the Supreme Soviet heard the Chairman of the USSR State Planning Committee, V. N. Novikov, announce that the year's industrial output had been overfulfilled. Novikov then added:

stage for its crystallization. He was not yet recommending a specific and drastically novel program.

Within that general framework the other Soviet leaders could focus on more specific issues, in keeping with their individual responsibilities. Thus Mikoyan, particularly after his trip to the United States, repeatedly urged improvements in methods of distribution of consumer goods and spoke of the need to increase wages, which in turn presumably implied also more consumer goods if inflation was to be avoided. The Trade Union Leader V. V. Grishin (promoted in January of 1961 to the Party Presidium) spoke mostly about improving social services and benefits, suggesting that surplus from overfulfillment of the heavy industrial plans should be channeled in that direction. Presumably because of the close connection between the Trade Union bureaucracy and the heavy-industry management, Grishin still tended to consider social advancement dependent on the further development of heavy industry.[1] The importance of light industry and technological progress for "the achievement of the highest standard of living" was stressed in speeches by A. N. Kosygin, brought into the Party Presidium by Khrushchev and given the task of directing industry and planning. Kosygin also echoed Khrushchev on the subject of balancing supply and demand, and explicitly gave Khrushchev the credit for measures designed to expand the light industry. Leaders more directly connected with agriculture, such as Polyansky, Voronov, and Podgorny, not surprisingly laid the primary emphasis on greater allocations to agriculture. Some of the other leaders connected more directly with Party affairs took a middle line: they proclaimed themselves to be in favor of further heavy industrial development, of better defenses, and of a higher standard of living. Typical in that respect were the speeches of P. N. Demichev, the Party Secretary of Moscow, coopted later into the Party Presidium and late in 1962 placed in charge of light industry, and L. F. Ilyichev, the Party CC Secretary in charge of ideological matters. Just as in the United States no responsible national leader could go on record as being *against* civil rights, no Soviet leader could publicly proclaim his opposition to a better deal for the Soviet man.

Absence of open opposition and Khrushchev's public endorsement of a shift in the traditional allocations policy were not tantamount to a policy. Khrushchev himself had to consider other commitments and priorities. Although he gave a great deal of personal attention to correcting the deficiencies of the Soviet economy (and made agriculture his pet project), foreign affairs increasingly preoccupied him personally. This meant that he could not make a clear-cut choice on behalf of a time- and energy-consuming domestic commitment, and effecting a major policy shift would have required his constant attention and personal pressure. No other Soviet leader could carry through such a major initiative, overcoming so many interlocking vested interests in industry, defense, and the central bureaucracy.

The extent of his travels shows Khrushchev's personal involvement in foreign affairs. During 1960, in the late winter and early spring, he visited southeast Asia and France, France again in May, Austria during the summer, and the United Nations in New York in the fall. In early 1961 he traveled to eastern Europe; in late spring he met with Kennedy in Vienna, then visited East Berlin. His frequent absences were also clear proof of his personal domination of the Soviet political scene. The only alternative conclusion would be that Khrushchev was only a figurehead, a dubious proposition in the light of his personal monopoly of all the top power positions, public policy initiatives, and powers of political appointment. His absences did mean, however, that he could not give his undivided attention to domestic problems, and that at that particular moment he himself did not attach the highest priority to them.

Independently of his own interest in them, foreign affairs as such had an impact on domestic Soviet policies. The middle of 1960 had seen an accentuation of international tensions, particularly in the wake of the U-2 affair and the breakup of the top-level Paris meeting in May 1960. Subsequently, however, tensions declined somewhat, while the American elections made the Soviet leaders hopeful that the new Kennedy Administration would be more amenable to meeting Soviet demands in Berlin and elsewhere. This period corresponded to the internal Soviet discussion summarized above. In April 1961, however, came the abortive Bay of Pigs intervention in Cuba, followed shortly afterward by the Khrushchev-Kennedy confrontation in Vienna. The Soviet leader went away from it without having obtained Western

clearly that "some comrades" were opposed, and at the very least they must have included the high echelons of the heavy industrial bureaucracy. They doubtless argued that such a shift was economically premature and that its consequences would be generally unfavorable to the Soviet economy and defense. Their arguments were primarily of the operational type (see Chapter Four). Within the context of the "Leninist style of work," encouraged by Khrushchev personally and by the CPSU's campaign against the "cult of the personality," there was now room for discussion, "log-rolling," debating, and urging. In the late spring and early summer of 1961 members of the Central Committee (among whom the largest group by far had a heavy-industry professional background), and heavy-industry ministers and managers were certainly busy drafting memoranda proving their particular cases, telephoning one another, attempting to convince individual Presidium members of their point of view. All of that impinged on the priorities and the views of the First Secretary, still engaged only in initiating a policy.

Other considerations also complicated the public dialogue. By 1960 and especially 1961 the decentralization reforms of 1957 were being steadily reversed in the name of improved coordination and efficiency. There is reason to believe that even more important was the Party bureaucracy's political fear of the emergence of local power centers. Khrushchev, who had initiated the 1957 reform in order to break up the state-economic bureaucracy which was opposing his march to power, was now actively engaged in the new recentralization designed to consolidate the state's control over the economy.

This shift, however, contributed to the prevailing atmosphere of confusion and ambivalence. It meant that the discussion about consumer goods was taking place within a highly fluid institutional context, with recently created *sovnarkhozy* (state economic councils) being reorganized, with economic bureaucrats shifting back to Moscow barely after having been relocated, with abolished ministries reappearing as state committees. Such conditions were not conducive to a rational, thoroughly planned, and systematically organized reallocation of economic resources, and they doubtless contributed to the confused character of many public utterances. In addition, Khrushchev and his advisers had previously acknowledged that improved production of consumer goods and better distribution could be achieved only by decentralizing and bringing closer to the consumer the industries concerned. The same was true of agriculture. Yet that went against the dominant trend in Soviet economic reorganization in 1960 and 1961.

The cumulative effect of international tensions, of conflicting domestic pressures and advice, of Khrushchev's own varied pre-occupations, was that by the middle of 1961 he was equivocating again. Toward the end of June Khrushchev warned the Soviet public that military allocations might be increased, and early in July the announcement was made that more than 3 billion rubles were being added to the defense budget. At the same time, the planned cuts in the size of the Army were suspended. In September, Soviet nuclear tests were resumed. In August, however, Khrushchev moved to reassure the Soviet people that a new program of austerity was not at hand. In a national television address he reiterated his belief that "the system that does a better job of satisfying men's material and spiritual requirements will triumph," announced a new 3-billion allocation to light industry (thereby neatly balancing the increased defense appropriation), and re-assured the population that "the tentative view of the Central Committee and the government" is that no further defense allocations are necessary. Exactly three weeks later, however, a statement of the Central Committee announced "a decision on increasing defense expenditures somewhat in 1961."

The meeting of the 22nd Party Congress in October gave Khrushchev and the other leaders an opportunity to define authoritatively the Party's views on economic development. The initiation of policy begun in January 1961 led not to a formal recommendation but rather to an adjustment of conflicting positions. In his address Khrushchev stated that "in the creation of the material-technological basis for communism a decisive role is played by heavy industry as the foundation of the whole national economy." This was somewhat weaker than the earlier formulation of the seven-year plan, which spoke of the heavy industry's "preponderant development," but stronger than Khrushchev's own earlier references to even development, and clearly a reassurance to the defenders of the established maxim. However, in an esoteric but meaningful change, the final version of the new Party program adopted by the Congress listed the heavy industrial sector's objec-

Kennedy's moderation or ambivalence was reflected in the voting on the three key issues involved in the 1957 civil rights bill. To prevent it from being bottled up in the Judiciary Committee (whose chairman was Senator Eastland of Mississippi), the bill's supporters moved that it be placed directly on the Senate calendar without reference to a committee. This move had the backing of virtually all the liberal Democrats and moderate Republicans. Kennedy and the conservative Frank Lausche from Ohio were the only senators of either party from the large midwestern and northeastern industrial states to oppose it. In the key vote on the substance of the bill, however, over whether to give the Attorney General power to intervene in civil-rights proceedings, Kennedy supported the pro-civil-rights position. On the third major issue, concerning the so-called jury-trial amendment proposed by a group of moderate senators to make the bill more palatable to the South, Kennedy again split from the more ardent northern liberals and voted for the amendment. Some northern Negro and liberal leaders saw Kennedy's votes on the bill as a "profile in cowardice." His biographer sums it up more accurately when he says that Kennedy

> showed a profile in caution and moderation. He walked a teetering tightrope; at the same time that he was telling liberals of the effectiveness of a bill that included the O'Mahoney [jury-trial] provision, he was assuring worried Southerners that it was a moderate bill that would be enforced by *Southern* courts and *Southern* juries—Kennedy's italics.[4]

As he became increasingly involved in his campaign for the presidential nomination, Kennedy tended more and more to associate himself with liberal causes and to work more closely with the liberals in the Senate. Even so, he remained less strongly committed on civil-rights issues than most other northern Democratic liberals. On nineteen controversial amendments to the 1960 civil-rights bill, Kennedy voted against the southern bloc sixteen times, more often than the majority of northern Democrats but less often than such stanch liberals as Douglas, Clark, Morse, Humphrey, and McNamara. In the race for the Democratic nomination, Kennedy continued to be a moderate on civil rights. Hubert Humphrey was an outspoken liberal; Lyndon Johnson was given credit for steering both the 1957 and 1960 civil-rights acts through the Senate; over the years even Symington, from the border state of

Missouri, had voted pro-civil rights more frequently than Kennedy. At the opening of the Democratic convention in July Kennedy was "the *least* popular among Negroes of all Democratic candidates. . . ." [5]

Yet Kennedy was nominated by the convention, and during the campaign that followed, civil rights and the Negro vote played a crucially important role. In terms of both ideology and strategy Kennedy had little choice on the question. The 1960 Democratic platform included the strongest civil-rights plank ever adopted by a major party. It referred approvingly to the sit-in movement which had begun the previous winter in Greensboro, North Carolina, and it called for: the elimination of literacy tests and poll taxes; a requirement that all school districts take "first steps" toward desegregation by 1963; technical and financial assistance to school districts facing special problems in desegregation; power for the Attorney General to file civil injunction suits in federal courts to prevent the denial of civil rights; creation of a Fair Employment Practices Commission; strengthening the existing Commission on Civil Rights; equal employment and the end of segregation throughout federal services, institutions, and in the performance of federal contracts; and an end to discrimination in all federal housing and federally assisted housing. The plank embodied the views of the northern civil-rights liberals.

A presidential candidate is not bound by his party platform. In this case, however, election strategy dictated a similar stance. Kennedy's success depended largely upon his carrying the large northern industrial states of New York, Pennsylvania, Ohio, Michigan, and Illinois. In all these states the Negro vote was crucial: Negroes made up 14 per cent of the population in New York City, 26 per cent in Philadelphia, 29 per cent in Detroit.[6] Kennedy consequently made a strong appeal on civil rights: he denounced the failure of President Eisenhower to eliminate discrimination in federal housing "by a stroke of his pen"; he asked Senator Clark and Representative Celler to draw up legislation embodying the Democratic civil-rights planks; and at the climax of the campaign in the last week of October, Kennedy directly identified himself with the Negro protest movement by telephoning the wife of Martin Luther King offering his help and sympathy on behalf of her husband, who had been locked up in a Georgia prison for participating in a civil-rights

public-opinion polls. In a poll among Negroes he outran the Republicans by thirty to one.[7] The Administration thus had good grounds for thinking that its Negro supporters could neither help nor hurt it in achieving its policy goals. Nor could the Negroes significantly affect its chances of re-election. Their overwhelming support for the Administration deprived the Negroes of leverage against it.

The Kennedy Administration's own sense of the needs of the nation combined with the differences between its policy and electoral constituencies thus led to a go-easy policy on civil rights during its first two years. The two chief needs of the Negroes, in the Administration's view, were to improve his economic position throughout the country and to increase Negro voting in the South. The best way to accomplish the first goal, the Administration held, was to stimulate the economy generally and to enact the Administration's social-welfare proposals. Hence, influence should be directed to getting these measures through Congress rather than proposing major new civil-rights legislation. "Suppose the President were to send up a dramatic message on civil rights," as one Presidential assistant put it, "and alienate enough Southerners to kill his economic program in Congress. Would the Negro be better off? I think he'd be worse off." [8] On the voting front, the Administration proposed to move forward with a vigorous enforcement of the Civil Rights Acts of 1957 and 1960. Between 1957 and 1961 the Eisenhower Administration inaugurated nine suits on behalf of Negro voting rights; during its first year in office the Kennedy Administration launched fourteen.[9] The Administration also established a new Presidential Committee on Equal Employment Opportunity, under the chairmanship of Vice President Johnson, to work against discrimination by government contractors, and it pushed the desegregation of interstate transportation facilities in the South. In other areas, however, the Administration held back, even from purely administrative action. Kennedy's campaign criticism of Eisenhower for failing to end discrimination in federal housing "by a stroke of his pen" came back to haunt him during the first two years of his Administration. Liberal and Negro groups demanded that Kennedy wield his pen. But the President was anxious to secure the passage of new housing legislation and to create a new Cabinet department devoted to housing and urban affairs. If moderate southern Democrats came to his support on these measures, he could hardly turn about and repay them by issuing the desegregation order. As a result, it was not until after the 1962 congressional elections that the presidential "stroke of the pen" ordered the end of discrimination in federally assisted housing.

In line with this general strategy the Administration kept its requests for civil-rights legislation to a minimum during 1961 and 1962. The only such measure it supported in 1961 was the extension of the Civil Rights Commission for another two years. In 1962 the Administration proposed two bills: a constitutional amendment abolishing the poll tax, which was passed with some southern support; and a bill to end literacy tests for voting, which was blocked by a Senate filibuster. Civil-rights legislation was pushed by other groups, but without Administration backing it had no chance of success in a conservative Congress that wanted to keep the status quo. Senator Clark and Congressman Celler, for instance, introduced the legislation based on the Democratic platform which they had drawn up in 1960 at the request of candidate Kennedy. In 1961, however, no support for it was forthcoming from President Kennedy. Similarly, the Administration opposed a bill sponsored by Representative Powell (one of the four Negroes in Congress and chairman of the House Labor and Education Committee) to prohibit federal support for apprentice training programs practicing discrimination.

The Administration's reluctance to push new civil-rights measures stimulated vigorous criticism from Negro and liberal groups. In 1962, for instance, the labor secretary of the NAACP charged that there were "dangerously nullifying tendencies" in the Administration's record on civil rights.[10] A year later, when the civil-rights issue was coming to a climax, other Negro leaders declared that the Administration had simply substituted an "inadequate" civil-rights policy for the "miserable" policy of the Eisenhower Administration. The President, Martin Luther King said, has approached civil rights simply as a political problem rather than as a moral one. This criticism coincided with the views previously expressed by liberal commentators, journalists, and professors that the President was failing to exert a positive moral leadership for his program, and that his approach was too strongly tempered to

in 1964. This, however, was beyond their power. What they could do, however, was threaten the civic peace and the American image abroad. The Administration was left with no choice but to take positive action. In the middle of June, James Reston neatly summed up the dramatic change in the Administration situation and its attitude:

> The Negro leaders of America . . . have made the President and probably a substantial majority of the Congress realize that this country is now faced not with a Negro "problem" but with a Negro revolution.
>
> This has changed many things here. It has changed the Administration's order of priorities. It has put the domestic revolution above the cold war on the President's catalogue of urgent business. It has destroyed the official assumption that the race question could be dealt with by political manipulation. It has forced a major bipartisan effort . . . for new civil rights legislation, probably at the expense of the rest of Kennedy's domestic legislative program.[13]

While the long-run aim of the President was to broaden civil rights, his immediate aim was to end the demonstrations and to restore civic order. His legislative proposals were designed precisely to do this. At the same time, pressure in the streets seemed to be the only way of producing the legislation which would end the demonstrations in the streets. "Let's face it," one Republican senator was quoted as saying. "The moderates will swing toward cloture [in the Senate] only if the mood of Negroes is ugly enough when it comes time for a showdown." [14] The threat of continued demonstrations and violence was thus a sword over the head of Congress, but it cut both ways. Too much pressure in the streets might also stimulate more opposition in Congress. The attitude of the Administration was thus curiously ambivalent. On the one hand, the President unsuccessfully urged the Negro leaders to change their plans for a "march on Washington" and to agree to a truce in anti-segregation demonstrations. "Unruly tactics or pressure," he warned, "will not help and may hinder the effective consideration" of his civil-rights proposals. On the other hand, his legislative lieutenants pointed to the same demonstrations as the major reason for timely action on these proposals.

The shift in the situation and the resulting change in Administration strategy involved serious political costs for the Administration. The bitter controversy which developed was itself a defeat for the Administration. President Kennedy was unable to maintain a "consensus" on civil rights. The Negro leaders, by dramatically breaking the consensus and polarizing opinion, had forced him to become leader of one side rather than the mediator between the two. From a high point of 76 in January 1963, the President's popularity rating dropped steadily as he became more and more involved in the issues, reaching a low point of 61 in June. Nor was he able to command a significant popular majority on the civil-rights question: in June, according to one poll, 49 per cent of the population favored the way he was handling the problem, while 51 per cent disapproved.

The general decline in his popularity was, of course, relevant both to the President's persuasiveness with Congress and to his prospects for re-election. In more specifically electoral terms, commitment on the civil-rights issues forced the Administration virtually to write off the South in the 1964 election. Southern politicians competed with each other in disavowing any connection with the Administration. The Republicans, who had significantly increased their vote in the South in the 1962 elections (before the civil-rights issue came to a head), now looked forward confidently to carrying the bulk of the South in 1964. In the 1960 contest, Kennedy had carried all southern states except Florida, Mississippi, Tennessee, and Virginia. In the summer of 1963 he was reported to be planning a 1964 strategy on the assumption that he would carry none of them except possibly Texas, Georgia, and Louisiana.[15] In 1963, the Administration's civil-rights bill seemed likely to cost it from 50 to 75 electoral votes in the 1964 election.

The electoral cost of civil rights also might not be limited to the South. The New Deal Democratic Party which Kennedy inherited was a combination of southern whites and northern low-income groups. In addition to losing the southern support, there was the possibility that the Administration would lose votes among northern wage earners and lower middle-class elements who would feel threatened by the new Negro demands for jobs, housing, and school desegregation. Defections from the northern Democratic coalition could easily cost the Administration Illinois, Ohio, and other in-

dustrial states in the 1964 election. In both South and North, the
civil-rights issue thus enormously complicated the Administration's
plans for re-election.

Top priority for the civil-rights bill also, of course, had its price
in terms of policy. The tax bill, which earlier had top priority, was
now downgraded. The prospects for other less urgent Administration measures dimmed appreciably in the face of a prolonged
Senate filibuster. In addition, the legislative coalition which the
Administration had been carefully piecing together to support its
domestic economic program was now shattered. By the early spring
of 1963 the Administration's two-year wooing of the southern
Democrats in Congress had appeared to be finally producing results. The civil-rights bill torpedoed this achievement. The Republican–southern Democratic legislative coalition reappeared on the
scene with the rise of the civil-rights issue.

Finally, the issue posed a major threat for the Administration
and the country. What if Congress did not pass a rights bill satisfactory to the majority of the Negro leaders? The alternative, in
the President's words, would "be continued, if not increased, racial
strife—causing the leadership on both sides to pass from the hands
of reasonable and responsible men to the purveyors of hate and
violence, endangering our domestic tranquillity, retarding our nation's economic and social progress, and weakening the respect
with which the rest of the world regards us." Yet in the summer of
1963 few would rule out the possibility that such might well be the
case. To break the Senate filibuster the Administration would need
the support of at least twenty-two Republicans. It could count with
assurance on the support of about a dozen. The problem was to
win the support of the additional number required without weakening the bill so much as to alienate the Negroes.

The Administration's bill fell into the classic pattern of American policy innovations. For a decade or more liberal and Negro
groups had been urging vigorous federal action on civil rights. The
Administration's bill embodied many of their demands. Administration witnesses defended it before Congress on the grounds of
morality, equality, and justice. Its presentation to Congress in June
1963, however, was the pragmatic response of the Administration
to the immediate need to "get the struggle off the streets and into
the courts." What gave the bill prospects for passage was not the

principles behind it but the threat of mounting disorder if it failed to pass. On the one hand, there was a minority group demanding "freedom" and "equality" immediately. Opposed was another minority invoking states' rights and property rights. Between the two the Administration steered a thoroughly pragmatic course, attempting to weave a new basis of consensus and to put an end to civil discord through a new definition of federal responsibilities in civil rights.

ENDS, MEANS, AND POWER

During his struggle for power Khrushchev identified himself with the needs of heavy industry and defense. Once securely in power, however, he moved toward a major innovation in Soviet policy by proposing to give consumer goods equal priority with industrial goods. During his struggle for the Presidency Kennedy became clearly identified with a strong pro-civil-rights and pro-Negro position. Once in office, however, he refused to throw his weight behind major civil-rights legislation. In this he was adjusting from the demands of his electoral constituency to the demands of his policy constituency. Khrushchev's emphasis on consumer goods in 1960 and 1961 fitted in with the over-all thrust of his policy: demobilization of land forces and more stress on strategic weapons, the emphasis on peaceful coexistence, the continued stress on economic competition and on overtaking the United States in industrial production and in standard of living. His proposed shift in policy, however, was a major innovation, ideologically and politically. There was silent but real opposition to it among Soviet bureaucrats and other Party leaders. In his pre-eminent position in the Soviet system, however, Khrushchev was able to push his proposal forward and to prepare the ground for this major change. Only when the domestic opposition was reinforced by a change in the international climate did Khrushchev moderate his position. It was that complex of "external" factors—the Soviet desire to do something on Berlin, the pressure from the Chinese, the stanch unwillingness of Kennedy to make concessions at Vienna—which led Khrushchev to moderate his own policy innovation. In effect, the pressure of events and of multiplying concerns and demands forced him to move from a position of commitment to one of ambivalence with respect to the priority of consumer-goods industry. Subsequently, the 1963 agricultural crisis finally did force reforms in the USSR, with striking reallocations to fertilizer production, light industry, and agriculture. The agricultural crisis played the same triggering role as the Negro demonstrations in the United States.

In the American case, the situation was similar—but reversed. The opposition to civil rights in Congress, the entrenched position of the southern Democrats there, the absence of Negro political sanctions against the Administration, and the President's own estimate that top priority should go to stimulating the economy and reestablishing American leadership in the Western alliance, all led him to equivocate on civil rights during 1961 and 1962. In 1963 an outside "trigger" forced him to shift from ambivalence to commitment. President Kennedy, it has often been reported, believed in the maxim, "When it is not necessary to change, it is necessary not to change." An implicit corollary of this conservative maxim is that there are times when change is necessary. In 1963 this became the situation with respect to civil rights. The Administration dramatically reversed its position and expeditiously moved to bring civil-rights legislation before Congress. Khrushchev was forced to modify his proposed innovation by developments over which he had no control outside the Soviet Union. Kennedy was forced to modify his position by developments over which he had no control within American society. There is no evidence that political pressure from Soviet consumers or consumer-goods industry was the decisive factor in leading Khrushchev to innovate. The timing and the nature of the action reflected Khrushchev's views, not those of another policy group. The consumers, an amorphous social force, were not represented directly by any policy group. The one group that came closest to sharing their interest, the light-industry managers, could not openly solicit and mobilize their support, unless backed by the apparat, and then only through the mouth of the First Secretary himself. Once the situation changed, and opposition pressures developed from the other policy groups, Khrushchev backed away from his innovation. Kennedy hesitated to innovate and then moved ahead when pressures favorable to innovation developed within society and when innovation seemed the only way of escaping from an intolerable political situation. From the first, the Negro demonstrations, as "news events," received full and generally sympathetic coverage from the mass media. This coverage stimulated additional demonstrations, promoted more general popular support for the Negro cause, and, in effect, put civil rights in the forefront of the national consciousness. Kennedy was thus subject to popular pressures which are unknown and unthinkable to the Soviet Union. The southern oligarchy in Congress was matched by the Soviet heavy industrial bureaucracy. In the Soviet Union, however, the mass media certainly would not dramatize the claims of and reveal the plight of the consumer. At no time did Khrushchev have to fear that demands of consumers for washing machines "all, here, and now!" might develop into a massive march on the Kremlin.

There have been cases when Khrushchev did have to contend with minor political demonstrations produced by his own initiative and then subsequent ambivalence. To gain power, he had felt that it was necessary to break with Stalinism. This brought him the support of the apparat, the military, and the public, all united in the desire never to have to go through Stalinism again. Yet at the same time, Khrushchev's "secret speech" to the 20th Party Congress in February 1956, and the unprecedented detailed public revelations of Stalin's crimes to the 22nd Congress in October 1961, both timed to suit Khrushchev's political needs, created a strong popular demand, especially among the youth and the intelligentsia, for a real "civil rights" campaign: for the punishment of Stalin's accomplices and for legal guarantees against the recurrence of terror. Youth demonstrations, public poetry readings, even some speeches to the 22nd Congress reflected this widespread reaction. But, unlike Kennedy and also unlike himself in the consumer-goods debate, Khrushchev could not accede to these demands without directly threatening the security of his power and of the ruling CPSU. A total rejection of Stalin through the punishing of his remaining living accomplices would have required Khrushchev's disavowal not only of his own past but also of most of his associates. This could hardly have been favored by the ruling apparatchiki or by Khrushchev himself. It would be as if Kennedy's civil-rights bill also necessitated a total and direct repudiation of policies deliberately pursued by Presidents Truman and Roosevelt. In the anti-Stalin campaigns, Khrushchev's initiative thus reflected specific political needs; his unwillingness to follow up reflected deep political fears. With open public pressure in itself constituting a threat to the security of the Soviet leadership, complicity in the past created ambivalence about remedying the present.

In the consumer-goods debate, the stakes were not fundamental and the outcome was thus in many respects similar to the early phases of Kennedy's civil-rights policies. Good intentions and broad promises were translated into limited adjustments. More than that was seen by the respective top leaders as inopportune, in the light of their other preoccupations, the likely political cost of overcoming established interests, and the general uncertainty over the best course of action. Khrushchev's dilemma was accentuated by the conflict between limited national resources and external Communist ambitions. Had he chosen not to press the Berlin crisis and the domestic issue at the same time, in all likelihood the outcome might have been different.

Precisely because the Soviet consumer discussion did not involve the security of the existing leadership it is more revealing of the operational limits of policy innovation in a complex political system, subject to all sorts of conflicting pressures and suffering from restricted resources. It confirmed once again that in the Soviet system, the politically important prerogative of initiative rests only with the top leader and depends on his power and interests. While other leaders may advance proposals *within* the leadership, only the top leader does so publicly. This permits him to rouse up support; his supporters can be vocal while his critics must remain silent. Broader support can hence be generated, thereby further isolating internal policy dissenters. The exclusive monopoly of public initiative is thus an important factor of power. In the United States, on the other hand, many groups can initiate proposals and get publicity for them. But measures for which there is much hostility in Congress receive serious consideration in Congress only when they have the top backing and support of the President. Dozens of civil-rights bills were introduced in 1961 and 1962, but, with two minor exceptions which did have Administration support, none received congressional approval. The President does not monopolize the initiation of measures, but he decisively influences the agenda of Congress. Innovation, however, rarely occurs except when the top leadership is under direct pressure from social forces and interest groups within society.

The consumer-goods debate also showed that lack of enthusiasm on the part of other leaders for the top leader's initiative is not the same thing as the opposition of power rivals, as had been the case with the decentralization of 1957 and with anti-Stalinism in general. Power rivals are usually peers, not the leader's appointees. Khrushchev's peers had been eliminated in 1957. The complex system of government and economy furthermore often requires conflicting expertises, and not every contrary opinion is a threat to power; neither is resistance to an initiative from specific policy groups, none of whom could provide alternative national leadership. Khrushchev frequently circulates little notes among his colleagues, suggesting various initiatives. Some of them have been subsequently implemented while some have not. The fact that the texts of the latter were included in his published papers on agriculture suggests that he himself does not consider his suggestions as binding and that their failure to be implemented is not seen by him as a reflection on his leadership.

In the United States the President's power, but not his position, can be threatened by strategically located voting blocs and by determined minority groups. He also lacks sufficient sanctions and inducements with which to insure favorable action on his proposals by Congress. Caught between these conflicting forces, the President has to pursue a course of compromise and moderation which will secure congressional approval of his most important policies without alienating the most important groups among his electoral supporters.

It also follows from the foregoing that equivocation about translating pledges into policy is not tantamount to the leader's loss of power, as was alleged in the West about Khrushchev during the consumer debate, nor is it proof of bad faith, as was sometimes suggested about Kennedy. From the leader's point of view, the initiative in the one case may still have served the useful purpose of shaking rigidly established patterns and interests, and of reconnoitering political and public reactions; the pause in the other case may have helped the President to let the situation mature and to tackle, in the meantime, more pressing priorities. When the top leader is torn by conflicting domestic and external goals, and hence is ambivalent in principal objectives, not every initiative is a full-scale commitment. In any complex political and economic system, be it the centralized Soviet one or the pluralistic American, it is often easier to equivocate than to innovate.

CHAPTER SEVEN

The Intractable Problem of Power: Agriculture

PROBLEMS always seem easier to solve to the contestant for power than to the leader in power. Both Khrushchev and Kennedy learned that lesson with respect to agriculture. During the United States presidential campaign of 1960 both Kennedy and Nixon spoke in sweeping terms of the new farm policies which their Administrations would implement after inauguration. The Soviet leader, prior to his firm consolidation of power, outlined grandiose programs of vastly increased agricultural productivity and consumption. With the responsibility of power came a greater recognition of the agricultural problem in the two countries. The promised radical, surgical solutions faded into palliatives, and palliatives frequently perpetuate rather than solve existing problems. Behind their glittering achievements in industry, nuclear energy, military power, and space, each society has a record of failure and frustration in agriculture. The economics of their agricultural problems differ greatly. The Soviet problem is underproduction; the American problem is overabundance. In terms of economics alone neither is insoluble. Yet in both countries politics and the predominant beliefs (or ideology) of the society inhibit economically rational remedial action. The world's two industrial giants stand baffled and stymied by the intractable problems of agriculture.

ECONOMIC CONTEXT AND CONTRASTS

The Soviet and American agricultures reflect in extreme form the more pervasive economic problem of each society: in the one case, the elimination of scarcity; in the other, the management of abundance. In recent years Soviet production has risen, but nowhere nearly as fast as the country's needs require. In 1953 the per-capita harvest of grain was one-fourth less than what it had been in 1914.[1] In the first five years after Stalin's death it increased by about 40 per cent, but grain production remains considerably

301

short of Soviet needs, which on several occasions had to be satisfied by extensive purchases abroad. The initial post-Stalin spurt of increased agricultural productivity tapered off by 1958, and in recent years the agricultural plans have been woefully underfulfilled (even while the Soviet government has continued to encourage a rapid population increase). By 1962-1963, the over-all food production was approximately one-third less than provided by the 1959-1965 Seven-Year Plan, that is, still at the 1958 level.

In contrast, American production has been larger than needed or wanted. In 1959-1960, United States farm output was about 7 per cent more than that which could have been sold at current prices on a free market.[2] In some commodities production far outran domestic needs. In 1960 American production of wheat (1,357,272,000 bushels) was more than twice the total domestic consumption (604,925,000). Corn production in 1960 was 4,322,-813,000 bushels; domestic corn consumption 3,395,778,000. At the beginning of 1962 the Commodity Credit Corporation had an inventory of farm products valued at roughly $5,250,000,000. Included in this inventory were 1,412,000,000 bushels of corn (about one-third of a year's production) and 1,130,000,000 of wheat (roughly equal to one year's production).

TABLE 1

GRAIN HECTARAGE AND PRODUCTION:
SOVIET UNION AND THE UNITED STATES

	HECTARAGE (1000 HECTARES)		PRODUCTION (1000 METRIC TONS)	
	USSR	USA	USSR	USA
1957-1958	119,915	76,310	102,631	158,178
1958-1959	121,094	77,313	138,533	182,648
1959-1960	115,602	74,878	123,192	169,250
1960-1961	116,742	74,056	130,807	181,428
1961-1962	121,753	65,168	132,848	164,333

Source: Food and Agriculture Organization, *Production Yearbook, 1960, 1961, 1962*, pp. 52-53, 60-61.

Soviet underproduction and American overproduction stem basically from differences in agricultural methods in the two economies. The area sown for grain in the United States, for instance, is about two-thirds of that in the Soviet Union, yet American grain production is 25 to 50 per cent higher than that of the Soviet Union. The Soviets typically attempt to expand their agricultural production by expanding the area under cultivation. The result is to bring marginal land into production and to achieve minor increase in total production with little or no increase in productivity per acre. Between 1940 and 1961, for instance, the Soviet Union increased its over-all crop acreage by 50 per cent, but its agricultural crop production went up by only 30 per cent. During the same period, the United States *decreased* its acreage by 13 per cent while increasing its production by 35 per cent.[3]

American productivity also far exceeded Soviet productivity when measured in terms of the labor input. In the United States, less than half as much labor was devoted to agriculture in 1961 as in 1940. Output per man hour, however, was three times as great in 1961 as in 1940. Soviet productivity per man hour has also increased, but at a much slower rate, and during the mid-1950s the Soviets also expanded their total labor input into agriculture. The gap in productivity between Soviet and American labor remained tremendous, as Khrushchev himself emphasized and as is revealed in the figures in Table 2.

The gap in productivity between Soviet and American labor and land is due in large part to differences in the use of machinery and fertilizer. In 1960 Soviet agricultural workers numbered about

TABLE 2

MAN HOURS USED PER QUINTAL OF OUTPUT: SOVIET UNION AND UNITED STATES

	USA	USSR	
			Collective
		State Farm	*Farm*
Grain (excluding corn)	1.0	2.1	7.2
Potatoes	1.0	4.2	5.1
Sugar beet	0.5	2.1	3.1
Cotton	18.8	29.8	42.8
Milk	4.7	14.2	20.8
Cattle (additional weight)	7.9	52.0	112.0
Pigs (additional weight)	6.3	43.0	103.0

Source: *SSR i SSha* (*Tsifry i fakty*), Moscow, 1961, p. 84.

30 million, American only about 8 million. American agriculture, on the other hand, utilized approximately four times as many tractors as the Soviet, twice as many grain combine harvesters, four times as many trucks, fifteen times as many tractor-trailers, four times as many tractor-drawn plows, not to speak of some 4.5 million automobiles, for which there is practically no Soviet equivalent.[4] The comparison is equally unfavorable with respect to electric power. Although Soviet leaders have frequently described their collective farms as representing an advanced form of economic organization, only about 70 per cent of them are supplied with electricity, whereas 96 per cent of American farms have it. Actual consumption of electric power in American farming is more than four times higher than in Soviet agriculture.

An additional factor contributing to the low agricultural productivity in the Soviet Union is the neglect of mineral fertilizers. Average Soviet usage per hectare is one-third that of the United States (and one-twentieth that of West Germany). Although Soviet production of mineral fertilizers doubled between 1953 and 1963, it is still insufficient to meet the needs of Soviet agriculture. Thus, in 1962, the collective and state farms received only 53 per cent of the corrosive chemicals they required, and it was also estimated that but for the absence of weed killer an additional 3.2 million tons of grain might have been harvested. In the United States, increased use of fertilizer and more sophisticated forms of fertilizer have played a major role in the dramatic increases in American production.

For the Soviet Union underproduction has meant difficulty in meeting the needs of a rapidly growing population, a depressed standard of living for approximately half the population (since the low productivity of the farmers makes higher rewards uneconomical), and high costs of foodstuffs to the urban consumer, in whose family budget food represents the single most important item. In the United States, agricultural overabundance has produced a decline in farm income, an oversupply of labor in agriculture (with perhaps 1 million agricultural unemployed), and increasingly heavy burdens on the taxpayer for the billions of dollars annually required to support agricultural prices, which, in turn, have to be paid by the urban consumer. Differences in climate and soil make agricultural production more difficult in the Soviet Union than in the

United States, yet they cannot explain Soviet underproduction and American overproduction. These two situations are as much the products of men as of nature. Obviously neither situation is economically desirable. Obviously, also, powerful forces must be at work perpetuating them.

THE STRUCTURE OF POWER

About 40 per cent of the Soviet population lives on farms. Only 8 per cent of the American population does. Agricultural interests and groups, it would seem, should play a far more important role in Soviet politics than they do in American. But in this case two and two do not make four—in either Soviet or American politics. The power of agriculture in Soviet politics is far less than it is in American politics. In the Soviet system, the needs of the cities, of industry, and of the military have ridden roughshod over the needs of agriculture; farm policy itself has been shaped by nonagricultural interests. In the American system, agricultural interests not only dominate the making of farm policy but also exercise a powerful influence over policy in other areas and occupy a strongly entrenched position in the national structure of power. These differences in political power lie at the root of the economic problem in each country. In the Soviet Union, the political weakness of agriculture has meant insufficient capital investment in agriculture and thus continued underproduction. In the United States, the political strength of agriculture has stimulated intense investment and thus contributed to overproduction.

The politics of Soviet agriculture also differ from those of American in that control over agricultural problems is relatively centralized in the former. The Presidium and the Secretariat are the key points of decision. In the United States, power over agricultural policy is fragmented among a large number of interest groups, farm organizations, and governmental agencies. These differences shape the ways in which the Soviet and American systems have attempted to come to terms with the agricultural problem.

While the contrast in power between Soviet and American agriculture may seem anomalous, the history of American agriculture suggests that the discrepancy between numbers and power in agriculture is not entirely unique. In the 1880s farmers composed

ing Administration and the Soil Conservation Service in turn attempted to develop their own local constituencies to counterbalance the Federation.

The farmers themselves participate directly in the policy-making process. Annually they elect county committeemen to supervise the administration of federal programs concerned with conservation and production controls. If the government wishes to impose marketing quotas on a crop, these must be approved in a referendum by a two-thirds majority of farmers producing that crop. In the spring of 1963 the Kennedy Administration, with the support of the Farmers Union and the Grange, proposed strict marketing quotas for wheat. The Farm Bureau Federation opposed them, and the wheat farmers defeated the controls by a vote of 597,000 to 547,000. In this way, those groups most directly affected by a government policy are given a formal veto on that policy.

American agriculture is thus organized into a formidable structure of power independent of control by the President, political parties, or popular majorities of the nation as a whole. The political position of Soviet agriculture stands in marked contrast to this. One important effect of the collectivization drive, and of the subsequent agricultural stagnation, was that agriculture became a low-priority area in the Soviet economy. The Soviet leaders both attached greater importance to and took greater pride in the industrial achievements of the state, and they tended to see in the backwardness of agriculture a confirmation of their ideologically influenced low estimate of the peasant. It was a classical example of the self-fulfilling prophecy. Furthermore, with neither the element of private interest to act as a spur nor sympathetic and powerful political representation within the top leadership, the agricultural sector was not able to make its needs effectively known to the top leader. Under Stalin, first A. A. Andreiev and then Khrushchev were charged with overseeing the country's agriculture, but neither of them, within the framework of Stalin's system, could act as a spokesman for the agricultural interests. Rather, they were the spokesmen of the ruling party, representing its interests and priorities, and both men limited themselves to recommending occasionally certain organizational changes in agriculture as a means of improving productivity and consolidating the Party's control over the countryside. Stalin himself took little interest in agriculture once the collectivization had been imposed.

That imposition, despite the wishes of the vast majority of the peasantry, required far-reaching and extensive centralization and bureaucratization of the agricultural sector of the economy. But this, too, made for the political weakness of agriculture. The centralization and bureaucratization forced the Party into close involvement with day-to-day administration; it stimulated administrative inefficiency; and it created opportunities for graft and corruption. Lines of command, on both the Party and the state level, have tended to be confused; jurisdictional conflicts have been frequent, causing in turn the abdication and evasion of responsibility, and excessive and disruptive interference. Even official instructions were often contradictory: the Kazakh First Secretary reported that "Nikita Sergeievich Khrushchev advises us to renounce petty tutelage of the territory organizations and to allow them more opportunity to show initiative, but at the same time to strengthen control over the fulfillment of the national economic plan in the virgin-land territory." [9] The Soviet press, and Khrushchev's speeches, abound in detailed accounts of paper shuffling, duplication of effort, lack of initiative among the bureaucrats. It even turned out that the Russian Republic's Ministry of Agriculture, located since 1961 in an experimental farm, was unable to work that farm productively, even though it has been profitable in the past. The representatives of power were thus omnipresent in agriculture, but agriculture had no political power.

The political weakness of agriculture perpetuated discrimination against it. There was no effective policy group with a vested interest in promoting it. Khrushchev on one occasion said:

> For a long time in the past no one was concretely answerable for the state of agricultural production. The district Party committees and district executive committees—these territorial organizations—approached guidance from a general point of view. They were occupied in equal degree with the district budget and with agricultural, public health, road-building, and mass cultural work. In these circumstances, agricultural affairs often landed at the bottom of the pile.[10]

Khrushchev was speaking of the lower ladders of power, but the same situation has prevailed at the top. In the Central Committee

The collectivization drive was justified by Stalin as necessary to the country's industrialization. Although Khrushchev has condemned Stalin publicly for many crimes, he has not criticized collectivization and has repudiated neither the forcible deportation of millions of peasants nor the terror used to force the peasants to give up their land and livestock. The official position is that the policy made available the capital and labor necessary to achieve rapid industrialization. Yet the fact is that the first industrialization five-year plan of 1928 called for only gradual collectivization, with 13 per cent of the target to be achieved by 1934, whereas Stalin suddenly ordered its forcible acceleration, and by 1934 more than 70 per cent of the peasantry had been forcibly collectivized. Had the original plan been followed, the calamity might have been averted, and Soviet agriculture would not have been unlike that of Poland or Yugoslavia today. Furthermore, it is difficult to sustain the case for collectivization on the grounds of the needs of industrialization, for prior to the forcible collectivization there was a surplus of labor in the cities and the rate of industrial growth was as high as or higher than the rate after collectivization. Indeed, there was urban unemployment, made worse by rural workers moving into cities, and they were not absorbed until some time after the collectivization.[12] Some non-Soviet communist leaders, such as Gomulka, who were more open-minded on the issue and less personally involved in actually executing the collectivization drive than Khrushchev, have conceded in recent years that the policy was unnecessary and also that it was the point of departure for the subsequent illegalities and violence of the Stalinist regime.*

---

* An important Soviet re-evaluation of the Stalinist collectivization drive, published in 1963, thus explained why the collectivization had been necessary: "It was dictated by historical necessity and by the vital requirements of the development of Soviet society. Without collectivization, it was impossible to overcome agriculture's lag behind industry, to create a homogeneous base for the Soviet system, to liquidate the remains of the exploiting class, to put the laboring peasantry on the path toward a prosperous, decent life, to strengthen the country's defenses and to build socialism." M. L. Bogdenko, "For a History of the Initial Stage in the Solid Collectivization of Agriculture in the USSR," *Voprosy istorii,* No. 5, May, 1963.

It is noteworthy that four of the six reasons given are political and ideological.

The only concession made by Stalin to the agricultural needs of the country and to the desires of the peasant was the provision permitting the collective farmer to retain a small private plot, usually with a cow and a few chickens. During World War II the Party even tolerated quiet and spontaneous extension in the size of these plots by the peasantry and their acquisition of additional livestock, very frequently from herds owned by the collective farms. This gave rise to widespread rumors, perhaps even encouraged by the Party, that after the war the entire collective system would be abandoned or at least modified, and this expectation had much to do with encouraging the farmers to maintain food supplies to the cities (in addition to requisitions) during the war. These hopes were quickly shattered after the conclusion of the war. In 1946 a Party resolution ordered the strict enforcement of the collective system.

Yet on the economic side recent Soviet statistics tell a remarkable and a highly pertinent story. They reveal that although less than 4 per cent of the sown area is in private plots, the peasants produce on it 46 per cent of the Soviet Union's meat, 45 per cent of the milk, 78 per cent of the eggs, and 45 per cent of the vegetables. Productivity in the private sector is appreciably higher than in the socialized sector: it is almost twice as high in yield of potatoes and somewhat more than twice as high in vegetables.[13] The average Soviet consumer is thus highly dependent on the private sector, even though more than thirty-five years have passed since the collectivization. The private sector is a major source of income to the 18 million peasant households in the Soviet Union. In the late fifties the Soviet Institute of Agricultural Economics calculated that about 40 per cent of the annual income of peasants came from their private holdings.

For the Soviet leaders, economic statistics are secondary to the ideological heritage of the collectivization drive. Khrushchev himself has simply dismissed the increased productivity of the private plots as irrelevant,[14] and at various times the Party leaders have spoken in a similar vein: "A great hindrance in agricultural development at collective farms is the fact that agricultural products produced by collective farmers on their private plots exceed those of collective farms." [15] In 1961 the Central Committee of the Party authoritatively stated that "without a well-developed agriculture,

practice at the price of poverty and waste. The myth rationalizes government technological assistance to agriculture which, in turn, enables the large farmer to increase his productivity. Similarly, government price supports are justified by the need to save the family farm as a way of life and prevent small farmers from being driven out of business. At the same time, however, the price supports encourage the larger farmer to maximize his yield and to increase his production. They thus exacerbate the problem of overabundance.

A substantial proportion of the American population is only one generation removed from the farm, and the agrarian myth consequently still has a sympathetic audience even in the cities. Whatever their personal sentiments, political leaders and governmental officials still have to pay deference to the Jeffersonian tradition. Soviet encomiums of collective agriculture are matched by American tributes to the family farm. "In America," President Eisenhower declared in 1956, "agriculture is more than an industry; it is a way of life. Throughout our history the family farm has given strength and vitality to our entire social order. We must keep it healthy and vigorous." [18]

The sanctity attached to the family farm and the rural way of life was well reflected in the response to the proposals of the Committee for Economic Development for an "adaptive program" for agriculture. This committee, composed of two hundred progressive-minded business and educational leaders, recommended, among other things, that 2 million workers be moved off the farms and into the cities during a five-year period. The reaction of the farmers to this proposal was devastating, and it was most explosive among the poorer farmers, the very ones who would most benefit by moving to the cities. The program, the Secretary of Agriculture declared, was a "threat to the American family farm" and its results would be "disastrous." The plan, one congressman suggested, "would usher in a system of vertical integration and contract farming, where our farmers would be relegated to the position of hired hands instead of owner managers. . . ." Furthermore, he went on to say:

> An important point which cannot be overlooked in any serious discussion of the future of American agriculture is the fact that our family farms have supplied many of our governmental, civic

and business leaders through the years. The youth raised on a farm or in a rural community learns early the value of diligent labor, responsibility and thrift. Whatever vocation he chooses, these traits stand him in good stead. The Nation will be poorer indeed if we lose the valuable training ground for leaders which is the family farm.[19]

If the dogmas of Jeffersonian agrarianism have survived one hundred and fifty years, it is hardly surprising that Soviet leaders remain entranced with Stalinist doctrines of socialized agriculture.

Both Soviet ideology and the American agrarian myth have prevented the economically rational organization of agriculture. Under the impact of the Soviet ideology, the more productive peasant plots are being slowly squeezed out by the less productive state and collective farms. Under the impact of the agrarian myth, hundreds of thousands, if not millions, of inefficient and underemployed farmers are not encouraged to find urban employment. Yet neither ideology nor myth in itself provides a satisfactory solution. For some time to come, Soviet collectivism will have to be tempered by continued reliance on the private plots for a substantial proportion of Soviet meat and vegetables. In America, the "independent" family farm can be maintained only by government intervention in agriculture. Pure collectivism in the Soviet Union would produce greater shortages of food, pure laissez-faire liberalism in American agriculture a quicker end to the small-scale family farm.

Soviet ideology has proclaimed the need to abolish the distinction between the countryside and the city by adapting factory-style organization to the farm. The American tradition, in effect, has argued that the city should be made like the countryside by incorporating into urban culture the rural values of the independent producer and the widespread diffusion of power. Neither goal, however, has been practical. The failure of Khrushchev's early scheme for "agro-cities" on the one hand has been matched by the frustrations of the backers of antitrust legislation on the other. Khrushchev wanted to mold agriculture in terms of a factory ideal; the rural opponents of monopoly wanted to mold industry in terms of an agrarian ideal. Paradoxically, the most efficient farms in the United States embody the industrial approach which is the ideal of Soviet agriculture. The most efficient producers in the Soviet Union,

ture. (Although still insufficient to meet agricultural needs, agricultural investments in the post-Stalin decade were three times higher than previously.[20])

In 1955 Khrushchev began to press for an expansion of acreage under corn in order to provide more feed-grain base for livestock. As in the case of the virgin lands, this too was undertaken as a crash program with enormous publicity. In 1961 at the 22nd Party Congress Khrushchev followed this up with an attack on the so-called Williams system of grassland rotational farming (which Stalin dogmatically imposed as "the most progressive system") and on the use of fallow land in the crop cycle. Instead, Khrushchev dictated much more intensive use of the land with annual crops of corn, wheat, peas, sugar beets, and other soil-depleting crops. Stalin had insisted on applying the Williams system in the drier Soviet regions, where it was not appropriate. In reversing Soviet policy, Khrushchev eliminated the Williams system even where it was appropriate and insisted on introducing annual crops in areas where they were not appropriate. Thus the pendulum of Soviet farm policy swung crazily from one extreme to another.

These diverse innovations in policy were paralleled by rapid institutional changes, designed to improve Party control over agriculture, agricultural planning, and organization. Khrushchev pushed forward the consolidation of the collective farms, and by the end of the decade their number decreased to less than fifty thousand, thereby streamlining their administration and also facilitating more direct control by Party organizations. Furthermore, Khrushchev favored the gradual transformation of the collective farms into state farms, where the farmers work for regular wages and generally resemble industrial workers. The share of the state farms (which numbered over nine thousand) in the total agricultural production had climbed from less than 10 per cent in 1953 to about 35 per cent in 1960. An even more dramatic organizational change involved the abolition in 1958 of the Machine Tractor Stations (MTS), which in Stalin's time were held to be of central importance to the "construction of socialism" in the countryside; their equipment was sold to the collective farms. In 1961 the old territorial administrative structure was abolished and replaced by a hierarchy of territorial production and procurement administrations, thereby providing a specialized structure charged specifically with agricultural matters. This reform was followed a year later by a reorganization of the Party hierarchy into two separate, parallel structures, industrial and agricultural. According to Khrushchev, henceforth Party organization would rest "on the basis of the production principle and thereby ensure more concrete Party guidance of industry, construction, and agriculture." Special Party organizers were to provide the impetus to the work of the fifteen hundred production administrations charged with supervising the country's fifty-five thousand state and collective farms. In 1959 Khrushchev had stated that "weak organizational work is the chief defect" of Soviet agriculture. This radical innovation in Party and state organization was designed to meet it.

The search for solutions also led to a rapid change in personnel. Between 1945 and 1963 Soviet ministers of agriculture averaged only two years and three months in office; in the decade after Stalin's death they averaged only one year and seven months. Bright stars regularly appear on the agricultural horizon, are rapidly promoted to top agricultural positions in the state and Party apparat, and then fade equally rapidly into disgrace when they fail to overcome the problem. In similar fashion, numerous shake-ups occur in the middle levels of the agricultural bureaucracies. Charges of corruption, inefficiency, violation of regulations, and bungling are regularly leveled at the middle-ranking bureaucrats by Khrushchev and other top Party leaders. The bureaucrats, in turn, can legitimately feel that the Party expects them to do too much while providing too few tools for doing the job. As a result, "family circles" develop for protection against punitive measures, and dismissals for inefficiency or corruption in many cases are followed by quick reassignment to other important posts. With terror no longer rampant and the top leadership relying more on administrative measures, the bureaucrats are able to rely on administrative self-protection and evasion. Agriculture, however, is again the loser.

In his efforts to stimulate production Khrushchev has devoted unprecedented personal attention to farm problems. He has criss-crossed the country, attending countless special conferences, inspecting collective farms and agricultural institutes, urging improvements, cajoling and threatening. In 1958-1962 more than 40 per cent of his formal public speeches were on the theme of agricul-

The Truman Administration made the first major effort in 1948, proposing a system of flexible price supports on basic crops. A coalition of farm spokesmen in the House of Representatives, however, insisted on freezing price supports at 90 per cent of parity for the next year, postponing flexible supports until 1950. The Administration then changed Secretaries of Agriculture and also changed policies. In 1949 it proposed a radical new approach, the so-called Brannan Plan, providing for high price-support programs and authority to impose production controls on all major crops, plus a free market for perishable products, with the consumer getting the benefit of the lower price and the farmer receiving direct income payments from the government instead of the government's purchasing his crop at a high support price. This plan represented a systematic, although controversial, approach to the farm problem. It was defeated in Congress through the opposition of the Farm Bureau Federation, larger farmers, Republicans, and southern Democrats. Instead, Congress continued the high price supports which had been scheduled to expire under the 1948 legislation.

The Eisenhower Administration challenged this policy frontally in 1954, proposing flexible supports (70 to 90 per cent of parity) for basic commodities to remove the incentives for overproduction. Although both the House and Senate Agricultural Committees favored high supports, the Administration was able to secure the basic authority it wanted. The marked decline in farm income which followed the end of the Korean War, however, furnished continuing incentives for congressional groups to challenge the Administration's approach. In 1956 Congress passed a bill restoring the 90-per-cent-of-parity price supports. The President vetoed the bill. Criticisms from the Democrats and the pressures of an election, however, forced the Administration to raise significantly its original support levels on several crops. Two years later Congress again tried to prevent a drop in supports, and the President again vetoed the bill. In 1959 Congress passed bills setting higher price supports for wheat and tobacco, and the President vetoed both. Meanwhile, in 1957, 1959, and 1960, Congress in turn refused to approve Administration proposals to reduce price supports still further and to hasten progress toward a free market in agriculture. Policy was at a stalemate. As farm income continued to sag and surpluses continued to accumulate, the popularity of Eisenhower's

Secretary of Agriculture, Ezra Benson, sank to record lows. In 1960 even Vice President Nixon carefully disassociated himself from any identification with the Eisenhower-Benson farm policies.

The election of Kennedy produced a shift in Administration outlook. Price-support levels were generally raised and elaborate proposals were drafted to impose strict production controls. Kennedy won an initial victory with a bill for emergency controls on feed grains, but his general proposals for restrictions on production based on amounts produced instead of acreage got nowhere in Congress. In 1962 Congress again rejected tight production controls for feed grains and dairy products. It approved a modified version of the controls which the Administration wished to impose on wheat but made them subject to a referendum by the wheat producers, who, in turn, vetoed them. Thus, Congress, which had strenuously resisted Eisenhower's efforts to reduce price supports, now seemed to oppose with equal vigor Kennedy's efforts to impose production controls. "Benson made a Democrat out of me," was a common remark in the farm belt in 1962, "and now Freeman [Kennedy's Secretary of Agriculture] is turning me back into a Republican." [24] In short, neither "solution" to the farm problem was politically acceptable to the farmers, and hence neither was politically feasible.

As a result, American agricultural policy in practice was a mishmash of conflicting approaches and ad-hoc compromises, the product of conflicts between Republicans and Democrats, President and Congress, and the tough pragmatic bargaining among regional and commodity interests on the basis of the principle, "You scratch my back and I'll scratch yours." No long-run policy emerged; instead there was a series of temporary expedients recorded in the major agricultural legislation passed almost on a biennial basis. Each agricultural act involved complex bargaining among the representatives of the six "basic commodities" (wheat, cotton, corn, tobacco, rice, and peanuts—so defined by legislation), not to mention the spokesmen for dairy products, cattle, wool, sugar, poultry, and miscellaneous other products. To receive majority support, each act usually had to include something for each major commodity group. In 1958, for instance, despite Republican charges of "logrolling," the House Agricultural Committee put together an "omnibus" bill dealing with five major commodities.

Even so, it was initially defeated in the House. In due course, however, cotton, rice, and feed grain representatives negotiated a compromise in which they got what they wanted in return for dropping
from the bill the wheat and dairy provisions which the Department
of Agriculture and the Farm Bureau found particularly objection-
able.[25] In pursuing their objectives agricultural interests not only
made deals with each other, but also traded off support with other
groups which had little or no interests in agriculture per se. In
1955, for example, Democrats favoring high price supports reportedly won the help of labor and urban Democrats by agreeing
to support higher minimum wages. Agricultural policy was thus
made in an environment in which each participant was constrained
"to place the special interest first and, when forced to look somewhat beyond it, to define the larger problem in the narrowest possible terms." [26]

In 1961 American farm output was one-third greater than it had
been in 1947. The realized net income of farmers, however, was
26 per cent less in 1961 than it had been in 1947. The per-capita
personal income of people on farms in 1961 was only $1373; that
of nonfarmers was $2345. Fifteen years of compromises and pallia-
tives had notably failed to solve the problem of too much farm
output and too little farm income.

THE POLITICS OF CHANGE

In both countries, change has been opposed by political interests
and rigid ideas. In both countries, palliatives have perpetuated the
status quo. Furthermore, and quite paradoxically, powerful factors
are at work in each country in favor of perpetuating the other
country's ideological and political status quo in agriculture. The
midwestern politician or grain exporter who wishes to sell to the
Soviet Union is helping to maintain the collective system in Soviet
agriculture. The Soviet apparatchik urging grain purchases from
the United States is helping to alleviate the dilemma of American
overabundance and to perpetuate its basic causes. But without
such external aid radical changes may eventually come in both
societies.

A radical solution of the American farm problem through an
abrupt return to the free market would reduce farm prices and
farm income by 30 to 40 per cent. Farm land values would also

drop precipitously, and the income gap between the larger, more efficient producers and the smaller, less efficient ones would widen.[27] The result would be economic deprivations for the farmer on a revolutionary scale, an American equivalent of what the Soviet farmer suffered during collectivization, except that in America the principal burdens would fall on the poorer farmers rather than on the wealthier ones. Such an overnight change *is* politically impossible. So also in the Soviet Union any drastic abondonment of socialized agriculture or even an abrupt shift in investment priorities from industry to agriculture seems most unlikely under the present conditions. In each society a fundamental solution of the farm problem depends upon prior changes in the ideological and political context in which farm policy is made. In each society, also, however, there are at least some indications that such changes may take place over a prolonged period.

As the population of the United States becomes farther and farther removed from direct contact with the rural way of life, the appeal of the agrarian myth inevitably declines. The validity of that myth is also being increasingly undermined by the revolution which is taking place on the farm itself. Just as the industrial revolution replaced home industries with the factory system, so also the agricultural revolution is replacing the small-scale farm proprietor with the large, highly capitalized farm business, which often unites in one enterprise production, processing, and distribution. Eventually, farming will come to be accepted as an industry little different in its essentials from other industries. At the same time, the bases of farm political power will probably weaken. The Supreme Court decision in *Baker v. Carr* in 1962, requiring more equitable distribution of legislative seats, threatens rural dominance of the state legislatures and, in due course, rural overrepresentation in the House of Representatives. In addition, the costs of the farm program have reached the point where the interests of urban groups in achieving a solution have become painfully obvious. In a pluralistic political system, no myth is forever unchallenged, while concentrated power eventually generates countervailing forces. The undermining of the agrarian myth and the overcoming of the farm bloc will not occur in a day. But the slow—glacially slow—processes of American politics are moving in that direction. In any other society, such a slow pace of change would sharpen social tensions and possibly unleash revolutionary forces. Fortunately abundance is a less pressing problem than scarcity, and for the United States agricultural overabundance is only the most extreme instance of a more pervasive condition. The general affluence of the American economy supports the burden of agricultural overabundance and buys time for the political system to work through its tortuous, slow processes toward a more fundamental solution.

Unlike the vague agrarian myth, the ideology of socialized agriculture cannot be openly challenged from within Soviet society. In Yugoslavia, however, Tito gave up collective farming after it had been in practice barely three or four years, and in Poland Gomulka reversed collectivization after five years. At the 22nd Party Congress Khrushchev recognized approvingly this "experience of socialist change in the countryside without nationalizing the land, but with consideration for the long-standing traditions of deep attachment which the peasantry has for private land ownership." [28] Unlike the Yugoslavs and Poles, the Soviets have invested thirty years of hard work and deep commitment in their socialized system. Perhaps at some point they too may find a face-saving device for major concessions to the peasants; for instance, formal ownership could remain collective but land could be "leased" to individual peasants. The same could be done with livestock and smaller-scale machinery. At the present time, however, the Party is committed and determined to make the existing system work. In spite of persisting difficulties, the pressure against the private plots has been maintained, and in 1958 and 1963 additional measures were adopted to restrict their economic significance. Furthermore, once more machinery and fertilizer is made available, there is no reason to assume that some further advances cannot be made in spite of collectivization. This in turn would serve to perpetuate the existing system.

Recent changes in the political organization of agriculture greatly increase the probability that more resources will be devoted to enhancing agricultural production. In 1962, and against some opposition within the Party,* Khrushchev moved to split the CPSU

---

* Cf. Khrushchev's references to "some comrades" who claimed that Party organizations in agriculture have worked well and that no reorganization was necessary. *Pravda,* March 14, 1963.

into two parallel hierarchies. Henceforth there will be separate rural Party organizations, containing only members involved in agricultural matters and led by officials who will have a direct stake in and experience in agriculture. For the first time agricultural interests would also be effectively represented at the top, by a special Central Committee Bureau for Agriculture, subject only to the Presidium and Secretariat. In effect, an amorphous social mass was being transformed into a policy group.

At this stage, it is impossible to foretell what will be the effects of this far-reaching reform. Clearly, Khrushchev's ideal is to involve Party members in promoting higher production and productivity. Reorganized on the production principle, the Party organs will be closer to actual conditions and, hopefully, they should provide better leadership, control, and representation within the power structure. There is also, however, a political danger in the reform. If the Party persists in it and develops a large cadre of leaders who have a vested interest in the agricultural sector, and who feel their own careers dependent on its success, in effect the reform will have created two separate political entities within the CPSU. It could lead to conflicts and tensions, and even to a measure of pluralism within the Communist Party. The post-reform discussions in the Party press reveal that the top leaders are not insensitive to this possibility. They have been stressing the proposition that the Party will remain united and that the march toward communism is in any case eliminating all differences between town and country. Conceivably also, at some point the reform may be undone in one of those characteristically sweeping reversals. But if it is not, and if it does create a political force based on the interests of one-half of the population, then, in one of the ironies of history, the political shape of the Soviet system may be radically altered by the least privileged and the most intractable sector of Soviet society.

In this event, the evolution of Soviet agriculture would have paralleled that of American. Soviet agriculture today is, in a sense, in a position comparable to American agriculture in the 1880s: numerically strong but politically weak. In the last part of the nineteenth century the rising needs of industry furnished the most dynamic and aggressive force on the American political scene. This also was the case in the Soviet Union between the 1930s and the

limited war. The political setting of the Zhukov affair involved the adjustment of the Soviet system to the death of Stalin and intense factional and institutional struggles to determine his successor. In each case, political discord—the struggle for power and the struggle over foreign policy—drew military officers and military institutions into unusual political roles. Some military leaders developed autonomous sources of power to the point where they appeared able to wield decisive influence on matters outside the normal military sphere. The "MacArthur problem" came to a head when it appeared (at least to Truman and his advisers) that MacArthur was directly repudiating and undermining the Administration's strategy. The issue, as one Truman assistant defined it, was: "Who is President?" Zhukov's challenge to Khrushchev was less overt but nonetheless serious. It came to a head in 1957 when it appeared (at least to Khrushchev) that Zhukov was challenging party control of the armed forces and was putting himself in a position to become an arbiter of conflicts among political leaders. For Khrushchev the problem was: "If Zhukov has this power, will I remain the top leader in the Soviet Union?" The cases of MacArthur and Zhukov thus involve political systems in crisis: they are not typical of the normal pattern of civil-military controversy in either country. But it is unusual circumstances that test the resiliency of political systems.

CIVILIAN CONTROL: SOVIET AND AMERICAN PATTERNS

Traditions of military subordination to civil power are deeply ingrained in both Russian and American politics. These traditions have their roots in both history and ideology. Unlike many autocracies, the czarist regime was not politically challenged by its military establishment, in spite of many defeats. Neither the Crimean War nor the humiliating defeat by the Japanese led to internal military coups. The Army officer corps, increasingly professionalized by the late nineteenth century and less and less the exclusive domain of the nobility, viewed itself as a custodian of state security and was one of the principal pillars of czarist rule. For many, it was also the most important avenue of social advance. In part, the intense loyalty of the military was also an expression of Great Russian nationalism, and the military were the principal means of maintaining Russian control over the Empire's 50-percent non-Russian population.

The Bolsheviks came to power with a deep sense of hostility to the military. They saw it—rightly—as one of the key instruments of "state oppression," and they were determined to destroy it. The exigencies of the Civil War, however, quickly shattered their more radical, anarchistic illusions, and the need for a centralized and disciplined military machine was recognized by the Leninist leadership. Under the personal command of Trotsky, a new Red Army of Workers and Peasants was forged, and Trotsky did not hesitate to recruit for it many thousands of ex-czarist professional officers. Under their command, but subject to central political leadership, that Army gave a creditable performance during the Civil War and the various frontier struggles that followed.

In Soviet Russia the czarist tradition of the military as the instrument of the state was reinforced by the ideology which the revolution made dominant. Subordination of the military is basic to communist ideology, just as it is to American political beliefs. That ideology provides a rationale for the Clausewitzian view that "war is the continuation of politics by other means," that strategy is the handmaid of policy, and that military forces are the instrument of the state. During and after their revolution, the Bolsheviks felt vulnerable to attack. For this reason, from the beginning, political supervision by the Bolshevik party was rigidly enforced. In the Civil War every front had its own political commissar, with powers of life and death over even the military commander, and every unit also was overseen by him. On occasion military commanders were removed and executed on the orders of the commissars. At the same time, a numbr of able young czarist officers and noncommissioned officers were given rapid promotions, and some of them, like the later Marshals Tukhachevsky and Budënny, commanded entire armies. They were the core of a new Bolshevik officer corps.

The conclusion of the war led to the reorganization of the armed forces on a peacetime basis, with the gradual release of many of the ex-czarist professionals and simultaneous training of younger cadres in the new Bolshevik military academies. As the new communist officer corps took shape, the political leadership was increasingly willing to grant it special privileges, previously denied.

Gradually, old military ranks were re-established, and so were the distinctive insignia; special medals were created, and more and more emphasis was put on military discipline. This trend culminated during World War II with the reintroduction of the traditional epaulets for officers, and shortly afterward the name of the military forces was changed from Red Army of Workers and Peasants to Soviet Armed Forces. The professionalization of the officers' corps and its new position as a more privileged and better-paid social class were again making the military into a pillar of state power, this time communist.

Political supervision, however, was not relaxed. Throughout the entire period the military establishment remained permeated by a triple network of controls. The commissars eventually gave way to the so-called *zampolity,* or deputy commanders for political affairs, but the change was principally one of name. The zampolity remained charged with overseeing the political loyalty and education of the officers and troops, and they themselves were part of a hierarchy directed at the top by the Main Political Administration of the Armed Forces, a special department of the Central Committee's Secretariat. No promotion could be made without approval of this political organ. In addition, in every military unit there was a Party cell, headed (depending on its size) by a Party secretary or organizer whose task was to assist the zampolit in his political education and to spread the message of the Party among the military. Finally, the secret police maintained its own Special Section (during World War II renamed SMERSH—abbreviation of Russian for "Death to Spies") to ferret out dissenters, and also its own armed forces. It is not surprising that with several such conflicting chains of command there were periodic clashes between commanders and the political supervisors. In the eyes of many officers such a system contributed to inefficiency. To the political leaders, however, with their ideologically deep-rooted fear of "Bonapartism," it was essential.

Political supremacy over the military was also asserted under Stalin by the simple expedient of physical liquidation. In 1937 and 1938 almost the entire high command of the Red Army, headed by Marshal Tukhachevsky and most of his closest associates (as well as his immediate family), was executed. The purge swept ruthlessly through the ranks of the officer corps, and it is estimated that approximately twenty thousand officers were destroyed—approximately one-half to one-third of the professional officer corps. There is some reason to believe that in part this destruction was motivated by Stalin's suspicion, skillfully fed by the German intelligence service, that they were planning a coup. It is still not clear, however, to what extent Stalin found such suggestions politically expedient, and the massive destruction of thousands of officers certainly cannot be explained in terms of a German provocation. It was clearly a determined political measure designed to weaken a potential source of power at a time of great internal stress in the Soviet Union.

The destruction of Tukhachevsky and others meant that military command passed into the hands of two broad groups of high officers: at the top were Tukhachevsky's old rivals and colleagues, men such as Voroshilov, Budënny, Timoshenko. They tended to be less professional, more politically minded officers, more akin to Stalin personally, in part because of their simple peasant background and very much so because of their personal loyalty to him. They shared Stalin's hostility to the more glamorous, usually more sophisticated officers like Tukhachevsky. With them came a second group, composed of junior officers, trained already in the Stalinist period and usually with personal ties to the Voroshilov-Budënny-Timoshenko clique. They stepped forward to occupy the higher posts suddenly made vacant.

While World War II led to a rapid expansion of the Army and to the appearance of highly decorated and popular war heroes, the postwar period was marked by the reassertion of political supremacy. The credit for winning the war was given entirely to Stalin and the Communist Party. It is true, however, that Stalin maintained complete political and military direction of the war. It was only after Stalin's death that the wartime exploits of the Army were again gradually given their due and the personal contributions of individual marshals acknowledged. Eventually, also, pressure built up for the rehabilitation of the purged officers. The destruction of Beria in late June 1953 and the resulting denigration of the secret police automatically increased the importance of the military establishment. Furthermore, military figures were prominently mentioned as participating both in the "trial" of Beria* and as addressing special meetings called to condemn the ex-police boss. The growing importance of the military was reflected in their increased representation in the Party councils and the Central Committee, and in their unavoidable involvement in the struggle for succession that dominated Soviet political life from 1953 to 1957.

The Soviet Union inherited a tradition of civilian control rooted in czarist concepts of absolute rule. The American colonists of the seventeenth and eighteenth centuries inherited a very different tradition of civilian control rooted in the belief that standing armies were threats to individual liberty. Unlike communist ideology, American political ideas have never been sympathetic to the use of the military as an instrument of the state. Instead, in the American tradition hostility to standing armies has been complemented by the Jeffersonian belief that every citizen should be a soldier. The need for a distinct military class or distinct military institutions apart from society has been denied. The Bolsheviks had to develop complex institutions to insure control of their military forces. The Americans were able to solve the problem through two entirely different means.

One method was simply to do away with military forces. This policy of "extirpation" got off to a notable start six months after the end of the Revolution, when Congress reduced the Continental Army to a total of eighty officers and men. Throughout American history, until 1945, the American armed forces were kept at minimum levels in peacetime. This policy derived partly from the blessings of geography, partly from ideological suspicion of military force, and partly from an unwarranted optimism concerning the effectiveness of the militia. During the nineteenth century the peacetime strength of the American army was almost never more than twenty-five thousand men. In the Soviet Union civilian control has been the product of a strong state; in the United States it has been largely the result of weak military forces.

The second traditional American method of securing civilian

---

* There is some doubt whether such a trial was actually ever staged. According to reasonably authoritative versions Beria was shot on the spot in the Kremlin. In that, however, the military played a very prominent role.

control has been through the fusion of the military with society, the introduction of civilian norms and practices into the military sphere, the mixing of political and military leadership. This blending was aided by the Constitution, in which the Founding Fathers attempted to guarantee against both too much power in the hands of the military and too much power over the military in the hands of any single civilian institution. For the czars and the Bolsheviks civilian control was a function of concentrated power. For the Founding Fathers it was a function of divided power. Congress was given the power to declare war, ratify treaties, approve the appointment of military officers, determine the structure and functions of the armed forces, and control their funds. The President was made Commander in Chief with the power to appoint officers and, presumably, to supervise operations. The state governments had control of their own militia forces, except when they were in the service of the United States. The Founding Fathers were as much interested in the separation of powers as in civilian control. As a result, they divided political controls over the military, and hence invited military participation in politics.

Hostility to military institutions remained a dominant theme in American thinking for one hundred and fifty years. The continuing American concern with "the man on horseback" resembles the later Bolshevik preoccupation with "Bonapartism." This concern kept the military forces small and the military profession, when it developed after the Civil War, weak and isolated. It did not, however, prevent politicians from becoming generals or generals from becoming political leaders. Twenty-one of the fifty-one major party presidential nominees before 1896 were generals or former generals. Eight of those were elected. Six of those eight were nonprofessional, Cincinnatus-style, civilian generals, and those two professional soldiers who were elected (Taylor and Grant) managed to convince the electorate that they were folksy and unmilitary. Thus, the American antimilitary tradition includes selecting unmilitary or antimilitary soldiers for the Presidency. By the end of the nineteenth century, however, the emergence of a professional officer corps brought to a halt, at least temporarily, military involvement in presidential politics. The last professional general in that century was nominated in 1880; the last amateur general was Benjamin Harrison in 1892. For sixty years thereafter no general was nominated for the Presidency. The easy interchange and close connections between military and civil leadership declined. The leaders of the military profession exercised little political influence or power.

The unprecedented challenge of World War II, however, brought about a revolution in American civil-military relations. Generals and admirals moved directly into the seats of power. They played a far more important role in directing the course of the war in the United States than their counterparts did in the Soviet Union. Soviet mechanisms of civilian control continued to function during the war. The American methods of civilian control were drastically altered. In effect, Congress surrendered its powers over the military budget. The civilian secretaries of War, Navy, and State were relegated to secondary positions. The strategy of the war was shaped by the President and the Joint Chiefs of Staff. The authority of the military extended into many areas not directly related to military operations. The Joint Chiefs, Admiral Leahy could declare in 1945, are "under no civilian control whatever."

This change, however, was not out of harmony with the traditional approach. Politics and war, in the American view, were two distinct activities. If the politicians and diplomats failed to maintain the peace, they must step aside and let the soldiers achieve victory. The American approach which refused to recognize the legitimacy of military forces in peace also refused to recognize the legitimacy of political goals in war. "I would be loath to hazard American lives for purely political purposes," General Marshall declared during the war. "The single objective," he said, "should be quick and complete victory." In World War II this view was shared by everyone: President, Congress, people, and military.

Between 1945 and 1950 the military continued to play a key role in the government. Generals Clay and MacArthur ruled as proconsuls in Germany and Japan. In Germany the American zone continued under military control after the French, British, and Russians had brought theirs under civilian authority. Military officers served as ambassadors and in executive positions. General Marshall was Secretary of State in 1947 and 1948. General Eisenhower was, formally and informally, the principal military adviser to the Truman Administration. Only after a bitter struggle was atomic energy shifted from military to civilian control. At the same time, however, that military men were performing a variety of civilian functions, the military budget was drastically reduced and limited. The military leaders may not have liked it, but, accustomed to the traditional "feast in war, famine in peace" approach to military spending and confident of the durability of the United States' atomic-bomb monopoly, they accepted those limitations.

MILITARY LEADERS: ZHUKOV AND MACARTHUR

It is against these backgrounds of ideology and institutions that the Zhukov and MacArthur controversies must be seen. Georgy Konstantinovich Zhukov was born in 1896 in a small village in Kaluga province. He was apparently of humble origins. During World War I he served first as a private and then as a noncommissioned officer. When the Civil War broke out he joined the Bolsheviks, and in 1919 he became a member of the Party. He rose to be troop commander in the Sixth Chongarsky Division, a crack unit in Budënny's cavalry army. The division was commanded by Timoshenko. After the war he remained in military service and was stationed in Byelorussia with the reorganized Budënny forces. In 1928 he was sent to the Frunze Military Academy, and in 1932, after completing his studies and serving briefly as a deputy regimental commander, he became regimental commander, again in the Byelorussian Military District, and again under Timoshenko, who was serving as a corps commander. Zhukov must have impressed his superiors favorably, for he was entrusted with the command of one of the first Soviet motorized cavalry regiments. By 1936 he was already a divisional commander.

His career so far suggests an officer of considerable ability. But his meteoric rise began with the purges. In 1937 he became deputy commander of cavalry in the strategically important Byelorussian district and in 1939 he was appointed to command the Soviet forces that were engaged in the frontier conflict with the Japanese at the Khalkin Gol river on the Manchurian frontier. This was the first important test of the Soviet Army, and such an appointment must have been made by Stalin himself. Zhukov distinguished himself [1] and was then sent to serve as deputy commander of the Kiev

Military District, now commanded by Timoshenko, who had also benefited by the purges. It is not known whether Zhukov came to Khrushchev's attention at that time.

After service on the front in the 1940 Finno-Soviet war, Zhukov went to Moscow (Timoshenko was now Commissar of Defense, having replaced the incapable Voroshilov), where he occupied successively the posts of Chief of General Staff, Commander of the Western Front, and First Deputy Commander in Chief of the Armed Forces. His period of tutelage was over, and he was already looming on the horizon as the most publicized military figure in the USSR. In 1944-1945 he led the First Ukrainian and Byelorussian Fronts and in that capacity stormed the German capital and was hailed as the victor of Berlin. Sometime during this period he had also been coopted into the Central Committee of the CPSU, a mark of political success.

His fortunes declined after the end of the war. Stalin was unwilling to share the laurels with anyone, and internal military jealousies may have also played a role. Zhukov was recalled from Germany in 1946, and between then and 1953 was assigned to progressively less important military posts. In 1946 also he was criticized within the Central Committee and expelled from it. One measure of his popularity and prestige, as well as the Army's standing, is the fact that, in spite of his unwillingness to confess his errors to the Central Committee (the charges have not been made public),* Stalin deemed it opportune not to apply direct personal sanctions against him, and in 1952 he was even appointed candidate member of the Central Committee.

MacArthur's background was very different from Zhukov's, but his career was at least equally brilliant and rapid. MacArthur, unlike Zhukov, was born in 1880 into the upper middle class and into the Army. His father, Arthur MacArthur, was a Regular Army captain who went on to become lieutenant general, conqueror of Emilio Aguinaldo's insurgents in the Philippines, and military governor there in 1900 and 1901. Douglas MacArthur apparently

---

* While it may be presumed that Stalin wished to degrade a potential Bonaparte, the ostensible motive may have been Zhukov's overemphasis on military discipline and training. In 1944 he is also known to have quarreled bitterly with Bulganin, who was then serving as the political commissar on the Byelorussian Front.

never considered any career but a military one. He was graduated from West Point in 1903 with top military and academic honors. Throughout his early assignments he made a record as a bright, able, and decisive, if somewhat difficult, officer. In 1913 he was assigned to the General Staff in Washington. After American entry into the war, he helped conceive and organize the so-called Rainbow Division and went with it to France. In little over a year he was promoted from major to brigadier general. At thirty-eight he was the youngest general and the youngest division commander in the Army. He was a dashing combat soldier, wounded twice, gassed twice, decorated over and over again. The newspapers called him "the D'Artagnan of the AEF"; the Secretary of War called him "our greatest front-line commander."

Although most Regular Army officers were reduced in rank after the war, MacArthur's ability, plus his personal and political connections, enabled him to stay a brigadier general. They also won him the coveted appointment of Superintendent of West Point. While in France, however, he had antagonized both General Pershing, commander of the AEF, and Pershing's aide, Colonel George C. Marshall (whom Pershing thought the finest officer of the war). Pershing became Chief of Staff in 1921, and MacArthur was assigned or "exiled" to the Philippines in 1922. Two years later, however, when only forty-four, he was promoted to major general, and in 1930 he became one of the youngest Chiefs of Staff in the history of the Army. In this position he fought hard for military appropriations, dramatically drove the "Bonus Army" of unemployed veterans out of Washington in 1932, and declined to promote George Marshall to brigadier general, "exiling" him instead to the Illinois National Guard. MacArthur remained as Chief of Staff for five years, an incongruous, romantic, heroic, and even somewhat disturbing military figure in Washington during the first days of the New Deal.* Fifty-five years old in 1935, MacArthur had ten years of active service left but no higher Army post to move on to. Consequently, he seized the opportunity to return

---

* In 1932 Franklin D. Roosevelt described the Louisiana senator and demagogue Huey Long as "one of the two most dangerous men in the United States today." Asked who the other was, Roosevelt replied, "Douglas MacArthur." Arthur M. Schlesinger, Jr., *The Crisis of the Old Order,* Boston, 1957, pp. 417-418.

with Malenkov and 1955-1957 by his conflict with the "anti-Party" group. In both phases, the military participated as an institution, strategy played a role as an issue, and Zhukov was involved as a military leader. At no time did the military reach out for political power, but their presence was felt simply because the internal institutional balance had been dramatically altered by the gradual elimination of the secret police as an important power institution, and also because the Malenkov-Khrushchev disagreement over allocations (see Chapter Five) involved the military as an interested policy group. They were even more directly concerned with the differences between Malenkov and Khrushchev over military strategy, all the more so since the strategic issue was related to the economic one.

Both Malenkov and Khrushchev realized that Soviet military doctrine had atrophied under Stalin and was in urgent need of revitalization. Both rejected Stalin's formalistic doctrine of five constant factors that were said to be decisive in a war: stability of the home front, morale of the military, the quantity and quality of divisions, their weapons, and the skill of command. They conceded that the nuclear age was at hand and that the utilization of nuclear weapons, on the basis of a new strategy, was the primary consideration. The implications they drew from these considerations differed, however. Malenkov argued that the Soviet Union's achievement of atomic and hydrogen weapons made possible effective deterrence of an American attack. Under those conditions he hinted that war was no longer inevitable, and his spokesmen even suggested "wise compromises" with the West (much like Khrushchev later, especially after the Cuban crisis). A corollary of this view, again of importance to the military, was the proposition that the Soviet Union could therefore channel more of its production toward consumer goods. Khrushchev's position at that time tended to be more conservative. He argued that the Soviet Union should be able not only to deter an aggressor but also to wage successfully a nuclear war, which in turn required further development of weapons, particularly of delivery systems.

The Soviet military's rejection of Stalin's constant factors and their growing interest in the problem of surprise, in addition to their natural desire for further development of weapons, made them sympathetic to Khrushchev's position. Furthermore, Zhukov explicitly rejected Malenkov's notion that war would mean the end of civilization, arguing that "one cannot win a war by atomic weapons alone." In keeping with this attitude, the military press more or less explicitly took issue with the Malenkov line late in 1954,[3] and his removal as Premier at the end of January 1955 was quickly followed by a series of enthusiastic military approvals as well as a virtual regeneration of Soviet military thought. The commitment to push rapid Soviet rocket development was probably made then also.

Marshal Zhukov benefited personally by Malenkov's fall. He now became Minister of Defense, and shortly afterward accompanied Khrushchev and Bulganin to Geneva. This was a major recognition of his new stature. He was soon heard in the Soviet press as expressing approval for the Khrushchev-initiated rapprochement with Yugoslavia, a matter then hotly debated within the inner Party counsels and violently opposed by Molotov. This was not only a matter of allying oneself with Khrushchev; it was also taking a stand on a political issue normally not within the purview of the military. But in the conditions of splintered leadership the support was welcomed by the First Secretary and in turn enhanced the marshal's position.

It is likely, however, that even Khrushchev, the chief beneficiary of Zhukov's support, was not unmindful of the implications of the marshal's unusual eminence in the Soviet political arena. He was probably also aware that within the military Zhukov had bitter rivals, particularly Marshal Ivan Konev, also a distinguished war hero, who had served during the war in the Ukraine in a close relationship with Khrushchev. He had replaced Zhukov on his removal from Germany in 1946. It was Marshal Konev who on the Soviet Army day, February 23, 1955, made it a point to praise Khrushchev's wartime role, whereas Zhukov in his comments and in an interview with the foreign press failed to mention the Party Secretary and took much of the credit for planning the Stalingrad operation for himself.[4] Perhaps because of that, Konev was chosen to deliver the tenth victory anniversary speech in May 1955 and was credited in the press a month later with planning the victorious Berlin operation. Skillfully playing on internal jealousies, Khrushchev may have been protecting his flanks even in 1955.

For the time being, however, Khrushchev's primary problem was

20th Congress in February 1956 Khrushchev hinted that injustices had also involved many officers, but he did not explicitly rehabilitate Tukhachevsky.

It may be assumed that Zhukov, as one of the beneficiaries of the purges, was in an ambivalent position. It may also be suspected that many of the higher officers who resented his pre-eminence—as well as apparent arrogance—saw in the rehabilitation a convenient means of embarrassing him. There was no doubt, however, that taken as a whole the officer corps favored the rehabilitations as a way of removing a blot from its past, and perhaps even as a way of ensuring that such a purge could not hit its ranks again. Finally, a rehabilitation would also remove the implied doubts concerning the military's loyalty to the communist cause, thereby in turn reducing the objective need for intense political controls. To the extent that the two issues were thus interrelated, Zhukov, who was known to favor a reduction in political controls and greater stress on military proficiency (he was basically a military purist), had no choice but to become identified with the military cause, his personal embarrassment notwithstanding.

During the summer of 1957 the military press ran several articles on Civil War heroes, including Stalin's later military victims. In this way, albeit indirectly, the process of rehabilitation was being initiated. At the same time, efforts to diminish the supervision of the military by their political watchdogs continued. Already in 1955, after Zhukov had become Defense Minister, the zampolity (political officers) were eliminated from the company level. In 1956 Zhukov flatly stated that outside efforts to criticize "the service activities of officers . . . must be punished," and asserted that ideological training should have increased military proficiency as its principal goal. He was echoed by his old friend, Marshal Timoshenko: "Communists and Komsomols must play the same tune as the officers." [6] In the fall, the military press criticized the work of Party organs in the military, and in May 1957 a new instruction, emanating from the Central Committee and accompanied by a special order by Zhukov, ordained that "criticism of the commands and decisions of commanding officers will not be permitted at Party meetings." Regimental and higher commanders were given the authority to direct Party work in their units.

These steps must have heightened Khrushchev's suspicions, but as long as the political leadership was torn by internecine conflict Zhukov, particularly his popularity, was valuable. The situation changed drastically after June 1957. The elimination of the "anti-Party" group left Khrushchev with the Party *apparat* now firmly in his grasp. The absence of rivals within the leadership, the earlier denigration of the state and economic bureaucracy, and the subordination of the secret police all meant that Zhukov's support was no longer a necessity, while his espousal of military rehabilitations and, even more important, of limitations on political controls could become politically embarrassing.

The trigger event which may have determined Khrushchev to remove Zhukov was the marshal's public speech to a mass meeting of Leningrad citizens in the middle of July, shortly after his election to the Party Presidium. It was an unusual speech in several respects. First of all, Zhukov made liberal use of the pronoun "I" (something which is normally the privilege of only the top leader), and this time claimed for himself also the pre-eminent role in the epic siege of Leningrad: "I was in command of the troops of the Leningrad front in the autumn of 1941, at the most difficult, critical moment . . . ; I saw the Leningraders defend their city . . . alongside the Soviet Army . . . ; later on, coordinating the actions . . . to breach the blockade, I once again admired the heroism of the Leningraders. . . ." Second, he failed completely to credit the CPSU for its wartime role, or that of individual communist leaders. Third, nowhere in the speech did he refer to Khrushchev, not even when speaking of the recent rout of the "anti-Party" group. Fourth, he hinted that the group ought to be expelled from the Party, which went considerably beyond the decision reached only two weeks earlier by the highest Party body. Fifth, he charged them with illegalities which he specified to his audience and which *Pravda* did not reprint. (He thus anticipated the detailed charges made by Khrushchev at the 22nd Party Congress four years later). Sixth, he ended his speech by assuring his audience that the armed forces "are standing confidently and firmly on guard over the interests of our country and are always ready to carry out the will of the people," again not including the Communist Party.

Judging from Zhukov's past, the speech was more likely a manifestation of personal vanity and of a certain political clumsiness

possible; that he had a portrait of himself painted "just like St. George the Dragon Slayer on an old icon" and had it hung in the Soviet Army Museum; and that he revised the scenario of a film about Stalingrad to glorify himself. A month after the publication of this article, Marshal Konev received the Order of Lenin.

To complete the ritual, the press also published a humble, even if somewhat qualified, confession by Zhukov. He admitted that the criticism "has in the main been correct," that it had been helpful to him, that he recognized his mistakes and promised to "completely eliminate my shortcomings." The November 3rd announcement concluded by stating that Zhukov had been removed from membership in the Presidium and in the Central Committee and that the Secretariat had been "instructed to give Comrade Zhukov other work." A few hours later, the launching of the second Soviet sputnik distracted public attention. Amid public jubilation over the new Soviet success, the marshal quietly faded from the public scene.

MacArthur's political history also did not end in triumph. The bipartisan rallying together at the outbreak of the Korean War was only a prelude to intense political acrimony and institutional conflict. These controversies arose from the conjunction of the war with the political weakness of the Truman Administration, the opposition of Republican leaders to the Administration's Far Eastern policy, and the political independence and military assurance of MacArthur. In the fall of 1949, the Truman Administration suffered two serious foreign-policy setbacks. First, the Soviet Union exploded an atomic device several years before the date predicted by most American intelligence experts. Second, the Chinese Communists completed their conquest of mainland China. These two events forced the Administration to launch a complete reappraisal of its foreign and military policies. By the spring of 1950 this had already led to the decision to go ahead with the hydrogen bomb and to approve tentatively a vast expansion of military programs and expenditures. Both the Soviet bomb and the Chinese Communist victory, however, gave new opportunities to the Administration's domestic critics. Further ammunition was provided by the apparent success of Soviet espionage. In January 1950 Alger Hiss was convicted of perjury and Klaus Fuchs was arrested for passing nuclear secrets to the Soviets. The following month Senator Joseph

R. McCarthy exploited these developments with his first charge of Communists in the State Department.

The structure of bipartisanship on foreign policy was also beginning to crack. Most Republican leaders had never been happy with the Administration's policies in the Far East. The "loss" of China seemed to reveal those policies as a complete disaster. Attention was now focused on the problem of Formosa. In January 1950 the Truman Administration made clear that it was unwilling to give military aid to Chiang Kai-shek and unwilling to commit itself to the defense of the island if the Communists attacked it. Congressional Republicans vigorously denounced both policies. In addition, the leadership of the Administration was not as strong as it had been. Neither Eisenhower nor Marshall nor Lovett was in the government. Acheson had been Secretary of State for a year and was rapidly exhausting the stock of congressional good will with which he had begun his term. The Secretary of Defense, Louis Johnson, was stanchly attempting to keep military expenditures down and on some foreign-policy issues did not attempt to conceal his sympathy with the views of the opposition. The relations between him and Acheson were seriously strained and were soon to break down completely. In the spring of 1950 the Truman Administration was thus in an especially vulnerable political position.

The course of the controversy over the conduct of the war was also shaped by the uniquely independent position which MacArthur occupied in Tokyo. This independence derived from three factors. First, American military doctrine traditionally stressed the autonomy of field commanders. In the American view, a commander was given a mission and the resources to accomplish that mission, and the rest was up to him. During the Pacific War MacArthur had taken full advantage of his autonomy. In the Korean War this respect for the independent judgment of the theater commander contributed to the misunderstandings between Washington and Tokyo. Nonetheless, MacArthur, as President Truman put it, "was commander in the field. You pick your man, you've got to back him up. That's the only way a military organization can work. I got the best advice I could and the man on the spot said this was the thing to do. . . . So I agreed." [7] Second, during and after World War II the theater commanders were responsible for political and diplomatic as well as military activities in their area. For a

criticism of the "restrictions" which Washington had imposed upon him. These were, he told one newsman, an "enormous handicap, without precedent in military history." The Administration promptly responded with a directive that all statements on foreign policy should be cleared with the State Department and that there was to be no direct communication of "military or foreign policy with newspapers, magazines, or other publicity media in the United States." Meanwhile, during all of December and much of January, it seemed quite possible that MacArthur's armies might be completely destroyed or driven out of Korea. The Administration's policy was to avert this as long as possible, to attempt to maintain a foothold on the peninsula, and under no conditions to expand the war. The latter, however, was just exactly what MacArthur wanted to do. Specifically, he recommended more reinforcements for the Far East, a blockade of China, air and naval bombardment of Chinese industry, use of Nationalist forces in Korea, and diversionary actions by the Nationalists against the southern Chinese mainland. The rationale behind these recommendations to expand the war outside Korea was the probability of defeat within Korea. Instead, the UN forces dug in, stopped the Communist advance, and launched a counteroffensive.

By the middle of March the UN forces were again approaching the 38th parallel. The issue which had been posed the previous October again came up. This time, however, the Administration had no intention of attempting to unite Korea by force. Consequently it made plans to attempt to negotiate a cease-fire on the basis of the status quo ante. Informed of these intentions, MacArthur promptly issued his own demand for the surrender of the Chinese forces. Through this action he effectively torpedoed the Administration's plans. This was a direct challenge to the President and his foreign policy. It was, in President Truman's view, "open defiance of my orders as President and as Commander in Chief. This was a challenge to the authority of the President under the Constitution. . . . By this act MacArthur left me no choice—I could no longer tolerate his insubordination." [8] Truman immediately ordered the Chiefs to remind MacArthur of the directive of the previous December against uncoordinated foreign-policy statements. The President had, however, also determined that MacArthur would have to be relieved. The final impetus came on April

5, when the Republican leader in the House of Representatives made public a letter from MacArthur. In this the general again endorsed the use of Nationalist troops in Korea, declared that Asia was where the Communists had "elected to make their play for global conquest," and said that he and his troops in Asia were fighting "Europe's war with arms while the diplomats there still fight it with words. . . ." The President, Secretary of State Acheson, Secretary of Defense Marshall, and the Joint Chiefs of Staff all agreed that MacArthur had to go. On April 11 the general was summarily relieved of his commands.

Zhukov's dismissal was followed by the ritual of degradation, MacArthur's by the ritual of adulation. The general came home to a tumultuous and hysterical popular reception. He was invited to address a joint session of Congress (an honor customarily accorded visiting Chiefs of State rather than cashiered generals). His eloquent speech touched off further ecstatic paeans. "We saw a great hunk of God in the flesh," exclaimed one congressman, "and we heard the voice of God." [9] In the following weeks the general was accorded record-breaking ticker-tape parades in the great cities of the nation. He was showered with praise, invitations to give speeches, offers of help and assistance. Such was the popular acclaim.

Among the more substantial elements of opinion, the division of support between President and general was more equal. The bulk of the "quality" press backed the President with reservations; the more popular press was more enthusiastically for the general. In Congress opinion also was divided—almost entirely along partisan lines. A congressional investigation was inevitable, of course, and the hearings formally opened on May 3 before the Senate Foreign Relations and Armed Services Committees. As the opening witness, MacArthur presented his case with skill and dexterity, if not always with clarity. He was followed by a long succession of Administration witnesses: Marshall, Bradley, Acheson, the Joint Chiefs. The weight of the Administration's case was carried by the military men in the Administration. This sharp division between the Washington generals and MacArthur repeated once again, this time on the open fields of politics, the previous splits between Marshall and MacArthur, the European generals and the Far Eastern ones. Those who opposed the Administration, in turn, had to oppose its gen-

within that party his most active and influential supporters came from the extreme right wing. The dominant forces in the Republican Party on the east coast did not hesitate to exploit the discontent with the Truman Administration which MacArthur helped to stimulate. But they disagreed seriously with the general on both domestic policy and foreign policy and were preparing the way for the nomination of MacArthur's wartime rival, Eisenhower. For all the popular enthusiasm he was accorded after his dismissal, only a few of the minority party leaders sympathized fully with MacArthur and his policy.

Zhukov's lack of political allies was underwritten at the Central Committee meeting following his ouster. In effect, the Committee gave the dismissal the collective seal of approval of the political (and military) elite. In a very different way, the congressional hearings on MacArthur performed a somewhat similar function. In this case the issue was wide open, and the principal effect of the hearings was to reduce MacArthur's serious supporters to a hard core of right-wing Republicans.

4. Both Truman and Khrushchev were helped by serious divisions within the military. The Konev-Zhukov rivalry was similar to and had much the same impact as the Marshall-MacArthur rivalry. In addition, in each case there was a distinct group of military chiefs upon whom the political leaders could count for support. Khrushchev's dismissal of Zhukov was followed by the appointment to top positions of many members of the so-called "southern clique"—Malinovsky, Grechko, Moskalenko, Galikov, Yeremenko —with whom Khrushchev had been closely associated during the war. The advancement of their power and the protection of Khrushchev's were both served by the dismissal of Zhukov. Similarly, the Truman Administration drew upon the support of the so-called "European clique" of General Marshall and his protégés. Marshall and Bradley, MacArthur subsequently alleged, "were both personally hostile to me." [12] When the chips were down, both MacArthur and Zhukov were to an astonishing degree isolated within their own profession. Only a few of Zhukov's immediate colleagues were removed following his dismissal. Many of MacArthur's subordinate commanders shared his strategic views. Yet they stayed on at their posts, not because it was impossible for the Truman Administration to dismiss them but because it was unnec-

essary to do so. If MacArthur could be fired, anyone else could also. Similarly, it is unlikely that Marshal Malinovsky or any other high officer has forgotten Zhukov's fate.

5. Truman and Khrushchev feared the popularity of their generals. But the ousters suggest that in neither political system is popular appeal a resource which can be effectively employed by a cashiered general against the incumbent political leadership. Zhukov, lacking access to the mass media and to sympathetic organizations, had no way to translate popularity into power. That popularity was also dimmed by the condemnation which followed his ouster and then the silence which followed that. MacArthur, after his dismissal, had all the opportunities which Zhukov lacked to capitalize on his popularity, but in democratic states popularity is ephemeral. It can be effectively employed in politics only when it is bolstered by concrete support from leading elements within the political system. In the future in both countries, moreover, it is unlikely that the generals will even have popularity. In the absence of another major conflict or crisis, the generals will increasingly be unknown bureaucrats rather than well-known commanders.

6. Both political systems discourage their generals from acquiring political skills, and both MacArthur and Zhukov lacked the skill and sophistication of the professional politicians they opposed. Each appears to have overrated his own political strength and particularly his indispensability to the political leadership. The political ineptitude of the generals was manifest in their political tactics. Unless Zhukov was contemplating an immediate military coup (which he apparently was not), his Leningrad speech was a monstrous political blunder. He challenged Khrushchev verbally but not politically. MacArthur's pronunciamentos reveal a similar lack of political sophistication. In 1944 he inadvertently and single-handedly destroyed Senator Vandenberg's MacArthur-for-President boom by an injudicious letter to a congressman. In 1950 and 1951 he seemed unable or unwilling to consider the impact of his public statements on the currents of domestic politics.

Many similar factors thus helped Truman and Khrushchev to restore political supremacy in their two systems. The fundamental causes of the challenges to that supremacy, however, rested not in the ambitions of arrogant generals but in the conflicts among ambitious politicians. The relation between the restoration of political supremacy and the restoration of political unity was very different in the two countries. In the Soviet Union the assertion of civilian control was the result of the end of political discord, the firing of Zhukov the last step in the consolidation of Khrushchev's power. In the United States, that assertion came before the restoration of political harmony. The firing of MacArthur was one battle in a political controversy which continued for two more years.

Once Khrushchev had defeated his enemies in the Party apparat and established firm control of the Presidium in June 1957, he had little to risk in ousting Zhukov and much to gain. Zhukov's ouster was followed, in turn, by the re-establishment of many traditional Soviet institutions of civilian control which had been weakened during the succession struggle. The tendencies fostered by Zhukov toward an autonomous military profession were reversed, and efforts were made to create "a higher Party-political consciousness throughout the armed forces." [13] The administrative subordination of the Army to the Party was again emphasized. Unlike Zhukov, Malinovsky was not made a member of the Presidium: although the military representation on the Central Committee was increased in 1961,* no general penetrated into the inner seat of political power, the Presidium. During the succeeding years, generals who had previously been closely associated with Khrushchev were rapidly promoted to higher offices as they became vacant. Thus, Khrushchev cemented both his and the Party's control over the military.

The meaning of these controls was clearly revealed in the course of military policy following Zhukov's dismissal. The predominance of Khrushchev is demonstrated in the partial demobilization which he ordered in 1959 and 1960, the suspension of nuclear tests at the same time, his proposals for greater allocations to nonindustrial production in 1961, his delaying of the complete rehabilitation of Tukhachevsky and his comrades until the 22nd Party Congress in 1961, and the rapid withdrawal of the missiles from Cuba. The military leaders may not have liked any of these actions, but there was little that they could do about them. Under strong and unified political leadership, the Soviet armed forces were once again the

---

* To 31, out of a total of 330. The 10-per-cent representation has been the average allotted to the military since 1939.

pliant instruments of the Party and the state. The generals were permitted to continue their internal debates on strategy and tactics, and the military press continued featuring many diverse opinions. But in doing that, they were acting as a major policy group,* not as a political alternative to the Party.

In the Soviet Union the achievement of political unity was a prerequisite to the assertion of political supremacy. Unlike Khrushchev, however, Truman could assert political supremacy in the midst of political discord and at a time when the authority and popularity of himself and his Administration were at a very low ebb. The Democrats had lost strength in the 1950 elections; McCarthy was attacking the Administration for being soft on Communists; Kefauver was investigating crime and corruption; the Senate had just completed a lengthy and heated "great debate" over the sending of troops to Europe. At the start of his second term in January 1949, some 69 per cent of the American people had approved the way in which Truman was handling his job as President. By January 1950 this rating had dropped to 45 per cent; in June 1950 it was 37 per cent; in February 1951 it was 26 per cent. The President's appreciation of his political weakness was one reason he had not relieved MacArthur in August or December 1950. The longer he delayed, however, the more precarious his position became. While Khrushchev seized his first opportunity to get rid of Zhukov, Truman reluctantly took what seemed to be his last chance to get rid of MacArthur. In the light of these circumstances, the amazing thing is that Truman was able to act at all. But in fact he was able not only to lead from political weakness, but to do precisely what Khrushchev could not do: re-establish political supremacy in the absence of political unity. It was as if Khrushchev had fired Zhukov in December 1956 rather than November 1957.

Truman was able to act this way for two reasons. First, the separation of powers, checks and balances, and calendar-fixed elections meant that short of impeachment there was no way in which his opponents could compel him to reinstate MacArthur. Since he acted within the accepted scope of his authority, the most his opponents could do was compel him to pay a high price in other

---

* See Chapter Four for discussion of the role played by policy groups in the Soviet system.

areas. This they did, but by April 1951 Truman was willing to pay it. Khrushchev's ouster of Zhukov cost him practically nothing politically. Truman's ouster of MacArthur cost him a lot. Most importantly, it deprived him of the ability to resolve the political discord which had been the root cause of the challenge to his authority in the first place. In effect, the Administration was backed into a corner where it could not achieve its policy goals in Korea (an armistice line in the vicinity of the 38th parallel) without employing the means (sustained military pressure) which the American people would have accepted only to achieve MacArthur's goal (military defeat of China). The result was a bitter and prolonged political stalemate at home comparable to the bitter and prolonged military stalemate in Korea.

Political supremacy and political harmony were easier to achieve in the American case because of the ability of the political system to assimilate military figures into positions of political leadership without damage to itself. Four years on the Central Committee and two years as a candidate member of the Presidium could not convert Zhukov into an apparatchik. He remained the representative of an institution which embodied a potential challenge to the supremacy of the party. In the American system, however, top-ranking officers such as Marshall, Bradley, and Eisenhower could become thoroughly involved in politics without threatening civilian control. Indeed, just the reverse was true: their very participation helped in the assertion of civilian control. In the Soviet Union the exercise of top political power by military leaders would have undermined Party supremacy. In the American system political supremacy is defied when a subordinate commander (such as MacArthur) challenges the policies of his civilian superiors. It is not necessarily challenged when military officers assume political posts. Instead, one means of civilian control is the absorption of military officers into the ways of democratic politics.

The permeability of the American system also made it possible for political harmony to be re-established through means which would have been out of the question in the Soviet Union. The problem of political discord was resolved by the election of Eisenhower. He brought into office the political strength to restore the conditions for consensus. "President Eisenhower," as Walter Lippmann pointed out, "signed an armistice which accepted the partition of Korea and a peace without victory because, being himself the victorious commander in World War II and a Republican, he could not be attacked as an appeaser. . . . President Truman . . . was not able to make peace, because politically he was too weak at home. He was not able to make war because the risks were too great. This dilemma of Truman's was resolved by the election of Eisenhower." [14] In effect, Eisenhower ended the war on Truman's terms, pacified the right wing by symbolic gestures ("unleashing" Chiang, replacing the Truman Chiefs of Staff), and sealed the American acceptance of the communist conquest of China. He restored harmony to the political system, and, as he himself has recognized, this was probably his single greatest accomplishment as President.*

Thus, in the Soviet system political supremacy depends directly on the institutional relationships between Party and Army. It takes a strong political leader to establish the political authority necessary for harmony and to fire a strong general. In the more complex and flexible American system, however, a weak President can fire a strong general, and a popular general can end an unpopular war. In the Soviet Union Khrushchev had to establish both unity and control. In the American system, Truman asserted control, Eisenhower restored unity. What the one political system secured through the concentration of power, the other achieved through flexibility and resilience.

---

* Asked after leaving the Presidency to identify his "greatest achievements," Eisenhower replied, "When I came to the presidency the country was in an unhappy state. There was bitterness and there was quarreling . . . in Washington and around the country. I tried to create an atmosphere of greater serenity and mutual confidence, and I think that it . . . was noticeable over those eight years that that was brought about." "Eisenhower on the Presidency," CBS telecast with Walter Cronkite, October 12, 1961; quoted in Emmett Hughes, *The Ordeal of Power,* New York, 1963, p. 331n.

years of rapid change. Yet in retrospect it seems that at first neither Soviet nor American leaders perceived the full implications of the domestic shifts that had taken place in the two countries. The Soviets tended to assume that the Hungarians would simply imitate their own post-Stalinist reforms, and that would be that. In America the collapse of Batista was seen as merely another upheaval in the regular cycle of Latin American coups. Neither understood that profound—indeed revolutionary—changes were taking place in the two small countries. To understand the reason for this failure of perception one must go beyond problems of intelligence analysis, diplomatic reporting, or the shortsightedness of leadership. Fundamentally, the initial failure was rooted in the character of the relationship that had prevailed for a number of years between the Soviet Union and Eastern Europe, and between the United States and Central America.

This relationship was one of indirect colonialism by means of satellite regimes. Both major powers, in their expansionist phase, had asserted their domination over a contiguous divided and weak region, and imposed upon it their own political supremacy and economic mastery. To be sure, there were significant differences in the pattern of domination. The Soviets, exporting an overt ideology already embedded in the institutions of Soviet society, insisted on an almost total imitation of the Soviet political, economic, and social system by the Eastern European states. This meant a violent social revolution, and it was carried out with means borrowed directly from the Stalinist experience in the Soviet Union. The political leadership imposed upon Eastern Europe was composed in the main of Stalin's personal agents, trained in his own apparat and directly subject to him. The economic institutions, such as collectivization and intense heavy industrial development, were also derived from the Stalinist model. The resulting Eastern European resentment was further stimulated by the unabashed exploitation of their economies by the Soviet Union, and by the fact that generally Eastern Europeans saw themselves as culturally and economically superior to the Russians. Thus Stalinist domination in almost every respect meant to them personal degradation. This feeling was intensified by the lack of respect shown by the Soviets for the national sensitivities of the dominated peoples, a majority of whom entertained a traditional antipathy toward the Russians.

The American pattern of domination was different in form and therefore also somewhat in substance. In effect, it reflected the pluralism of the American society, just as the Soviet pattern reflected the peculiar qualities of Stalinism. There was no overt and purposeful export of American institutions, even though most of the Central American republics adopted American-style constitutions. This, however, was merely a front for a system of domestic rule profoundly different from that prevailing in the United States. In its essence, local government involved a rotation of cliques, usually combining military power with economic privilege, in which the palace coup replaced the electoral process. The United States required only that the regimes respect American property rights and be able to maintain "law and order" domestically. Since American primacy in the region was not challenged by any other power, there was no need to subordinate overtly the foreign policies of these states to the United States, especially since foreign-policy issues involved, in the main, minor local disputes among them. The United States could thus act as an arbiter, thereby also increasing its sway, while on broader issues it could rely on their automatic support. In economics, domestic concessions for American companies, protection for American capital, and American withdrawal of locally derived profits made for a relationship of domination and exploitation. Although the standard of living in these countries was considerably below that of the United States and in many respects there were local economic benefits in the relationship with the United States, the prevailing attitude of the people tended to be one of hostility, reinforced in part by the feeling that Latin American culture is superior to the mercantile Anglo-Saxon values of the Yankees.

In Hungary the general pattern described above was expressed in the rule of First Secretary Matyas Rakosi, an old-time Stalinist, directly imposed on the country by the Soviet Union. Rakosi's rule was marked by brutality unusual even in Stalinist Eastern Europe. Its terror was directed at both Communists and the nation at large. The violent purges of the Party, culminating in the hanging of the one-time Party Secretary Laszlo Rajk (one of the few domestic— not Moscow-trained—communist leaders) and many of his associates, created fear and demoralization in the ruling elite. By 1953 the massive terror of the regime and the radical character of the internal social and economic reforms created in Hungary an atmosphere of almost unprecedented social stress.

When Stalin died in March 1953, the new leadership initiated in the Soviet Union a series of gradual reforms, designed to reduce popular bitterness and also to weaken the power of the secret police, which threatened even Stalin's successors. The Soviet leaders felt that it was only natural for the satellite leaders to do likewise, and thus they encouraged Rakosi in the summer of 1953 to accept a "New Course" in Hungary. The Soviet leaders personally even chose the man who, as the new Prime Minister, was to carry out the reform program. They selected Imre Nagy, an old Communist; he had spent many years in Moscow, and so the Soviet leaders had no reason to mistrust him. Nagy proceeded to reduce the pace of industrialization, to cut back on the collectivization, and, most important, to free many concentration-camp prisoners. His program was resented by Rakosi, who still retained control over the Party machinery, and who steadfastly agitated against the New Course. Taking advantage in early 1955 of the internal Soviet difficulties, and the consequent reduction in direct Soviet management of satellite affairs, Rakosi staged a comeback. Nagy was removed and the New Course abandoned. This, however, merely intensified the tensions in Hungary. Many Party members saw in Nagy the only hope for communism in Hungary, while the increasing Soviet courtship of Tito encouraged them in the belief that Nagy represented the views of the more forward-looking Soviet leaders. Violent agitation within the Party, increasing outspokenness of the intellectuals, ferment among the youth rose in intensity, and Khrushchev's sudden attack on Stalin in February 1956 made Rakosi's position untenable. He resigned in the summer of 1956, and was replaced not by Nagy but by Erno Gero, a man closely associated with Rakosi, hand-picked by the Soviet leaders to reduce domestic tensions gradually without yielding the predominant position of the Communist Party or changing Hungary's relationship with the Soviet Union. Three months before the outbreak of the revolution, the Soviet leaders were still unresponsive to the increasingly apparent signs of turmoil in Hungary.

Their blithe self-assurance about conditions in Eastern Europe and their underestimation of the impact of de-Stalinization on an area in which communist institutions were still relatively new and were associated in the public mind with foreign domination thus inhibited timely initiatives which might have reduced the ferment and stabilized the political scene. The situation was further complicated by the simultaneous Soviet wooing of Yugoslavia, in the hope that Tito's return to the Soviet camp would strengthen its internal unity. In fact, the courtship of Tito merely helped to intensify internal pressures against the old Stalinist lieutenants in Eastern Europe, while the absence of a clear-cut Soviet line tended to produce widespread confusion and demoralization within the ruling elites. The problem was made even worse by the struggles within the Soviet leadership: not only did those struggles produce sudden zigzags in Soviet policy, but they were in turn reproduced on a smaller scale within the Eastern European leaderships, with various leaders desperately trying to attach themselves to different Soviet rivals in the hope of sharing in the spoils of victory. This made for an even more confused political picture.

In Cuba, Fulgencio Batista's dictatorship was established under the benevolent surveillance of the United States and enjoyed the sympathetic backing of several American ambassadors, usually considered the second most important men in Havana. Although Batista was not imposed on Cuba by the dominant power in the way Rakosi had been on Hungary, it seems clear that timely American disapproval would have sufficed to undermine his power. But the United States was not interested in the internal character of the Cuban regime or in its relationship to its own people. The decisive criterion was Batista's attitude toward the United States and toward American interests in Cuba. Since on both scores it was deemed satisfactory, Batista's dictatorship enjoyed in effect benevolent, though passive, American sponsorship, and thus many anti-Batista Cubans saw him primarily as an American puppet. Many Cubans probably recalled that their country was an American creation and that the United States had intervened in the past in their affairs.[2] It seemed logical, therefore, to associate Batista with America. What is more, certain American economic interests did back Batista directly. Thus, although Cuba did prosper economically and became one of the most developed Latin American countries, there was a strong sense of political deprivation, linked with growing anti-American sentiment. As in Hungary, this nationalism was to become an important factor in the intensifying dynamic of the revolution, and, as in Hungary, the dominant power tended to be unaware of it.

In the fifties, internal dissatisfaction began to erupt in sporadic outbreaks of violence. Although Batista was opposed by many groups, including the active and popular Catholic student movement, resistance to him was dramatized most effectively by Fidel Castro's guerrilla band. It was given considerable publicity by the American press and its eventual triumph in December 1958 was hailed in the United States as marking the end of another corrupt and backward Latin American tyranny. But beyond such vague sympathy of the public, and a statement of approval from the United States government, little thought seems to have been given to the longer-range implications of this change or to the social and political character of the new regime. The unstated assumption presumably was that Castro would become a more up-to-date, a more modern, and a more democratic star in the American constellation. Costa Rica, led by José Figueres, seemed to provide the precedent.

The subsequent strong reaction against Castro was thus partly a product of excessive and false expectation. The American public was not prepared for the wave of executions which followed his advent to power, and there was little in the American tradition to make a Central American Robespierre very popular. The mounting anti-Castro sentiment was fed in part by a campaign launched against him by some of the American interests likely to be affected by his reform programs and also by the refugees from Cuba who began to stream into Florida. The impact of the latter became particularly strong when former anti-Batista opponents began to leave Cuba, charging Castro with heading in a communist direction. In Cuba itself, anti-Americanism soon became the central motif of Castro's propaganda, while the internal shifts of power in his regime made it quite clear by late 1959 that anticommunists, such as the first President, Manuel Urrutia Lleo, or the anti-Batista Catholic student leaders, were being systematically eliminated. In late 1959 two leading communist associates of Castro, Che Guevara and Antonio Jiménez, were appointed to key governmental positions: to head the Cuban National Bank and the Institute of Agrarian Reform respectively.

American assessments of the Cuban scene—and here one must

generalize about often conflicting Congressional statements, press editorials, and official pronouncements—were complicated by a growing feeling in America that there was an urgent need for revision of the United States policies toward Latin America in general. There was mounting sentiment for a policy designed to support democratic movements, to isolate the old-fashioned dictatorships, and to associate America with the forces of progress and reform. Castro was therefore viewed with both sympathy and ambivalence. There was fear that a policy of hostility toward him not only would again identify the United States with the conservative or reactionary elements, but might drive Castro into communist hands. As a result, much of the public emotion and debate over American policy toward Castro tended to focus on the question whether he was himself a Communist. There was little discussion of the more fundamental and difficult problem concerning the broad nature of the Cuban revolution, of the inherent thrust of a combined political revolution from above and anti-Americanism from below, of the logic of a social and nationalist revolution rolled into one. And, as in the Soviet case, the problem of analysis was further obfuscated in the United States by the approaching political contest for power and the consequent growing partisanship.

When finally the Soviet and the American decision-makers had to respond to the crises in Hungary and Cuba respectively, their initial reaction involved an almost mechanical application of lessons derived from relatively recent and seemingly analogous situations. The first Soviet response to the Hungarian challenge was almost a repetition of Soviet conduct in East Berlin in 1953. As the Hungarian masses clamored on October 23 for the return to power of Nagy—and hailed the recent return to power of Gomulka in Poland, which they saw as a precedent for themselves—the Soviet tanks appeared on the streets of Budapest. The Soviet leaders simply did not perceive that they were dealing with both a national revolution and an uprising in the ranks of the ruling Communist elite, and that Budapest in 1956 was not East Berlin of 1953. Similarly, when Cuban-American relations became strained in 1959 and 1960, and Cuban activities outside Cuba took on an openly communist revolutionary character, while in Cuba armed resistance to Castro began to mount, the reaction of the Administration portrayed a similar misunderstanding of the novelty of the

the Soviet Union, revisionist tendencies might be encouraged, to the detriment of the Party's position, while the Army leaders were voicing the urgent need to protect the Soviet strategic position in Central Europe. Inaction, followed by a chain of disruptive consequences, could be even worse for Khrushchev's position than an implicit acknowledgment of error followed by decisive remedial action.

The debate within the leadership was accompanied by top-level efforts to obtain a clear understanding of the situation. When the October crisis first began in Poland, a Presidium delegation, headed by Khrushchev, flew to Warsaw, to investigate at first hand what was happening. The fighting going on in Budapest made it too risky to expose the entire leadership to danger, but still two members of the Presidium, Mikoyan and Suslov, were sent on October 24 to make a personal appraisal. It is noteworthy that this mission was not delegated to any second-level leader; both Mikoyan and Suslov occupied pre-eminent positions. Furthermore, it may be surmised that they also reflected the basic lines of division within the Presidium, thus assuring it of reasonably unbiased accounting. The two men made their way into Budapest from the airport in a tank and conferred with the highest Hungarian leaders. After assessing the situation they allegedly strongly condemned Gero for calling in the Soviet troops which turned a demonstration into an uncontrollable revolt. On their return to Moscow their initial report must have urged restraint, for within days the Soviet pullout began, while the Soviet press on the whole maintained the line that Nagy was being attacked by the reactionaries and that the Soviet action had been on his behalf.

The result of the internal debate, of the Polish case, of Tito's advice, and presumably of the Mikoyan-Suslov mission was the final realization that a drastically new Soviet policy toward East Europe was an urgent necessity. This was openly admitted on October 30, with a special declaration issued on behalf of the Soviet government and the Soviet Communist Party. It was meant to be a charter for new Soviet–Eastern European relations. The declaration openly admitted past iniquities in these relations, promised to take into account Eastern European grievances against Soviet economic exploitation and to remove the offensive presence of Soviet "advisers" in Eastern European armies, and pledged that henceforth the Soviet Union would respect the independence and sovereignty of its Eastern European neighbors. The declaration hedged, however, on the subject of Soviet troops and bases; these might be removed, it stated, in agreement with all the Warsaw Treaty members, thereby making Soviet withdrawal from Hungary or Poland also dependent on the approval of the USSR or Czechoslovakia or Rumania, and the other members. Nonetheless, it was an effort to reassure both Hungary and Poland, as well as Yugoslavia and China, that the Soviet Union no longer insisted on the Stalinist pattern of relations. Presumably to convince Nagy of this, as well as to take stock again of the internal Hungarian scene, both Mikoyan and Suslov returned to Budapest on the day the declaration was issued.

They must have found the situation, from their standpoint, to be deteriorating rapidly. The Hungarian Communist Party had collapsed almost entirely; noncommunist parties were rapidly growing in strength; the Hungarians, embittered by the first Soviet intervention and emboldened by the subsequent withdrawal, were insisting on a total Soviet pullout from Hungary. On the day of the Soviet leaders' arrival a multiparty system was restored, and on the next day the Hungarian leaders requested formal negotiations for Hungary's withdrawal from the Warsaw Treaty. Although, according to Khrushchev's later accounts, the Soviet leaders were divided on the subject of renewed intervention, these developments must have strengthened the case of the pro-intervention group (which, again according to Khrushchev, included him). In any case, the military preparations for such a contingency were rapidly being completed.

It may be assumed that the decision to intervene was triggered by the combined impact of Nagy's announcement on November 1 of Hungary's neutrality and renunciation of membership in the Warsaw Treaty, and of the Anglo-French ultimatum to Egypt of October 30, resulting in the Suez crisis. In the eyes of the Soviet leaders, accustomed to Marxist-Leninist black-and-white thinking, Nagy's action was one of betrayal. "Who is not with us is against us" is an old Leninist-Stalinist maxim, and the Soviet leaders subscribed to it. The simultaneous Suez crisis must have reassured the Soviets that the likelihood of Western engagement on Hungary's behalf had been substantially reduced, especially in view of the sharp divisions within the Western camp, and the Anglo-French-Israeli aggression could even have been read by them as an implicit suggestion from the West that each side use the opportunity to set its house in order. Under those circumstances, and given the stakes, nonintervention would have been contrary to all the precepts of Marxist-Leninist strategy. Or, as Khrushchev put it more pungently, "We would have been called fools, and history would not have forgiven us this stupidity."

The intervention, begun on November 4, was carried out in sufficient force to crush all organized Hungarian resistance within days. It was not deterred by the outcry of world opinion or by the protests of the United Nations. Once the Soviet leaders perceived the novelty of the Hungarian situation, they adjusted rapidly. They first sought accommodation within limits of tolerance defined by themselves. When that failed, they imposed these limits by crushing the opposition.

Unlike the Soviets', American policy toward Cuba never involved a clear definition of the limits of tolerance for Castro's revolution. It never sought a real accommodation with it, nor did it attempt effectively to crush it. Perhaps accommodation was impossible, considering the special dynamic factors inherent to the Cuban revolution. But accommodation within clearly defined limits, and with the alternative of massive use of force clearly conveyed to Castro, might have been possible. It would, however, have involved a systematic effort to spell out why nationalization of American property, socialization, and even anti-American neutralism may be permissible while the establishment of a communist dictatorship, of close links with the communist camp, and political and military cooperation with the Soviet Union in Latin American subversion is not. To be sure the effort to define the limits, difficult in itself, would have been further complicated by Castro's efforts to blur any such distinctions. But instead, the lack of any broad theory of revolution, and the traditional insistence on certitude about the immediate present, tended to turn almost all discussion of Cuba into a quarrel about Castro's being or not being a Communist. (As if the crucial concern of the Presidium in 1956 had been whether Nagy was a CIA agent.) At the same time, the desire to obtain Latin American backing against Castro induced the United States to underplay the possibility of the use of force, because of the general Latin American sensitivity to "Yankee intervention" and the growing feeling in the United States that a new pattern of relations with Latin America must be established.

The year 1960 was an election year in the United States, and the Cuban problem was bound to be an issue. At first, public debate was dominated primarily by Congressional spokesmen, and these, both Republican and Democratic, favored American economic sanctions against Cuba, in reprisal for Cuban expropriation of American property. In part responding to this pressure, and in part calculating that economic sanctions might induce Castro's government to change its attitude toward the United States, the Eisenhower Administration cut off the Cuban sugar quota. At the same time, steps were taken within the Administration to prepare for further contingencies. The State Department was instructed to plan an over-all political and economic program directed against Cuba, but with the very important proviso that it be coordinated with the other Latin American nations. Much of American diplomacy in 1960 was directed at gaining reluctant Latin American support. Almost simultaneously, however, the CIA began to train the exiles and to form them into military formations. Furthermore, during the summer and fall of 1960, American support for anti-Castro guerrillas rapidly increased, and frequent air drops and sea deliveries were made to assist the growing campaign of diversion and sabotage. It is noteworthy, however, that there is little evidence for any broad strategic plan for this campaign. It seems to have been developed merely as a response to the growing internal opposition to Castro, and it lacked any systematic doctrine of the sort developed by Mao, Giap, or even Guevara. Furthermore, both in the case of the State Department and in that of the CIA, there was considerable delegation of responsibility, and the record suggests that the President, the National Security Council, and the Cabinet did not concern themselves very closely with the Cuban matters.

The presidential election debates, especially the direct confrontation between the two candidates, did much to arouse public opinion and also to confuse it. The Democratic candidate went far in urging an active policy of support to anti-Castro forces in order to prevent a communist beachhead in the western hemisphere. The Republican candidate, presumably discomfited by the knowledge of

preparations precisely to that end, adopted publicly a more moderate posture, warning against American intervention. The general
effect, however, of the presidential campaign was to commit both
candidates to a policy designed to remove Castro from power.

Cuba thus became a top item on the agenda of the new Democratic Administration, installed in January 1961. Its point of departure was a public recognition of the need for a broad new
American approach to Latin America. In that spirit the Alliance
for Progress was officially inaugurated in mid-March. It was,
broadly speaking, an attempt to put hemispheric relations on an
entirely new plane, not unlike the Soviet declaration to the Soviet
bloc on October 30, 1956, although in some ways the Soviet statement went further than the American in the admission of past
iniquities. Roughly at the same time, a close presidential adviser
was charged with the task of formulating a broad indictment of the
Castro regime, this time placing the primary emphasis not on
legalistic American objections to Cuban expropriations but on the
theme of the betrayal of the Cuban revolution by Castro and his
regime. Both initiatives thus involved a break with the past and a
recognition of the novelty of the challenge.

At the same time, however, the new Administration was addressing itself to the much more concrete problem of action. The
exile units had been formed, armed, and made ready. The CIA
had prepared a plan of attack, which in March was submitted to
the President and his advisers. The President's military staff confirmed the feasibility of the undertaking. It involved a concentrated
landing of a brigade of men, backed by limited air strikes and presumably aided by internal uprising. It is to be noted that this undertaking, planned by lower echelons, was the only plan of action presented to the Chief Executive. Its rejection would have
been tantamount to abandonment of direct action and would have
meant continued reliance on economic sanctions and diplomatic
activity—in other words, the Eisenhower policy explicitly criticized
by Kennedy during the campaign. Furthermore, the rejection of
the plan would raise the additional problem of the disposal of the
armed men, of their morale, and of the fate of the anti-Castro
guerrillas on the island. Finally, the President was warned that
within a short period of time Castro was to be equipped with MIGs,
and hence even a brief delay would make subsequent action of this

sort much more hazardous. The warning was thus the trigger event, while the success of the previous CIA-led Guatemalan operation provided an important element of reassurance. The decision was made to land.

The Kennedy Administration, however, significantly modified the invasion plan originally prepared by the CIA and approved by the Joint Chiefs of Staff. This plan had provided for American air intervention if necessary to establish air supremacy over the beach-head and to protect the invasion forces. The President and his State Department advisers, however, insisted that there must be no direct and overt American military participation in the initial landings. Several reasons led them to impose this limitation. (1) Unlike the direct Soviet intervention in Hungary, which was imperative to preserve the bloc and was supported by a majority of bloc leaders, a direct United States intervention would almost certainly have ruptured the new and still delicate fabric of good will toward Latin America, which the new Administration was attempting to weave. (2) Unlike the Soviets, the United States had at its disposal an armed force composed of the citizens of the country involved, and it assumed (wrongly) that they would be backed by large-scale defections from Castro. (3) Cuba was only one of several trouble spots confronting the Administration, and the possibility of Soviet counteraction elsewhere would be less likely if the United States did not become directly involved in Cuba. As a result, a revised plan without direct American military participation was prepared and approved by the CIA and Joint Chiefs. The operation was still further weakened the night before the landing when the President canceled a second air strike against Castro's Air Force as a result of protests and concern expressed by UN Ambassador Stevenson and State Department officials. Thus, the doubts in some quarters of the Administration about the wisdom and morality of the invasion produced compromises and limitations which reduced its already slim chances of success. The invasion was launched in spite of a major gap between means and ends, and it was quickly crushed.

This was a major United States setback. The initiative aroused much hostility in Latin America and elsewhere, in spite of the absence of direct American involvement. Its failure reflected badly on the new American Administration and on the general posture

commitment lapsed because it did not involve a commitment to a full-scale intervention. Hence, the next one was that the United States would not permit the establishment of a Soviet base in the Western Hemisphere. Once that took place, refuge was taken in the distinction between offensive and defensive weapons, and the commitment was made not to permit the armed export of the Cuban revolution to Latin America and not to permit the Soviet troops in Cuba to stage a new "Hungary" by suppressing an anti-Castro revolution. However, since there is little reason to believe that a Castro-type revolution in another country need involve direct armed intervention by Castro forces, while the limitations imposed by the United States on the anti-Castro activity of the Cuban exiles make a domestic rising much less likely, neither commitment is equivalent to policy.

Second, the outcome was affected by the character of the respective leaderships. While much of the initial hesitation on both sides was due in one case to divisions within the leadership and in the other to the election, there were important differences in the degree of top-level attention to the problem and of control of operations. The Hungarian crisis was given the personal attention of several top Presidium leaders even before it had reached the October stage of urgency. Intensive top-level involvement in the United States occurred only in March 1961. Furthermore, the Soviet decision was made by a group of men professionally skilled in politics and in the application of force, accustomed to weighing risks against stakes. Aside from the President, the participants in the American decision were in large part political novices. The list that follows compares the two groups of top decision-makers responsible for the decision to intervene and for the character of that intervention.

USSR	USA
1. Party leader with twenty-two years of executive responsibilities in Party apparat, as republic premier, as wartime Front Commissar, three years	1. Chief Executive for two and a half months, member national legislature for fourteen years, wartime naval lieutenant.

(USSR)

(USA)

CPSU First Secretary, seventeen years full member of Presidium (Politburo).

2. Former revolutionary, high-level apparat executive for thirty-five years, former USSR premier and Foreign Minister, full member of Presidium for thirty years.

2. Secretary of State for two and a half months, foundation executive for eight years, earlier Assistant Secretary of State, wartime colonel.

3. High-level executive for thirty years, Defense Minister for three years, wartime Commissar of a Front and Army Marshal, full member of Presidium for eight years.

3. Presidential assistant for national security for two and a half months, former college professor and dean, wartime captain.

4. Party executive for twenty-five years, with special responsibility for purges, Premier for two years, wartime member of the Soviet State Defense Committee, full member of Presidium for ten years.

4. Secretary of Defense for two and a half months, former auto-industry executive, professor of business administration, junior wartime planner.

5. Former revolutionary, Party executive for thirty-three years, with special interest in foreign affairs and personal familiarity with Hungarian politics, wartime member of State Defense Committee, full member of Presidium for twenty-one years.

5. Central intelligence executive during World War II and 1951-1961, lawyer, former diplomatic official.

6. High-level apparat executive for fifteen years, specialist in ideological matters, with per-

6. Lawyer and law professor, former presidential brain-truster and Assistant Secre-

time its fear of war, its unwillingness to let "American boys" be involved (especially in a protracted counter-guerrilla activity which might have followed Castro's fall), its underlying conservatism, which would have impeded the necessary reforms in Cuba. All this complicated the response: on the one hand it made impossible the abandonment of the Cuban venture and on the other it encouraged strong reservations and imposed such limits that it prejudiced the outcome. Thus in both cases the respective natures of the political systems in large measure shaped the destiny of the two interventions.

ALLIANCE-MANAGEMENT: FRANCE AND CHINA

Dealing with enemies is usually simpler than dealing with friends. The choices are clearer, the goals more direct. Allies, however, can translate their weakness into power, their recalcitrance into a bargaining advantage, their alliance into an entanglement, their interpretation of the common goal into a unilateral objective. This lesson was taught to both the United States and the Soviet Union by France and China respectively; by early 1963, relations among the respective allies had become so strained that President Kennedy could not arrange for a visit to Paris and Secretary Khrushchev and Chairman Mao Tse-tung not only exchanged and rejected invitations to visit each other but also publicly traded insults.

There were several striking similarities between the Franco-American strain and the Sino-Soviet rift. In each case, the weaker and more dependent ally (France, China) was a country with an old history, a long tradition in diplomacy and warfare, and an ancient culture. To each, the United States and the Soviet Union were upstart nations, compensating for their lack of culture and background with a heavy-handed reliance on their relative power, wealth, and technological superiority. The resentment against a dominant yet culturally and intellectually inferior partner was intensified by the actual and past dependence of France and China on American and Soviet support respectively. America had contributed heavily to the recovery of France (more than 9 billion dollars), and seventeen years after the war France was still dependent on the American deterrent for its national survival. China had also received extensive Soviet credits (approximately 2 billion dollars), and its security was certainly reinforced by the Soviet nuclear commitment. For both states, the alliance was far from symmetrical, and this fact weighed heavily on the relationship.

China and France, furthermore, had reasons to feel that their interests had not been fully recognized by their more powerful allies, and they could even point to circumstances in which this lack of recognition resulted in their national humiliation. The memory of Suez in 1956 was a strong factor in the French self-assertion of 1960. The Chinese must have also resented the Soviet failure to support them in the Quemoy-Matsu crisis of 1958, and they were openly outraged by the Soviet military and political support for the Indians in 1962. In French and Chinese eyes, the equanimity with which the American and the Soviet leaders viewed French and Chinese national interests respectively stood in sharp contrast to the willingness of the two major powers to run considerable risks, affecting the entire world, when their own interests were involved. To the French, the American response to the Cuban crisis of October 1962 was another proof that the alliance meant the subordination of French interests. To the Chinese, the Soviet engagement in Cuba, as well as the Soviet preoccupation with Berlin, also suggested that Moscow was willing to risk much for itself but little for its ally.

These more immediate French and Chinese complaints, reflecting both a legacy of national frustration and a mounting mood of self-assertion, rested on more deeply rooted and more underlying feelings of resentment. Both France and China had tasted national greatness more than once and had not forgotten their past preeminence. Yet in the present era each had been widely abused as the "sick nation" of Europe or Asia, and each had had to follow the leadership of a dominant foreign power. Furthermore, both had been imperial nations—and they could not help noting that their decline coincided with the emergence of America and Russia. While the French could hardly blame the United States for the loss of Indochina and Algeria, there was widespread resentment because of American efforts to achieve French colonial disengagement and strong suspicion that American interests benefited by the French withdrawal. The Chinese, too, objected to the spread of Russian influence to territories traditionally subject to Chinese suzerainty, and for many years the Chinese had been unwilling to

wiped out from Moscow, and central Europe from Washington. And who can even say that the two rivals, after I know not what political and social upheaval, will not unite?" [7] American unwillingness to arm France was then seen as proof that the original assumption and the resulting policy had been right. (Conversely, American willingness to aid that nuclear development, even if it cast doubt on the original assumption, would not have changed the policy.)

Mao Tse-tung, likewise, made no attempt to hide his disapproval of Khrushchev's willingness to engage in close negotiations with the United States and particularly of Khrushchev's visit to President Eisenhower. The Chinese press openly ridiculed the "Camp David" spirit, and it held up as an example of pacifist and revisionist thinking Khrushchev's statement that President Eisenhower truly desired peace. While the Chinese made no public demands for Soviet aid in the development of nuclear weapons, it is now known that they desired it, were not satisfied with the level of Soviet aid in 1957-1958, and resented bitterly the 1959 Soviet decision to discontinue it. [8] Yet the paramount reason for the Chinese desire to obtain such weapons from the Soviets was to achieve military-political independence from the Soviet policies, which increasingly they viewed as self-defeating. Under the circumstances the not-surprising Soviet unwillingness to provide that aid was seen as confirmation of the reasons which first motivated the request for it.

It is against this background that the dilemma of alliance-management, as faced by the American and the Soviet leaderships, must be examined. To the two leaderships the challenge raised unprecedented problems. Neither had any experience in alliance-management, and both Kennedy and Khrushchev had inherited coalitions in a state of profound flux and change. Since 1945 the United States had been heading a coalition of states inferior to it in wealth, technology, and military power; since 1945 the Soviet leadership had been directing a complex of satellites, while China's involvement in the Korean War made for even greater Chinese dependence on the USSR than otherwise would have been the case. Neither the American nor the Soviet leadership had any training for leading an alliance of equals, and both showed remarkable lack of sensitivity to the psychology, the wounded pride, and the sense of frustration of the French and the Chinese. As a result, neither leadership apparently was ready for the sudden change in the prevailing relations that occurred between 1958 and 1963.

The relatively restricted American experience in alliance relations involved primarily coalitions which were of short duration and highly focused. They were a response to an outside threat and were designed to meet it. This was true of World War I, of World War II, and even of the initial postwar American commitments to Europe. Each instance involved reasonably tangible objectives. This was, happily for Washington, very much in keeping with the traditional American approach to politics: to take up each issue "as it arises" and to resolve it without seeing it in a broader pattern of development. In large measure because of that past experience, the United States was simply unprepared for the sudden emergence in the late fifties of a new spirit of self-assertiveness in France, a spirit made possible by the recovery and the rapidly progressing modernization of French society. Almost in a defensive reflex, much of the initial American reaction was based on the assumption that this was merely a temporary aberration in Franco-American relations, due largely to the personal (hence transitional) impact of the French leader's temperament on these relations. Little or no effort was made to analyze the deeper causes of the difficulty; only belatedly did American policy-makers begin to realize that a profound shift in the general pattern of America-Europe relations was taking place, a shift that had been brought about mainly by earlier American efforts to speed European recovery and promote the re-emergence of Europe on the international scene.

The initial American reaction was simply to temporize: the problem will resolve itself when the general fades from the scene. The French decision to develop an independent French nuclear deterrent, a move justified by de Gaulle in terms of long-term French political needs, and by General Pierre Gallois, the French nuclear theorist, in terms of France's strategic requirements, was widely ridiculed by American policy-makers as another example of de Gaulle's "Don Quixote" mentality. A more serious American objection involved the fear that France's development would precipitate a general proliferation of nuclear weapons, in both the East (China) and the West (Germany). It was thus seen as countering Soviet-American efforts to achieve some stable arms control and eventually disarmament arrangements. Congressional spokesmen,

French inferred that henceforth conventional forces were to be the "sword," and noted that this crucial shift was made in the relatively informal atmosphere of a brief consultation between the heads of two Anglo-Saxon states. This again seemed to confirm de Gaulle's basic thesis.

The French also had deep-seated doubts concerning the general quality of American leadership. In the initial postwar period, qualms of this sort had to be subordinated to the urgent need to provide for the recovery of Europe and for its defense. Furthermore, the character of President Truman's leadership, the far-sighted nature of the Marshall Plan, and Secretary Acheson's dedication to the cause of Europe contributed much to European confidence in America. By 1958, however, the situation had changed a great deal, and it deteriorated sharply after Secretary Dulles' death, although the turning point was reached during the Suez crisis. Increasingly, Europeans spoke of American drift and indecision, and European doubts became particularly intense shortly after President Kennedy's inauguration. The Bay of Pigs fiasco had a particularly strong impact on Europe. United States failure to respond to the construction of the wall in Berlin in August 1961, which clearly reduced Western rights, also contributed to the feeling that European interests were not in the forefront of Washington's concerns. Washington's subsequent willingness to negotiate with the Soviet Union concerning West Berlin, contrary to de Gaulle's recommendation that Soviet proposals be simply rejected, gave impetus to the sudden German interest in de Gaulle's conceptions and leadership.

President Kennedy's skillful handling of the Cuban crisis in October 1962 did much to re-establish both American and his own prestige in Europe, and at the end of 1962 it was reliably reported that President Kennedy saw in that event the beginning of the reassertion of American leadership in the West. Paradoxically, however, much as even de Gaulle praised the American conduct and supported the American stand, it served again to confirm to the French the imperative need to push on with their military and political conceptions. To them Cuba demonstrated that the United States had the capacity and the means to defend *its* own national interest, and that the United States was prepared to act unilaterally when necessary. Thus while the episode served to reassure the

French about the character of American leadership, it did not convince them that it was in the interest of France to accept it. Quite the contrary, the Cuban affair and the Nassau Anglo-American agreement gave additional impetus to French efforts to shape a Europe independent of Anglo-American influence. President de Gaulle's news conference excluding Britain from the Common Market and reaffirming French determination to pursue separate nuclear development followed in January 1963. It brought into the open the profound differences in French and American thinking on military strategy and on the future of Europe. The issue was now directly joined.

Yet even then the American response was wide of the mark. In an observation typical of much of Washington's thinking, former Secretary of State Acheson ascribed France's insistence on its own nuclear deterrent to a "lack of knowledge of the facts, for which the United States has been largely responsible." [13] He argued convincingly that the French efforts were misguided on technological and strategic grounds, and he criticized the American policy of nuclear secrecy for abetting French ignorance. There was little recognition in his remarks of the essential and dominant political dimension of the problem, and this lack of recognition characterized the American response in general. Just as earlier, at the Athens meeting of 1962, the American proposal to place five Polaris submarines under NATO control simply evaded the political problem, since it still involved the retention of ultimate American firing control, so, after the issue was openly posed, new American overtures simply ignored the overriding political character of France's challenge. Instead, the American response relied on well-argued, well-reasoned, and probably quite accurate military-technological arguments designed to prove the military futility of the French effort, thoroughly overlooking the fact that the French position, and the increasing European support for it, involved fundamentally the emancipation of Europe from American tutelage. The American plans for a multilateral deterrent, still based on the American veto, were seen by the French (and by other Europeans) merely as a complex screen for maintaining American predominance, without any continued forward-looking, affirmative partnership of goals between America and Europe. Under those circumstances, American leadership had to be rejected, and Washington's handling of

level meeting in Bucharest to confront the unsuspecting Chinese with a series of sudden accusations. Although later that year, in November and December, a collective meeting in Moscow of eighty-one Communist Parties succeeded in producing a common statement, the process of drafting involved several weeks of bitter negotiations between the Chinese and the Soviets. Furthermore, in the course of the closed debates the Soviets openly attacked the one party which supported the Chinese—the Albanian—and demanded that it subordinate itself to the Soviet position.

In 1961 at their own Party Congress, attended by other party leaders, including the Chinese, the Soviet leaders further intensified their tensions with Peking by launching, this time, an open attack on the Albanian Party and unilaterally expelling it from the communist camp. This step brought the Sino-Soviet divergence into the open, and the Chinese Party responded by asserting that no one party has the right to decide who belongs to the communist camp. By appealing to other parties for support, the Chinese now made equality of parties one of their primary issues with the Soviets and, in effect, were challenging also their primacy.

Although urged by several parties to exercise self-restraint, the Soviet leaders acted in 1962 as if determined to bring the Chinese leadership to its knees. The Soviet leaders used the opportunity provided by a number of Party Congresses to exorcise the Albanians and to ridicule, attack, and reject the Chinese views on Marxism-Leninism, on strategy, and on world affairs. Increasingly, the epithet "Trotskyism" crept into the Soviet vocabulary. At the same time the Soviet leaders began to improve their relations with Yugoslavia, a prime target of Chinese (and Albanian) attacks on revisionism. The anti-Chinese campaign reached a crescendo in the fall of 1962, at the East German Communist Party Congress, when the Yugoslav delegate (attending for the first time since 1948) was cheered, the Chinese spokesman was jeered when he attempted to argue that Yugoslavia was a revisionist state, and the North Korean delegate was prevented from speaking when he wished to back his Chinese colleague. For this turn of events the Chinese blamed the Soviets, who were clearly in a position to determine the procedures of the Congress.

The years 1957-1963 thus saw a steady intensification of the Sino-Soviet dispute. Beginning as a divergence in views on strategy and foreign policy, first it led to a gradual worsening in Party relations; then the unilateral Soviet violation of the nuclear agreement quickly contributed to a sharp deterioration in state relations; Chinese accusations from 1960 on elevated the dispute to a sharply doctrinal one, with far-reaching reciprocal charges of deviationism; the doctrinal dispute automatically also became a struggle for leadership within the international communist community. Furthermore, at one or another point both sides tried to take advantage of internal leadership conflicts within Moscow and Peking: Khrushchev hinted strongly in 1961 that Molotov had foreign backing for his anti-Khrushchev position, and there were allegations that the Soviet leaders had attempted to intrigue against Mao Tse-tung's leadership. Early in 1963 both parties engaged in open polemics designed to mobilize support on their behalf within the international movement, while the Cuban crisis of 1962 and the almost parallel Sino-Indian dispute led to mutual charges of adventurism and ineptness in foreign policy. The Chinese were particularly outraged by Moscow's unwillingness to support them in their conflict with India, and they saw in this a fundamental betrayal by Moscow of both their revolutionary and their national interests.

In 1963 a new element was added to the dispute: the territorial. Late in 1962 the Chinese had chided Khrushchev for his lack of revolutionary courage during the Cuban crisis, and Khrushchev, personally outraged, responded by mocking the Chinese leadership's restraint over Hong Kong and Macao. He compared it with India's forceful assertion of her claim to Goa. This in turn produced an unexpected Chinese response, which in years to come could assume major importance in the Sino-Soviet relationship. The Chinese pointedly reminded the Soviets that in the past Russia had imposed three unfair territorial settlements on China, and noted, "We know very well, and you know too, that you are, to put it plainly, bringing up the question of Hong Kong and Macao merely as a figleaf to hide your disgraceful performance in the Caribbean crisis." [14] By specifying the treaties involved, the Chinese also implicitly pointed a finger at the territories at stake: they involved what is today the Soviet Maritime Province, including Vladivostok, as well as territories in Central Asia, with a total area of more than 750,000 square miles. Because of the traditional Soviet sensitivity to frontier issues, as well as China's growing

in Moscow in July 1963 and was punctuated by bitter reciprocal ideological condemnations.

Why did these two similar controversies evolve in such different ways? Undoubtedly many factors contributed, but pre-eminent among them are the natures of the two political systems. The fact that both the United States and the Soviet Union inherently tended to ally themselves with states which had certain affinities to each of them even further accentuated the dominant aspects of their respective political styles. The Western alliance stressed pragmatism, compromise, adjustment; the communist alliance, ideological purity, primacy, and the elevation of differences into matters of "principle." Thus, first of all, the absence of a strong ideological outlook on the American side and de Gaulle's emphasis on the more traditional concept of national interest on the other contributed decisively to the containment of the disagreements. Once the basic issues emerged to the surface, both sides were capable, with their intellectual and political tradition, of adjusting to an implicit agreement to disagree. The concept of national interest, furthermore, in spite of its basic vagueness, had the advantage of establishing a certain reciprocity: the very fact of insisting on French national interest made the French President also responsive to a clear-cut definition of the American. In doctrinal conflict, on the other hand, all claims tend to be absolute and cumulative—disagreement breeds hostility, hostility breeds suspicion of deviation, deviation breeds charges of heresy.[15] The Western political style, in addition, is at home within a pluralistic and diverse context; the Marxist-Leninists stress dichotomies or uniformities. With enemies, the relationship is one of absolute hostility; with friends, of monolithic unity. Internal divisions tend to be ignored until they have become antagonistic. Once they have become antagonistic, the strategy of conflict can be applied. Such an approach does not lend itself to effective resolution of divergencies within an alliance of equals.

Second, the characters of the respective leaderships had much to do with the pattern of the two disputes. Despite the gap in style and outlook between the French (and generally Continental) leadership and the American, and the tendency of the French to be contemptuous of the American operational preoccupation with day-to-day events, a community of shared experience has been established between the two leaderships since World War II. In both countries, the political "Establishment" contains a large cadre of men deeply involved in the development of NATO and of European unity, and in the application of American aid to the recovery of France; this has created a special bond of understanding and shared interest. In each country there were prominent individuals pleading for reciprocal restraint and cooperation. To the United States, individuals such as Jean Monnet or Robert Schumann were an important source of reassurance that the basic ties were not being severed. To the French leader, the voices of General Norstad, Ambassador Gavin, and Governor Rockefeller meant that his conceptions had important American interpreters, and this too was vital in maintaining a relationship of continuing discussion.

Because of the monolithic structure of the Soviet and Chinese systems, any such informal and indirect ties would have automatically threatened the stability of their respective leaderships. Formal communication exhausted all communication, with no safety valve of the indirect approach and no commonly shared experience in constructive understandings as a cushion. The Soviet and Chinese leaders met only on several formal occasions; there was simply no "Sino-Soviet Establishment" to plead the cause of unity and to moderate the increasingly immoderate language of the debate. Any effort to compensate for this handicap through approaches to individual leaders was inescapably construed as an intrigue, and, in fact, neither leadership had any alternative except intrigue. But this, in turn, further intensified the hostility, as Khrushchev's charges against Molotov in 1961 demonstrated.

Third, and directly relevant to the foregoing, the decision-making process in the United States and France was carried on in the context of a broad debate on foreign policy, with many governmental and nongovernmental "Establishment" participants. The openness of the debate tended to reassure both sides concerning ultimate ends, even if it often contributed additional elements of grievance (particularly in the case of the highly personal anti-de-Gaulle tenor of some American press comments). The writings of such pro-de-Gaulle French experts as Gallois or the more critical contributions of Raymond Aron on the one hand, and in America of Acheson and the more pro-French Kissinger on the other, created a fluid and more elastic context than the rigid and directly

national division between Moscow and Peking. The openness of
the debate, furthermore, tended to inhibit sudden, unilateral moves
by either Washington or Paris, with their exacerbating effect. The
two notable exceptions—the Kennedy-Macmillan Nassau agreement and de Gaulle's January 1963 press conference (excluding
England from the Common Market)—had precisely that negative
effect on the dispute. Yet that was the general pattern in the Sino-
Soviet case. All decisions were made in secrecy; the two vital Soviet
moves—the attack on the Chinese position at the Bucharest conference and the condemnation of Albania—were made suddenly
and without warning; neither side was willing to give a hearing to
the other's arguments, with the consequence that the Chinese were
forced even to use the illegal device of their students in Russia for
distribution of their materials. Once the Soviets and the Chinese
lost hope that a change in the other's leadership might mean the
acceptance of their own postulates, the conflict was handled as a
political-warfare operation.

Fourth, unlike Russia and China, America and France were
bound together as states and societies in a variety of formal and
informal ways. The structure of the Western international system
requires reliance on many multilateral bodies with special common
interests. These provide additional arenas for the articulation of
one's point of view without precipitating a head-on confrontation.
France and the United States could thus meet at NATO, the
OECD, GATT, or the various informal bodies of the Atlantic
community. Russia and China could only confront each other
directly. China did not belong to the Warsaw Treaty or to the
Council of Economic Mutual Assistance. No multiplicity of organs
provided even a limited safety valve for the accumulated grievances. In addition, both America and France had countless personal ties: millions of Americans visit France, thousands of French-
men travel to America; economic investments cut across national
divisions, and the common experience of having fought on the
same side and together in two world wars created a certain national
affinity. On that level, too, both Russia and China were at a disadvantage. There were practically no social ties between the two
countries, each isolated itself from the other, economic relations
had been used as a tool of the conflict, and there was no common

national tradition of alliance. No social affinity provided a break for the doctrinal and political conflict.

These political contrasts suggest more directly relevant reasons for the relative American success and Soviet failure in alliance-management than does the frequently emphasized gap in stages of economic development between Russia and China, or the Chinese challenge to Soviet leadership, or the inherent national conflict between China and Russia. As far as stages of development are concerned, it is to be remembered that until the Soviet leadership responded forcefully to the Chinese challenge the communist leaders of the two most developed communist states, Czechoslovakia and East Germany, were showing obvious sympathy for the Chinese position. Their outlook could hardly have been determined by stages of economic development. Similarly, it is to be noted that the Chinese challenge to the Soviet leadership arose as an objective consequence of the dispute between them. To the Soviets, the defiance of their leadership was sufficient to produce a sharp reaction, and they demonstrated this on two other occasions, with respect to Yugoslavia and Albania, when no direct threat to Soviet leadership was involved. Thus the challenge to leadership was the effect and not the cause of the dispute. Finally, the argument that "national" factors were decisive can always be used to explain a dispute ex post facto; it can also be used to explain collaboration even in cases such as that between Poland and the Soviet Union, in spite of strong anti-Russian national sentiment in Poland. However, the introduction of the territorial dispute did contribute an element of direct national conflict, although it came into play at a stage when the conflict was already acute.

Factors peculiar to the American and the Soviet political systems were of decisive importance in shaping the character of the two disputes; in delaying adequate responses, and in aggravating the misunderstandings with allies. The same factors, however, allowed a gradual containment of the dispute in the Franco-American case, while they pushed the Sino-Soviet relationship into a spiraling hostility. Analysis of the two interventions and of the two alliances suggests that the Soviet system is better suited for dealing with enemies and that the American system is more effective in coping with friends.

Conclusion

STRENGTHS AND WEAKNESSES

THE Soviet political system was created to serve as an instrument of communist rule and reform. The American political system was created to provide a loose governmental framework for American society. The peculiar strengths and weaknesses of each system reflect these original intents, in spite of extensive changes since the original inception of the two systems. On the operational level, the Soviet political system appears to be more vigorous, more capable of mobilizing national resources for specific political ends, more likely to be led by skilled practitioners of power. At the same time, the weaknesses of the Soviet system seem potentially more disruptive than those of the American system.

The strengths of the Soviet system flow from the supremacy of its political ideology and institutions over Soviet society and the political leaders' ability to control that society. Conversely, the weaknesses of the Soviet system flow in large part from the disruptive consequences of overconcentrated personal power, from the restrictive impact of official ideology on the country's economy and intellectual life, and from the resulting tensions between the political system and other social forces and institutions. The strengths of the American system, on the other hand, derive primarily from the close unity between society and polity and from the unceasing dynamic adjustments between the two. Its weaknesses, in turn, are due to its subordination to society, which often prevents clear-cut formulation of long-range goals and timely and effective political action.

Soviet ideology gives its leaders a useful conceptual framework for dealing with many contemporary political problems. As an ideology of conflict, it has given them a more effective basis for a strategy of conflict than American statesmen have in their relatively amorphous, compromise-oriented political beliefs and practices. Soviet ideology has helped Soviet leadership combine strategic purposefulness with tactical flexibility. It has provided a basis for

409

all dissent to the point that internal unity can be harmful to the system.

The structure of American leadership is better adapted than the Soviet structure for avoiding leadership crises and promoting regular reassessment of policy. The institutionalized office of the Presidency provides executive continuity at the top, even though a great deal depends on the special talents and personality of the man who fills it. Although the personality of the leader may determine the difference between an energetic, assertive administration and a passive one that allows other political institutions to dominate the scene, nonetheless the state is always led by a legitimate leader, accepted as such by the political system and society as a whole. The transfer of power in America is smooth and quick. This is not the case in the Soviet Union. There legitimacy follows the seizure and consolidation of power by a leader. Until he emerges from the succession struggle, legitimacy rests vaguely in the ruling Communist Party, precluding the claim to power of anyone outside it but not preventing bitter and destructive conflicts within.

In the American system, the top echelons of the executive branch are changed periodically, even if somewhat abruptly. In the Soviet Union, the change is more gradual, accelerating only during power changes. This means that newcomers to the Soviet national leadership are absorbed into the prevailing outlook, and new initiatives must overcome the inherent resistance of set patterns. In the United States, there are periods of "learning" as a new administration, composed in part of political "rookies," takes over, but there is also more room for initial experimentation and re-evaluation. During periods of stability, the higher professional quality of the Soviet leadership is probably a more important asset than the greater structural elasticity of the American system. On the other hand, it is easier to remedy the absence of professionalism than to reform a major structural defect. In fact, a new professionalism is emerging in the United States, while there is still no evidence that workable provisions for a smooth and effective succession have been devised in the Soviet Union.

In the Soviet Union only rarely do the top leaders of the Party have to bargain extensively with the leaders of social forces and specialized bureaucracies. The leaders virtually monopolize initiation and decision on major policy issues. Through the Party apparat, they mobilize support for their policies and supervise their execution. In the United States, the major functions of the policy-making process—initiation, persuasion, decision, and implementation—are dispersed among many more groups than in the Soviet Union. These groups assert their right to participate in decision-making not only because they wield autonomous economic or social power but in some cases because they possess special knowledge. The compartmentalization of expertise in the Soviet Union means that specialists have highly focused interests, and their views are judged on political grounds by professional politicians. This ensures the application of more politically relevant criteria in decision-making, whereas in America the criteria are often confused. As a result, consensus-building takes much time and energy in the American system.

The concentration of power over policy in the Soviet Union means that its leaders are more frequently able to make clear-cut choices among major alternatives than American political leaders, whose choices are almost invariably marginal or ambiguous. The Soviet leadership is also better able to coordinate policies in various areas, and, because of the greater scarcity of resources, the need for such coordination is far greater in the Soviet Union than in the United States. The concentration of the responsibility for initiating policy in the top leadership means that the Soviet system may be slow in responding to gradually developing policy problems. In the American system the agitation of the affected groups is likely to bring the problem to the attention of the top leadership more quickly. Once the problem is recognized by the Soviet leaders, however, their concentrated power enables them, if they wish, to deal with it vigorously and to reverse, if necessary, earlier policies. Policy innovations invariably are slow in the United States.

All the strong points of the Soviet system—in ideology, in leadership, in policy-making—would be impossible to duplicate in a society which protects the liberty of the individual. One should not be oblivious to the costs of the system to the Soviet citizen. On the other hand, despite the optimistic assertions of Western liberals, the absence of liberty in the Soviet Union does enable the Soviet political system to be strong in ways which are denied to Western liberal democracies.

Whatever their specific political weaknesses, neither system apart, and literature to develop according to the autonomous initiatives of scientists, artists, and writers and to what extent are they to develop according to the ideology determined by the Party? To what extent are the key positions of political leadership to be pre-empted by apparatchiki and to what extent are they to be shared with industrial managers, military chiefs, scientists, and professional bureaucrats? To what extent are these groups to play a role in policy-making? To what extent are the Party-determined needs for politization to pre-empt the educational and communication processes? The problem of the leadership is to keep the exercise of Party authority between that minimum which is essential to maintain Party supremacy and that maximum beyond which the exercise of control would seriously impair the technical functioning of a modern society. To solve this problem the leadership is attempting to adapt new scientific and technical developments to the purposes of Party control and direction.

The threat to Party supremacy from the demands of other elite groups is one of slow erosion. It is also limited. Ideology cannot replace engineering, physics, military science, or even economics. Nor can engineers, scientists, generals, or economists manage a modern state without becoming politicians. Conceivably, the apparatchiki could be displaced by a military coup d'état or a managerial revolt. The probability of this, however, is very low. It could occur only if the Party apparat were first weakened by an assault not from below but from above, not from the pluralistic tendencies in Soviet society but from the autocratic ones.

The Soviet system requires a supreme political leader. This leader, however, is a potential threat to the supremacy of the Party and its apparat. In Stalin this threat materialized to the point where it almost led to the disruption of the system in the struggle for power after Stalin's death. Every absolute ruler eliminates his peers and encourages "new men." During the Great Purge Stalin eliminated the Old Bolsheviks, the aristocrats of the Communist Party, and replaced them with younger men, the "Class of '38," who were dependent upon Stalin for their position. The last ten years of Stalin's rule saw the steady decline of the Party organs and groups. The competition among various chains of command which at lower levels serves to strengthen Party leadership was extended to the top levels of the Party to weaken that leadership. Zhdanov and

Malenkov were encouraged to compete for the number-two spot. Under Beria the MVD developed immense powers. The state bureaucracy was strengthened. Stalin's private police and control agencies were developed. The dictatorship of the Party was replaced by the dictatorship of the dictator. The apparat was undermined by the autocrat.

The effects of personal dictatorship on the Soviet system became clear after the death of Stalin. All the principals in the succession struggle (except Zhukov) were apparatchiki. But the struggle among them was not confined to the apparat. Instead, each apparatchik had his own institutional base of power: Beria in the secret police, Malenkov among some groups of economic administrators, Khrushchev in the Party apparat. At crucial points in the struggle the military played an autonomous role. This struggle was possible only because Stalin had reduced the power of the Party apparat vis-à-vis these other bureaucracies. The victory of Khrushchev between 1953 and 1957 was also the victory of the apparat. It marked the reassertion of the position of the Party as the supreme institution of Soviet society and the drastic reduction in power of the secret police, the industrial managers, and the military. The victory of Khrushchev and the apparat, however, again raised the problem of the relation between the leader and the apparat. In the 1960s some steps were taken which tended to reduce the unity and the power of the apparat. To date, however, Khrushchev has not wanted or has not been able to follow in Stalin's path and transform his leadership into a personal autocracy. The incentives to do so must be as great as the obstacles. For the moment, the balance is maintained, and sovereignty rests in the central organs of Party leadership. That sovereignty is now being vigorously asserted and exercised. Thus the Party attempts to minimize the dangers of overthrow from above and erosion from below.

It is unlikely that the near future will see in the Soviet Union a linkage between social pressure for greater freedom from below with partial, fragmented elite support from above. Yet that has usually been the precondition for politically significant liberalization not only in noncommunist societies but also in communist ones, as the recent histories of Poland and Hungary in 1956 and of Communist China in 1957 show. There is still some disruptive potential from below in Soviet society, particularly among some of the younger intellectuals, the peasants, and the non-Russian nationalities. The new generation of workers, no longer so terrorized, is also anxious for a better deal. These groups could perhaps be stimulated into a violent reaction against the system in the event of a breakdown within the leadership. The millions of former concentration-camp inmates could even provide a hardened spearhead in the event of disturbances. But in such an event the Army would probably step in as a custodian of the Soviet state and would mobilize the intensifying nationalism, particularly of the Great Russians, to preserve the Soviet Union. Events of this sort would depend essentially on unpredictable factors, such as accident, personality, coincidence. Nonetheless, because of the foregoing considerations, a major upheaval is more likely in the Soviet Union than in the United States.

The probabilities of breakdown in the Soviet system or crisis in the American one should not be overrated. The American system of government, a product of the eighteenth century, has functioned successfully without a major breakdown for almost a hundred years. The Soviet system is a product of the twentieth century, but it has functioned successfully without a major breakdown for almost fifty years. Americans are accustomed to thinking of their government as one of the oldest in the world. Despite its twentieth-century origins, the Soviet system also can claim honorable mention in the struggle for survival. Apart from Finland's, it is the only political system to emerge out of the collapse of the Habsburg, Ottoman, Hohenzollern, and Romanov empires in World War I that is still in existence. Since World War I nine countries have essayed major roles in world politics. Of these, France has had four political systems; Germany, Italy, and China three each; Japan and India two each. Only the United States, the United Kingdom, and the Soviet Union have avoided drastic changes in the last forty years.

The Soviet and American governments thus belong to a small club of successful systems. Simply because they *are* able to govern, they have much in common which distinguishes them from the faltering, incomplete, and ineffective systems found in Asia, Africa, and Latin America. The Soviet and American systems are effective, authoritative, and stable, each in its own way. They are endowed with legitimacy by distinct sets of political ideas. They

are rooted in homogeneous political cultures. Lacking an aristocratic heritage, they recruit their political leaders from broad strata
of the population and have relatively open systems of social mobility. They have both demonstrated an ability to replenish their leadership cadres and to adapt their policies and goals to fundamental
changes in their environment. Both systems are dynamic. They
are changing—in part spontaneously and in part through purposeful human action. The task that remains is to identify the direction
and content of these changes.

CONVERGENCE OR EVOLUTION

The Communists believe that the world will converge, but into
an essentially communist form of government. In the West, on the
other hand, the widespread theory of convergence assumes that the
fundamentally important aspects of the democratic system will be
retained after America and Russia "converge" at some future, in-
determinate historical juncture. Although probably there will be
more economic planning and social ownership in the West, the
theory sees the Communist Party and its monopoly of power as
the real victims of the historical process: both will fade away. Thus
on closer examination it is striking to discover that most theories
of the so-called convergence in reality posit not convergence but
submergence of the opposite system. Hence the Western and the
communist theories of convergence are basically revolutionary:
both predict a revolutionary change in the character of one of the
present systems. The Communists openly state it. In the West, it
is implicit in the prevalent convergence argument.

Leaving aside for the moment the further implications of this
parallel, it is important to examine the assumptions on which this
view of the future rests. The argument, as noted in the Introduction, rests on the assumption of a cumulative impact on the political system, particularly the Soviet, of four factors: the industrial
culture, the organizational and operational implications of the industrial system, affluence, and international involvement.

Undoubtedly certain universal traits inherent in the modern industrial and urban order affect the style and the values of contemporary mass culture and leisure. The Soviet leaders today are
far more similar in clothing, in social behavior, even in some of
their private aspirations, to their Western counterparts than was the

case twenty-five years ago. The same is true of an average Soviet citizen. In that sense there has been, and there will be, a steady convergence of the West and the East, including China. Every factory built in some isolated Chinese town reduces the time, the cultural, the economic, and the social gap between, let us say, Chikurting and Chicago. But the question is, does it reduce the political difference? Is the form of leisure, mass culture, and working habits a determinant for political organization?

The archaic society was characterized by the economic similarity and the political diversity of its institutions. A common economic "base" and a pastoral culture thus did not dictate the character of the political "superstructure." Today both China and India are at similar levels of development—yet no one would seriously argue that their political systems are becoming more alike. Nonetheless, at the heart of the widely held view that modern industrialization imposes certain common social and political consequences is the assumption that there is a direct causal relationship between the stage of economic development and politics. It is this view that leads to the generalization that Russia and America are becoming basically alike. The example of the archaic society indicates at the very least that not every common economic pattern dictates a common political structure. Perhaps the more complex, technological, and more socially impinging industrial economy does, but this proposition of causality remains to be proven.

Here, too, one can point to many examples which suggest that industrial complexity and maturity do not necessarily cause political uniformity and moderation. Essen under the Nazis was similar to Detroit in an economic and technological, as well as cultural, sense, yet the similarity did not preclude the Nazis from imposing on the society a relationship of mobilization and control quite unlike the one prevailing in Detroit. Similarly, Poland and Hungary today are in the critical and disruptive "stage of transition" from agrarian to industrial societies and so, according to the theory, should be radical and totalitarian. Yet they are both more moderate and less doctrinaire, more politically "mature," than the much more developed and economically advanced East Germany and Czechoslovakia, both of which "took off" in industrial development many years ago and should, therefore, according to the theory, be politically more moderate.

The objection may be made that the cases of India and China, Essen and Detroit, Poland and East Germany do not invalidate the general theory because in all the above situations specific historical factors were decisive. But if that is so, these specific "historical" reasons become much more important and decisive than an over-all theory. Should they not also be given their due in the case of America and Russia? In effect, no one-to-one correlation exists between economic and political change. A political system is influenced and shaped by continuing cultural, social, historical, and traditional forces. Even more important, a political system has its own staying power and helps shape the course of economic and social development.

Any consideration of the influence on politics of social-economic modernization must take into account the means used in the past to modernize the antecedent society, since the means tend to affect the very character of the development. The methods used and the political institutions developed in the course of the industrialization and modernization themselves establish between the political system and society a specific pattern of relations, with its own vested interests and inherent developmental pressures. The democratization and liberalization of Western societies, and even their adoption of many socialist measures, was achieved because social and political pluralism preceded and accompanied these economic processes, and many pluralist groups, some possessing economic power (the new middle class), some political power (the liberal aristocracy), allied themselves with and provided the leadership for the masses craving social and/or political reform. Political pressure from below and pluralist social-political leadership from above was—and usually is—the basic prerequisite for wrenching domestic concessions from the established political system.

In analyzing the relationship between politics and economics in America and Russia it is, therefore, very important to look closely at *both* the character of the political system and the character of economic growth. If, in the Soviet and American cases, both the political systems and the character of economic growth are different, it is reasonable to conclude that the influence of economics on politics, and vice versa, is also likely to be quite different in the two societies. In the Soviet Union, a relatively backward society was to a degree industrialized and modernized (it is sometimes forgotten that the Soviet Union is still only a quasideveloped society) through total social mobilization effected by terroristic means wielded by a highly disciplined and motivated political elite. The very nature of this process is inimical to the emergence of political pluralism, while the liquidation of the private economic sector and of all informal leadership groups creates a social vacuum that must be filled through political integration on a national scale. In very broad terms, it would seem that in the Soviet case we are dealing with a process of very rapid industrialization which was politically directed and involved purposeful social "homogenizing." In the American case it was far more spontaneous, with national political coordination gradually emerging when social, economic, and political pluralism had already taken firm root.

These patterns of development have resulted in a strikingly different relationship between society and politics in each country. The American Revolution freed a society from the bonds of an irrelevant and restraining aristocratic order and made possible its subsequent, largely spontaneous, organic growth. The diversity, the pluralism, the fear of central control which characterized the early settlers, living in isolation not only from the world but also from one another, expressed itself in a political and social system designed to protect that diversity. One sees it in the segmented school system, in all the efforts to preserve regional and group autonomy, in the assertion of local community identity. The purposes of the political system were conservative insofar as society itself was concerned. This in turn inhibited the development of a political elite with a defined political outlook, since neither the social basis nor the consciousness of political purpose was present to sustain and justify the existence of such an elite. Today, in some respects, a modern American society, characterized by industrial dynamism and corporate efficiency, is governed by an anachronistic political system designed for the unique conditions of early-nineteenth-century America. This accounts for the weaknesses already noted.

In Russia, on the other hand, the Soviet political system came into being before the emergence of the Soviet society. Indeed, the political system was set up and organized for the specific purpose of creating a Soviet society. A power-motivated political elite was the *sine qua non* of the system, while the stupendous task of destroying the old social order and then of constructing a new one meant that power had to be centralized, wielded by professional political leaders, and exercised with sustained ruthlessness, skill, and ideological commitment. Governing a continental society, changing the way of life of 200 million people, consciously shaping the future of an entire social order is no mean task, and for this reason the emphasis of the leadership inevitably has been on the development of novel techniques of governing commensurate with this undertaking. Thus if it can be said that American politics can best be understood in terms of American society, Soviet society can best be understood in terms of Soviet politics. In the latter, political power preceded economic power; in the former, economic power preceded political. And it would be ironic indeed if a fading Marxism's last intellectual victory were to convince the West that economics shaped politics in the Soviet Union. Marxism cannot explain a communist state.

Accordingly, factors such as ideology or professional political bureaucracy play a less important role in determining the future in the United States than in the Soviet Union; and, conversely, factors such as economic change and the activities of interest groups play a greater role in the United States than in the Soviet Union. (It is this difference which also establishes a greater affinity between the Soviet experience and the current problems of the new, developing nations.) Thus, changes in Soviet economic management and methods of planning and allocation need not challenge the ideological and power monopoly of the ruling Party. As Peter Wiles has argued, because of its introduction of computers, linear programming, and the various modern techniques usually associated with the concept of "economic rationality and maturity," "central planning or, better, the so-called command economy can now be rationally conducted. Large enterprises, forced investment programs, equal incomes, even centralized control, will no longer be obstacles to rational resource allocation. That equally unattractive institution, the beehive state, will also be able to achieve this end. The wasteful and arbitrary command economy imposed by Stalin is no longer the only kind possible." [2] The ruling Party can now afford to give up its antiquated theory of value in exchange for a more efficiently operating economy. The increasingly complex development of the economy no longer forces the Party to choose between the Marxist theory of value—which, in turn, prevents economic rationality—and the introduction of the market mechanism—which would threaten the ideological-political structure of the system. Indeed, the advance in techniques of economic control and coordination may make possible for the first time *both* further economic development and the retention of the ideological-political structure.

Everything that the Party leaders have said and done in recent times suggests that they will consciously strive to protect that structure from erosion. They intend to keep scientific and technical expertise compartmentalized, with the Party bureaucracy monopolizing the politically and socially necessary and decisive function of integrating the complex society. A multiplicity of expertises (inherent in any modern society) is not the same thing as social-political pluralism based on group autonomy (inherent in a particular form of development). The recent history of various groups in the USSR (see Chapters Four, Five, and Eight) shows this clearly. Attacks by the Party leaders on the intellectuals and on the notion of ideological coexistence advocated by some Soviet intellectuals indicate that the bureaucrats know the main source of the danger to the stability of the political system: any decline in the ideological and political monopoly of the ruling Party. If tomorrow the Soviet Union were to open its frontiers to foreign books, newspapers, and criticisms of the system, the effect could be politically dramatic. For this reason the Party has been striving to combine economic rationalization, which it does not fear per se, with ideological revitalization. This it is trying to do by linking the Party with technological innovation and improvements in the people's standard of living. In effect, it is attempting to link tightly social consciousness, shaped in part by politization, with the social-economic institutions of the country. Its obvious long-range goal is to close the gap between doctrine and reality, a gap which eventually might tend to erode the ideology.

It is here that the role and character of affluence come in. First of all, it is again essential to bear in mind the nature of the efforts used to attain that affluence. Affluence achieved by a mixed economic process, involving both the political system and independent individual and group activity, consolidates social diversity and creates new loci of social and political power. The economic and political power of the trade unions in the Western democracies is a case in point. Furthermore, the American pioneers were first both free and poor, so subsequent affluence could at worst diminish their freedom and at best consolidate it, but not bring it about. Indeed, the case could be made that contemporary affluence has produced far more conformity, interdependence, and social malleability in America than heretofore. In the Soviet Union, affluence is being brought about by means of political control, wielded by a political elite which already has acquired the characteristics of the entrenched "New Class" attacked by Milovan Djilas in his well-known book. When affluence comes to the Soviet Union—that is, when in several decades from now the Soviet standard of living approximates the American of 1960—it will have come to a society which was always both poor and unfree. It will also come to a society that still will be *less* affluent than many others, given present western European and American trends. Thus the feeling of "relative nonaffluence" will still be there, and the pressures for political moderation inherent in general well-being may be weaker than is the case with the "absolute affluence" of the American variety—no country is richer and hence there is no one to envy. Furthermore, if affluence (of either kind) does create greater conformity and interdependence, as already suggested in Chapter Two, it could even reinforce social control.*

In any case, affluence is likely to diminish the tension-producing tendency of the Soviet political system to make demands on its society which are almost impossible to meet. Greater resources and higher awards will make less necessary the "storming," the crash campaigns, and the often unattainable goals which the Soviet political leadership has often felt compelled to impose on either the agricultural sector or industry. These demands in turn usually resulted ultimately in counterclaims on the regime for greater allocation of resources by the groups directly involved, with conse-

---

* A suggestive parallel involves the Teamsters' Union in the United States. In many respects its members have more benefits than other unionists. Yet in part the success of the union leadership in achieving this has helped to consolidate the rigid hierarchy and authoritarianism. It is also worth noting that in such matters as controls, access to foreign press, travel abroad, or even travel inside, the Soviet Union is still more coercive than Nazi Germany of 1938-1939.

A special factor influencing the development of political systems in our age is the unprecedented impact of international affairs and new, rapid means of communications. This is true particularly in the cases of the United States and the Soviet Union; both are most heavily involved in and committed to the present international rivalry. In assessing the impact of international affairs one must take note of several conflicting tendencies. The direct competition with the United States, especially the technical-economic one, has encouraged in the Soviet Union a tendency toward a more instrumental approach, highlighted by Professor Kapitsa's well-known statement to the effect that many of the Soviet space successes would have been impossible if the views of the "philosophers" (read: ideologues) had fully prevailed. In that, the leadership increasingly concurs. This has led it to accept scientific and scholarly exchanges with the West in the expectation that Soviet technical progress will gain by them. At the same time, the exchanges have aroused the fears of some Party leaders, especially those charged with ideological matters, that Western humanists and philosophers, admitted in part as the necessary price for the scientific exchanges, will undermine the official ideology. It seems that by 1963 Soviet leaders had not resolved this issue and that there was an internal debate on the advantages and risks of the enterprise.

Similarly, the expansion of communism on the one hand has provided apparent proof for the correctness of the communist prophecy, but on the other hand has generated inter-Communist debates, thereby undermining somewhat the image of the doctrine as a universal creed. The expansion of communism from the Soviet Union into adjoining countries, furthermore, has meant that the Soviet Union is now exposed to the flow of competitive ideas from other communist states, more culturally akin to the West, which act as "transmission belts" for novel ideas, garbed in the common doctrine but reflecting a more European outlook. This, too, helps to weaken the control which the political system has maintained over the individual's exposure to ideologically undesirable views. Finally, the competition for the underdeveloped nations has involved a commitment of badly needed resources and the tacit acceptance of various regimes' claims to socialism, an acceptance that could eventually threaten domestic orthodoxy.

On the other hand, the very fact of the competition justifies the internal mobilization of resources, not to speak of armaments, and the related attempts to generate popular hostility to the United States. The new sense of Soviet nationalism is merged with the ideological interests of the ruling bureaucracy, and the competition with America is their natural expression. It is also important to bear in mind that the communist system was created as an institution of revolution and conflict and hence in some ways is less threatened by international tensions than by protracted international harmony. To be sure, both America and Russia may learn from each other ("codiscovery"), while the mutual balance of terror forces them to coexist. But this is not tantamount to becoming more alike, nor indeed is there much reassurance that their becoming more alike would necessarily diminish tensions between them. A common communist system has not prevented bitter hostility between China and Russia, and most European wars were fought by countries with very similar social and political structures.

This last point is particularly important because much of the emotional commitment to the convergence theory rests on the belief that it represents the only hope for peace. History shows that social-political uniformity and peace need not go hand in hand. In fact, the latter may be a more comforting conclusion than the proposition—shared by both the Marxists and the "convergists" —that peace depends on uniformity. Such a premise is both curiously escapist and utopian. By now, the Communists particularly should realize that a communist America and a communist Russia would be likely to engage in a competition more intense than the relatively unequal struggle between Russia and China. Noncommunist believers in convergence also have no reason to assume that a noncommunist Russia, with its nationalist ambitions, would be less likely to strive to dominate the Eurasian continent than a communist Russia.

The theory of convergence thus minimizes or ignores the totality of the Russian and the American historical experience—political, social, and economic—and exaggerates the importance of one factor alone. It minimizes also the uniqueness of the historical process and forces it into a common pattern with fundamentally the same outcome for all. It asserts the repetitiveness of the historically familiar and ignores the probability that the future will see in both the United States and in the Soviet Union novel forms of government which will *evolve* out of the present on the basis of the *uneven* importance of political and social-economic determinants in the two countries.

In the Soviet Union the sense of purpose and commitment of the ruling professional Party bureaucracy; its organizational efficiency and its ability to recruit the ablest citizens; its capacity to continue directing the socialization and politization of the people; the availability of new means of social and economic control, designed to integrate and develop the society; finally, but very important, the personal character of the leader and the duration and methods of the struggle for succession—all these factors are likely to be more important than the intrusion of experts, of common patterns of industrial culture and leisure, of affluence, and of limited contacts with other countries. Barring some unforeseeable paralysis of the system during a struggle for succession, the Soviet trend involves a continuity in the pattern of political control and indoctrination on the basis of growing collectivist consensus. In the United States there is no convincing evidence for the argument that change either in the character of the leadership, including its increased professionalization, or in the social-economic aspects, particularly the new self-assertiveness of groups demanding a more equitable distribution of national wealth, points in the direction of the Soviet model. The broad trend, including the impact of the Cold War, seems to be toward a system involving a more politically conscious elite, more politically distributed social welfare, but within the framework of continued political and social pluralism. Thus the structure of power, the access to leadership, the role of ideology, and the relationship of the political system to the individual are not likely to undergo a radical change in either system.

Mere changes in mood and style, or reductions in terror and fear, are not enough to advance the process of Soviet political democratization. Positive political reforms are also needed. These reforms would have to go beyond the introduction in the Soviet political system of more formal and regular procedures which in themselves would not undermine one-Party rule or challenge the Soviet social-economic system. To be sure, any formalization in the long run would result in some democratization, but it is possible to consider reforms which would not involve direct revolutionary consequences. For example, the following minimum of five reforms primarily affecting the ruling Party would be an important step toward more regularity and order without disastrous consequences for the present rulers:

(1) Adopting regular periods of incumbency for the First Secretary and for the Chairman of the Party Presidium in order to rest that office on regularity and legitimacy rather than on sheer political power, which inevitably introduces the dynamic of conflict into the leadership.

(2) Making the Prime Minister's incumbency correspond to that of the Party leader, in order to prevent the post of Prime Minister from becoming an alternative seat of power.

(3) Adopting regularized, formal procedures for replacing the leader at the end of his term, perhaps by a vote of the Central Committee or the Party Congress, out of several candidates, each of whom would be allowed to solicit support openly.

(4) Allowing open discussion and voting within the Central Committee, with the acceptance of majority versus minority votes instead of the present practice of requiring unanimity, which inhibits debate, encourages conformity, and abets dictatorial rule.

(5) Giving Party members the right to criticize specific Party policies, thereby making it possible to generate support for alternative programs even while restraining tendencies toward splits by the practice of "democratic centralism."

Such reforms would introduce elements of regularity, orderly procedure, and limited dissent into the top bodies of the ruling bureaucracy. This would be a step forward. However, political struggles would still involve a relatively small number of people in the higher echelons of the Party, controlling bureaucratically the levers of power. Political change would become more institutionalized but not yet necessarily more democratic. The political system would remain a bureaucratic oligarchy.*

---

* It is also not certain that most people desire freedom and democracy. As Carl J. Friedrich observed: ". . . past as well as contemporary experience provided by history, sociology and psychology suggests that human beings desire a *minimum* of freedom, rather than a maximum. All human beings enjoy making *some* free choices, but not many, let alone all. It is only an unusual man who desires to be as fully autonomous as possible. . . . When tested in a democratic context, where an

Turning to America, one sees portents of the future in the new type of political leadership that is now emerging in both the Democratic and Republican parties. The common emphasis on a "public image," even on youthful energy, obscures the more basic and more important development of a new generation of much more politically professional leaders, surrounded by "brain trusts" and eagerly devouring policy papers on international and domestic problems. This reflects what seems to be a general trend toward more craft and less art in policy-making. It is likely that this trend, combined with the inescapably persisting pressures of international politics, will push the national government, irrespective of which party is in power, toward broader national management, gradually altering the present relationship between the political system and the individual. Inevitably, the government will be forced more and more to disseminate its own interpretation of reality (that is, "manage the news") in order not only to shape public opinion but perhaps occasionally to mislead foreign opponents and influence foreign friends. Eventually the American government may begin to approach in that respect the practices and skills that have been applied already for many years in England and France. Similarly, the socialization of the citizen is likely to acquire more direct political overtones, as, for instance, in the spreading courses on communism. The present efforts to protect civil rights of Negroes also give the central government a new role in social affairs. The future may see the central government intervening more actively in arbitrating labor-management disputes, and the strike leader may increasingly give way to the arbitrator-bureaucrat.

But all that will still be balanced by the pluralism of the political and economic structure of the country and by the traditional pragmatism of the social and political elites. This pragmatism inhibits

---

opportunity for maximizing freedom is provided, most or at any rate many men exhibit a decided preference for values other than freedom, such as justice and security, and a consequent willingness to be content with something decidedly less than the maximum possible. When opportunity for participation is provided, they do not participate, and when opportunity is provided for private activity, they do not engage in it. Many men seem to prefer having most decisions made for them, and practically all men prefer to have some decisions made for them. What holds for decisions, holds equally for actions, opinions, and the rest." *Man and His Government* (New York, 1963), p. 362.

the emergence of a political orthodoxy, which usually in turn generates even further pressures toward a power monopoly. The pluralism—weakening in certain areas—is being reinvigorated by the emergence of new groups clamoring for their rights and asserting their political claims. The Negroes are but one such constituency. Others include the educational and urban spheres, and the scientific-technological community. The influence of some of these groups may not rest primarily on economic resources but may be derived from an increasing social perception of the importance of these groups to the general national welfare and to American power in the context of the Cold War. The continuing importance of the Congress will also tend to offset the expansion of administrative power, even though Congress may act not as an arena for the varied interests of the country but primarily as a forum for the conservative interests, especially rural and regional. The new claimants, lacking the territorial basis and the economic wealth to acquire effective congressional representation, may therefore seek more direct access to the administrative branch.

In the Soviet Union, the increasing technical and scientific competence of the communist bureaucracy means that the modernization of society will continue apace and, as the French experience under de Gaulle suggests, modernization, economic rationalization, and further industrialization need not bring liberalization in their wake—but rather may bring the opposite. The complexities of central control, of long-range planning, of advance and often irrevocable commitment of large resources, and of scientific know-how are pushing the modern world into a greater concentration of decision-making in fewer hands. In that respect, America is still far behind even such countries as Britain or Germany, not to speak of France.

France particularly has taken giant steps in the direction of what the French technocrats, drawn mainly from the polytechnical circles, call democratic planification. It involves a concerted effort to wed technocratic rationality, on the basis of modern computing devices applied to economic planning, to democracy on the societal level. The political-economic decision-making thus tends to be concentrated within a relatively narrow circle of experts, but the plans allow for contingency revisions on an annual basis in response to popular reactions and the operations of the market. This is both a more advanced and a more rational model of command structure than the Soviet pattern, with its dogmatic aberrations, and than the American system, with its interlocking, segmented decision centers. Its roots must be sought in the strong French tradition of poly-technical education, emphasis on rationality and logic brought to the surface by the combined impact of external and domestic crises. This is a major development in the French political system, and, while de Gaulle helped to crystallize it, it is likely to outlast him.

It is noteworthy that this experiment might be very appealing to young Soviet technocrats, who sense that their own Soviet attempt, pioneering though it was, has gone sour because of the bureauc-ratization of dogma and because of the traditional tension in Russia between anarchism and the resultant need for organizational disci-pline. To them, the French planning system might also be more appealing than the revisionism of either communist Poland or Yugoslavia, which essentially harks back to the old traditional no-tions of democracy and is based on the failure of centralized plan-ning, not on its modernization. Precisely because the French system leaves little room for traditional democratic parties, and for the time being relies on the personal role of de Gaulle for the link between the society and the state, it could be all the more appeal-ing to the younger Soviet technocrat.

However, what distinguishes this general trend from the Soviet version is that in the advanced countries it is accompanied by the maintenance of civil liberties and individual rights and above all by the political system's acceptance of pluralism in popular outlook and expression. Perhaps the modern world, with its new com-plexities and need for professional technically skilled leadership, is seeing a new divorce between the political decision-makers and the masses—a gap traditional to the aristocratic order and only recently closed by the liberal democracy—but, at least for the foreseeable future, the society in countries such as France remains democratic, and this inevitably influences and restrains the state. In the Soviet Union, however, the society is subject to control and mobilization by the state, and the superiority of the Party-state is paramount. Furthermore, since the Party-state fears any challenge to its doctrinal primacy, it will not tolerate anything which ap-proaches "ideological coexistence" even within the society. Thus the further modernization of the Soviet Union is likely to be accompanied by efforts to maintain both the political and the ideological monopoly of the Party bureaucracy and the interdiction of any politically significant social or ideological pluralism. To that end, the unity of the ruling bureaucracy is the basic requirement. Although the late 1962 division of the CPSU into an industrial and an agricultural hierarchy could strain this unity, the Party has nurtured the tradition of discipline and unity, and the fear of factionalism is deeply ingrained. Furthermore, the inherent thrust of a modern bureaucracy is usually in a centralizing direction. Even so, one can still anticipate new clashes between the ruling bureaucracy, protecting both its power and hence its ideology, and the aspirations of various groups, particularly under the influence of external contacts that might be difficult and harmful for the leadership to cut off entirely. These clashes will probably be the dominant dilemmas of the Soviet political scene, but with the bureaucracy likely to prevail in its orthodox approach.

This suggests that the frequent talk of "democratization" in relation to the Soviet political bureaucracy is as irrelevant as it would be to the evolution of American industrial bureaucracy. The real question is one of orderly procedures, flexibility, and bureaucratic rationality. The Ford Motor Company in this sense has changed very significantly from the time when it was a personal autocracy of Henry Ford. But it would be misleading to describe the process as one of "democratization." To be sure, the recent experience of France or Mexico suggests that modernization on the basis of essentially one-party rule, with relatively centralized controls monopolized by a state bureaucracy, does not require as extensive social mobilization as is practiced in the Soviet Union. In that sense, it can be argued that the scale of controls insisted upon by the CPSU is counter to its own ends, consumes much of its energy, and creates needless discontent. Here, however, it is important again to remember that the legacy of the past has its own momentum; in that respect the behavior and the demands of the Soviet political bureaucracy reflect the specifics of the Russian history, of the Leninist Revolution, and of the Stalinist transformation of Soviet society. Even a limited democratization of the Soviet society—that is, freedom of expression and of travel—would threaten the present political leadership, whereas in both Mexico and France, for equally good historical reasons, politics can remain the domain

of a limited elite without seriously impinging on individual freedom. Similarly, in America, the growing role of the political system
is not likely to affect drastically the character of American democracy, although increasingly the political system and society will
be struggling with the problem of how to keep a free society in
close touch with the policy-making process without paralyzing the
exercise of effective leadership. Yet this is quite a different dilemma
from the one, mentioned earlier, that is likely to dominate the
Soviet scene.

The Soviet and the American political systems, each in its own
way, have been highly successful. Because they have been successful, they are not likely to change drastically. Yet for the two
systems to converge there would have to be a drastic alteration of
course—in a historical sense, a revolutionary change of direction
—in the path of development of one of them. Every healthy political system changes, but if the change is gradual it tends to be
shaped by the present and the past. Unless it is possible to prove
that there has been or will be a major shift in the development of
either the American or the Soviet system's relationship with society,
or unless it is possible to prove that the past models of development
of the two societies are fundamentally alike, then the very fact of
evolution makes convergence unlikely. It is too simple to assume
that the complexity of the human condition is reducible to a single
social-economic or political mold. The evolution of the two systems, but not their convergence, seems to be the undramatic pattern for the future.

APPENDIX

REFERENCE NOTES

INDEX

Soviet and American Societies

DEMOGRAPHIC DATA
(1963)

	USSR	USA
Total population	223,100,000 (est.)	188,447,000
Urban population	115,100,000 (52%)	133,625,000 (71%)
Rural population	108,000,000 (48%)	54,625,000 (29%)
Agricultural employment	38,900,000 (est.)	4,946,000
Nonagricultural employment	65,600,000 (est.)	63,863,000
Unemployment	No data	4,166,000 (5.7%)

SOCIAL DATA
(1961-1962)

Communications:

	USSR	USA
Telephones in use	3,167,000	80,964,000
Radios in use	44,000,000	170,000,000
Television sets in use	8,300,000	56,300,000
Letters sent	4,239,000,000	64,933,000,000
Telegrams sent	252,000,000	117,236,000
Daily newspaper circulation	39,555,000	58,900,000
Daily newspapers per 1000 population	181	326
Railroad length	127,000 km	346,312 km
Railroad passenger km	189,300,000,000 km	32,459,000,000 km
Motor road length	143,000 km	5,709,000 km
Motor vehicles used	3,983,000	73,590,000
Automobiles used	638,000	65,644,000
Passenger vehicle km	81,500,000,000	1,180,056,000,000
Airline length	400,000 km	216,715 km
Airline passengers carried	27,000,000	52,712,000
Air passenger km (scheduled)	20,300,000,000	64,099,758,000
Foreign tourists visiting	862,700	1,331,383*
Citizens going abroad	772,000	2,159,857*
Exchange: USSR-USA	USSR tourists in USA: 1849	USA tourists in USSR: 16,156

* Not including Mexico and Canada temporary visits.

ECONOMIC DATA

Consumer goods
(1962 sales figures):

Refrigerators	812,000	3,775,000
Washing machines	1,734,000	3,795,000
Radios	4,068,000	12,000,000
Television sets	1,997,000	6,485,000
Vacuum cleaners	586,000	3,713,000
Motor vehicles (trucks, cars)	578,000	8,173,000
Footwear (produced)	490,000,000	619,407,000

Work time per consumer goods
(1961 estimates for an average worker):

Bread (1 lb.)	11 minutes	5 minutes
Sugar (1 lb.)	1 hour, 24 minutes	3 minutes
Butter (1 lb.)	3 hours, 11 minutes	19 minutes
Man's suit	86-350 hours	21 hours, 8 minutes
Man's shoes	62 hours, 20 minutes	3 hours, 48 minutes
Eggs (1 doz.)	3 hours	14 minutes
Potatoes (1 lb.)	13 minutes	1.5 minutes
Beef (1 lb.)	1 hour, 45 minutes	27 minutes
Milk (1 qt.)	34 minutes	7 minutes
Pork (1 lb.)*	approx. 2 hours	16-24 minutes
Cigarettes (20)*	13 minutes	7 minutes

Industrial Data
(1962 production figures):

Steel	76,300,000	metric tons	89,213,000	metric tons
Pig iron	55,300,000	" "	61,324,000	" "
Iron ore	128,100,000	" "	72,946,000	" "
Oil	186,200,000	" "	355,000,000	" "
Natural gas	75,200,000,000	cubic meters	375,088,000,000	cubic meters
Coal	517,000,000	metric tons	381,408,000	metric tons
Electric power	369,000,000,000	kwh	855,490,000,000	kwh
Cement	57,300,000	metric tons	56,718,000	metric tons
Paper	2,800,000	" "	14,831,000	" "
Cotton fabrics	4,900,000,000	sq. meters	7,753,992,000	sq. meters
Woolen fabrics	469,000,000	" "	255,847,000	" "

* 1960 estimates

Sources:

Statistical Abstract of the United States for 1963

U.N. Statistical Yearbook 1962

SSSR v Tsifrakh v 1962 godu

Free Europe Committee, Library and Reference Services, 3 December 1962

(Table prepared by David Williams.)

REFERENCE NOTES

Introduction

1. W. W. Rostow, *The Stages of Economic Growth* (Cambridge, 1960), pp. 133, 162.

CHAPTER ONE: POLITICS AND POLITICAL IDEAS

1. John K. Jessup et al., *The National Purpose* (New York, 1960). President's Commission on National Goals, *Goals for Americans* (Englewood Cliffs, N.J., 1960).
2. The most comprehensive of recent Soviet statements is O. V. Kuusinen, ed., *Fundamentals of Marxism-Leninism* (Moscow, 1960).
3. See his *Philosophical Notebooks* and *Materialism and Empirio-Criticism.* For a general discussion, see A. Meyer, *Leninism* (Cambridge, Mass., 1957).
4. P. U. Chaadaev, *Philosophical Letters* (1829).
5. Quoted in Leonard Schapiro, "The Pre-Revolutionary Intelligentsia and the Legal Order," in Richard Pipes, ed., *The Russian Intelligentsia* (New York, 1961), p. 20.
6. Cf. A. Gerschenkron, "The Problem of Economic Development in Russian Intellectual History of the Nineteenth Century," in E. J. Simmons, ed., *Continuity and Change in Russian and Soviet Thought* (Cambridge, Mass., 1955), p. 21.
7. Schapiro, in Pipes, op. cit., pp. 29-30.
8. Gerschenkron, in Simmons, op. cit., p. 36.
9. Seymour Martin Lipset, *Political Man* (Garden City, N.Y., 1960), pp. 68-72; William Kornhauser, *The Politics of Mass Society* (Glencoe, Ill., 1959), pp. 142-158.
10. Louis Hartz, *The Liberal Tradition in America* (New York, 1955).
11. See ibid., pp. 145ff.
12. These changes are carefully analyzed in Eric F. Goldman, *Rendezvous with Destiny* (New York, 1952), and Richard Hofstadter, *The Age of Reform* (New York, 1955).
13. See John Dewey, *Freedom and Culture* (New York, 1939).
14. See James G. March and Herbert A. Simon, *Organizations* (New York, 1958) for discussion of "analytic" and "political" means of resolving controversies.
15. Carl J. Friedrich et al., *Problems of the American Public Service* (New York, 1935), p. 12.
16. See Walter Lippmann, *The Coming Tests with Russia* (Boston, 1961); N. S. Khrushchev, *For Victory in Peaceful Competition with Capitalism* (New York, 1960), pp. 85-106.
17. Lippmann, op. cit., p. 15. Khrushchev, op. cit., p. 88.
18. Khrushchev, op. cit., p. 91.
19. Lippmann, op. cit., pp. 9, 19.
20. Khrushchev, op. cit., p. 102.
21. Lippmann, op. cit., p. 35.
22. *New York Times,* Aug. 28, 1958 (italics added).
23. *New York Times,* Nov. 29, 1961.
24. James Reston, *New York Times,* Dec. 29, 1961.

25. See Clyde Kluckhohn, "Have There Been Discernible Shifts in American Values During the Past Generation?" in Elting E. Morison, ed., *The American Style* (New York, 1958), pp. 145-217.
26. See Chapter Seven.
27. President Wilson's address to Congress, Jan. 8, 1918.
28. Walter Lippmann, *The Communist World and Ours* (Boston, 1959), p. 13.
29. See Dwight Perkins, *The American Approach to Foreign Policy* (Cambridge, Mass., 1952), pp. 76ff.

CHAPTER TWO: THE POLITICAL SYSTEM AND THE INDIVIDUAL

1. See Amitai Etzioni, *A Comparative Analysis of Complex Organizations* (New York, 1961), pp. 141-150, for a discussion of normative and utilitarian "complex organizations."
2. This grouping of objects is an extension and alteration of those suggested by David Easton, "An Approach to the Analysis of Political Systems," *World Politics*, April 1957, pp. 383-400.
3. V. O. Key, Jr., *Public Opinion and American Democracy* (New York, 1961), p. 313. Herbert Hyman, *Political Socialization* (Glencoe, Ill., 1959), pp. 58-59, 63. David Easton and Robert D. Hess, "The Child's Political World," *Midwest Journal of Political Science*, August 1962, pp. 235-236.
4. S. Mikhalkov, "All-Union Conference on Questions of Ideological Work," *Pravda*, Dec. 28, 1961.
5. "The Daily Life of Workers under Communism," *Novy Mir*, July 1960.
6. Nicholas DeWitt, *Education and Professional Employment in the USSR*, (Washington, 1961), p. 120.
7. See Harry Schwartz, *New York Times*, July 4, 1962.
8. Fred I. Greenstein, "The Benevolent Leader: Children's Images of Political Authority," *American Political Science Review*, December 1960, pp. 934ff. Easton and Hess, *Midwest Journal*, p. 242. Robert D. Hess and David Easton, "The Child's Changing Image of the President," *Public Opinion Quarterly*, Winter 1960, pp. 632-644.
9. Hyman, op. cit., pp. 58-59.
10. Richard Centers, "Children of the New Deal: Social Stratification and Adolescent Attitudes," *International Journal of Opinion and Attitude Research*, 1950, p. 331, quoted in Hyman, *Political Socialization*, pp. 62-63.
11. Hyman, op. cit., pp. 46-47; see also pp. 19, 75, for similar points.
12. See George Belknap and Angus Campbell, "Political Party Identification and Attitudes Toward Foreign Policy," *Public Opinion Quarterly*, Winter 1951, 601-23. Key, op. cit., pp. 449-452.
13. D. Zemlianskii, S. Mezentsev, "Ideological Commissions of Party Committees," *Kommunist*, No. 5, March 1962.
14. A. Bulgakov, Secretary of the Central Council of Trade Unions, *Pravda*, Dec., 28,1961.
15. See: Erik H. Erikson, *Childhood and Society* (New York, 1950), pp. 275-277. Robert E. Lane, *Political Life* (Glencoe, Ill., 1959), p. 207. Eleanor E. Maccoby, Richard E. Matthews, Anton S. Morton, "Youth and Political Change," *Public Opinion Quarterly*, Spring 1954, pp. 23-29.

16. Easton and Hess, *Midwest Journal,* August 1962, p. 239.
17. Seymour M. Lipset, *Political Man* (New York, 1960), p. 180.
18. Cf. Jeremy R. Azrael, "Is Coercion Withering Away?" *Problems of Communism,* November-December 1962, pp. 9-17.
19. Lane, *Political Life,* pp. 53-54, 75; Angus Campbell et al., *The American Voter* (New York, 1960), p. 91.
20. Cyril E. Black, "Soviet Political Life Today," *Foreign Affairs,* July 1958, pp. 569-581.
21. Campbell, op. cit., p. 91.
22. Alexander Heard, *The Costs of Democracy* (Garden City, N.Y., 1962), pp. 40-42, 46-47, 421.
23. *Renascita,* January 1962.
24. *Komsomolskaia Pravda,* Sept. 8, 1961.
25. Cf. "In Aid of the Workers of Rural Soviets," a series of pamphlets providing detailed instructions and guidelines, published by the State Juridical Publishing House, Moscow.
26. See: Lipset, *Political Man,* Chap. 4; Samuel A. Stouffer, *Communism, Conformity, and Civil Liberties* (Garden City, N.Y., 1955), Chap. 2; H. Hyman and P. B. Sheatsley, "Trends in Public Opinion on Civil Liberties," *Journal of Social Issues,* No. 3, 1953, pp. 6-16. But cf. Campbell, *American Voter,* pp. 512-515; and Key, *Public Opinion,* pp. 135-138.
27. E.g., *Spravochnik Druzhinnika* [The Druzhinnik's Handbook], (Moscow, 1961); N. V. Dementiev, G. M. Sergeiev, *Tebia Tovarishch Druzhinnik* [To You Comrade Druzhinnik] (Moscow, 1961).
28. J. L. Woodward and Elmo Roper, "Political Activity of American Citizens," *American Political Science Review,* December 1950, p. 874.
29. Renate Mayntz, "Citizen Participation in Germany: Nature and Extent" (Paper, International Political Science Association, 5th World Congress, Paris, 1961), pp. 13-14. John G. Scott, Jr., "Membership and Participation in Voluntary Associations," *American Sociological Review,* June 1957, p. 320. Charles R. Wright and Herbert H. Hyman, "Voluntary Association Memberships of American Adults," Ibid., June 1958, p. 287.
30. Lane, *Political Life,* p. 260. W. Lloyd Warner and Associates, *Democracy in Jonesville* (New York, 1949), pp. 137-143.
31. First Secretary of the Latvian Communist Party, A. Pel'she, *Sovietskaia Latviia,* January 28, 1960.
32. *Kommunist* (Armenia), Feb. 25, 1962 (italics added).
33. *Pravda,* April 5, 1962.
34. William Kornhauser, *The Politics of Mass Society* (Glencoe, Ill., 1959), pp. 108-109; and see *passim* for a brilliant analysis of alienation and mass society.
35. Murray B. Levin, *The Alienated Voter: Politics in Boston* (New York, 1960), p. 58.
36. Kornhauser, op. cit., p. 61.
37. *Nauka i Zhizn,* No. 3, 1962.
38. *Kommunist,* No. 8, 1962.
39. Richard Hofstadter, *The Age of Reform* (New York, 1955), pp. 5, 62.
40. Kornhauser, op. cit., p. 191.

41. For an account of a "slanderous" wall-newspaper, see *Trud,* Jan. 8, 1957. For an account of student expulsion for raising embarrassing questions about the 20th Party Congress; see *Komsomolskaia Pravda,* Aug. 9, 1956. For accusations of revisionism among young writers, see *Literaturnaia Gazeta,* Dec. 28, 1958.
42. Cf. Azrael, *Problems of Communism,* November-December 1962, especially p. 11.
43. Hofstadter, op. cit., p. 21.
44. Raymond L. Garthoff, "The Marshals and the Party," in Harry L. Coles, ed., *Total War and Cold War* (Columbus, Ohio, 1962), p. 261.
45. A. I. Berg, ed., *Kibernetiku na Sluzhbu Kommunizmu* (Moscow-Leningrad, 1961); English translation, U.S. Joint Publications Research Service, *Cybernetics at the Service of Communism* (Washington, 1962).
46. I. B. Novik, "Some Methodological Problems of Cybernetics," in Berg, *Cybernetics,* p. 66.
47. A. I. Kitov, "Cybernetics and Control of the National Economy," in Berg, *Cybernetics,* p. 283.
48. Stanley Kelley, Jr., *Professional Public Relations and Political Power* (Baltimore, 1956), pp. 101-102.
49. Leila Sussmann, "The Personnel and Ideology of Public Relations," *Public Opinion Quarterly,* Winter 1948-1949, p. 708, cited in John A. R. Pimlott, *Public Relations and American Democracy* (Princeton, 1951), p. 236.
50. See Kelley, op. cit., pp. 107ff.

CHAPTER THREE: POLITICAL LEADERSHIP

1. Leonard Schapiro, *The Communist Party of the Soviet Union* (New York, 1959), p. 538n. *New York Times,* Oct. 11, 1962, p. 6.
2. Donald R. Matthews, *The Social Background of Political Decision-Makers* (Garden City, N.Y., 1954), p. 23, and *U.S. Senators and Their World* (Chapel Hill, N.C., 1960), pp. 20-21. W. Lloyd Warner et al., *The American Federal Executive* (New Haven, 1963), pp. 10-15, 28-38, 326. Wendell Bell, Richard J. Hill, Charles R. Wright, *Public Leadership* (San Francisco, 1961), pp. 99-104.
3. John A. Armstrong, *The Soviet Bureaucratic Elite* (New York, 1959), p. 48.
4. Schapiro, *Communist Party,* p. 567. S. Bialer, "Comparative Communist Elites" (Ph.D. Thesis, Columbia University, 1964.
5. H. D. Anderson, "Educational and Occupational Attainments of Our National Rulers," *Scientific Monthly,* June 1935, p. 516, cited in Matthews, *Social Background,* p. 23.
6. C. Wright Mills, *The Power Elite* (New York, 1956), pp. 400-402.
7. Schapiro, op. cit., pp. 171-172.
8. See Andrew Hacker, "The Elected and the Anointed," *American Political Science Review,* September 1961, pp. 541-542.
9. David Granick, *The Red Executive* (Garden City, N.Y., 1961), p. 38.
10. E. G. Burroughs, *Who's Who in the Red Army* (London, 1944), cited in Julian Towster, *Political Power in the U.S.S.R., 1917-1947* (New York, 1948), p. 355.
11. Alex Inkeles and Raymond A. Bauer, *The Soviet Citizen* (Cambridge, 1959), p. 77.

12. Mills, op. cit., p. 402.
13. Armstrong, op. cit., p. 37.
14. See Bell et al., *Public Leadership,* pp. 101-102.
15. S. Bialer, op. cit.
16. Floyd Hunter, *Top Leadership: USA* (Chapel Hill, 1959), pp. 195ff.
17. Joseph A. Schlesinger, *How They Became Governor* (East Lansing, Mich., 1957), p. 11.
18. Merle Fainsod, *How Russia Is Ruled* (Cambridge, rev. ed., 1963), pp. 181, 206-207.
19. James Bryce, *The American Commonwealth* (London, 1891), II, 52.
20. These figures are all from Mills, op. cit., pp. 228-231.
21. Hunter, op. cit., p. 208
22. Douglas Cater, "A New Style, a New Tempo," *The Reporter,* March 16, 1961, p. 28.
23. John Fischer, "Truman & Co., Limited," *Harper's,* July 1949, p. 19.
24. For a general discussion of the control of intermediate groups, see William Kornhauser, *The Politics of Mass Society* (Glencoe, Ill., 1959), p. 82.
25. Soviet 1959 Census; *Partiinaia zhizn,* No. 1. Nicholas DeWitt, *Education and Professional Employment in the USSR* (Washington, 1961).
26. Commission on Organization of the Executive Branch of the Government, *Report of Task Force on Personnel and Civil Service* (Washington, 1955), p. 218.
27. Robert Michels, *Political Parties* (New York, 1959), pp. 99-100.
28. F. Kozlov, "CPSU—Party of the Entire People," *Problemy Mira i Sotsializma,* No. 6, 1962, p. 5.
29. See Myron Rush, *The Rise of Khrushchev* (Washington, 1958).
30. Myron Rush, "The Khrushchev Succession Problem," *World Politics,* January 1962, pp. 260-261.

CHAPTER FOUR: POWER AND POLICY

1. See Robert A. Dahl and Charles E. Lindblom, *Politics, Economics and Welfare* (New York, 1953), Chaps. 12, 13.
2. E.g., Marshal Malinovsky, in *Kommunist,* No. 7, 1962, p. 21.
3. See Sidney Verba, *Small Groups and Political Behavior* (Princeton, N.J., 1961), pp. 27-29.
4. *Staffing Procedures and Problems in the Soviet Union,* Committee on Government Operations, U.S. Senate, 88th Congress, 1st Session, 1963, p. 25.
5. For helpful discussion of the phases of the policy-making process, see Harold D. Lasswell, *The Decision Process* (College Park, Md., 1956), and Paul H. Nitze, "Organization for National Policy Planning in the United States," Paper prepared for Annual Meeting, American Political Science Association, Sept. 10-12, 1959, Washington, D.C.
6. See: Dahl and Lindblom, *Politics, Economics, and Welfare,* p. 230. Alvin W. Gouldner, ed., *Studies in Leadership* (New York, 1950), p. 19.
7. Dean Acheson, "Thoughts about Thought in High Places," *New York Times Magazine,* Oct. 11, 1959, pp. 20ff.
8. A. Hoeffding, "The Soviet Industrial Reorganization of 1957" *American Economic Review, Papers and Proceedings,* May 1959, pp. 65ff.

9. *Izvestia,* October 22, 1961. Also Bulganin's admissions to the CC Plenum of December 1958.
10. Thomas Bernstein, "Soviet Educational Reform" (MA Thesis, Columbia University, 1962), pp. 13-14.
11. See: Herbert Simon, *Models of Man: Social and Rational* (New York, 1957), pp. 66-68. Richard E. Neustadt, *Presidential Power* (New York, 1960). Dahl and Lindblom, op. cit., pp. 341-44. Richard F. Fenno, *The Presidential Cabinet* (Cambridge, 1959), Chap. 6. Samuel P. Huntington, *The Common Defense* (New York, 1961), pp. 146-166.
12. See Roger Hilsman, "Congressional-Executive Relations and the Foreign Policy Consensus," *American Political Science Review,* September 1958, pp. 725-44.
13. See Bernstein, "Soviet Education Reform," pp. 106ff.
14. Hoeffding, *American Economic Review* (May 1959), pp. 65ff.
15. See, for example, the 1950 decision on rearmament, NSC 68, and the 1953 expansion of Continental defense, both of which were approved despite the opposition of officials directly responsible for them. Paul Y. Hammond, "NSC 68: Prologue to Rearmament," in Warner R. Schilling, Hammond, Glenn H. Snyder, *Strategy, Politics and Defense Budgets* (New York, 1962), pp. 267ff.; and Huntington, op. cit., pp. 47-53, 326ff.
16. *Ekonomicheskaia gazeta,* November 17, 1962.
17. Henry A. Kissinger, *The Necessity for Choice* (New York, 1960). Charles E. Lindblom, "The Science of 'Muddling Through,'" *Public Administration Review,* Spring 1959, pp. 79-88.
18. Warner R. Schilling, "The H-Bomb Decision: How to Decide without Actually Choosing," *Political Science Quarterly,* March 1961, pp. 24-46.
19. Ernest S. Griffith, *Impasse of Democracy* (New York, 1939), p. 182.
20. Victor A. Thompson, *Modern Organization* (New York, 1961), p. 91.

CHAPTER FIVE: THE STRUGGLE FOR POWER

1. See J. Armstrong, *The Politics of Totalitarianism* (New York, 1961), pp. 107, 228. Also Armstrong, *Soviet Bureaucratic Elite* (New York, 1959), pp. 147-148.
2. For revealing and authentically documented discussion of the stresses of an agricultural obkom's work, see Merle Fainsod, *Smolensk under Soviet Rule* (Cambridge, Mass., 1958).
3. See Robert Conquest, *Power and Policy in the USSR* (New York, 1961), p. 242.
4. Conquest, op. cit., p. 243.
5. See *Kommunist,* No. 10, 1957.
6. Cf. Merle Fainsod, "What Happened to Collective Leadership?" *Problems of Communism,* July-August, 1959, p. 5.
7. H. Rigby, "How Strong Is the Leader," *Problems of Communism,* September-October 1962, p. 3.
8. Cf. Conquest, op. cit., p. 317.
9. The most detailed analysis of the coup and its failure is in R. Pethybridge, *A Key to Soviet Politics* (New York, 1962).
10. These remarks are based on Theodore H. White, *The Making of the President: 1960* (New York, 1961), pp. 30, 93, 104, 108, 136n.

11. Herbert E. Alexander, "Financing the Parties and Campaigns," in Paul T. David, ed., *The Presidential Election and Transition 1960-1961* (Washington, 1961), pp. 120-124.
12. Ibid., p. 120.
13. White, op. cit., pp. 35, 109-110. Herbert E. Alexander, *Financing the 1960 Election* (Princeton, N.J., Citizens' Research Foundation, Study No. 5), p. 26. *New York Times,* April 15, 1960.
14. White, op. cit., p. 137.
15. *Congressional Quarterly Weekly Report,* Jan. 13, 1961, pp. 32-42.
16. Stanley Kelley, Jr., "The Presidential Campaign," in David, ed., op. cit., p. 68.
17. Earl Mazov et al., *The Great Debates* (Santa Barbara Calif.: Center for the Study of Democratic Institutions, 1962), pp. 4-5. Cf. Sidney Kraus, ed., *The Great Debates* (Bloomington, Ind., 1962), especially Chaps. 7, 11, 13, 14.

CHAPTER SIX: THE AMBIVALENCE OF POWER

1. See his speech of Aug. 14, 1961. A valuable summary of the views of Soviet leaders is contained in an unpublished research paper by D. L. Williams, "The Allocations Debate Within the Soviet Leadership," Columbia University, 1962.
2. *Krasnaia Zvezda,* Jan. 20, 1960.
3. *Pravda,* Sept. 14, 1961.
4. James M. Burns, *John Kennedy: A Political Profile* (New York, 1960), pp. 204-205.
5. Theodore H. White, *The Making of the President, 1960* (New York, 1961), p. 354.
6. Ibid., p. 232.
7. See "The Negro in America," *Newsweek,* July 29, 1963, pp. 28-29.
8. *New York Times,* March 6, 1961, p. 1.
9. *Congressional Quarterly Almanac,* 1961, p. 393.
10. *Newsweek,* April 16, 1962, p. 30.
11. *New York Times,* June 9, 1963, p. E12.
12. *New York Times,* Jan. 16, 1962, p. 14.
13. *New York Times,* June 16, 1963, p. E10.
14. *New York Times,* June 7, 1963, p. 4.
15. See *U.S. News & World Report,* Aug. 19, 1963, pp. 34-36.

CHAPTER SEVEN: THE INTRACTABLE PROBLEM OF POWER

1. *Kommunist,* No. 13, 1963.
2. Lauren K. Soth, "Farm Policy for the Sixties," in President's Commission on National Goals, *Goals for Americans* (Englewood Cliffs, N.J., 1960), p. 215.
3. *Wall Street Journal,* March 5, 1962, p. 18.
4. U.S. Department of Agriculture, Economic Research Service, *The Agricultural Situation in 1961-62 in the Soviet Union and Other Eastern European Countries* (Washington, 1962), p. 14.

5. Paul T. David and Ralph Eisenberg, *Devaluation of the Urban and Suburban Vote* (University of Virginia, Bureau of Public Administration, 1961), pp. 10, 14.

6. Andrew Hacker, *Congressional Districting: The Issue of Equal Representation* (Washington, 1963), pp. 84-87.

7. Charles M. Hardin, "Farm Political Power and the U.S. Governmental Crisis," *Journal of Farm Economics,* December 1958, pp. 1648-1649.

8. Charles O. Jones, "Representation in Congress: The Case of the House Agricultural Committee," *American Political Science Review,* June 1961, pp. 359-361.

9. *Kazakhstanskaia Pravda,* Dec. 26, 1962.

10. *Pravda,* March 14, 1963.

11. *Kommunist,* No. 6, 1963, p. 23. See also *Pravda,* Dec. 16, 1958.

12. Data on labor can be found in S. M. Schwarz, *Labor in the Soviet Union* (New York, 1951) and in W. Nutter, *The Growth of Industrial Production in the Soviet Union* (Princeton, 1962). The subject is ably discussed by Peter Wiles, "The Importance of Being Djugashvili," *Problems of Communism,* March-April 1963, in which he presents comparative growth rates before and after the collectivization.

13. J. A. Newth, "Soviet Agriculture—the Private Sector," *Soviet Studies,* October 1961, 160-171.

14. Cf. Chapter One, pp. 39-40.

15. *Zarya Vostoka,* June 10, 1959.

16. See Richard Hofstadter, *The Age of Reform* (New York, 1955), Chapter 1, "The Agrarian Myth and Commercial Realities."

17. Edward C. Higbee, *Farms and Farmers in an Urban Age* (New York, 1963), pp. 45-46.

18. Special Message to Congress, Jan. 9, 1956, quoted in Dale E. Hathaway, *Government and Agriculture* (New York, 1963), p. 7. Mr. Hathaway, who worked in the Executive Office of the President when this message was drafted, reports that these views were not merely an effort to project an image but were believed by "people very influential with the President, and perhaps the President himself."

19. *Congressional Record,* 108 (Aug. 28, 1962), 17977.

20. *Kommunist,* No. 13, 1963.

21. Radio Free Europe, *Background Information: USSR,* Jan. 11, 1963. Khrushchev's speeches, policy proposals, and memoranda devoted to agricultural matters have been published in a large seven-volume collection: *Stroitel'stvo Kommunizma v SSSR i Razvitie Sel'skogo Khoziaistva,* Moscow, 1963, vols. I-VII.

22. *Pravda,* Dec. 29, 1959.

23. G. Grossman, "The Soviet Economy," *Problems of Communism,* March-April 1963, p. 33. A. Bergson and S. Kuznets, eds., *Economic Trends in the Soviet Union* (Cambridge, Mass., 1963), especially Chap. V.

24. Higbee, op. cit., p. 137.

25. Jones, *American Political Science Review,* June 1961, pp. 361-362.

26. Hardin, *Journal of Farm Economics,* December 1958, p. 1658.

27. Willys R. Knight, "Agriculture," in Walter Adams, ed., *The Structure of American Industry* (New York, 1961), p. 37. Soth, in President's Commission, *Goals for Americans,* p. 220.

28. *Pravda,* Oct. 19, 1961.

CHAPTER EIGHT: CIVIL POWER IN POLITICAL CRISIS

1. For a detailed account of his performance, see P. Ruslanov, "Marshal Zhukov," *The Russian Review* (April, July 1956), 122-129, 186-195.
2. Walter Millis in Walter Millis, Harold Stein, and Harvey C. Mansfield, *Arms and the State* (New York, 1958), p. 265.
3. See Robert Conquest, *Power and Policy in the USSR* (New York, 1961), pp. 331-333. On the doctrinal debate, see Raymond Garthoff, *Soviet Strategy in the Nuclear Age* (New York, 1958), Chap. 4; and Herbert Dinerstein, *War and the Soviet Union* (New York, 1959), Chaps. 2, 3, 4.
4. *Pravda*, Feb. 13, 1955.
5. See D. Floyd, *Daily Telegraph* (London), Sept. 11, 1957.
6. *Krasnaia zvezda*, April 27, 1956, as quoted in W. Leonhard, *The Kremlin Since Stalin* (New York, 1962), p. 254, from which the citation is drawn.
7. Quoted in Richard E. Neustadt, *Presidential Power* (New York, 1960), p. 128.
8. Harry S. Truman, *Memoirs*, Vol. II, *Years of Trial and Hope* (Garden City, N.Y., 1956), pp. 441-442.
9. *Congressional Record*, 97 (April 19, 1951), p. 4129.
10. *New York Times*, April 27, 1951, p. 4.
11. Courtney Whitney, *MacArthur: His Rendezvous with History* (New York, 1956), pp. 490-491.
12. *New York Times*, Feb. 9, 1956, p. 25.
13. Raymond L. Garthoff, "The Marshals and the Party: Soviet Civil-Military Relations in the Postwar Period" in Harry L. Coles, ed., *Total War and Cold War* (Columbus, Ohio, 1962), p. 262.
14. *New York Herald Tribune*, Aug. 24, 1956, p. 12.

CHAPTER NINE: FOREIGN DILEMMAS OF POWER

1. Useful background studies on Hungary include P. Kecskemeti, *The Unexpected Revolution* (Stanford, Calif., 1961), F. Vali, *Rift and Revolt in Hungary* (Cambridge, Mass., 1961), and P. Zinner, *Revolution in Hungary* (New York, 1962); on Cuba, Theodore Draper, *Castro's Revolution, Myths and Realities* (New York, 1963), Tad Szulc and Karl E. Meyer, *The Cuban Invasion: The Chronicle of a Disaster* (New York, 1962), and Paul C. Davis, *The Strategic Perspective in American Foreign Policy*, forthcoming.
2. It was only in 1934 that the Platt Amendment, giving the United States the legal right to intervene in Cuba, was abrogated.
3. Stanley Hoffmann, "Restraints and Choices in American Foreign Policy," *Daedalus*, Fall 1962, p. 681.
4. Tad Szulc and Karl E. Meyer, op. cit., p. 76.
5. Quoted in *Newsweek*, March 4, 1963, p. 24.
6. Stewart Alsop, "The Lessons of the Cuban Disaster," *Saturday Evening Post*, June 24, 1961, p. 70.
7. President de Gaulle's statement of November 10, 1959.

8. Cf. Chinese government declaration of August 15, 1963. See also A. Hsieh, *Communist China's Strategy in the Nuclear Era* (Englewood Cliffs, N.J., 1962).
9. Cf. Charles de Gaulle, *Unity*, Memoirs of the War Years, Vol. II, 1942-1944 (New York, 1959), Chap. 4.
10. Testimony before the Senate Foreign Relations Committee, April 21, 1959.
11. *Foreign Affairs*, October 1962.
12. Henry Kissinger, "NATO's Nuclear Dilemma," *The Reporter*, March 28, 1963.
13. "The Practice of Partnership," *Foreign Affairs*, January 1962, p. 258.
14. *Jen Min Jih Pao*, March 8, 1963.
15. Cf. Z. Brzezinski, "Deviation Control—the Dynamics of Doctrinal Conflict," *American Political Science Review*, March 1962.

CONCLUSION

1. See, for example, James N. Rosenau, *National Leadership and Foreign Policy* (Princeton, 1963), especially pp. 345-360.
2. Peter Wiles, "Will Capitalism and Communism Spontaneously Converge?" *Encounter*, June 1963, pp. 84-90.
3. Cf. the new Party Program; various speeches by Khrushchev; Prof. S. Strumilin's articles, notably in *Novy Mir*, July 1960; Stepanian, in *Oktyabr*, No. 7, 1960.

Index

Acheson, Dean, 204, 208, 353, 357, 396, 397, 405
Adams, John, 38
Africa, 61, 67, 418
Agitprop. *See* Communist Party of the Soviet Union, Secretariat
Agriculture, Chapter 7; collective farms, 304, 310, 311, 313, 314, 318, forced collectivization, 48, 226; Machine Tractor Stations (MTS), 46, 212, 320; Soviet price increase, 219, 270, 323; the Soviet problem, 39, 52, 198, 214, 221, 242-43, 263, 267, 270, 275, 277, 296, 301-306, 308-14, 316-23, 326-27, 328, 435; in the United States, 301-308, 310-11, 314-18, 323-26, 327, 329-30
Aguinaldo, Emilio, 340
Aksakov, K., 25
Algeria, 389
Albania, 33, 400, 406, 407
Albanian Communist Party, 400
Alliance for Progress, 286, 380, 381
American Communist Party, 105, 120, 121
American Farm Bureau Federation, 307, 308, 323, 326
American Nazi Party, 105
American Red Cross, 103
Americans for Democratic Action, 44
Andreiev, A. A., 308
Anti-Masonic Movement, 116
Arbenz Guzmán, Jacobo, 374
Aristov, A. B., 149
Armenian Communist Party, 106
Aron, Raymond, 405
Arzak, N., 118
Asia, 9, 13, 24, 67, 401, 418

Baker v. Carr, 327, 415
Bailey, John M., 264
Barnett, Ross, 199

Batista y Zaldívar, Fulgencio, 368, 371, 372
Batten, Barton, Durstine & Osborn, Inc., 126
Beliaev, K. I., 322
Benson, Ezra Taft, 325
Beria, Lavrenti P., 122, 161, 236, 263, 417; eliminated, 241, 266, 335-36, 343
Birch Society, The John, 121
Black, Cyril, 94
Boulding, Kenneth, 125
Bowles, Chester, 229
Boy Scouts of America, 83
Bradley, Omar, 357, 360, 364
Brannan Plan, 324
Brezhnev, Leonid I., 40, 162, 186n., 201, 243, 250, 279
Bryce, Lord James, 103, 156
Bucharest Conference of Communist leaders, 406
Budënny, Marshal S. M., 333, 335, 339
Bukharin, N. I., 236, 237, 244, 311
Bulganin, Marshal N. A., 245, 246, 249, 340n., 346; ousted, 252; opposed to Khrushchev, 213, 250, 251-52
Burke, Edmund, 77, 79
Bundy, McGeorge, 387, 395

Camp Fire Girls, 83
Canada, 131
Castro, Fidel, 371-73, 374, 378, 379, 380
Celebrezze, Anthony, 134
Celler, Emmanuel, 285, 289
Chaadaev, P. U., 25
Chiang Kai-shek, 353, 365
China (Communist), 13, 21, 41, 64, 74, 81, 195, 352, 355, 375, 377, 417, 418, 420, 421, 429; American policy toward, 354, 365; and the Korean War, 355-56, 392; and

China (Communist) (*cont'd.*)
  Sino-Soviet dispute, 388, 389, 390, 391, 392, 398-403, 405
China (Nationalist), 355, 356, 357
Chinese People's Party (Communist Party of China), 375, 400, 401ff.
Clark, Joseph, 284, 285, 289
Clay, Lucius, 266, 338
Committee for Constitutional Government, 44
Committee for Economic Development, 316
Common Market. *See* European Economic Community
Communist Party of the Soviet Union (CPSU)
  Apparatus and membership: apparat, 68, 122, 132, 195, 197, 220, 223, 229, 250, 295, 311, 416; apparatchiki in post-Stalin succession crisis, 54, 122, 151, 214, 241-243, 244-45, 247-50, 254-55, 263-264, 265, 267, 272, 297, 359, 417; Azerbaijanian party organization, 236; background of apparatchiki, 138-40, 141-46, 148-50, 151, 155, 162, 168, 169, 170, 172; Georgian party organization, 236; Leningrad party organization, 142, 236, 244, 264; membership, 93, 99, 139, 182; membership background, 168-70; Moscow party organization, 142, 236; reorganization of, 170, 197n., 214-15, 226, 270, 435; Ukrainian party organization, 236, 244, 255, 264; youth organizations, 81-83
  Central Committee: expansion of, 177-78; limitations on First Secretary, 3, 193, 195-96, 207, 229, 270; membership, 135, 144, 150, 151-54, 155, 252, 310; military representation in, 336, 340, 350; minority representation in, 131-32; plenums of, 88n., 105, 205, 215, 249, 261, 322n., 351; policy-making role of, 197ff., 204, 213, 217, 280ff.; and the struggle for power, 188, 248, 249, 251, 263, 265, 347; turnover in, 177-181
  Party Congresses: Sixth, 136;

Nineteenth, 242; Twentieth, 53, 55, 206, 220, 247-48, 297, 322, 346, 348; Twenty-first, 220, 252; Twenty-second, 40, 50, 53, 87, 96, 155, 220, 251, 279, 281, 297, 310, 320, 328, 349, 362, 400
  Presidium: anti-party group in, 251, 264; background of members, 132-33, 135, 136, 150, 151, 155, 161-66, 310; cooperation within, 160, 199-201; enlargement of, 162, 177-78, 228; and the Hungarian revolution, 376ff., 384-386, 387; ideologues in, 40-42, 162; policy-making role of, 197ff., 204, 211, 213-14, 217, 227-28; and the struggle for power, 184-186, 187, 195, 237ff., 245, 246, 248, 250-51, 252, 265, 346-47; turnover in, 177-78, 181-82
  Secretariat: agitation and propaganda (Agitprop), 40, 41, 86-87, 244; background of members, 132-33, 150, 155, 161, 163; Bureau of Agriculture, 329; Bureau for Russian Socialist Federal Soviet Republic, 186, 239, 248; cooperation within, 199; enlargement of, 162; *nomenklatura*, 197; Personnel Department of, 147; in the struggle for power, 184-86, 187-188, 241, 244, 248, 249, 263. *See also* Ideology; Policy-making process; Political leadership; Political socialization
Convergence, Theory of, 9-14, 419-429
Costa Rica, 372
Council for Mutual Economic Assistance (CEMA), 406
Crimean War, 332
Crotty, Peter, 157, 265
Cuba, 62, 110, 286; Bay of Pigs invasion, 277, 367, 380-82, 384-88, 396
Cuban, Institute of Agrarian Reform, 372; missile crisis, 201, 202, 344, 396, 389; National Bank, 372; refugees in the United States, 372, 379, 380, 382, 384; People's Revolutionary Movement (MRP), 382;

revolution, 371-73; Revolutionary Council, 382; sugar quota, 379
Cybernetics, 123-25
Czechoslovakia, 375, 377, 407, 420

Daley, Richard J., 157, 259, 265
de Gaulle, Charles, 74, 390, 391, 393, 394, 396ff., 402ff., 433-34
Demichev, P. N., 276
Democracy in America (Tocqueville), 7, 29, 102, 103, 104, 207
Democratic National Convention, 253, 257-60, 265, 285
Democratic Party, access to leadership of, 130; and civil rights, 283, 284, 293; and Kennedy campaign, 237, 253-54, 258-59, 260ff., 263-264
Democrats, 126, 193, 257, 261, 262; and agricultural policy, 307, 323ff.; and Korean War, 343, 352, 353, 364; opposed to New Frontier, 284, 286-88, 293-94
Denisov, M., 273
de Sapio, Carmine, 259
de Tocqueville, Alexis, 7, 29, 102, 103, 104, 207
Dewey, John, 32
Dillon, Douglas, 266
Djilas, Milovan, 117, 425
Docking, George, 265
Douglas, Paul H., 284
Dulles, John Foster, 375, 396

Eastern Europe, 61, 68, 277; destalinization in, 248, 368, 370; relations of with Soviet Union, 368, 376-77, 380, 400; revisionism in, 118-19
East Germany (GDR), 367, 373, 374, 407, 420, 421
East German Communist Party, 400
Eastland, James O., 284
Eden, Sir Anthony, 246
Ehrenburg, Ilya, 113
Eisenhower, Dwight D., 170, 237, 246, 261, 265, 343, 358, 360, 364, 365, 392, 394; Administration of, 115, 154n., 158-60, 172, 174, 183, 288, 289, 323, 324, 373, 379; as adviser to Truman, 338, 353; and agricultural problems, 316, 323ff.;

and civil rights, 115, 285, 288, 289; Cuban policy of, 379-81, 387
Engels, Frederick, 21
England. *See* Great Britain
Estes, Billie Sol, 107, 108
EPIC Movement, 116
European Economic Community, 397, 406

Figueres, José, 372
Finland, 418
Finno-Soviet War, 340
Fischer, John, 159
Ford, Henry, 435
Foreign Affairs, 89, 395
France, 34, 74, 94, 102, 103, 180, 188, 418, 432, 433-34, 435; relations with United States, 388-98, 404-407
Freeman, Orville, 325
Free Soil Movement, 116
Freud, Sigmund, 112
Friedrich, C. J., 34, 431n.
Frost, Robert, 43
Fuchs, Klaus, 352
Furtseva, Ekaterina, 54n., 143

Gagarin, Yuri, 48
Galbraith, John K., 8, 172
Gallois, Pierre, 393, 405
Gavin, James, 405
General Agreement on Tariffs and Trade (GATT), 406
Germany. *See* East Germany; West Germany
Gero, Erno, 370, 376
Ghana, 74
Gheorghiu-Dej, Gheorghe, 375
Giap, 379
Girl Scouts of America, 83
Goldwater, Barry N., 20, 54, 199
Golikov, F. I., 360
Gomulka, Wladislaw, 21, 312, 328, 373
Grant, Ulysses S., 337
Great Britain, 29, 32, 34, 74, 80, 94, 103, 131, 141, 160, 180, 191, 215-16, 394, 397, 406, 418, 432, 434
Grechko, Marshal A. A., 360
Greenbackers, 116, 306

Griffith, Ernest, 226
Grishin, V. V., 201, 276
Gronouski, John A., 134
Guevara, Che, 372, 379

Hamilton, Alexander, 115
Harriman, Averell, 152, 156, 175
Harrison, Benjamin, 337
Herter, Christian, 394
Hiss, Alger, 352
Hitler, Adolf, 65
Hoffman, Stanley, 383
Hoover, Herbert, 237
Humphrey, Hubert, 239, 255, 256, 257ff., 264, 284
Hungarian Communist Party, 369, 370, 374, 377
Hungarian revolution, 248, 346, 370, 373, 374-78, 383, 384; effect of on Soviet workers and intellectuals, 110, 118. *See also* Union of Soviet Socialist Republics, military intervention in Hungary
Hungary, 110, 346, 370, 377, 382, 417, 420
Hunter, Floyd, 157, 175

Ideology
    American: *See* Political beliefs
    Soviet: and the agricultural problem, 301, 310-14, 317-18, 326, 328; analyzed, Chapter 1; and foreign policy, 56-70, 382-83; functions of, 45-56; historical origins of, 24-29, 30-35; influence of on Soviet leadership, 41-42, 49-54, 409-10; intellectuals' response to, 54-55; revision of, 20-22, 53-55, 61; and social deviation, 108, 113-114, 119; and the struggle for power, 40-44, 61; value and viability of, 56-70
Ilyichev, L. F., 13, 40, 53n., 276
Imperialism—The Highest Stage of Capitalism, 58
India, 13, 24, 401, 418, 420, 421, 426. *See also* Sino-Indian Dispute
Ireland, 131, 426
Iskra, 32
Italy, 94, 131, 418
Ivanov, I., 118

Izvestia, 35, 89, 213, 273. *See also* Mass media

Japan, 11, 13, 59, 73, 74, 339, 342, 354, 418
Jefferson, Thomas, 22n., 69, 314, 315ff., 336, 426
Jiménez, Antonio, 372
Johnson, Louis, 353
Johnson, Lyndon B., 43n., 175, 239, 255, 256, 257ff., 260, 264, 266, 284, 288, 415; career of, 166-67

Kadar, Janos, 382
Kaganovich, Lazar M., 147, 241, 263; against Khrushchev, 53, 205, 213, 214, 248, 251, 265; against Malenkov, 244, 245; demoted, 248; ousted, 252
Kamenev, L. B., 236
Kapitsa, P., 111-12, 428
Kardelj, E., 118
Kefauver, Estes, 253, 283, 363
Kennan, George F., 65
Kennedy, John F., 22n., 35, 43, 170, 229, 237, 253, 260, 261, 277, 286, 295, 296, 391; Administration of, 37, 115, 133-34, 154n., 157-60, 172, 174-75, 270, 277, 287, 288, 289, 291ff., 294ff., 308, 323, 380, 395; and the agricultural problem, 253-54, 260, 301, 308, 323, 325; and the Alliance for Progress, 380, 381; Cabinet appointees of, 134, 170; and civil rights, 115, 229, 271, 283-95, 296-99; Cuban policy of, 202, 286, 379-81, 383-84, 387, 396; economic policy of, 283, 286, 290, 294; on foreign policy, 253, 260, 283, 286, 290; and Franco-American relations, 388, 390, 391, 392, 395-98; political outlook of, 36-37; relations with Congress, 54, 229, 283-85, 286-87, 294, 298; and the struggle for power, 239-240, 253-62, 263-368
Kennedy, Robert F., 256, 260
Khrushchev, Nikita S., 9, 10, 11, 14, 18, 22, 35, 139, 140, 147, 182, 198, 204, 217, 246, 277, 295, 345, 376; agricultural policies of, 39-40n., 52, 198, 214, 242-43, 263,

267, 270, 275, 277, 303, 308-10, 312, 313, 317, 318-23, 328-29; background of, 135, 170, 308; on consumer goods, 272-83, 295, 296, 298, 344, 362; and the Cuban missile crisis, 344, 362, 401; on defense spending, 275-80, 281, 295, 362; and destalinization, 247, 248, 263, 267, 297, 299, 346, 375; and economic reorganization, 205, 206, 213-14, 230, 246, 249, 250, 261, 266, 267, 270, 280, 299, 346; educational reform proposals of, 206-207, 213, 214, 215, 270; and foreign policy, 60-61, 246, 250, 267, 277, 295, 298, 344; on heavy industry, 243-44, 263, 267, 273, 275, 279, 282, 295; and Hungarian revolution, 248, 377; ideological outlook of, 35-36, 38-40; and intellectuals, 102, 110; manipulation of party machinery by, in succession crisis, 54, 122, 151, 189, 241-243, 244-45, 247-50, 254, 255, 263-64, 265, 267, 272, 297, 359, 417; and Marxism-Leninism, 35-36, 40; rapprochement of with Tito, 246-47, 267, 345, 370, 371, 375; relations of with military, 279-80, 348-52, 258-64; reorganization of party-state machinery by, 214-15; in the succession struggle, 40-41, 53ff., 61, 122, 185-86, 187, 198, 206, 235, 238-39, 241-252, 254, 255, 263-68, 344-47, 417, against the anti-party group, 213, 238, 299, 344, 346-47, 349, 362—Bulganin, 213, 251-52, Kaganovich, 53, 205, 213, 214, 248, 251-52, 265, Malenkov, 41, 53, 122, 193, 205, 214, 242, 243-44, 245, 246, 251-52, 264, 266, 267, 272, 344, 345, Molotov, 53, 54, 205, 213, 214, 246, 247, 248, 251-252, 301, 345, 405, Pervukhin, 213, 251-52, Saburov, 213, 251-252, Shepilov, 251-52, Voroshilov, 251-52; and Zhukov, 122, 332, 345, 348-52, 358-64
King, Martin Luther, 199, 285, 289
Kirichenko, A. I., 246, 251, 264, 322

Kirov, S. M., 151
Kissinger, Henry, 395, 405
Know-Nothing Movement, 116
Kolakowski, 118
Kommunist, 89, 112, 246
Komsomol. *See* Young Communist League
Konev, Marshal Ivan, 345, 350, 351, 352, 360
Korean War, 62, 324, 342-43, 352ff., 355-57, 364, 392
Kosygin, A. N., 40, 201, 276
Kozlov, Frol, 40, 201, 279
Kuusinen, O. V., 40, 201, 279
Kuznetsov, F., 350

Laos, 286
Lausche, Frank, 284
Lawrence, David, 157, 259, 265
League of Women Voters, 103
Leahy, Admiral William, 338
Lee, Ivy, 126
Lenin, V. I., 22, 28, 31, 32, 38, 40, 41, 58, 151, 182, 186, 399
Leninism. *See* Marxism-Leninism
Lincoln, Abraham, 22n., 80
Lippmann, Walter, 35, 36, 364
Lipset, Seymour M., 98
Locke, John, 20, 23, 69
Loveless, Herschel C., 265
Lovett, Robert A., 353
Lukacs, 118

MacArthur, Douglas, 332, 338, 340; biographical data on, 340-42, 343; during and after World War II, 342, 353-54; and Korean War, 352-53, 355-57, 359; dismissed by Truman, 357-58, 359-64
Macmillan, Harold, 394, 395
Madison, James, 38
Malenkov, Georgi M., 151, 243, 244, 263, 344, 345, 417; demoted, 238, 245, 241, 251, 264, 266, 267; opposed by Khrushchev, 41, 53, 122, 193, 205, 214, 248, 251, 264, 265, 272, 344, 345; ousted, 252; as protégé of Stalin, 147, 186, 240, 242
Malinovsky, Marshal Rodion, 278-279, 350, 351, 360, 361, 362
Mao Tse-tung, 21, 41, 74, 379, 388, 390, 391, 392, 398, 401

Marshall, George C., 338, 341-42, 353, 357, 360, 364
Marshall Plan, 396
Marx, Karl, 20, 21
Marxism, anti-Soviet, 10; in Czarist Russia, 28, 32
Marxism-Leninism, appeal of, 12, 67; in Soviet ideology, 21-22, institutionalized in CPSU, 39-42, 49; influence on Soviet leadership, 37, 39-42, 57, 140, 232, 378; Khrushchev's interpretation, 35-36, 40; and Sino-Soviet differences, 399, 400, 402, 403; and social change, 69, 114; and Soviet revisionism, 119
Mass media, in presidential campaigns, 125-26, 261-62, 379-80; in the Soviet Union, 88-89, 297; in the United States, 88-89, 196
Mazurov, K. T., 143
McCarthy, Joseph R., 163, 352-53, 363, 414
McCarthyism, 102, 116, 283
McCloy, John J., 175, 266
McClure's, 32
McCormack, John, 253
McDonald, Iverach, 35
McKinley, William H., 31
McNamara, Patrick, 284
McNamara, Robert S., 203, 395
Merriam, Charles, 125
Mexico, 73, 75, 435
Meyner, Robert B., 265
Michels, Robert, 175
Michelson, Charles, 126
Mikoyan, Anastas I., 40, 53, 161, 201, 239, 246, 251, 252, 276, 376, 377
Mills, C. Wright, 136
Molotov, V. M., 54, 149, 241, 246, 347; demoted, 248; ousted, 252; opposed by Khrushchev, 53, 205, 213, 224, 247, 248, 250, 251, 264, 265, 345, 401, 405; and Malenkov, 244, 245
Mongolian People's Republic, 390
Monnet, Jean, 405
Montesquieu, Baron de, 427
Morse, Wayne, 284
Moscow meeting of 81 Communist Parties, 400

Moskalenko, Marshal K. S., 350, 360
Nagy, Imre, 370, 373, 374, 375ff., 382
Nassau Agreement, 395, 397, 406
Nasser, Gamal Abdul, 66
National Association for the Advancement of Colored People, 120, 289
National Association of Manufacturers, 86, 88
National Farmers Union, 307, 308, 323
National Grange, 116, 306, 307, 308, 323
Nehru, Jawaharlal, 66
New Deal, 121, 147, 149, 230
Nitze, Paul, 211
Nixon, Richard, 260, 261, 262, 267, 301, 325, 379-80
Nkrumah, Kwame, 74
Norstad, Lauris, 405
North Atlantic Treaty Organization, 204, 296, 354, 394, 397, 405, 406
Norway, 94, 95n.
Novikov, V. N., 273-74
Novotny, A., 375

Oppenheimer, J. Robert, 125
Orenburg House for Political Education, 87
Organization for Economic Cooperation and Development, 406

Parent-Teacher Assocations, 76, 103
Paris Summit Conference (1960), 264, 277, 399
Pavlov, I. P., 112
Periodical literature. *See* Mass media
Pershing, John J., 341
Pervukhin, M. G., 149, 213, 246, 251, 264; demoted and ousted, 252
Philippines, 340, 341, 342, 354
Pobedonostsev, Konstantin, 25n., 31
Podgorny, N. V., 201, 276, 322
Politburo. *See* Communist Party of the Soviet Union, Presidium
Poland, 24, 33, 110, 118, 131, 312, 328, 373, 398, 407, 420, 421, 434; destalinization in, 248, 346, 417; political crisis in, 118, 346, 373, 374, 375, 376

Policy-making process, Chapter 4; bargaining and deciding in, 193-202, 214, 318, 413, 414; decision-making in, 202, 216-20, 413; execution of policy, 202, 220-23, 413; initiation of, 202, 203-209, 413; innovation in, 52-54, 228-32, 318, 411; integration in, 226-28; persuasion in, 202, 209-16, 413; selection of alternatives in, 224-26; and struggles for power, 191-93, 198-99, 202, 205, 241-44, 249, 250, 260, 267, 270, 311, 319

Political beliefs
    American: and the agricultural problem, 301, 310-11, 314-18, 326; analyzed, Chapter 1; and foreign policy, 56-70; functions of, 5, 45-56; historical roots of, 29-35; and invasion of Cuba, 383-384; leadership attitudes toward, 36, 42-44; revision of, 53-55; and social change, 114; value and viability of, 56-70
    Soviet: *See* Ideology

Political leadership, Chapter 3; in bureaucratic structures, 148; changing character of, 156-57, education and training for, 5, 141-146, 151-73, 412; ethnic and social origins of, 130-39; generalists among, 41, 141, 269; influence of ideology on, 49-54; interchangeability of roles within, 148-49, 152-55, 161-62, 168-73; outlook of, 35-44, 139-40; patron-protégé relationships in, 147, 236; and policy initiation, 2-3, 209, 280, innovation, 294, 296, 298, persuasion, 209-16, decision, 216-20, and execution, 220-23; possible changes in American, 432-33, 435; power struggles among, Chapter 5, 40-44, 61, 147, 157, 184-90, 191-93, 198-99, 202, 205, 237, 239-40, 253-62, 263-68, 293-94, 343-47, 412; turnover within, 173-184, 412; typology of Soviet, 40-42. *See also* John F. Kennedy, Nikita S. Khrushchev and the struggle for power

Political parties, 46, 126, 263, 308; factional struggles within, 235-37, 258-59; and policy-making, 191-192; and political socialization, 84-86, 93. *See also* Communist Party of the Soviet Union

Political socialization, Chapter 2; interest groups and, 84, 86, political participation and control in, 90-104; and science, 69, 122-25; socialization and politization, 76-90; of the Soviet elite, 144

Politization. *See* Political socialization

Polyansky, D. S., 40, 143, 186n., 201, 251, 276

Ponomarenko, P. K., 149, 243; career of, 164-66

Populism, in Russia, 26; in the United States, 31, 116, 306

Powell, Adam Clayton, 289

Pravda, 89, 213, 244, 351. *See also* Mass media

Prendergast, Michael, 259

Progressive movement, 116

Quemoy-Matsu crisis, and Sino-Soviet relations, 389

Radical Right in America, 116

Rajk, Laszlo, 369

Rakosi, Matyas, 369, 370, 371, 382

Rayburn, Sam, 188, 265

Red Army of Workers and Peasants. *See* U.S.S.R. Armed Forces

Reflections on the Revolution in France (Burke), 77

Republican Party, 126; access to leadership of, 130; and civil rights, 284, 287, 288, 291, 293, 294

Republicans, 126, 192, 266; and agricultural policy, 307, 323, 325; Far Eastern policy of, 354; and the Korean War, 343, 352, 353, 357; and the MacArthur controversy, 358, 360; opposed to New Frontier, 286-87, 294

Reston, James, 290, 292

Reuther, Walter, 199

Rockefeller, Nelson, 229, 405

Rockwell, George L., 105

Romanov, E., 418

Roosevelt, Eleanor, 260, 265

Roosevelt, Franklin D., 22n., 31, 126, 188, 230, 237, 297, 341n.
Roosevelt, Theodore, 44n., 83
Rostow, W. W., 12
Rotary Clubs, 103
Rousseau, J. J., 426
Rumania, 375, 377
Russia (Czarist), 12, 24-28, 33, 99, 136, 209; eastward expansion of, 130-31; industrialization of, 27-28; intellectuals in, 24-27; military in, 332-33, peasantry in, 24, 25-26, 27
Russian Orthodox Church, 24, 32, 119
Russo-Japanese War, 332
Rykov, A. I., 236, 237, 244

Saburov, M. Z., 42, 213, 246, 251, 264; ousted, 252
Schaff, Adam, 118
Schlesinger, Arthur, Jr., 20
Schumann, Robert, 405
Share the Wealth Movement, 116
Shelepin, A. N., 40
Shepilov, D. T., 249, 251, 265; purged, 248, 252
Sino-Indian dispute, 389, 401
Sino-Soviet dispute. *See* U.S.S.R., alliance management by
Smathers, George, 265
Smith, Adam, 315
Socialization. *See* Political socialization
Social Justice Movement, 116
Society for the Dissemination of Political and Scientific Knowledge, 86
Sokolovsky, Marshal V., 350
South Vietnam, 62, 290, 389
Soviet Armed Forces. *See* U.S.S.R., Armed Forces
Spain, 75
Stalin, J. V., 10, 33, 40, 46, 53, 74, 113, 117, 140, 151, 182, 187, 193, 195, 217, 232, 236, 237, 238, 265, 272, 273, 301, 311, 319, 321, 339, 340, 343, 344, 346, 350, 370, 399, 416, 417; agricultural policy of, 308, 309, 311, 312ff., 319; military purged by, 334-36, 343; as patron of Malenkov, 147, 186, 241

Stalingrad, Battle of, 345, 351, 352
Steffens, Lincoln, 32
Stevenson, Adlai, 36, 175, 239, 253, 255, 256, 257ff., 260, 263, 264ff., 381
Strauss, Lewis L., 166-67
Strumilin, Stanislav, 58n., 80
Student Non-Violent Coordinating Committee, 120
Suez Crisis, 63, 66, 389; effect of on Hungarian revolution, 377-78
Suslov, M. A., 40, 201, 239, 246, 251, 252, 279, 376, 377
Sweden, 74
Switzerland, 94
Symington, Stuart, 239, 255, 256, 257ff., 264, 284

Taft, Robert A., 358, 415
Taft-Hartley Act, 71
Taylor, Maxwell, 175
Taylor, Zachary, 337
Tennessee Valley Authority, 52
The Federalist, 20, 38
Times, London, 35
Timoshenko, Marshal S. K., 335, 339, 340, 348, 351
Tito, J. B., 328, 370, 371, 375, 399
Titov, German, 48
Tomsky, M. P., 236, 237
Touré, Sekou, 66
Townsendite Movement, 116
Trotsky, L. D., 40, 42, 151, 193, 236, 237, 333
Truman, Harry S., 3, 154, 194, 260, 265, 297, 323, 324, 396; Administration of, 154n., 158-60, 172, 174, 183, 323, 324, 332, 338, 352, 353, 354, 355ff., 360, 363, 414; Korean policy of, 343, 353, 354, 355-57, 359, 364-65, 414; and MacArthur, 332, 352, 353-57, 358-364
Tukhachevsky, Marshal M. N., 333, 334, 347, 362
Turner, Frederick J., 426
Tydings, Millard, 126

Union of Soviet Socialist Republics (USSR), alienation and dissent in, 54-55, 104-14, 116-19, 411; alliance management by, Chapter

9, 64, 68, 277, 295, 388ff., 391, 392, 398-403, 404-409, 410; amorphous social forces in, 195, 296; anti-semitism in, 101, 117; and arms control, 62, 220, 393-94, 399; as an affluent society, 424-28; Berlin policy of, 62, 277, 278, 295, 298, 389; bureaucratic "family circles" in, 222-23, 321; bureaucrats in, 3, 52, 149, 191, 196, 212, 213, 229, 242, 245, 246, 249, 267-68, 272, 280, 295, 297, 416; Civil War, 333, 339, 348; and the Cold War, 62-63; comrades' courts in, 101-102; in the convergence theory, 9-13; and the Cuban missile crisis, 201, 344, 362, 401; destalinization in, 10, 53, 110, 113, 220, 247, 248, 263, 267, 297, 299, 346, 398; East European policy of, 371, 376-77, 380, 400; economic planning in, 9, 96, 124-125; economic modernization of, 434-35; economic reorganization of, 122, 162, 196, 205, 206, 213-214, 230, 246, 249, 250, 261, 266, 267, 270, 280, 299, 346; education of adults, 86-87; education and political socialization in, 79-80; educational reform in, 206-207, 212-13, 214, 215, 270; elections in, 4, 93-95; foreign policy of, 61, 63, 226, 231, 246, 250, 267, 277, 295, 298, 344, 398, 428-29; industrialization of, 9, 308, 312, 421-422; intellectuals in, 43-44, 54-55, 102, 110-14, 136, 196, 198, 416-18, 424; local administration in, 96-97; managers in, 3, 10, 137-138, 168-170, 196, 213, 244, 249, 263, 417; military intervention of in Hungary, Chapter 9, 110, 118, 369-71, 373, 374-78, 381, 382-83, 384, 387; minority groups in, 34, 119, 130, 196, 271, 410; party-state reorganization of, 214-215, 226; Permanent Productivity Councils in, 96, 110; policy groups in, 196, political reform of, 431; population growth of, 48; public discussion in, 97-98, 212-213; Regional Economic Councils (*sovnarkhozy*) in, 96, 280; revisionism in, 118-119; secret police in, 10, 162, 334, 417; social engineering in, 123-25, 127; specific interest groups in, 196, 212, 214, 215; statistical data on, 447-448; strengths and weaknesses of, 415-10, suppression of East German rising by, 367, 373, 374; technical experts in, 44, 122-23, 138, 139, 424; trade unions in, 97, 101; and the U-2 incident, 264, 277, 399; and the underdeveloped world, 63, 66-67; and Yugoslavia, 246-47, 267, 328, 345, 370, 371, 375, 377, 399. *See also* Agriculture; Communist Party of the Soviet Union; Ideology; Policy-making process; Political leadership; Political socialization; Russia (Czarist)

USSR Academy of Pedagogical Sciences, 212

USSR Administration of Labor Reserves, 212

USSR All-Union Society for the Dissemination of Political and Scientific Knowledge, 119

USSR Armed Forces, 334, 347, 348, 359, 362-63, 364; created by Trotsky, 333; in Hungary, 374, 376, 377; leadership of, 152, 376, 416; leadership of and policy-making, 196, 197, 198, 203, 207, 212, 278-280; leadership of purged, 334-36, 343, 346, 347-48, and rehabilitated, 362; Main Political Administration of, 334, 350; Military Councils of, 351; politization of, 122-23; reduced in size, 278-81; and the struggle for power, 198, 244, 247, 249, 251, 252, 263, 265, 267, 272, 297, 332, 343-47; under civilian control, Chapter 8, 333-336, 364-65; and Zhukov controversy, 332, 344-52, 359-64

USSR Central Statistical Administration, 282

USSR Council of Ministers, 206, 217, 238, 239, 240, 243, 274, 431

USSR Institute of Agricultural Economics, 313

USSR Ministry of Aviation Industry, 213
USSR Ministry of Defense Industry, 213, 351
USSR Ministry of State Control, 213
USSR State Economic Commission (*Gosekonomkomissiia*), 205
USSR State Planning Commission (*Gosplan*), 214, 249
USSR Russian Republic Ministry of Agriculture, 309
USSR Russian Republic Supreme Court, 107
USSR Supreme Soviet, 3, 14, 107, 213, 214, 216, 273, 131-32
USSR Ukrainian Academy of Agricultural Sciences, 52
United Nations, 63, 354, 355-56
United States of America, administrative turnover in, 180-181; alienation and dissent in, 54-55, 108-110, 114-16, 119-21, 411; alliance management by, Chapter 9, 63, 66, 388, 389, 390ff., 393-98, 404-407, 410; bureaucratic politicians in, 170-73; changes in political system of, 432-33, 435; China policy of, 290, 354, 365; civic associations in, 102-104, civil rights movement in, 115, 120, 271, 283, 284, 285-95, 296, 297, 432; Civil War in, 27, 30, 115, 116, 156, 271, 337; and the Cold War, 62-63, 75, 433; Constitution of, 20, 34, 46, 50, 80, 115, 120; and the Cuban missile crisis, 202, 344, 389, 396; Cuban policy of, 277, 371-73, 374, 378-79, 383-84, 387, 396; Declaration of Independence, 120; education and political socialization in, 79-80; elections in, 4, 93-95, 126, 192, 253-62, 289; electoral politicians in, 43, 141-42, 146, 147-50, 151, 156, 157, 170; the "Establishment" in, 139, 151, 152, 155, 157, 170-73, 175; ethnic composition of, 131; foreign policy of, 56-70, 215, 231, 286, 290; Founding Fathers of, 20, 46, 49, 337; intellectuals in, 31, 43-44, 54-55; interest groups in, 46, 55, 84, 86,

196, 199, 423; Latin American policy of, 286, 368, 369, 373, 379ff.; military intervention in Cuba by, Chapter 9, 277, 367, 380-82, 384-88, 396, and Guatemala, 367, 374, 381, 382, 383; military strategy of, 395-96, 397; political participation and control in, 90-104; pragmatism of 31, 32, 67, 432-33; radical movements in, 116; religion in, 23, 32, 90, 261; social engineering in, 125-126; statistical data on, 447-48; strengths and weaknesses of, 414-15, 418; technical experts in 43-44, 125; and the U-2 incident, 264, 277, 399; and the underdeveloped world, 63, 66-67, 391; Vice President of, 136, 156; and Vietnam, 62, 290, 389. *See also* Agriculture; Policy-making process; Political beliefs; Political leadership; Political parties
U.S. Army, 142, 144, 238
U.S. Armed Forces, civilian control of, Chapter 8, 336-39, 353, 364-365; historical development of, 336; Joint Chiefs-of-Staff of, 174, 338, 355, 356, 357, 365, 380, 381; the MacArthur controversy, 331, 352, 353-58, 359-64
U.S. Bureau of the Budget, 228
U.S. Central Intelligence Agency, 374, 379, 380, 381, 382
U.S. Commission on Civil Rights, 285, 289
U.S. Commodity Credit Corp., 302
U.S. Congress, 4, 148, 235, 288, 338, 343, 373, 379, 415; and agricultural policy, 307, 316, 323-24, 325; background of members of, 134-35, 136-37, 146; and civil rights, 286-87, 289, 291, 292ff., 296ff.; leadership of, 286, 306; legislative process in, 203, 209-10, 218-19, 224-25, 226, 232; and the MacArthur controversy, 357, 358, 360; policy-making relations of with the President, 54, 157, 191ff., 200, 210-11, 218, 220-21, 269,

290, 294, 298, 299, 414-15; turn-over in, 173, 175, 176
U.S. Department of Agriculture, 326
U.S. Department of State, 343, 353, 356, 379, 380, 381
U.S. Fair Employment Practices Commission, 285
U.S. House of Representatives, 44, 144, 218, 324, 357; Agricultural Committee, 286, 307, 324, 325; Appropriations Committee, 306; Armed Services Committee, 286, 306; Banking and Currency Committee, 306; Education and Labor Committee, 289, 306; "fourth term crisis in," 148; leadership of, 175-176, 286; Negroes in, 134; Rules Committee, 218, 286, 287; rural overrepresentation in, 306, 327; Speaker of, 136, 156; Ways and Means Committee, 286, 306
U.S. National Security Council, 211, 379
U.S. Presidency, 136, 156, 182, 183, 190, 191, 218, 220, 228, 290, 307, 337, 412; and administrative turn-over, 174-75, 180-81; Cabinet appointees of, 133, 134, 135, 156, 160-61, 194, 210, 237; consensus-building role of, 210, 269-70; con-test for, 157, 184, 237, 239-40, 253-62, 263-68, 293-94, 301; re-lations with Congress of, 148, 157, 200, 209-11, 229, 287; scope and limits of power of, 193-94, 201, 218, 221, 232, 269, 286-87, 298-299; succession to, 186. *See also* Policy-making process; Political leadership
U.S. Presidential Committee on Equal Employment Opportunity, 288
U.S. President's Commission on Na-tional Goals, 49-50
U.S. Production and Marketing Ad-ministration, 307-308
U.S. Senate, 44, 47, 218, 253; Agri-cultural Committee, 307, 324; Ap-propriations Committee, 227; Armed Services Committee, 357; and civil rights, 283-94; Foreign Relations Committee, 283, 357;

the "inner club" of, 148; Judiciary Committee, 284; leadership of, 175, 286; and the MacArthur con-troversy, 363; rural overrepre-sentation in, 306
U.S. Soil Conservation Service, 308
U.S. Supreme Court, 20, 47, 120, 136, 154, 156, 228, 232, 327
Urrutia Lleo, Manuel, 372
Ustinov, D. F., 40

Vandenberg, Arthur H., 361, 415
Vasilevsky, Marshal A. M., 350
Voronov, G. I., 201, 276
Voroshilov, Marshal K. E., 251, 335, 340; ousted, 252
Voznesensky, N. A., 42

Wagner Act, 71
Walker, Edwin, 163
Warsaw Treaty Organization, 377, 406
Weber, Max, 130
Western Europe, 8, 11, 67, 68, 72n., 73, 94, 99, 114, 130, 208, 209
West Germany, 74, 94, 103, 131, 304, 393, 418, 433
Wiles, Peter, 423
Williams, G. Mennen, 265
Wilson, Woodrow, 58

Yefremov, L. N., 201
Yeremenko, Marshal A. I., 360
Yesenin-Volpin, A. S., 117-18
Yevtushenko, Yevgeny, 110, 113
Young Communist League (Kom-somol), 81-83, 96, 319; and *druzhinniki*, 82, 101
Young Democrats, 83
Young Pioneers, 81
Young Republicans, 83
Yugoslavia, 33, 75, 110, 118, 312, 328, 350, 371, 400, 407, 434

Zhdanov, A. A., 236, 416
Zheltov, A., 350
Zhukov, Marshal G. K., 122, 243, 278, 340, 345ff., 351; biographical data on, 339-40, 342; ousted by Khrushchev, 238, 248, 252, 266, 332, 345, 349-52, 357, 358-64, 417
Zinoviev, G. Y., 236, 237